BUSINESS AND CORPORATE LAW

Prof. P. Saravanavel
M.Com., M.Phil., M.L.
Senior Advocate, Bar Council of Tamil Nadu,
Kumarn Illam, No. 20,
Parisutham Nagar,
Thanjavur - 613 007

Prof. S.R. Mohapatra
FCS, FICWA, MBA (XIMB), Ph.D.
Dean (Management), BPUT.
Principal, Centre of IT Education (CITE),
Bhubaneswar, Odisha.

S. Balakumar
M.Com.
Director,
SESUBA Consultants,
Kumaran Illam,
20, Parisutham Nagar,
Thanjavur - 613 007

First Edition : 2011
Reprint : 2024

Published by : Mrs. Meena Pandey
for **HIMALAYA PUBLISHING HOUSE PVT. LTD.,**
"Ramdoot", Dr. Bhalerao Marg, Girgaon, Mumbai - 400 004.
Phone: 022-23860170, 23863863; **Fax:** 022-23877178
E-mail: himpub@bharatmail.co.in; **Website:** www.himpub.com

Branch Offices :

New Delhi : "Pooja Apartments", 4-B, Murari Lal Street, Ansari Road, Darya Ganj, New Delhi - 110 002. Phone: 011-23270392, 23278631; Fax: 011-23256286

Nagpur : Kundanlal Chandak Industrial Estate, Ghat Road, Nagpur - 440 018. Phone: 0712-2721215, 2721216

Bengaluru : Plot No. 91-33, 2nd Main Road, Seshadripuram, Behind Nataraja Theatre, Bengaluru - 560 020. Phone: 080-41138821; Mobile: 09379847017, 09379847005

Hyderabad : No. 3-4-184, Lingampally, Besides Raghavendra Swamy Matham, Kachiguda, Hyderabad - 500 027. Phone: 040-27560041, 27550139

Chennai : No. 34/44, Motilal Street, T. Nagar, Chennai - 600 017. Mobile: 09380460419

Pune : "Laksha" Apartment, First Floor, No. 527, Mehunpura, Shaniwarpeth (Near Prabhat Theatre), Pune - 411 030. Phone: 020-24496323, 24496333; Mobile: 09370579333

Cuttack : Plot No. 5F-755/4, Sector-9, CDA Markat Nagar, Cuttack - 753 014, Odisha. Mobile: 09338746007

Kolkata : 3, S.M. Bose Road, Near Gate No. 5, Agarpara Railway Station, North 24 Parganas, West Bengal - 700 109. Mobile: 09674536325

DTP by : Kumar Computers, Tanjavur - 613007

Printed at : Geetanjali Press Pvt. Ltd., Nagpur. On behalf of HPH (P).

PREFACE

Business and Corporate Law is an important constituent of the business and corporate environment. No corporate entity can effectively work and survive without meeting legal obligations. The law relating to contracts is perhaps the most significant and all pervasive amongst the various Business and Corporate Laws. This text is presented to the students of MBA of BPUT with the coverage given below:

Module - I : The Indian Contract Act and The Sale of Goods Act

Module - II : Economic Laws comprising: The Competition Act, The Consumer Protection Act, Intellectual Property Rights, The Industries (Development & Regulation) Act, The Foreign Exchange Management Act.

Module - III : The Companies Act

The Indian Contract Act, 1872 which governs contract in India is the earliest piece of legislation which the country has produced. Since the book is meant for students of Law, Commerce and Management Institutes, the authors have dealt with the provisions of the Act topic-wise for facilitating better understanding of the subject. Examples, case laws etc. have been given to illustrate the provisions of the Act. Section numbers have been given at appropriate places to enable the readers to make reference to the Companies Act for further details. Suitable headings and sub-headings have been given to focus the attention of the reader on important aspects of company law.

The chapter arrangement in this text have been made in a systematic and logical way with examples, illustrations and charts. The important judicial decisions on the various issues have also been included.

We express our deep gratitude to the several authors whose contributions have helped us to write this book. We are grateful to Shri Niraj Pandey and Mr. Bijoy Kumar Ojha of Himalaya Publishing House, Bhubaneswar for their constant encouragement in publishing the book in a short period time. A creative feedback from the learned readers, bringing to our notice any mistake, error or omission or discrepancy that might have crept in this book in spite of our sincere efforts to avoid those, is almost welcome, for it will help us to improve the overall quality, style and presentation of the book in the forthcoming editions.

P. SARAVANAVEL,
S.R. MOHAPATRA,
S. BALAKUMAR

CONTENTS

MODULE - I (LAW OF CONTRACTS)

MODULE - II (ECONOMIC LAWS)

MODULE - III (COMPANY LAW)

DETAILED CONTENTS

MODULE - I (LAW OF CONTRACTS)

MODULE - II (ECONOMIC LAWS)

MODULE - III (COMPANY LAW)

MODULE - I
LAW OF CONTRACTS

1. **Law of Contract: Agreement and Contract**
2. **Offer and Acceptance**
3. **Consideration and Capacity**
4. **Free Consent**
5. **Legality of Object**
6. **Contingent and Quasi-Contracts**
7. **Discharge of Contract**
8. **Breach of Contract and Remedies**
9. **Contract of Guarantee**
10. **Contract of Bailment and Pledge**
11. **Contract of Agency**
12. **Contract of Sale of Goods**
13. **Performance of Contract of Sale**

Chapter

AGREEMENT AND CONTRACT

The law of contract is applicable not only to the business community, but also to others. Everyone of us enters into a number of contracts almost every day, and most of the time we do so without event realising what we are doing from the point of law. A person seldom realises that when he entrusts his scooter to the mechanic for repairs, he is entering into a contract of bailment; or when he buys a packet of cigarettes, he is making a contract of the sale of goods; or again when he goes to the cinema to see a movie, he is making yet another contract; and so on.

Besides, the law of contract furnishes the basis for the other branches of Business Law. The enactments relating to sale of goods, negotiable instruments, insurance, partnership and insolvency are all founded upon the general principles of contract law. That is why the study of the law of contract precedes the study of all other sub-divisions of Mercantile Law.

THE INDIAN CONTRACT ACT, 1872

The law relating to contracts is codified in the form of ***Indian Contract Act***, 1872. The main object of the law of contract is to introduce definiteness in business transactions.

Basic Assumptions underlying the Act

Before we take up the discussion of the various provisions of the Indian Contract Act, it will be proper to see some of the basic assumptions underlying the Act. These are :

1. Subject to certain limiting principles, there shall be freedom of contract to the contracting parties and the law shall enforce only what the parties have agreed to be bound. The law shall not lay down absolute rights and liabilities of the contracting parties. Instead it shall lay down only the essentials of a valid contract and the rights and obligations it would create between the parties in the absence of anything to the contrary agreed to by the parties.

2. Expectations created by promises of the parties shall be fulfilled and their non-fulfilment shall give rise to legal consequences. If the plaintiff asserts that the defendant undertook to do a certain act and failed to fulfill his promise, an action at law shall lie.

Law of Contract creates *right-in-personam* and not *right-in-rem*. *"Right-in-personam"* means right against a particular person or group of persons. A contract creates a right in personam only i.e., against a particular person. On the contrary *Right-in-rem* implies rights against the whole world.

Illustration : A takes a loan of ₹ 1,000 from B. B has a right to recover the said amount from A. The right of B against A is a personal right. It is called *right-in-personam* as it is available to B alone and none else. Again, this right is against A only and none else.

Right-in-rem means right against the whole world.

Illustration : X purchased a house from Y. X is the owner of the house. So he has a right of quiet possession and enjoyment against the whole world and not against Y alone. It is called *right-in-rem*. Law of Contract does not create right-in-rem, it creates right-in-personam only.

Scope of Indian Contract Act, 1872

The scope of the Indian Contract Act, 1872 may be broadly classified into two main groups, namely :

1. **General Principles of Contracts (Secs. 1 to 75) :** General Principles of contracts include :

- rules and laws relating to communication, acceptance and revocation of proposals (Secs. 2-9),
- voidable contracts (Secs. 10-19A and 22-23),
- void agreements (Secs. 11, 22-30, 32, 36, 56, 57 and 64-67),
- contingent contracts (Secs. 31-36),
- performance of contracts (Secs. 37-67),
- certain relations resembling those created by law i.e, Quasi - contracts (Secs. 68-73), and
- consequences of breach of contract (Secs. 73-75).

2. **Specific or Special Kinds of Contracts :** The remaining part of the Act deals with three special types of contracts discussed in Secs. 124 to 238 of the Act. These are contracts of :

- Indemnity and Guarantee (Secs. 124 to 147),
- Bailment and Pledge (Secs. 148-181),
- Agency (Secs. 182-238),
- Sale of Goods (Secs. 76-123), and
- Partnership (Secs. 239-266)

The provisions relating to contracts of Sale of Goods (Secs. 76-123) and Partnership (Secs. 239-266) were repealed and separate Acts called the 'Sale of Goods Act' and the 'Indian Partnership Act' were passed in 1930 and 1932 respectively.

AGREEMENT

Contract arises as a result of an agreement purporting to create and define rights and obligations between two parties. It is therefore quite essential to understand what an agreement is and how it can be arrived at.

Definition of Agreement : When an offer made by one (offerer) is accepted by the other, it becomes a promise. Section 2 (e) of the Indian Contract Act states that *every promise and every set of promises, forming the consideration for each other*, is an agreement. It implies that an agreement is an accepted proposal. It follows that every agreement is made of a proposal from one side and its acceptance by the other.

Characteristics of an Agreement

1. **Plurality of Persons :** Agreement is an expression of common intention of two or more persons. The first characteristic of an agreement is thus plurality of persons. It is impossible for one person to make an agreement with himself. For instance, when a person in his official capacity, as a director of a company, makes a promise to himself as an individual, no agreement is formed by an acceptance in the latter capacity.

2. **Consensus ad-idem :** The persons making an agreement must consent to some determination with a view to create a right in one party and corresponding duty on the other party. These determinations are known as *promises*. Promises are formed only when there is meeting of the minds of the parties who must agree to the same thing in the same sense. This is known as *consensus ad-idem* which is the other important characteristic of an agreement.

For instance, if A intends to sell his white horse to B and B intends to buy his black horse, there is no consensus ad-idem and hence no agreement. The real test as to whether there is consensus ad-idem depends on whether under the circumstances, one party was reasonably led to believe that there was an offer and the other party to believe that there was an acceptance.

Mental Condition : Generally, a person 'promises' orally or in writing what transpires in his mind. Arising from such mental condition, promise or contract signifies two ideas; namely, agreement and obligation which are otherwise described as *consensus-ad-idem* and *vinculum juris*. Agreement implies consent of the parties and consent has to do with the state of the mind as recorded in words, oral or written. *Agreement, in other words, is the outcome of consenting minds or consensus-ad-idem.*

The other component, namely *the vinculum juris* or *the legal tie*-arises

(a) if there is agreement

(b) between two parties

(c) with reference to definite acts and

(d) which relates to legal matters and not mere social engagements.

Because the legal tie or obligation may arise also from circumstances other than agreement e.g. a tort, judgements of courts, etc. *Salmond* has made the famous observation that the *law of contracts is not the whole law of agreements; nor is it the whole law of obligations; it is the law of those agreements which create obligations and of those obligations which have their source in agreements.*

3. **Promise or Reciprocal Promises :** An agreement has been defined as *every promise and every set of promises, forming the consideration for each other.* A promise is an accepted proposal. When the person to whom the proposal is made significer his assent thereto, the proposal is said to be accepted. Offer and acceptance together constitute an agreement. Agreement is thus a promise or a set of "reciprocal promises". *"Promises which form the consideration or part of the consideration for each other are called reciprocal promises"* [Section 2(f)].

KINDS OF AGREEMENTS

1. **Social Agreements :** They are of social nature and do not enjoy the benefits of law. They are not enforceable and cannot be called 'contracts'. An agreement to attend a dinner at a friend's house or to attend a marriage or a religious function, to see a movie etc., are the examples of social agreement.

2. **Legal (Valid) Agreement :** It is the sum of (a) an agreement and (b) an intention to create legal obligation. Obligations require the parties must do or obstain from doing something. However, such an act or abstinence may relate to social or legal matters. It is a valid agreement which is enforceable at law.

3. **Void Agreement :** An agreement not enforceable by law is said to be *void*. [Section (g)].

4. **Voidable Agreement :** A voidable agreement is one which is enforceable by law at the option of one or more of the parties thereto, but not at the option of other [Section 2(i)].

5. **Unenforceable Agreement :** Such an agreement is valid in the eyes of law, but cannot be enforced in the courts because of some *technical defect in procedural matters of formation and enforcement. eg., want of stamping, registration etc.*

6. **Illegal Agreement :** An illegal agreement is one which is against the provisions of the law.

7. **Agreements to Agree in Future :** An agreement to agree in future is a contradiction. It is absurd to state that a man enters into an agreement till the terms of the contracts are settled. Until the terms are settled, he is free to retire from the bargain. Moreover, there can be no binding contract unless all the material conditions of contract have been agreed upon. Thus agreement to agree in future is not a contract.

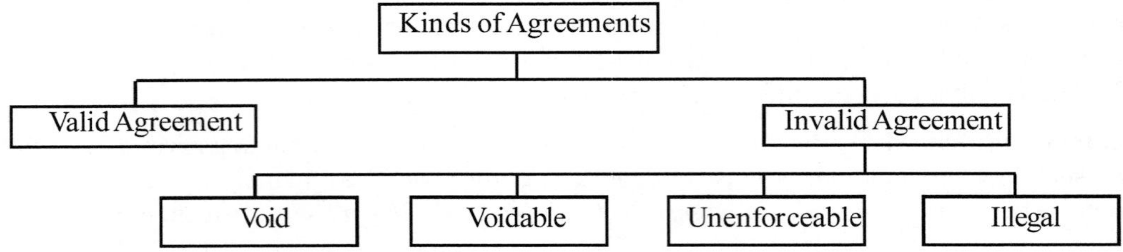

CONTRACT

Definition of Contract

A contract is a valid or legal agreement. In other words a contract is an agreement made between two or more parties whereby legal rights and obligations are created which the law will enforce. According to Sec. 2(h) of Indian Contract Act, 1872 ***an agreement enforceable by law is a contract.***

As mentioned already, an agreement connotes that (a) at least two parties have expressed themselves, (b) with sufficient certainty, and (c) in terms which correspond on the subject. An agreement is a very wide term. It may be a social agreement or a legal agreement. A social agreement does not give rise to contractual obligations and is not enforceable in law court. It is only those agreements which are enforceable in the law courts are called ***contracts.***

According to Section 10, ***all agreements are contracts if they are made by the free consent of parties competent to contract, for a lawful consideration and with a lawful object, and are not hereby expressly declared to be void.***

Some *definitions* given by leading authors may here be noted :

Salmond : Contract is an agreement creating and defining obligations between the parties.

Sir William Anson : Contract is a legally binding agreement between two or more persons by which rights are acquired by one or more to acts or forbearances on the part of the other or others.

ESSENTIALS OF A CONTRACT

A Contract in order to be enforceable by law must have the following ten essential elements :

1. **Plurality of Persons :** There must be two persons or groups of persons to form a contract. There must also be privity (knowledge) of contract between the two parties.

2. **Offer and Acceptance :** There must be a lawful proposal or offer by one party and a lawful acceptance of that proposal by the other party - thus resulting in an agreement. The terms of the offer and acceptance must be definite. The acceptance of the offer must be absolute and unconditional. It must also be according to the terms prescribed and must be communicated to the proposer. A proposal when accepted becomes a promise or agreement. The offer and acceptance must be *'consensus ad-idem'*, which means that both the parties must agree on the same thing in the same sense (i.e., identity of wills or uniformity and meeting of minds).

3. **Legal Relationship, Legal Consequences, Promises & Obligations recognized by law :** When two parties enter into an agreement, their intention must be to create a legal relationship between them. If there is no such intention, there can be no contract between the parties. In *Balfour Vs. Balfour (1919)* a husband agreed to pay $ 30 to his wife every month while he was abroad. On failure to pay, his wife sued him for the recovery of amount. It was held that it was a domestic agreement which did not intend to create legal relations. In *Weeks Vs. Tybald* the defendant in the course of casual conversation stated to the plaintiff that he would give $100 to any one marrying his daughter with his consent. The plaintiff having married his daughter with his consent, sued for the amount. It was held that there was no legal offer as the statement was not capable of creating legal relation.

4. **Lawful Consideration :** The agreement to be enforceable by law must be supported by consideration. The term *consideration*, in simple words, means something in return. The agreement is legally enforceable only when both the parties give something and get something in return. A promise to do something, getting nothing in return, is usually not enforceable by law. The intention of the parties to create legal relationship can only be ascertained by the presence or absence of consideration. The consideration need not necessarily be in cash or kind. It may be an act or abstinence (refraining from doing something) or promise to do or not to do something. The consideration may be past, present or future. But it must be real, definite, lawful and of some value in terms of money.

5. **Contractual Capacity (Competency) of Parties :** The parties to the agreement must be capable of entering into a valid contract. Every person is competent to contract if he (a) is of the age of majority, (b) is of sound mind and (c) is not disqualified from contracting by any law to which he is subject. Incapacity to contract may arise from minority, lunacy, idiocy, drunkenness, professional, status etc. If a party suffers from any flaw in the required capacity, the contract becomes invalid except in some special cases.

6. **Free and Genuine Consent :** It is essential to the creation of every contract that there must be a free and genuine consent of the parties to the agreement. The consent of the parties is said to be free when they are of the same mind on all the material terms of the contract. The parties are said to have identity of mind or agreed on the same thing in the same sense when all the terms of the consent are put in the form of an offer or proposal by one party and the other party says "yes" to it. There is absence of free and genuine consent if the agreement is induced by coercion, undue influence, fraud, misrepresentation, mistake etc.

7. **Lawful Object :** The object of the agreement must be lawful. It is lawful unless it is forbidden by law, or is of such a nature that, if permitted, it would defeat the provisions of any law, or is fraudulent, or involves or implies injury to the person or property of another, or is immoral or opposed to public policy. In simple words, the object of the agreement must not be (a) illegal, (b) immoral, or (c) opposed to public policy. If an agreement suffers from any legal flaw, it would not be enforceable by law.

8. **Agreement not declared Void :** The agreement, though it might possess all the essential elements discussed above, must not have been expressly declared void by any law in force in the country.

   Sections 24 to 30 of the Indian Contract Act specify certain types of agreements which have been expressly declared to be void. Some of those agreements are : (a) An agreement in restraint of marriage, (b) An agreement in restraint of trade, (c) An agreement in restraint of legal proceedings and (d) A wagering agreement.

9. **Certainty and Possibility of Performance :** The terms of the agreement must be certain and not vague or ambiguous. The terms of the agreement must also be such as are capable of performance.

***Illustration* :** A agrees to sell B 100 tons of oil. There is nothing in the agreement to show what kind of oil is intended. In this case, it is not clear as to what kind/brand of oil is intended to be sold. That means, the agreement is vague or uncertain, and so, it is void. However, if A, a dealer in coconut oil, agrees to sell to B 100 tons of oil, the terms of the agreement are considered to be definite, in spite of the fact that the kind of oil is not specified, because, in the case of a dealer in coconut oil, the oil contemplated is naturally the coconut oil.

An agreement to do an act impossible in itself cannot be enforced. This is based on the maxim *lex non cogit ad aimpossibilia* which means that *law does not compel to do what is impossible.*

Pre-contractual Impossibility : A contract which at the time it was entered into was impossible to perform, is *void ab initio* and creates no rights and obligations, e.g., a promise to bring honey from moon for one's honeymoon, to promise to put life in to a dead body or even a promise to discover treasure by magic.

Post-contractual Impossibility : A contract, which at the time it was entered into was capable of being performed may subsequently become impossible to perform or unlawful. In such cases the contract becomes void. This is known as the doctrine of *Supervening Impossibility*. It is also known as the *Doctrine of Frustration.*

10. **Legal Formalities :** The agreement may be oral or in writing. Where it is to be in writing, it must comply with the necessary legal formalities as to writing, stamping, registration and attestation. Further, an agreement is to be made in the presence of requisite witness. If the agreement does not comply with these legal formalities, it cannot be enforced by law.

Some of the contracts which must be *in writing* otherwise they will be invalid are:

1. A promise to pay a time barred debt
2. An arbitration agreement
3. Lease agreement for a period of more than three years
4. Contracts of insurance
5. Negotiable instruments e.g., bills of exchange, cheques, promissory notes etc.
6. Memorandum and Articles of Association of a company
7. Contracts relating to transfer of immovable property, and so on.

Some of the contracts which must be *registered* : are

(i) A promise made without consideration on account of natural love and affection between the parties standing in near relation

(ii) Documents of certain transactions which are compulsorily to be registered under Sec. 17 of the Registration Act.

(iii) Contracts relating to transfer of immovable property under the Transfer of Property Act, 1882,

(iv) Memorandum and Articles of Association, mortgages and charges under the Companies Act, 1956 and so on.

According to the Indian Stamp Act, 1894 certain instruments are chargeable with duty of stamp of the amount indicated in Schedule I of the Act e.g., Bills of Exchange, Promissory Note, Insurance Policy, Partition Deed, Share/Debenture Certificate, Pledge, Mortgage Deed, etc. If the instrument is not duly stamped (i.e. unstamped or under stamped or improperly stamped) it shall not be admitted in evidence in a court of law.

All the above essential elements must exist together in a contract. An agreement with all the above elements is a legal or valid agreement or simply called a contract and therefore enforceable. But if any one of the elements is missing, the contract is either voidable, void, illegal, or unenforceable in the eyes of law.

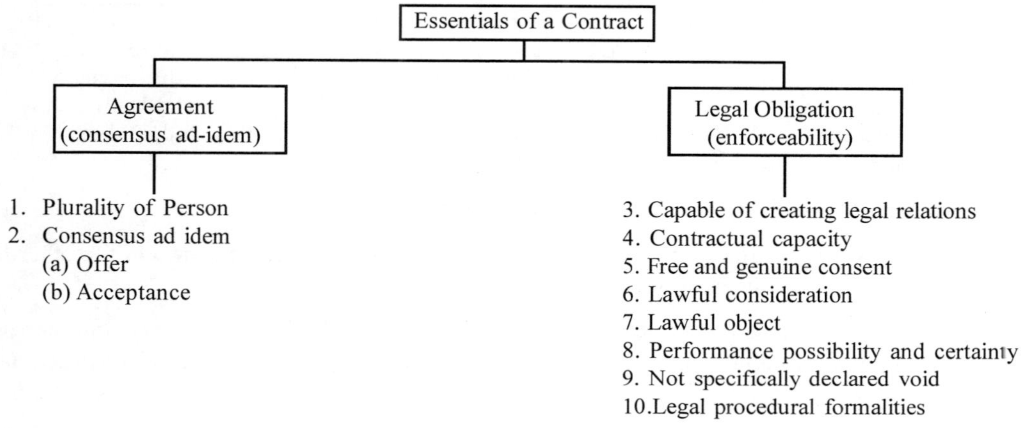

CLASSIFICATION OF CONTRACTS

I. **Classification according to Validity :** *Valid* and *Invalid.*

Void Agreement : An agreement not enforceable by law is said to be void.

Void Contract : A contract which ceases to be enforceably by law becomes void when it ceases to be enforceable [Sec. 2(j)]. It is valid when it is entered into, but something happens subsequent to the formation of the contract which makes it void.

Voidable Contract : An agreement which is enforceable by law at the option of one or more of the parties thereto, but not at the option of the other or others, is a voidable contract [Sec. 2(i)].

Illegal Contract : A contract is illegal if it involves the transgression of some rules of basic public policy and is criminal in nature and where it is based on immoral.

II. **Classification according to Formation :** (a) *Express Contract* : Contracts entered into between the parties by works spoken or written. (b) *Implied Contract* : It is a contract in which the terms are not expressly stated but which are inferred from the circumstances of the case and conduct of the parties. (c) *Quasi-Contract* : It is an obligation imposed by law, regardless of agreement.

III. **Classification on the basis of the Obligation to Perform :** (a) *Unilateral Contract* : It is a contract where only one party has yet to perform his obligation. (b) *Bilateral Contract* : It is a contract where both the parties have yet to perform their obligations.

IV. **Classification on the basis of Execution :** (a) *Executed Contract* : It is a contract which is wholly performed by both the parties. (b) *Executory Contract*: It is a contract in which promises of both of parties have yet to be performed.

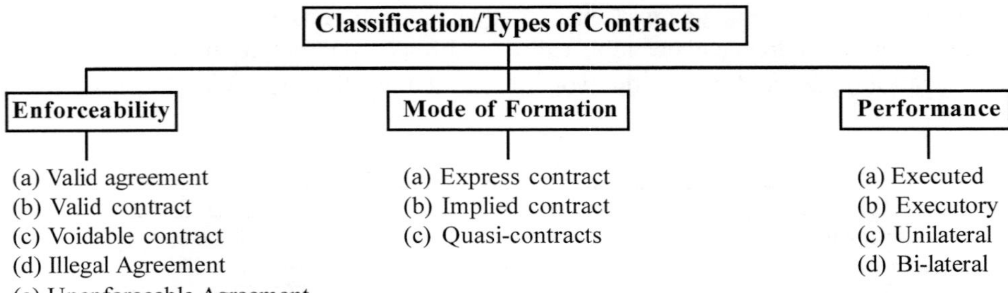

1. Difference between Agreement and Contract

(i) **Enforceability :** Offer and acceptance together constitute an agreement. On the other hand, agreement and enforceability together constitute a contract.

(ii) **Legal obligation :** Certain agreements may not create any legal obligation, but a contract necessarily creates an legal obligation. It is therefore said that "all agreements are not contracts but all contracts are agreements".

(iii) **Binding on Parties :** An agreement is not always a binding contract. Whereas a contract is always a concluded and binding agreement.

(iv) **Speciality :** An agreement is a *genus* i.e., wider concept than a contract, a section in itself. Contract is a *specie* of an agreement.

2. Differences between Void Agreement and Voidable Contract

(i) **Legality :** A void agreement cannot be enforced by either party whereas a voidable contract can be enforced by the party at whose option it is voidable i.e, avoidable or enforceable.

(ii) **Time of Enforceability :** Void agreement is unenforceable from the very beginning, whereas a voidable contract becomes unenforceable only when the party at whose option the contract is voidable, rescinds it.

(iii) **Restitution :** In case of void agreements, restitution is always followed unless the void nature of the agreement was known to the parties at the time of its formation. On the other hand, in a voidable contract when rescinded, the benefit received will be restored as far as possible.

(iv) **Compensation :** Since a void agreement is unforceable, the question of compensation does not arise on the non-performance of such an agreement. But under a voidable contract, any person who has received any benefit must compensate or restore it to the other party who rightfully rescinds it.

(v) **Collateral transactions :** A voidable contract does not affect collateral transactions. But if the agreement is void on account of the object and consideration being illegal or unlawful, the collateral agreement will also become void.

3. Differences between Void and Illegal Agreement

(a) **All Inclusive :** The word *Void* is used in broader sense, it includes illegal aspects. 'Illegal' as a word is used in narrow sense, it does not include void. *All illegal agreements are void but all void agreements are not necessarily illegal.*

(b) **Proofs :** Void agreements are not illegal until they are proved to be illegal. But illegal agreements remains so from the very beginning.

(c) **Collateral Transaction :** A void agreement does not involve collateral transactions. But an illegal agreement vitiates not only primary transactions but also collateral transactions.

Examples

(i) P engages B to kill C and borrows ₹ 10000 from D to pay B. Here the agreement with B is illegal. The agreement with D is collateral to it, if D is aware of the purpose of the loan. In this case the loan transaction is void and D cannot recover the money. But if D is not aware of the purpose of the loan, it may be argued that the loan transaction, is not collateral to the other illegal agreement, is valid.

(ii) W enters into a wagering agreement and borrows ₹ 100 for the purpose. The main agreement is void but the loan transaction being merely collateral to it is valid even though the creditor is aware of the purpose of the loan.

(d) **Punishability :** Void agreements are not always punishable. But illegal agreements are always punishable.

4. Differences between Illegal and Unenforceable Agreement

(a) **Defect in Subject/Procedure :** Illegal agreements are against public policy and law in force in India. Unenforceable agreements are not enforceable because of some technical or procedural defects.

(b) **Timing of Unenforceability :** Illegal agreements are void from the very beginning and cannot be enforced by court of law under any circumstances. An unenforceable agreement is valid in itself but it is not enforceable by court because of some technical defects. Some of these agreements can be enforced if the technical defect is removed.

(c) **Collateral Transactions :** In case of an illegal agreement, not only primary transactions but collateral transactions are also affected by illegality. In case of an unenforceable one, it is a flaw in procedural matters. Some of these agreements can be enforced if the technical defect in question is removed.

(d) **Punishment :** Illegal agreements may cause penalty. In case of unenforceable agreements, no penalty is imposed.

Thus, all illegal agreements are unenforceable. But all unenforceable agreements may not be illegal.

REVIEW QUESTIONS

1. Define the term (i) Agreement, (ii) Contract.
2. All contracts are agreements, but all agreements are not contracts - Discuss.
3. "Offer and acceptance bring the parties together but the law required some further evidence of their intention to create legal relationship". Comment.
4. Write short notes on : (a) valid contract, (b) void contract, (c) void agreement (d) Illegal contract, (e) unilateral contract (f) bilateral contract.
5. Distinguish between (a) Void agreement and Voidable contract, (b) Void and Illegal contract, (c) Void and Unenforceable contracts, (d) Agreement and Contract.

❑ ❑ ❑

OFFER AND ACCEPTANCE

A contract is made by the process of lawful offer by one party and the lawful acceptance of the offer by the other party to whom it is made. Thus, an offer is the starting point of making a contract. The term *proposal* is used in the Indian Contract Act in the place of the word *offer* which conveys same meaning as proposal. Hence a detailed discussion about 'offer' is given in this chapter.

Meaning of Proposal : The term (Offer) Proposal is defined in Section 2(a) of the Indian Contract Act, 1872, thus, when one person signifies to another his willingness to do or to abstain from doing anything with a view to obtaining the assent of that other to such act or abstinence, he is said to make a proposal. The person making the offer is known as *offeror* or '*proposer* or *promisor*' and the person to whom the offer is made is called *offeree* or *promisee.*

Illustration : A writes to B that he is willing to sell his house if B is willing to pay ₹ 4,90,000. A is said to make an offer and if B writes agreeing to that offer, it is called an *acceptance*, and A is called the offeror or proposer or promisor and B is the offeree or promisee.

Characteristics of Offer : The definition of offer involves the following important points : 1. It must be an expression of willingness to do or to abstain from doing something. 2. It must be made to another person. 3. It must be made with a view to obtain the assent of the second party to such act or abstinence. 4. The expression of willingness must be made with a view to create legal obligations.

Types of Offer

1. **Express and Implied Offers :** If an offer is made by words, spoken or written, it is called an *express offer*. If offer is made otherwise than in words, the offer is called an *implied offer*. The following are the examples of implied offer.
   (a) A transport company runs buses on a particular route. There is an implied offer from the transport company to carry passengers on the route who are prepared to pay the specified fare.
   (b) In a restaurant, there is an implied promise to pay for consuming the eatables.
   (c) A video-game machine kept at a Video-Game Parlour is an implied offer to use the machine for the game by inserting the necessary coin. A person who inserts the coin is said to have accepted it.
   (d) Weighing machine in the market place, request for ticket in lottery, cinema house or other public places, cloak room, taxi running on the streets, tram car, public buses, an invitation to existing share holders or debenture holders to take up right issue or conversion etc., are example of *continuous offer.*
2. **Specific and General Offers :** When offer is made to a definite class of persons, it can be accepted by that particular person or class of persons only. Such an offer is called *specific offer*. When offer is made to the world at large which could be accepted by anyone e.g., reward to a person supplying information pertaining to something, it is called a *general offer* or *offer at large.*

3. **Positive and Negative Offers :** The offer may be positive or negative. Thus, an offer may be to do something or not to do something. An offer to do something, is a *positive offer.* And an offer not to do something is a *negative offer*.

Offer and Invitation to Offer (Chaffer) : An offer must be distinguished from mere invitation to offer. Invitations to offer are negotiate or offers to receive offers. On the other hand, offer is a final expression of willingness by the offeror to be bound by his promise, should the other choose to accept it.

LEGAL RULES AND ESSENTIALS REGARDING OFFER

The Contract Act contains various rules regarding offer/proposal. They can be summed up as follows:

1. **The offer may be Express or Implied** *(Supra).*
2. **The offer may be Positive or Negative** *(Supra).*
3. **Offer must intend to create legal relationship :** An offer will not become a promise even after it has been accepted unless it has been made with a view to create legal obligations. It was held in *Weeks Vs. Tybald.* (1605) that mere statement of intention in the course of conversion will not create binding promise.
4. **Terms of offer must be certain :** The offer must not be ambiguous, uncertain and vague. The terms of the offer must be definite, unambiguous and certain. If the offer is indefinite, or vague, it will not be regarded as offer.
5. **An Offer may be made to specific person or class of persons or to any one in the world at large:**

Illustration **:** If A issues a public advertisement to the effect that he will give ₹ 1000 to anyone who brings back his (A's) missing son. It is an offer at large or a general offer, and any member of public can accept it by searching for and bringing back 'A's missing son.

Carlill Vs. Carbolic Smoke Ball Co. (1892) **:** Messrs Carbolic Smoke Ball Co. had issued an advertisement in which they offered to pay $ 100 to anyone who might contract influenza after having used the smoke balls manufactured by them three times daily for two weeks, according to the printed directions. In the advertisement, they also stated that they had deposited $ 1,000 in Alliance Bank to show their sincerity in the matter On the faith of this advertisement, Mrs. Carlill bought and used the balls as prescribed but in spite of it caught influenza. She brought an action case for $ 100. The court held that it was an offer made to the world at large and could ripen into a contract with anybody who performed the conditions. The company was, therefore, held liable to pay.

6. **The offer must express the final willingness of the offeror :** The terms of the offer should be such that they contain final willingness of the offeror. Sometimes, a party does not express his final willingness. On the contrary it proposes certain terms on which he is willing to negotiate. In such cases, he is not making an offer because he is not expressing his final willingness to enter into a contract.
7. **Every offer must be communicated to the offeree :** An offer is effective only when it is communicated to the offeree. There is no question of acceptance of an offer unless the acceptor knows the offer.

Fitch Vs. Snedkar (1886) **:** S offered a reward to anyone who would returns his lost dog. F brought the dog without any knowledge of the offer of reward. Held, F is not entitled to the award as "he cannot be said to have accepted the offer when he was not all aware of it".

Lalman Shukla Vs. Gauri Dutt, (1913) **:** G's nephew had absconded from his home. He sent his servant L to search his missing nephew. When the servant had left, G then announced that anybody who discovered the missing boy would be given the reward of ₹ 500. The servant discovered the missing boy without knowing a reward. When the servant came to know about the reward, he brought an action against G to recover the same. But his action failed. It was held that the servant was not entitled to the reward because he did not know about the offer when he discovered the missing boy.

Mode of Communication of Offer : An offer may be communicated to the offeree or offerees by word of mouth, by writing, or by conduct. A written offer may be contained in a letter, telegram, fax etc. A circular or advertisement or a notice may be written in such a language that it amounts to an offer. A tramway car and a bus going along a street and picking up passengers are examples of offers by conduct.

Offer by post and telephone : An offer may be made by post. An offer may also be accepted by post, if there is no other mode of acceptance specially prescribed by the proposer. When a proposal is made through the post, the post office is by implication the agent of the proposer. Offers can also be communicated through the telephone and cellphone. But there are certain conditions regarding oral communication. It had been held that the offer and acceptance must be audible, heard and easily understood. If these conditions are satisfied and the other essential elements of the contract exist, the parties are bound through a telephone and cellphone conversation.

8. **An Offer must be distinguished from** (i) invitation to make/receive offers, quotations, circulars etc., and (ii) declaration or statement of intention, tender etc. (iii) an answer to a question.

9. **Offer must be made with a view to obtaining the assent :** The offer to do or not to do something must be made with a view to obtaining the assent of the other person to whom it has been addressed and not merely with a view to disclosing the intention of making an offer. The communication of acceptance cannot be dispensed with by any of the terms of the offer.

10. **Offer should not contain a term, the non-compliance of which would amount to acceptance :** The offer should not impose on the offeree, an obligation to reply. The offeror cannot say that if acceptance is not communicated within a fixed period of time, the offer would be considered as accepted. If the offeree does not reply, there is no contract.

11. **An offer may be conditional :** Where an offer is subject to certain conditions it must be clearly written, expressed or communicated to the offeree. It is immaterial if the terms are hard and ridiculous. If a person accepts such an offer, he cannot plead ignorance of conditions later on. The offerer may even prescribe the mode of acceptance. Thus, if the offeror asks for sending the acceptance 'by telegram' and the offeree sends the acceptance 'by post', the offeror may decline to treat the acceptance as a valid acceptance provided he gives a notice to that effect to the offeree. If the offeror does not inform the offeree to that effect, he is deemed to have accepted the acceptance.

Offer with special conditions : If there are special terms or conditions in an offer, these must be brought to the notice of the offeree at the time of making a proposal. Moreover, they must be presented in such a manner as to ensure that a reasonable man can become aware of them before he accepts the proposal.

Standing Offers : Sometimes a 'Proposal' may take the form of a 'continuous offer'. Such offers are called '*Standing offers*' or '*Open Offers*'. A standing offer is in the nature of a tender. It is an offer to supply certain commodity for a certain price upto a certain period. The quantity to be supplied, however may or may not be specified.

Contracts for the supply of goods over a period of time are sometimes so worded that the buyer has an option as regards the quantity to be purchased and the time of purchase. Such contracts are called "*Standing Contracts*" or "*Open Proposals*".

***Illustration* :** P signed a tender addressed to the London County Council (L.C.C), agreeing, on acceptance, to supply all the goods specified in the schedule, to the extent ordered. The tender was accepted but the

L.C.C. did not order any goods. Held, the L.C.C. was not bound to order any goods, but if it did so, P was bound to deliver the goods as and when ordered. *Percival Ltd.* Vs. *L.C.C. (1918).*

In such cases as above, a contract comes into existence when a definite quantity is ordered. *Bengal Coal Co.* Vs. *Wadia (1900) Bom.*

Cross offers : Two offers similar in all respects, made by two parties to each other, in ignorance of each other's offer are termed as '*cross offers*'. Cross offers do not amount to acceptance of one's offer by the other and do not constitute a complete (formal) agreement. Hence no contract is formed.

Example : X of Chennai sends a letter by post to Y of Mysore offering to sell his car for ₹ 11akh. The letter is posted on 1st January and the same day Y of Mysore sends a letter by post to X of Chennai offering to buy X's car for ₹ 11 lakh. These two letters cross each other. Y's letter is merely an offer and not the acceptance of X's letter. Here, both the parties are making offer and no party has accepted the offer therefore no contract has been entered into, if they want to enter into a contract, at least one of them must send his acceptance to the offer made by the other.

ESSENTIALS OF A VALID OFFER

1. An offer may be express or implied.
2. The offer may be positive or negative
3. It must be intended to create legal relations.
4. The terms of the offer must be definite and certain.
5. The offer must be communicated to the offeree.
6. The special terms of the offer must be brought to the notice of the offeree.
7. An offer may be general or specific.
8. It must be made with a view to obtain acceptance.
9. It must be distinguished from "Invitation to offer" or "declaration of intention".
10. The offer should not contain any terms the non-compliance of which amounts to acceptance.
11. Two identical cross-offers do not result in a contract.

Termination of Offer

Section 6 deals with various modes of terminating (revocation or lapse) of an offer. In all these cases, an offer comes to an end.

1. **By notice of revocation :** An offer can be revoked at any time before acceptance, the offeror doing so **by giving notice** of revocation to offeree. A revocation of offer must be communicated to the offeree, otherwise the revocation does not prevent acceptance. It is necessary that the communication of revocation should be from the offeror or from his duly authorised agent.
2. **By lapse of time :** A proposal is revoked by the lapse of time prescribed in such proposal for its acceptance. If no time is prescribed that proposal is revoked by the lapse of a reasonable time [Sec. 6(2)].
3. **By failure of the acceptor to fulfil a condition precedent to acceptance. [Sec. 6(3)] :** If there is a condition in the proposal, before fulfilling of which, the acceptor cannot accept the proposal, the proposal will naturally be revoked if the acceptor fails to fulfil that condition precedent.
4. **By failure to accept according to the mode prescribed :** An offer is revoked, if the offeree fails to accept it according to the mode prescribed by the offeror. If no mode is prescribed, the offer must be accepted according to some reasonable or usual mode.

5. **By death or insanity of the offeror [Sec.6(4)] :** Death or insanity of the offeror puts an end to the offer, provided the fact of the death or insanity comes to the knowledge of the offeree before acceptance. But if the offeree accepts the offer in ignorance of death of offeror, the acceptance is valid as against the heirs of offeror.
6. **By Rejection :** An offer lapses as soon as it is rejected by an offeree. An offer is rejected, if the offeree (i) communicates his rejection to the offeror or (ii) makes a counter-offer or (iii) accepts the offer subject to conditions. Rejection of an offer may be expressed or implied. It is express, if it is communicated to the offeror by express words, spoken or written. It is implied, if the offeree makes a *counter-offer* or gives a *conditional offer*.
7. **By subsequent illegality or destruction of subject matter :** An offer lapses if it becomes illegal or the subject matter itself is destroyed after the offer is made but before it is accepted.

TERMINATION OF AN OFFER

1. An offer terminates when revoked by notice of revocation.
2. An offer lapses after stipulated or reasonable time.
3. A conditional offer terminates when condition is not accepted.
4. It terminates by not being accepted in the mode prescriber or in usual and reasonable manner.
5. An offer lapses by the death or insanity of the offeror or the offeree before acceptance.
6. An offer lapses on rejection by counter offer or conditional offer.
7. It terminates by subsequent illegality or destruction of subject matter.

Differences between Revocation of Offer and Rejection of Offer

1. Revocation of an offer takes place at the instance of the offeror, whereas rejection of an offer takes place at the instance of the offeree.
2. An offer may be revoked by the offeror at any time before its acceptance is complete as against the offeror. On the other hand, an offer may be rejected by the offeree at any time.
3. Revocation of an offer by the offeror must be always express. But rejection of an offer by the offeree may be expressed or implied.

Counter-Offer : To ensure a binding agreement, there must be absolute and unconditional acceptance of the terms of the offer. If the acceptance varies the terms of the offer, it is called a *counter offer* and not an acceptance of the original offer. A 'Counter-offer' is a rejection of the original offer and making of a new offer. A party who makes a counter-offer and subsequently changes his mind and wishes to accept the original offer cannot do so, as the first offer lapses, and he cannot treat it as still open.

***Illustration* :** A offers to B to sell his house for ₹ 5,00,000 and B says that he agrees to buy the house for ₹ 4,50,000. This is a counter-offer from B.

Communication of revocation of Offer : According to Section 3 of the Act, the revocation of a proposal or an acceptance is deemed to be made by any act or omission of the party by which he intends to communicate such revocation, or which has the effect of communicating it. The communication of revocation is complete : (i) as against the person who makes it, when it is put into a course of transmission to the person who makes, when it is made, so as to be out of the power of the person who makes it; (ii) as against the person to whom it is made, when it comes to his knowledge.

***Illustration* :** P makes a proposal to Q. Q sends a letter of acceptance. Subsequently Q changes his mind and revokes his acceptance by telegram. Q's revocation is complete, as against Q when the telegram is despatched, and as against P when it reaches him.

ACCEPTANCE

An offer in itself does not imply legal relationship. The legal relationship results only when the offer is accepted. Thus acceptance of an offer is necessary to create legal relationship.

Acceptance is an expression by the offeree of his willingness to be bound by the terms of the offer.

Definition of Acceptance : An acceptance is defined as, *When the person to whom the proposal is made signifies his assent thereto, the proposal is said to be accepted. A proposal when accepted becomes a promise* [Sec. 2(b)]. Thus, acceptance is the manifestation by the offeree of his assent to the terms of the offer. The offeree or promisee after acceptance becomes acceptor.

ESSENTIALS AND LEGAL RULES OF A VALID ACCEPTANCE

1. **Acceptance must be absolute and unconditional :** In order to convert a proposal into a promise, the acceptance must be absolute and unqualified. A proposal must be accepted in total and must correspond with the terms of the offer. Part or partial acceptance is no acceptance.
2. **Acceptance by usual mode as desired by the offeror :** Acceptance must be expressed in some usual and reasonable manner, unless the proposal prescribes the manner in which it is to be accepted. If the proposal prescribes a manner in which it is to be accepted, and the acceptance is not made in such manner, the proposer may, within a reasonable time after the acceptance is communicated to him, insist that his proposal shall be accepted in the prescribed manner, and not otherwise; but if he fails to do so, he is bound by the acceptance. Thus, if the offer says "wire reply please" and the reply is sent by post; there is no acceptance of the offer, if the offeror informs the offeree that the acceptance is not according to the mode prescribed.
3. **Acceptance cannot precede an offer :** There can be no acceptance before the communication of offer : An acceptance cannot precede the offer. There can, therefore be no acceptance before the communication of the offer. In a company, shares were allotted to a person who had not applied for them. Subsequently, when he applied for shares, he was unware of the previous allotment. Held, the allotment of shares previous to the application was invalid.
4. **Acceptance may be express or implied :** Acceptance must be communicated to the offeror by spoken or written words or conduct. When acceptance is made by words spoken or written, it is an express acceptance. If it is accepted by conduct it is an implied acceptance *(Carlill Vs. Carbolic Smoke Ball Co. (1893))*. The acceptor must have done something to signify his intention to accept. Mere intention or mental acceptance, if uncommunicated, will lack essence. If the acceptor never communicates his acceptance to the proposer, there will be no binding agreement. For the validity of an agreement it is essential that the proposer must know that his proposal has been accepted.

   Though the general rule is that an acceptance must be communicated to the proposer, yet it is possible to accept a proposal by performing the conditions of such proposal; the fulfilment of the conditions will be sufficient to signify the mental assent to the proposal. But the performance of the conditions of the offer must indicate that : (i) the proposal must be accepted by a definite person; and (ii) something must happen to ensure that the proposal has been accepted by the specified person.
5. **Acceptance must be given within a reasonable time :** If any time limit is specified acceptance must be given within that period. If no time is stipulated, it must be given within a reasonable time.
6. **Acceptance must show to fulfil a promise :** Acceptance, in order to be valid, must be made under circumstances which would show that the acceptor intends to fulfil the terms of the promise. If no such intention is present, the acceptance is not valid.

7. **Acceptance must be by an ascertained person i.e., the Person to whom the offer is made (offeree) :** While an offer may be made to unascertained persons or the world at large, acceptance must be by an ascertained individual.
8. **Offer once rejected cannot be accepted until it is renewed :** Once a proposal refused, it cannot be accepted unless it is renewed. Thus, if A makes a proposal to sell his house for ₹ 5,00,000 and B says that he will pay ₹ 4,00,000, he cannot under any circumstances bind A to sell the house even though he is ready to pay the amount demanded by A. However, variations which are immaterial do not vitate the acceptance.
9. **Acceptance of offer means acceptance of all terms attached to the offer :** However, if the terms are to a large extent apparent in the face and no reasonable caution is taken to draw the attention of the acceptor then, these terms will not be binding, e.g., where the attention of a passenger was not drawn to the clause, "*Luggage at owner's Risk*" meaning that the company is not liable for any loss of luggage, it was held in a suit for the loss of luggage, that the company was liable.
10. **Acceptance must be made before the lapse or revocation of an offer.**
11. **The acceptor must be aware of the proposal at the time of the offer:** Acceptance follows offer. If the acceptor is not aware of the existence of the offer and conveys his acceptance, no contract comes into being. There must be a knowledge of the offer before anyone could consent to it. An act done in ignorance of the offer of a reward cannot be called an acceptance.

Lalman Shukla Vs. Gauri Dutt (1913) D sent P who was in his service in search of his missing nephew. Subsequently D announced a reward of ₹ 500 for information relating to the boy. But before P saw the announcement he had traced the boy. In a suit to recover the promised award, it was held that there can be no acceptance unless there is a knowledge of the offer.

12. **Silence does not imply acceptance :** A mere mental acceptance not evidenced by words or conduct is in the eyes of law no acceptance. Acceptance must be something more than a mere mental assent.

Exceptions : The following exceptions to the rule that **'silence does not imply acceptance'** may be noted :

(i) Where because of previous dealings, the offeree has given the offeror reason to understand that his silence means that he accepts.

(ii) Where the offeror has dispensed with the communication of acceptance. This may be gathered from the circumstances of the case, or the terms of the offer.

(iii) Where the offeror imposes certain conditions in the offer, performance of all the conditions even without communication of notice of acceptance is also a sufficient acceptance of the offer.

(iv) Where the offeree having reasonable opportunity to reject the offer, takes the benefit of the offer, it will amount to acceptance.

ESSENTIALS OF VALID ACCEPTANCE

1. Acceptance must be absolute and unqualified.
2. Acceptance must be in the prescribed manner or usual mode.
3. Acceptance must be in response to offer.
4. Acceptance may be express or implied; Silence does not imply acceptance
5. Acceptance must show to fulfill a promise
6. Acceptance must be made within reasonable time.
7. Acceptance must be by the offeree.

8. Acceptance must be accepted only when acceptor is aware of proposal.
9. Acceptance must be communicated to the offeror.
10. Acceptance must be made before the offer lapses.
11. Acceptance must be accepted before rejection unless the offer is renewed.

Rules for Communication of Acceptance [Sec 4] :

It has following two aspects :

(i) *As against the person who makes it :* When it is put into course of transmission to the person to whom it is made, so as to be out of the power of the person who makes it; and

(ii) *As against the person to whom it is made* : When it comes to his knowledge.

Revocation of Proposal : A proposal may be revoked at any time before the communication of acceptance is complete as against the acceptor, but not afterwards.

Illustration : A proposes, by a letter sent by post, to sell his house to B. B accepts the proposal by a letter sent by post. A may revoke his proposal at any time before or at the moment when B posts his letters of acceptance, but not afterwards. B may revoke his acceptance at any time before or at the moment when the letter communicating it reaches A, but not afterwards.

Rules for Communication by Post

Where the proposal and acceptance are made by letters sent by post, the rule is that the communication is complete and the *contract is made at the time when and the place where the letter of acceptance is posted* and not at the place where the offer is posted or acceptance is received. Therefore, no cause of action arises at the place where the offer is posted or acceptance is received. The rules relating to the communication of offer and acceptance through the post may be stated as follows :

1. An offer sent through post may be accepted by post, unless the offeror indicates some other *mode of communication*. Even if the offer is not sent through post, acceptance may be sent by post, if the circumstances indicate that the parties intended that the post might be used. **An offer sent by post is communicated only when it reaches the offeree.**
2. An acceptance sent through post is completed, the moment the letter of acceptance *properly addressed and stamped* is posted. The posting of an acceptance letter by the offeree binds the offeror, as he (offeror) is deemed to have received the acceptance, at the moment when it is so despatched so as to be "*out of power of the acceptor*", and it becomes a promise on which the offeree (acceptor) can sue even though the letter never reaches the offeror (i.e., is lost or delayed in postal transit).
3. An acceptance binds the acceptor only when it reaches the offeror. This is done to give an opportunity to the acceptor to revoke his acceptance before the letter communicating the acceptance reaches the latter.
4. The place where the letter of acceptance is posted will be the place where the contract is made.
5. Regarding revocation of an offer, the letter of revocation must have been posted before the letter of acceptance is posted by the offeree.

When a proposal is made through the post, the post office is by implication the agent of the proposer. Therefore a letter of acceptance duly addressed and posted is sufficient acceptance even though the letter does not actually reach the proposer. (Notice to an agent is considered to be notice to the principal). The letter must, however, be duly stamped and correctly addressed. The letter must be actually posted. It is not enough to give it to somebody to post.

Illustrations

(i) G applied for shares in a company. A letter of allotment was posted but the letter did not reach G.Held there was a binding contract and G was a shareholder of the company. *Household Fire Insurance Co. Vs. Grant. (1877)*

(ii) A registered envelope was tendered by the postman to the addressee, who refused to accept it. It is to be presumed that the addressee has the knowledge of the content thereof. *Har Charn Singh* v. *Shiv Rani and Others. (1981) SC*

Rules for Contracts over the Telephone or the Telex, Fax / E-mail: Nowadays most of the commercial transactions are carried on through telephones, cellphone, telex, fax, e-mail, etc. These contracts are treated on the same line as if the parties are facing each other. No contract can arise unless the offeree's acceptance is audible, heard and understood by the offeror. "During conversation if the line goes dead and the offeror fails to hear the words of acceptor, he should once again establish the contact with the acceptor and his words should be heard" - *Justice Anson (Law of Contract)*

The High Court Judgement about this matter is quoted below. "Now, when the parties negotiate a contract orally in the presence of each other or over telephone and one of them makes an oral offer to the other, it is plain that an oral acceptance is expected, and the acceptor must ensure that his acceptance is audible, heard and understood by the offer. The acceptance in such a case must be by such words which have the effect of communicating it". *Kanhaiylal v. Dineshwar Chandra (1959).*

In an English court it was held that a communication, sent through a telex or a teleprinter machine in the office, is valid. A contract made by 'telex' was no exception to the general rule that acceptance is not complete until communicated. *Entores Ltd. v. Miles Far Eastern Corporation. (1955).*

Microphone : There was an auction sale of plots of land. The terms, including certain restrictive conditions, were announced by a microphone. The Supreme Court held, "Microphones have not yet acquired notoriety as carriers of binding representations. Promises held out over loudspeakers are often claptraps of politics" *Banwari Lal v. Sukhdashan Dayal. (1973) S.C.*

Difference between Offer and Acceptance

1. Offer constitutes the first stage in the formation of a contract, whereas acceptance constitutes the second stage in the formation of a contract.
2. An offer is made by the offeror to the offeree. But an acceptance is given by the offeree to the offeror.
3. An offer is not held to be made until it is brought to the knowledge of the offeree (i.e., communicated to the offeree). On the other hand, an acceptance may, in certain circumstances, be held to be made, though it has not come to the knowledge of the offeror (i.e., though it is not communicated to the offeror).

REVIEW QUESTIONS

1. What is an offer? State the essentials of a valid offer.
2. Why is the intention to create legal relations an essential of a valid contract? Give three examples of obligations arising from agreement which are not legal obligations.
3. Distinguish between an offer and an invitation to offer.

4. When is an offer complete? How and when may an offer be revoked?
5. Define 'acceptance', and state the legal rules governing valid acceptance.
6. "Acceptance is to an offer what a lighted match is to a train of gun powder". Discuss the statement in the context of acceptance of an offer.
7. 'A mental resolve to accept an offer does not give rise to a contract'. Discuss.
8. State the law relating to contract by post, telephone, telex and fax.
9. A teaches his parrot to recite an offer and then sends his parrot to B. The bird repeats the recitation. Is this a valid offer?
10. Over a cup of coffee at a restaurant, A invites B to a dinner at his house on a Sunday. B hires a taxi and reaches A's house at the appointed time, but A fails to perform his promise. Can B recover any damages from A?
11. H telegraphed to F asking him to inform him whether he would sell White horse and if so what price. F informed H that the lowest price was ₹ 50,000 but did not say that he was willing to sell at that price. H telegraphed that he would buy at that price. F gave no reply to the telegram. Is there a contract ?
12. P sees a rare book displayed in a shop. It is labeled "First Edition ₹ 15", P enters the shop and puts ₹ 15 on the counter and asks for the book. The bookseller refuses to sell saying that the real price of the book was ₹ 50 and that it had been marked as ₹ 15 by mistake. Is the bookseller bound to sell the book for ₹ 15?
13. An auctioneer advertised in the newspapers that a sale of office furniture would be held at Delhi. A, a broker of Mumbai reached Delhi on the appointed date and time. But the auctioneer withdrew all the furniture from the auction sale. The broker sues him for his loss of time and expenses. Will he succeed ?
14. P advertised in the newspapers to sell his house for ₹ 40,000. Q wrote to P "I offer ₹ 35,000 for your house". P refused the offer. Therefore, Q wrote to P offering ₹ 40,000 for the house. P refused to accept that offer also. Can Q compel P to sell the house to him (A) for ₹ 40,000?
15. A offers to sell his house to B for a sum of ₹ 1,00,000. B replies that he would like to buy the house but for ₹ 90,000. Is it acceptance of the offer ? What will be the position if A were to reply back that he would like to sell the house for ₹ 95,000.
16. The defendant on 6th June offered to sell an estate to the plaintiff for ₹ 10,000. On 12th June, in reply, the plaintiff made an offer of ₹ 9,000 which was refused by the defendant on 16th June. Finally on 20th June the plaintiff wrote to the defendant that he was now prepared to pay ₹ 10,000. The defendant refused to sell the estate. The plaintiff filed a suit against the defendant for breach of contract. How would you decide? State your reasons.
17. The plaintiff, who could not read, asked her neice to take excursion ticket for her. On the face of the ticket were printed the words "excursion for conditions see back" and the conditions on the back excluded company's liability for any injury. The plaintiff was injured while on excursion. The plaintiff filed a suit for damages. Decide.
18. P and her husband hired a room at a hotel and paid for a week's boarding and lodging in advance. When they went to occupy the room there was a notice on one of the wall which excluded proprietor's liability for articles lost or stolen unless handed to the manager for safe custody. Owing to the negligence of the hotel staff a thief entered their room and stole their property. Can P hold the proprietor of the hotel liable for the loss?

19. A gave a brand new woollen suit costing ₹ 400 to a dry cleaner for dry cleaning. The suit is lost by the mistake of the dry cleaner. On A's claiming the full value, the dry cleaner contends that as per the terms of the contract printed on the reverse of the 'receipt' which was also signed by A, he is liable to pay only ten times the amount of dry cleaning charges, the charges being only seven rupees.

20. The plaintiff offered by means of a letter to purchase his uncle's horse by writing. "If I hear no more, I will consider the horse mine at ₹ 1,500" The uncle sent no reply to this but told the defendant, his auctioneer not to sell the horse as it was already sold to his nephew. The auctioneer, by mistake, put up the horse for auction and sold it. The plaintiff sued the auctioneer on the ground that under the contract the horse has become his property and defendant's unauthorized sale amounted to conversion. Decide the case.

21. A in Delhi rings up B of Mumbai offering to sell too bales of cotton at a certain price. B accepts the offer made by A but A is not able to hear B's acceptance because a mechanical defect develops in A's telephone. Is there any binding agreement between A and B ? Give reasons for your answer.

22. On June 1, 2011, A advertised in a newspaper that he would pay ₹ 150 to anyone who would find his lost dog before July, 1, 2011. On 10th June, A advertised in the same newspaper that he had cancelled his offer of June 1, 2011. On 15th June, B, who had read the first advertisement but not the second one, found the lost dog and claimed ₹150 from A, which A refused. Has B any legal remedy against A.

23. A chemist advertised that he would pay a reward of £10 to anyone who contracted influenza after using a prescription supplied by him if used according to the directions supplied with it. Peter and Paul both purchased the prescription and used it and contracted influenza. Peter had seen the advertisement but Paul had not. Can they or either of them recover £10 from the chemist ? State briefly the principles involved.

24. A post of a clerk is offered by A to B, B asks for a day to consider the offer, to which A agrees. At the end of the day, B returns to A to signify his acceptance of the offer, but he is told by A that the post has been given to a third party. Has the contract come into existence in the above case?

25. A offers to take B's house on certain terms, the answer to be given within five weeks. Within that time, B writes to A a letter purporting to accept the offer but in fact the letter contained a material variation of the terms. A then withdraws his offer. B writes again still within five weeks, correcting the error in his first letter and accepting the terms originally proposed by A.

    State with reasons whether a contract has been formed between A and B and if B has any remedy available against A.

26. A resident of Delhi, posted an offer on 1st October to B of Lucknow to sell specified property for ₹ 50,000. The offer was to remain open for a week. B posted his letter of acceptance on 6th October, which reached A on 8th October.

27. A offers to sell a house in Delhi to B for a sum of ₹ 10,000. He communicates the offer by an express letter to B who is in Bombay. The letter is delayed in the Censor's Office. A, by a telegram, revokes the offer which reaches B just before he received the express delivery letter. Under these circumstance can any contract result by B's acceptance?

28. X at Delhi on 1st August, 2010 sends a letter to Y in Mumbai offering to sell his car to Y for ₹16,000. Y on 2nd August, 2010, sends a letter to X accepting the offer. This acceptance letter reaches X on 4th August, 2010. But on 3rd August, 2010, X has sold the car to Z and wired to Y revoking the offer. This wire reaches Y on 3rd August, 2010 itself. Is there a breach of contract committed by X ? Give reasons.

29. P, a merchant, sent his son, S, to Agra with a letter for R, an Agra merchant. In the letter P offered to sell to R a quantity of cloth and required R to give his reply to S. R sent away S without a reply but decided later to accept P's offer by telegram. The telegram reached P before S's return. State with reasons whether a valid contract has come into existence.

30. An offer was made by S to P in the following words : "I intend to sell my house for ₹ 4,00,000. If you are willing to have it, write to K at his address." Instead of writing to K, the purchaser, P, sent an agent in person to K and agreed to purchase the said house for ₹ 4,00,000. P asked S for handing over the said house to him. S contended that it was not a valid acceptance as the only manner in which the acceptance of the offer could be made was by writing to K at his address. How would you decide?

31. P applied for the principalship of a local college and the Governing Body passed a resolution appointing him. The appointment was not formally communicated to him but one of the members privately told him of his selection after the meeting. The resolution was subsequently rescinded. P claimed the post of principal. Will he succeed?

32. A offers to purchase a bar of gold from B at Mumbai, B accepts the offer by letter. But the letter is lost in transit. B sends the bar to A by value payable post. The price of gold has fallen when the parcel reaches A. Is a bound to accept the parcel ? Give reasons.

33. A sold his business to B without disclosing to his customers C, a customer, sent an order for goods to A by name. B, the new owner, accepted it. Is there a contract between the two?

❐ ❐ ❐

CONSIDERATION AND CAPACITY

Section 2(d) of the Indian Contract Act defines *"Consideration"* as

When, at the desire of the promisor, the promisee or any other person has done or abstained, from doing or does or abstains from doing, or promises to do or to abstain from doing, some thing, such act or abstinence or promise is called a *consideration for the promise.*

Elements of Consideration

The analysis of this legal definition shows that following are the essential parts of the consideration :

1. The consideration is an act, or abstinence.
2. Such act, or abstinence should be done at the desire of the promisor.
3. Such act or abstinence may be done by the promisee or any other person.
4. Such act or abstinence is either already executed, or is in the process of execution or may be still executory.

Illustration **:** A agrees to sell his car to B for ₹ 2,40,000. In this case B's promise to pay the sum of ₹ 2,40,000 is the consideration for A's promise to sell the car. A's promise to sell the car is the consideration for B's promise to pay the sum of ₹ 2,40,000.

LEGAL RULES REGARDING CONSIDERATION

1. **Consideration is required both for formation and discharge of an agreement or contract :** According to Sec. 25 of the Indian Contract Act, 1872 *"An agreement without Consideration is void".* Hence the rule *No consideration, no contract* with few exceptions provided under Sec. 25 and Sec. 185 of the same Act.
2. **Consideration may be past, present or future :** The words "has done or abstained from doing, or does or abstains from doing, or promises to do or to abstain from doing" indicate that consideration may be past, present or future.
3. **Consideration may be either positive or negative :** According to Section 2(d) of the Indian Contract Act, the Consideration may be a promise to do something or to abstain from doing something. Thus, a consideration may be an act '*to do*' or '*not to do*' something, i.e., it may be positive or negative.

   Consideration may be forbearance to sue : The term '*forbearance to sue*' means that the plaintiff has a right of action against the defendant or any other person, and on a promise by the defendant, the (plaintiff) refrains the bringing legal action. *The forbearance to sue is regarded as a valid consideration.*
4. **Consideration must move (i.e., must be done or promised to be done) at the desire of the promisor :** The act or abstinence must be done at the desire of the promisor and not at the desire of any other person. The desire of the promisor can be implied from the conduct of the parties. An act done without any request by the promisor is a voluntary act and does not come within the definition of consideration. But

it is not necessary that what is done by the promisee by way of consideration should benefit the promisor. Any benefit conferred by promisee or any other person at the request of promisor is taken to be good consideration in terms of promise. In other words, an act shall not be a good consideration for a promise unless it is done at the desire of the promisor.

5. **Consideration may be furnished by the Promisee or any Other Person:** Consideration may move from the promisee or any other person. Indian Contract Act recognises consideration moving from a third party other than the promisee. Thus consideration furnished by a third party will also be valid if it has been done at the desire of the promisor. Accordingly, even a stranger to the consideration can sue upon a contract, provided he is a party to the contract. This is called as the '*doctrine of constructive consideration*'. In other words, *consideration may move from a stranger,* but it must flow at the desire of the promisor. Consideration moving from a third party who is a *minor is no consideration.*

6. **Consideration must be lawful :** According Sec. 10 - "*All agreements are contracts if they are made ... for a lawful consideration...*"

   Sec. 24 further provides "if any part of a single consideration for one or more objects, or any part of any one of the 'several considerations for a single object, is unlawful, the agreement is void'. Thus, where part of the consideration is unlawful the whole agreement is void unless the part which is unlawful can be separated from the one which is legal.

7. **Consideration must be real and not illusory :** Though consideration need not be adequate, yet it must have some value in the eyes of law i.e., it must be real. Real consideration is one which is not physically or legally impossible and it is not illusory or sham or uncertain.

8. **Consideration must be of some value in the eyes of law :** The word '*something*' in the definition indicated that whatever is moved, as consideration, should have some value in the eyes of law.

9. **Consideration need not be adequate :** An agreement to which the consent of the party is freely given is not void merely because the consideration is inadequate; *but the inadequacy of the consideration may be taken into account by the court in determining the question whether the consent of the promisor was freely given.*

10. **Consideration must not be the performance of existing duties :** The term '*existing duties*' includes legal obligations or contractual obligations. A person may be bound to do something by law. The consideration must be something more than that what the promisee is already bound to do by law. *The performance of legal duty is not consideration for promise.*

Illustration **:** A's wife was caught in fire in a burning building. A offered reward to anyone who would rescue his wife, dead or alive. B, a fireman, at a great risk to his life and health, rescued A's wife. He was allowed to receive the amount of reward because the court found that as a fireman of the city, he was not legally bound to risk his life in this rescue operation.

- *Forbearance to sue* is a kind of abstinence and has always been considered as valuable consideration.
- *Compromise of disputed claim*, doubtful rights, etc., have been regarded as sufficient consideration.
- *Part-Payment* by a third party may be a good consideration for the discharge of the whole of the debt.
- Compromise of a pending suit is a good consideration provided the dispute is bona fide.
- *Payment of a lesser sum* is a good satisfaction for a larger sum where this is done in pursuance of an agreement of compromise entered into by the debtor with his creditors.
- Payment of a lesser sum before time, or in a different mode, or at a different place that appointed in the original contractor or "the gift of a horse, hawk or robe etc., in satisfaction is good".

NO CONSIDERATION, NO CONTRACT

The general rule is that *an agreement made without consideration is void* (Section 25). However, the Indian Contract Act contains certain exceptions to this rule. In the following cases, the agreements, though made without consideration, are taken to be valid and enforceable.

Exceptions to the Rule *No Consideration No Contract*

(A) **Natural Love and Affection :** An agreement made in writing and registered and is made on account of natural love and affection between parties standing in a near relation to each other [Sec. 25)].

An agreement without consideration is valid under Section 25(1) only if the following requirements are complied with :

(i) The agreement is made in a *written* document,

(ii) The document is *registered* according to the law relating to registration in force at that time,

(iii) The agreement is made on account of *natural love and affection.*

(iv) The parties to the agreement stand in *near relation to each other.*

Venkataswamy Vs. Rangaswamy (1903) : An elder brother V on account of natural love and affection, promised to pay the debts of his younger brother, R. The agreement was put in writing and was registered. But V did not repay the debt. The brother R repaid the debt out of his own and then sued the former for recovery of the money. Held, the younger brother has the right to do so because the agreement was valid, under Section 25(1).

Rajlukhee Debee Vs. Bhootnath (1900) : The defendant, a Hindu husband, after referring to quarrels and disagreements between him and his wife, executed a registered document in favour of his wife agreeing to pay for her maintenance, but no consideration moved from his wife. Held the agreement was void for want consideration. It was not made out of natural love and affection. Therefore, it was not a valid contract.

(B) **Compensation for past voluntary service :** An agreement made without consideration is also valid and enforceable if it is a promise to compensate, wholly or in part, a person who has already voluntarily done something for the promisor, or something which the promisor was legally compelled to do. In order that a promise to pay for past voluntary services is binding, the following essential conditions must exist :

(i) The services should have been rendered voluntarily.

(ii) The services must have been rendered for the promisor, and not anybody else. If the services are rendered involuntarily but at the desire of the promisor, then it is covered under 'past consideration' and not under this exception.

(iii) The promisor must be in existence when the services were made

(iv) The promisor must have intended to compensate the promisee.

(v) The promisor should be competent to contract at the time when the act was done.

(vi) It is to be noted that there is no need of having any written contract for this purpose. [Sec. 25(2)].

(vii) The services rendered should be immorator illegal.

(C) **Promise to pay Time-barred debt :** A promise in writing signed by the person to be charged therewith or by his agent, to pay a debt barred by the law of limitation would constitute a valid contract, even though it is not supported by any consideration [Section 25(3)]. The following essential conditions should be a noted in connection with this exception :

(i) The debt must be an ascertained and specific sum of money.

(ii) The promise to pay time-barred debt must be made in writing and signed by the promisor or his agent authorised on that behalf.

(iii) The promise must not be an acknowledgement of the debt.

(iv) The promise may be absolute or conditional. If it is conditional, it can be fulfilled only after the conditions have been performed.

(v) The promise may be to pay the whole or any part of the debt.

(vi) The debts must be such that the only bar to recovery is limitation, but otherwise the debt should be perfectly lawful and binding on the debtor.

(D) **Completed gift :** In the case of a gift actually made, not being an agreement to make a gift, *no consideration is necessary although the donor and the donees* may not be standing in near relation to each other, and even if they do, there may not be any natural love and affection between them.

(E) **Agency :** Besides the above exceptions mentioned in section 25 of the Act, there are also other types of agreements which are enforceable by law even without consideration. For instance, Section 185 of the Act Contract specifically says that, "*No, consideration is necessary to create an agency*".

(F) **Remission :** Under section 63 of the Contract Act, no consideration is necessary for an agreement to receive less than what is due, known as *remission in India* and *accord and satisfaction in England.*

(G) **Bailment :** A gratuitous bailment means giving an article to a person for a certain purpose and it is to be returned after the purpose is fulfilled; but no remuneration is charged for the favour. *Gratuitous bailment is, in essence, without consideration.*

(H) **Guarantee :** *A contract of guarantee is made without consideration* (Section 127 of the Contract Act 127).

Note : There is *no consideration in an accommodation bill* under the Negotiable Instruments Act, 1881.

STRANGER TO CONSIDERATION AND STRANGER TO CONTRACT

It is necessary, in this context, to distinguish between a stranger to a consideration and stranger to a contract. If consideration is furnished not by the promisee but a third person, the promisee becomes a *'stranger to the consideration'*, and as such, he cannot enforce the promise. However, it should be noted that a 'stranger to consideration' can sue the contract provided he is a party to the contract and the consideration must flow from him at the desire of the promisor. Similarly, a person who is not a party to a contract, cannot claim any rights under the contract even though the contract may be for his benefit, and such a person is known as 'stranger to the contract'.

DOCTRINE OF PRIVITY OF CONTRACT

As a contract is entered into by two or mroe persons thereby creating rights and obligations for them, it is a party to the contract only who can enforce his rights as against the other party (i.e., the promisor). The basic principle underlying law of contracts is that a stranger to a contract cannot maintain a suit for a remedy. The law entitles only those who are parties to the contract to file suits for exercising their rights. This is known as 'privity of contract'. This rule can be traced to the fact that the law of contracts creates just in personam as distinguished from jus in rem. Therefore, *a stranger to a contract cannot maintain a suit.*

Example : A is indebted to B. A sells certain goods to C.C gives a promise to A to pay off A's debt to B. In case C fails to pay, B has no rights to sue C, being a stranger to the contract between C and A. In other words C is not in privity with B. However, C is in privity with A.

The concept of privity of contracts is illustrated below figure.

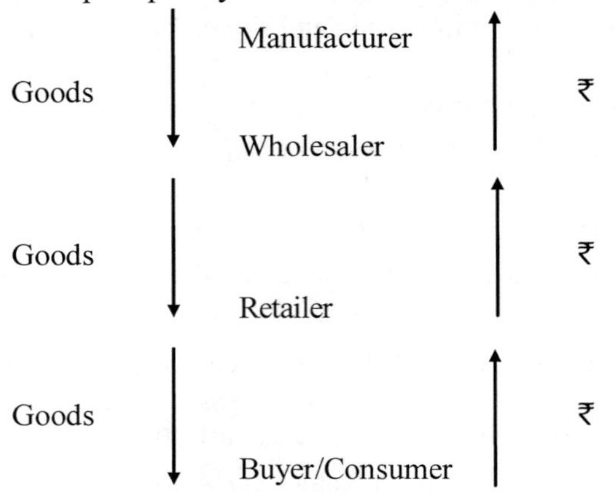

Buyer is in privity of contract with Retailer only but not with Wholesaler and Manufacturer

EXCEPTIONS TO THE RULE : A STRANGER TO CONTRACT CANNOT SUE ON THE CONTRACT

It is now a settled law in India that a *stranger to contract cannot sue on the contract*, (third parties to a contract have no rights and no liabilities under it) owing to the absence of privity of contract. However, in the course of its judgement, the Supreme Court itself has referred to certain well recognised exceptions.

1. **Beneficiary in a trust or charge :** In the case of trust, the beneficiary though a stranger to the contract between the trustee and the author of the trust, can sue in his own name to enforce the trust.
2. **Acknowledgement of payment or Estoppel :** In the case of acknowledgement of liability or where the principle of estoppel begins to operate, a stranger to the contract can sue the party in question.

Illustration : Y receives money from X for payment to Z and acknowledges this fact to Z; Z can sue Y to recover the money, though he is a stranger to the contract. Acknowledgement of collection by Y to Z, makes Y the agent to Z.

Where the promisor by his conduct, acknowledges himself as an agent of the third party, a binding obligation is thereby incurred towards him. Thus in *Khirode Behari Dull Vs. Man Govinda Pande* (1933) the landlord was allowed to recover unpaid rent from the sub-tenant whereas under an agreement between a tenant and his sub-tenant the sub-tenant was paying the rent directly to the landlord.

3. **Agreement creating a charge on land :** Where a person makes a promise to an individual for the benefit of a third party and creates a charge on specific immovable property for carrying out that promise, the third party, though a stranger to the contract can enforce it.

Khawaja Mohammad Khan Vs. Hussaini Begum (1910) P.C. : In that case, in a agreement executed between fathers of bridegroom and bride, it was agreed that father of the bridegroom will pay ₹ 500 every month in perpetuity as Kharche Pandan (Pin money) to the bride, if she marries his son. For this purpose, a charge was created on a specific immovable property in favour of the bride by a document executed by the father of the bridegroom and the father of the bride. On subsequent refusal to pay, the bride sued her father-in-law to recover the amount with arrears for 40 months. It was held by the Privy Council that though she was not a party to the contract, Yet 'she was clearly entitled in equity to enforce her claim'. Hence Privy Council awarded her claim with interest on the arrears of instalments.

4. **Family settlements :** Family arrangements or compromises made among male members for the benefit of female members of the family can be enforced by the female members, although the female members are not a party to these agreements. Thus, where an agreement is made in connection with marriage, e.g., partition agreement and a provision is made for the benefit of a person, that person may take advantage of that agreement although he or she is no party to it.
5. **Assignee of a contract :** Under certain circumstances a party to a contract can transfer his rights under the contract to third parties. For example, the holder of a bill of exchange can transfer it to any person he wishes. In such cases the transferee or the assignee can sue on the contract even though he was not a party to it originally. Assignment may occur through operation of law. For example, when a person becomes insolvent, all his properties and rights vest in the Official Assignee/Official Receiver who can sue upon contracts entered into by him.

CONTRACTUAL CAPACITY

One of the essential conditions for the enforceability of an agreement, is that the concerned parties must be competent to enter into an agreement. Section 10 of the Indian Contracts Act specifically requires that the parties must be competent to contract. Thus, an agreement is valid and enforceable only if the parties to it are competent enough to enter into contract.

Meaning of Contractual Capacity : The '*capacity to contract*' means the competence (i.e. capability) of the parties to enter into a valid contract. The term '*capacity to contract*' is defined in Section 11 of the Indian Contract Act, which reads as under :

*"Every person is competent to contract who is of the **age of the majority** according to the law to which he is subject and who is of **sound mind**, and is **not disqualified from contracting** by any law to which he is subject".*

In other words, a person who is major, of sound mind, and is not disqualified from contracting by law, is competent to enter into a valid contract.

PERSONS OF SOUND AND UNSOUND MIND

Meaning of Sound Mind : A person is said to be of sound mind for making a potential business contract, if at the time when he makes it, he is capable of understanding it and of forming a rational judgement as to its effects upon his interests (Section 12).

Section 12 further states that (i) a person who is usually of unsound mind, but occasionally of sound mind may make a contract when he is of sound mind, and (ii) a person who is usually of sound mind but occasionally of unsound mind may not make a contract, when he is of unsound mind.

Explanations

1. A patient in a lunatic asylum, who is at intervals of sound mind, may contract during those intervals.
2. A sane man, who is delirious from fever or who is so drunk that he cannot understand the terms of a contract or form a rational judgement as to its effect on his interest, cannot contract whilst such delirium of *drunkenness* lasts.

Even persons who have been *hypnotised*, persons who are delirious from fever and persons who have suffered *mental decay* on account of old age or disease become persons of unsound mind. Thus unsoundness of mind may arise (i) idiocy, (ii) lunacy, (iii) drunkenness, (iv) hypnotism and (v) mental decay.

Effects of Agreements made by Persons of Unsound Mind : Agreements by persons of unsound mind are *void*. But an agreement entered into by a lunatic or a person of unsound mind for the supply of necessaries for himself or for persons whom he is bound to support (e.g., his wife or children) is valid as a quasi-contract under Section 68 of the Act. Only the estate of such a person is liable. There is no personal liability.

The guardian of a lunatic can bind the estate of the lunatic by contracts entered into on his behalf. The mode of appointment of such a guardian and his powers are laid down in the Lunacy Act.

Examples

1. A person 'agreed' to sell a property worth about ₹ 25,000 for ₹ 7,000. His mother proved that he was a congenital idiot and she pleaded for cancellation of the contract. The court held the agreement to be null and void. *Inder Singh Vs. Parmeshwardhari Singh (1957).*
2. If an agreement entered into by a person of unsound mind is for his benefit, it can be enforced. *Jugal Kishore Vs. Cheddu (1903).*

Tests of Soundness of Mind : The test of soundness of mind are (i) the capacity to understand the contents of the business concerned, and (ii) the ability to form a rational judgement as to its effect on his interests. If a person is incapable of both these elements, he suffers from unsoundness of mind. Unsoundness of mind may arise from insanity, lunacy, idiocy, drunkenness, hypnotism, mental decay brought about by old age or disease and similar other factors. In each case, it is a question of fact to be decided by the Court. There is always a presumption in favour of sanity and if any person relies on the unsoundness of mind, he must prove it sufficiently to the satisfaction of the Court.

Mental Incompetents

(a) **Idiots :** An idiot is a person who is devoid of any faculties of thinking or of forming rational judgement. Idiocy is a congenital defect caused by lack of development of the brain. The agreement with an idiot is absolutely *void.* However his properties are liable for necessaries supplied to him and to his dependents.

(b) **Lunatics and insane persons :** A lunatic is one, whose mental power has been deranged. Insane persons are those persons who are sometimes sane and sometimes *insane.* Such persons may enter into contract during their lucid intervals i.e., period in which they are in senses. Such persons can always plead lunacy or insanity as a ground for avoiding a contract. It is for the plaintiff to prove that the contract was entered into during the lucid interval of the defendant.

(c) **Drunkards :** A person under the influence of intoxication of drug or liquor stands on the same footing as a lunatic. He also suffers from temporary incapacity to contract. *Contract by a drunken person is absolutely void and cannot be ratified.* But in order to make a contract by a drunkard void, the drunkenness should be effective and absolute, so that rational judgement cannot be formed by the contracting party. The drunken person is usually incapable of understanding the contents of the contract and its legal consequences. A drunken person's property is liable for necessaries of life supplied to him or his dependents during the period of his drunkenness. That means, if he does not have property to pay for such necessaries, the supplier has to lose the amount.

MINOR (INFANT)

Meaning of Minor : Minor is a person who has not completed the age of 18 years. However, a minor for whom a guardian has been appointed by court or when his property is managed by the court of wards, he becomes a major only on his completing 21 years (Sec. 3 of the Indian Majority Act, 1875).

Nature of Minor's Contract : The Contract Act does not expressly specify whether a minor's contracts are void or voidable. In ***Mohori Bibi Vs. Dhurmodas Ghose (1903)***, the Privy Council declared categorically that all contracts made by a minor are *null and void ab initio* and they cannot be ratified by him on his attaining majority.

Facts of the case : A minor executed a mortgage for a sum of₹ 20,000 on which he took an advance of₹ 8,000. Later on, the minor sought to set aside the mortgage on the ground of minority. The mortgagee contended that since a contract with a minor is voidable, the minor should refund the advance taken by him. The Privy Council negatived the contention and held that a contract with a minor is *void ab-initio* (ie., void in the very beginning). Being a void contract the minor cannot be asked to refund the advance taken by him. Otherwise, the court will be giving effect to a contract which never came into existence.

Thus money paid or lent to minors under contracts (mortgage, promissory notes etc.) cannot be recovered either from them or their estates even under Section 64 and 65 of the Contract Act. Hence *a minor cannot be asked to refund any benefit he received under a contract. However, he can enforce the contracts made by him and sue the party involved; only they are void against him.* Any money paid by minors under contracts not yet performed, can be recovered by them. But the question whether the money paid by a minor under contract, already performed, could be recovered by him depends on whether complete restitution is possible. If it is possible, that is, if the parties could be placed in the positions they occupied before the contract, the court will order restitution and direct the other party to return the money to the minor. *If restitution is not possible, the minor cannot recover the money.*

Contract for the benefit : A minor can be a promisee. In *Raghva Chariar Vs. Srinivasa,* the Madras High Court held that a mortgage executed in favour of a minor who has advanced the mortgage money is enforceable by him or by any other person on his behalf. Similarly, in case of sale of goods by a minor, he is entitled to recover the price from the buyer.

Contracts by Guardian : Contracts entered into by the guardian of a minor or the manager of his estate, can be enforced (under Hindu Law) against or by the minor if (a) the guardian has powers to enter into them on behalf of a minor and (b) they are for the benefit of the minor. The powers of a guardian are determined by the personal law of the minor and by the Guardian and Wards Act?

However a minor's estate will be liable for the debts incurred by him even for necessaries of life. Further, the liability is not personal, but is only that of the minor's estate. Thus, it has a little contractual element.

No Estoppel against a minor : A minor can always put forth the plea of minority and will not be estopped, i.e., prevented from doing so, even when he has entered into a contract falsely representing himself to be a major.

A minor who falsely represents himself to be a major, and thereby induces another person to enter into an agreement with him, can nevertheless plead minority as a defence in an action on the agreement. There can be no estoppel against a minor. *Saidk Ali Khan Vs. Jaikishore*. In the English case, *R. Leslie Ltd. Vs. Sheill*, the Court of Appeal held that where an infant obtains a loan by falsely representing his age, he cannot be made to pay the amount of the loan as damages for fraud, nor can he be compelled in equity to repay the money. But in India it has been held that the court can direct the minor to pay compensation to the other party in such cases. *(Khan Gul. v. Lakhs Singh. (1928) Lah).*

The Principle of Estoppel : The principle of estoppel is a rule of evidence. When a man has, by words spoken or written, or by conduct, induced another to believe that a certain state of things exists, he will not be allowed to deny the existence of that state of things. *"Estoppel arises when you are precluded from denying the truth of anything which you have represented as a fact, although it is not a fact".* (Lord Halsbury)]

No Ratification : An agreement made by a minor (during his period of minority) cannot be ratified (confirmed or approved) by him on attaining majority because minor's agreement is *void ab initio*. Even, if a new agreement given by a minor relating to an earlier agreement (during minority) cannot be enforced because the new agreement (during major) is not supported by any new consideration.

In *Indran Ramaswamy Vs. Ananthappa*, a person on attaining majority, gave a promissory note in satisfaction of one executed by him for money borrowed when he was a minor. It was held that the claim under the promissory note could not be enforced because there was no consideration. In *Anant Rai Vs. Bhagan Rai*, a person on attaining majority paid the debt incurred by him during minority. It is treated as valid.

Restitution : A minor is not liable to repay any money or compensate for any benefit that he might have received. The court on considerations of equity, will order restitution, i.e., compel the minor to return to the trader, the goods or the property into which it has since been converted if it is traceable. If the goods or the property cannot be traced, the court will not direct the minor to pay money as compensation to the trader, for *"restitutions stops where repayment begins"*. Restitution is not available if the party entitled to it (i.e., major) has been unscrupulous, aware of minority, has not been influenced by the minor's false representation and failed to satisfy the court as to the required proof.

No liability in contract or in tort arising out of contract : The term '*tort*' may be defined as any wrong for which a civil suit can be brought (except for breach of contract or breach of trust). We have already discussed that a minor's agreement is absolutely void. Moreover, he is not liable either for breach of contract or for damages on account of tort of deceit (fraud). If a minor enters into an agreement by misrepresenting his age, he cannot be sued either in contract or in tort for deceit (i.e. fraud). Because if the injured party is allowed to sue, it would be an indirect way of enforcing the void agreement. It may, however, be noted that the *minor is not liable for tort, only where the tort is directly connected with the contract*.

Fraudulent representation of age by minor : According to Sections 30 and 33 of the Specific Relief Act, 1963, in case of a fraudulent misrepresentation of his age by the minor inducing the other party to enter into a contract, the court may award compensation to the other party. The Lahore High Court in *Khan Gul Vs. Lakhs Singh* held that where the contract is set aside, the *status quo ante* should be restored and the court may direct the minor on equitable grounds to restore the money or property to the other party if the money or property could be traced.

Contract for supply of necessaries : A person who has supplied the necessaries to a minor or to those who are dependent on him is entitled to be reimbursed from the property of such minor. (Section 68)

Meaning of necessaries : The term necessaries includes articles required to maintain a particular person in the state, degree and station in life in which he is. According to Section 2 of English Sale of Goods Act, the necessaries mean the goods which are suitable to the condition in life of a minor and to his actual requirement at the time of sale and delivery. In India, food, clothing, shelter, education and marriage of a female have been held to be necessaries. Section 68 covers the reimbursement for the supply of such items or loans for the same.

Example : In case of *Nash Vs. Inman*, a minor bought eleven fancy coats from N for his own use. It was held that eleven coats at a time cannot be a necessity.

Section 68 also covers the rendering of necessary services to a minor. For example, the lending of a money to a minor for the purpose of defending him in prosectuion is deemed to be a service rendered to the minor.

Claim against property and not against person : A claim for the payment of necessaries supplied can be made against the minor's property and not against the minor personally. In other words, a minor cannot be asked to expend labour in exchange nor can his income.

Liability for minor's guardian : The parent or guardian of a minor cannot be held liable unless those goods/ services are supplied/rendered to a minor or to whom he is bound to support as the agent of the parent or guardian.

Validity of minor's agreement jointly with a major person : The agreements made by a minor jointly with a major person are void vis-a-vis the minor but can be enforced against the major person who has jointly promised to perform.

No specific performance : An agreement by a minor being void, the court will never direct specific performance of such an agreement by him.

No insolvency : A minor cannot be declared insolvent even though there are dues payable from the properties of the minor.

Partnership by minor : A minor cannot enter into a contract of partnership. But he can be admitted into the benefits of a partnership with the consent of all the partners.

A Minor can be an agent : A minor can draw, make, indorse and deliver negotiable instruments so as to bind all parties except himself. A minor agent cannot be adjudicated an insolvent. Where a minor and a major jointly enter into an agreement with another person, the minor has no liability but the contract can be enforced against the major if his liability can be separately ascertained. If an adult stands surety for a minor, the adult is liable on the agreement although the minor is not.

Minor as a shareholder of a company: A minor can become a shareholder or member of a company if (a) the shares are fully paid shares and (b) the articles of association do not prohibit so.

MOTHER CAN ACT AS GUARDIAN OF MINOR

The Supreme Court in a landmark judgement in Feburary, 1999 on "guardianship" of a "minor" under Section 6(a) of the Hindu Minority and Guardianship Act, 1956, and under Section 19(b) of the Guardian and Wards Act, 1890 has ruled that the mother "can act as natural guardian of the minor" and all her actions would be valid even during the life time of the father, who would be deemed to be "absent" for the purposes of Section 6(a) of the 1956 Act and Section 19(b) of the 1890 Act, under given circumstances.

The Chief Justice. Dr. Justice A.S. Anand, delivering the judgment held that "in all situations where the father is not in actual charge of the affairs of the minor either because of his indifference or because of an agreement between him and the mother of the minor - (oral or written) and the minor is in the exclusive care and custody of the mother or the father for any other reason is unable to take care of the minor because of his physical and / or mental incapacity, the mother can act as natural guardian of the minor". "Both parents are duty bound to take care of the person and property of their minor child and act in the best interest of the minor's welfare".

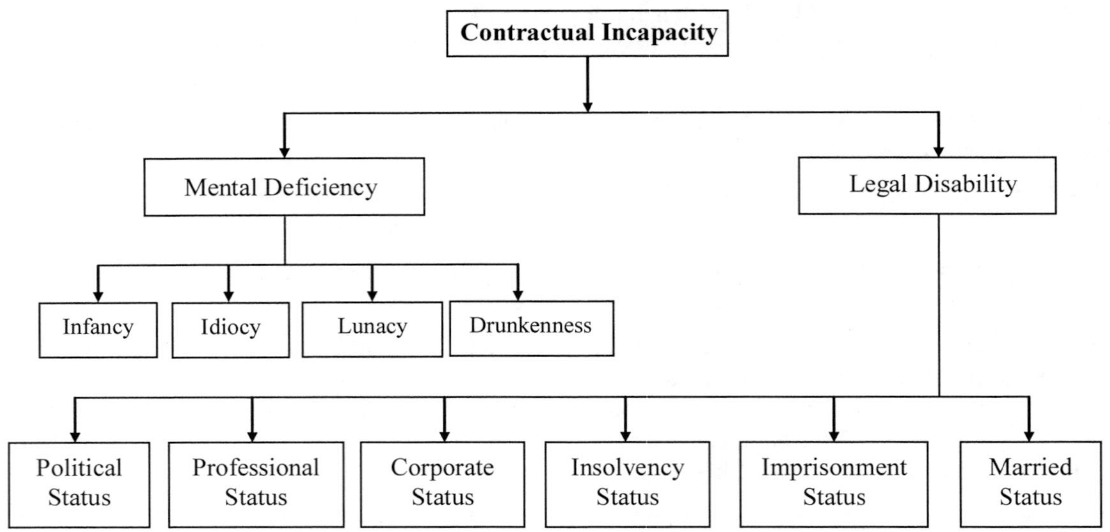

LEGAL DISABILITY

On the ground of status, some degree of incapacity is imposed by law.

(a) **Foreign Sovereigns, Ambassadors and Envoys *(National Status)* :** One has to be cautious while entering into contracts with foreign sovereigns and ambassadors, because whereas they can sue others to enforce the contracts entered upon with them, they cannot be used without obtaining the prior sanction of the Central Government. Thus they are in a privileged position and are ordinarily considered incompetent to contract.

(b) **Alien enemy *(Political Status)* :** Alien enemy is a person (including an Indian citizen) who is domiciled in a country which is at war with India. It is therefore, *the place of residence of an individual that decides whether he is an alien enemy or not*. An alien enemy cannot enter into contracts with an Indian citizen nor can he file a suit in an Indian Court.

(c) **Professionals *(Professional Status)* :** In England, barristers, doctors (physicians) are not permitted to enter into contracts pertaining to their profession or to sue for their fees or be sued. So also are members of the Royal College of Physicians. But they can sue and be sued for all claims other than their professional fees. For example, if a barrister or a member of the Royal College of Physicians engages a contractor of building a house he can sue for the enforcement of the contract.

In India these personal disqualification do not exist. It has been held in *Nihal Chand Vs. Dilwar Khan*, that *a barrister can sue for his fees in India*.

(d) **Corporation *(Corporate Status)* :** The contractual capacity of corporations, (corporate bodies) is restricted by the statutes governing them. They cannot enter into contracts which are beyond their object and powers (i.e., *ultra vires*); nor can they make contracts which are associated with physical existence like contract to marry, because they are only artificial persons.

(e) **Bankrupt (*Insolvent Status*) :** An undischarged insolvent cannot be appointed as a Magistrate, or director in a company or elected to any office of local authority. He is also disqualified from being elected, sitting or voting as member of any local authority. (Section 103 A of the Presidency Towns

Insolvency Act, 1909 and Section 73 of the Provincial Insolvency Act, 1920). The law relating to contracts entered into by an insolvent is as follows:

1. An adjudicated insolvent cannot enter into contracts of sale relating to his property. Only the official assignee or official receiver can deal with the property of an adjudicated insolvent. However, he can enter into certain other types of contracts, such as incurring debts, purchasing property, contract of service, etc.

2. Before discharge, an insolvent also suffers from certain other disqualifications. For instance, he cannot be a magistrate or a director of a company or a member of a local body.

3. After obtaining discharge, an insolvent becomes an ordinary citizen. So, he can enter into any valid contracts, and such contracts can be enforced against him and also by him. He also becomes free from other disqualifications.

(f) **Felons and Convicts (*Imprisonment Status*) :** Persons undergoing sentences of life imprisonment cannot enter into contracts, nor can they sue in Courts, except when they have a licence called *ticket of leave* (i.e., the *parole*). Their capacity to enter into a contract, and to sue is only suspended during the period of sentence and is regained after its expiry. The law of limitation would be held in abeyance during the period of sentence.

(g) **Marriage (*Marital Status*) :** According to our constitution, the right of a woman to be treated on a footing of equality with man is a fundamental right guaranteed to her. A Hindu woman formerly was under a disability in the enjoyment as an heir of the estate of a deceased male or female relative, in that she could enjoy only what was called a woman's or widow's estate, but the Hindu Succession Act, 1956 enables a Hindu woman to acquire absolute rights even in the property inherited by her from her male or female relations. It may also be noted that under the same Act, *for the purpose of succession to the property of a male or female Hindu, a daughter is placed in the same position as a son.*

REVIEW QUESTIONS

1. Define consideration. Distinguish it from motive. Is the existence of consideration essential for the validity of the contract?
2. "A contract without consideration is void". Are there any exceptions to this rule? If so, explain.
3. 'A stranger to a contract cannot sue, but a stranger to a consideration can sue'. Elucidate the statement.
4. "Inadequacy of consideration is of itself no ground for rescinding a contract. But it may be an evidence of undue influence". Explain.
5. Define the term 'capacity to contract'. State the law relating to the competence of the parties giving suitable examples.
6. Explain the meaning of "Capacity of Contract". To what extent can a minor under the Indian Contract Act be held liable for necessaries supplied to him?
7. Minor's agreements are absolutely void. Is there any agreement with a minor which can be enforced in a court of Law? If so, discuss with examples.
8. "A person who is usually of unsound mind, but occasionally of sound mind may make a contract when he is of sound mind". Explain.
9. State the legal disability of a person arising on the ground of status as imposed by law.

10. X sells his car which he purchased a month ago at a cost of₹ 20,000 for ₹ 2,000. Afterwards he seeks to set aside the contract on the ground of inadequacy of consideration. Can he seek to set aside the contract on the ground of inadequacy of consideration? Can he succeed?

11. X promised Y, his nephew, a reward of₹ 1,000 if he refrained from drinking for two years. Y does so. Is he entitled to the reward?

12. Two seamen deserted a ship and the remaining seamen agreed to take the ship to the port in return for extra wages. The ship safely reaches the port. Are they entitled to extra wages?

13. During a strike by a workers in a coal mine, the police authorities thought it enough to provide a mobile force for the protection of the mine. The colliery manager wanted a stationary guard. It was ultimately agreed to provide the latter at a rate of payment by the company owing to colliery, which involved a sum of₹ 2,200. Subsequently the company refused liability to pay, pleading absence of consideration. How should you decide.

14. X offered a reward to anyone who would rescue his wife dead or all from a burning building. A fireman risking his life brought out the wife's dead body. Is he entitled to recovery of the reward?

15. A promises to make a gift of₹ 3,000 towards the repairs of a temple. The trustee of the temple on the faith of his promise incurs liabilities. A does not pay. Can the trustee recover the promised amount from A ? Give reasons for your answer.

16. A promised B to subscribe a sum of money for the construction of a Town Hall. On the faith of A's promise, B called for plans, entrusted the work to contractors and thereby undertook certain pecuniary liabilities. A subsequently refused to subscribe any amount. Does B have any cause of action against A ?

17. A took a house from B and agreed to pay rent and to repair. He failed to pay rent or to repair. B agreed that if A paid up all the arrears of rent he (B) would do the repairs. Is it a valid agreement?

18. A writes a letter to B, his son, wherein he promises to pay₹ 10,000 to the latter without any consideration but on account of natural love and affection. Can B enforce the contract?

19. A husband executed a registered document in favour of his wife. After referring to quarrels and disagreements between them he promised to pay for separate maintenance and residence. On his failure to pay, the wife seeks your advice. Advise her.

20. A fell into a river. B rescued him and in gratitude A made an oral promise to pay B₹ 1,000. A now refuses to pay the money. Has B any remedy against A?

21. A and B are neighbours in Kalkatta. A was out of station for some days. During that time, a fire broke out in the house of A and B extinguished the fire after making an expenditure of₹ 1,500. A on return promises to pay the money spent by B. Is the promise enforceable?

22. A and B are friends. B treats A during A's illness. B does not accept payment from A for the treatment and A promises B's son. X, to pay him ₹ 1,000. A, being in poor circumstances, is unable to pay, X sues A for the money. Can X recover?

23. D bought tyres from Dunlop Rubber Co. and sold them to S, a sub dealer, who agreed with D not to sell below Dunlop's list price and to pay to Dunlop Co. ₹ 75 as damages on every tyre he undersells. S sold two tyres at less than the list price and thereon the Dunlop Co. sued him for the breach. Will the Dunlop Co. succeed?

24. A agrees with B to give car to B's son in consideration of his marrying A's daughter. Can B's son sue A on the agreement?

25. X, the uncle of Y, promised to pay ₹ 2,000 to Y if he refrained from drinking for two years. Y does not drink for two years and thereby saves his money. Can he now claim ₹ 2,000 from X?

26. A is aged 17 years. He enters into an agreement with B for hiring out certain machinery for running a factory belonging to B. After the agreement was signed, A backs out of the agreement and B wants to enforce the same. Discuss with reasons whether B will succeed or not.

27. A, a minor, lends ₹ 10,000 on the strength of a mortgage executed in his favour. Is the borrower liable to repay the money?

28. For a loan of ₹ 1,50,000 to be received in three annual installments, A (the borrower) executed a simple mortgage of his property in favour of B (the lender) - the borrower receiving ₹ 50,000 towards the first installment, at the time of executing the mortgage deed. Examine B's rights on the mortgage deed, and respecting the moneys paid over to A :

(i) If B did not know that A was a minor.

(ii) If B knew that A was a minor.

(iii) If a fraudulently misrepresented his age.

(iv) If the moneys paid to A were required for advanced studies abroad.

29. A, a minor, fraudulently represents himself to be a major and takes delivery of a car, executing a promissory note to favour of the dealer. S, A fails to pay as per the note. Can S recover the car from A or sue him on the basis of the promissory note?

30. P sold some articles from his shop to S on credit, not knowing that S was a minor. The time fixed for payment expired and no payment was made. Some time later when S attained majority P sued him for the price. What relief should the Court give P under the law?

31. A, minor aged 17, represented to B, a money-lender, that he was 19 years old and then asked for a loan of ₹ 5,000 starting that the amount was urgently required by him to complete his Higher Secondary Education. The money lender, without making any further inquiry, lent the amount to A.

32. P, a film producer, engaged R, a minor girl to act in his films and for this he entered into an agreement with R's father, P fails to pay R salary under the agreement and the girl sues the producer, through her father, for the arrears of the salary. Will she succeed?

❐ ❐ ❐

Chapter

FREE CONSENT

Definition of Consent : To make a contract valid not only the presence of a consent of the other party is necessary but this consent should be '*free*' and '*genuine*'. Section 12 defines '*consent*' as follows : *Two or more persons are said to consent when they agree upon the same thing in the same sense.* If parties do not consent. i.e., they do not understand the same thing in the same sense, there can be no agreement, because consent is like the very roots of an agreement. If there is no consent, the parties are not said to be *ad idem*, i.e., of the same mind.

Factors vitiating the Consent of the Parties

Consent is free if it is not caused by (i) Coercion, (ii) Undue Influence, (iii) Fraud, (iv) Misrepresentation and (v) Mistake. Consent thus gets vitiated by the presence of coercion or undue influence or misrepresentation. Accordingly, these are known as *vitiating elements*, and when any one of them is present in the consent given, there is said to be flaw in consent.

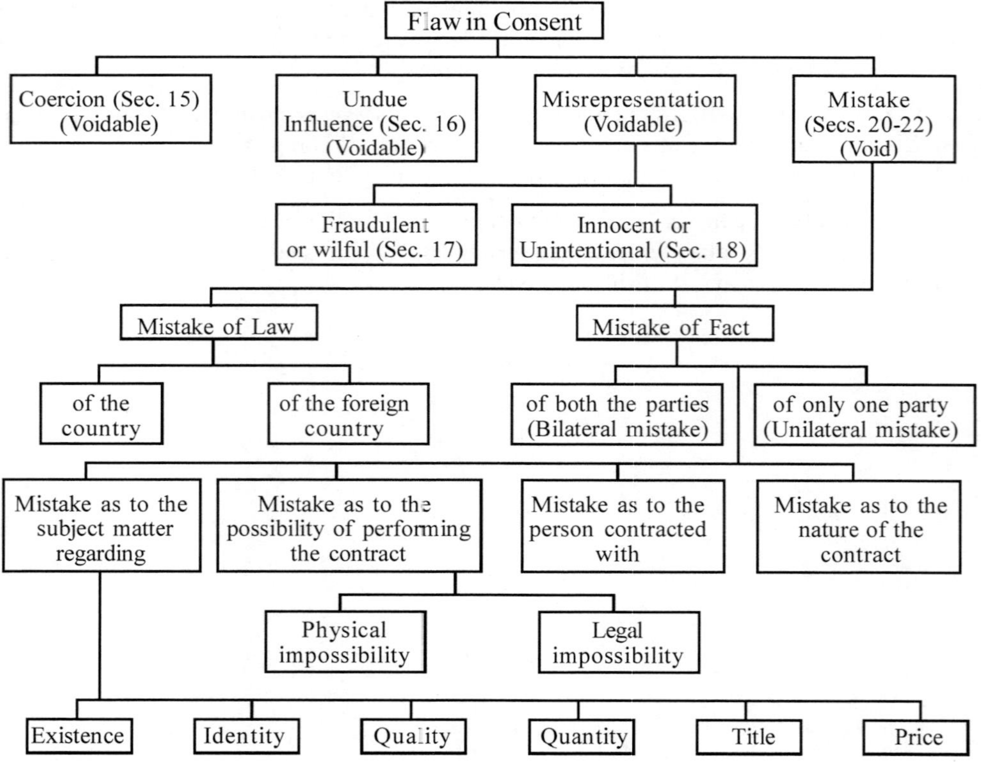

COERCION

When a person is compelled to enter into a contract by the use of force by the other party or under a threat, coercion is said to be employed. Coercion is defined in Section 15 of the Act as follows : *Coercion is (i) the committing or threatening to commit any act forbidden by the Indian Penal Code, or (ii) the unlawful detaining or threatening to detain any property to the prejudice of any person whatever, (iii) with the intention of causing any person to enter into an agreement. It is immaterial whether the Indian Penal Code is or is not in force in the place where the coercion is employed.*

Example : P threatens to shoot Q if he does not let out his house to P, and Q agrees to do so. The agreement has been brought about by coercion.

Essential Elements of Coercion

According to the above definition, coercion is :

(i) **The Committing of any act forbidden by the Indian Penal Code :** Thus, in *Ranganayakamma Vs. Alwar Setti,* (1889), a Hindu widow of 13 years was made to agree to adopt a boy by her husband's relative who prevented the removal of the dead body of her husband until she consented to the adoption. Held, the agreement to adopt a child was not binding on her.

(ii) **The Threat to Commit any act forbidden by Indian Penal Code (IPC) :** In *Amiraju Vs. Seshamma,* (1918), a release deed was obtained by a person from his wife and son under a threat of committing suicide. The transaction was set aside on the ground of coercion, as any attempt or threat to commit suicide is forbidden by Indian Penal Code Year?

(iii) **The Unlawful Detention of any property :** Thus, where an agent appointed for a period of time refused to hand over to his principal or to the new agent, the books of account regarding the business at the end of his term of office, unless the principal released him from all liabilities in respect of acts done by him an agent, and the principal, because of this coercion, did give the release it was held that the release deed was avoidable at the option of the Principal on the ground of coercion *(Muthian Chettiar Vs. Karuppan Chetty* (1927].

(iv) **Threatening to detain any property Wrongly :** Threatening to detain any property belonging to the other party to the contract or any other party.

(v) **The Intention to get consent to the agreement :** The act amounting to coercion must be committed with the intention of causing any person to give his consent to the agreement.

(vi) **Coercion may proceed from any party :** It is not necessary that the act amounting to coercion must be committed by a party to the contract. It may proceed from (i.e., it may be committed by) any party, even from a stranger to the contract.

(vii) **Coercion may be directed against any person :** It is not necessary that the threat or act amounting to coercion must be directed against the other contracting party. It may be directed against any person, even against a third person.

Illustration **:** The Government gave a threat of attaching the property of P for the recovery of the fine due from C, the son of P.P. paid the fine. Held, the contract to pay the fine was induced by coercion. *(Bansaraj vs. The Secretary of State).*

(viii) **IPC is or is not in force in the place :** It does not matter whether the Indian Penal Code is or is not in force in the place where the coercion is employed. If the suit is filed in India, the above provision (i.e., Sec. 15) will apply.

A, on board an English ship on the high seas, causes B to enter into an agreement by an act amounting to criminal intimidation under the Indian Penal Code. A afterwards sues B for breach of contract at Calcutta. A has employed coercion although his act is not an offence by the law of England and although the Indian Penal Code was not in force at the time when or the place where the act was done.

Certain Special Cases

In the context of examples of coercion, it is better to consider certain special cases and see whether they amount to coercion or not.

1. **Does a threat to prosecute a man or file a civil or criminal suit against a man amount to coercion:** A threat to prosecute a man or to file a civil or criminal suit against a man does not amount to coercion, as it is not forbidden by the Indian Penal Code. But a threat to file a suit against a man on false charge amounts to coercion, because such an act is forbidden by the Indian Penal Code. *(Askeri Mirza Vs. Bibi Jai Kishori).*
2. **Does a threat to charge high prices amount to coercion :** A threat to charge high prices does not amount to coercion, because such an act is not forbidden by the Indian Penal Code.
3. **Does a threat to charge high rate of interest amount to coercion :** A threat to charge high rate of interest on the amount due does not amount to coercion, because it is not forbidden by the Indian Penal Code.

Effects of Coercion

A contract brought about by coercion is *voidable* at the option of the party whose consent was so caused (S.19). The aggrieved party can have the contract set aside or he can refuse to perform it and take the defence of coercion if the other party sought to enforce it. The aggrieved party may, if he so desires, abide by the contract and insist on its performance.

Burden of proof : The onus of providing that the consent of a party to a contract was caused by coercion and that he would not have entered into it had coercion not been employed, *lies on the party who wants to relieve himself* of the consequences of coercion.

UNDUE INFLUENCE (Moral Coercion)

A contract is said to be induced by undue influence where (i) one of the parties involved is in a position to dominate the will of the other, and (ii) he has been in a position to obtain an unfair advantage over the other [Sec. 16(10)].

A person is deemed to be in a position to dominate the will of another:

(a) where he holds a real or apparent authority over the others e.g., master and servant,

(b) where he stands in fiduciary relation to the other; e.g., father and son,

(c) where he makes a contract with a person whose mental capacity is temporarily or permanently affected by reason of age, illness, or mental or bodily distress e.g., an old illiterate person [Sec. 16 (2)].

Burden of Proof : Where a person who is in a position to dominate the will of another, enters into a contract with him, and the transaction appears, on the face of it or on the evidence adduced, to be unconscionable, the burden of proving that such a contract was not induced by undue influence shall lie upon the person in a position to dominate the will of the other. [Sec. 16(3)].

To prove that undue influence has been exercised, the plaintiff or the defendant, as the case may be, must satisfy the Court : (i) that the other party was in a position to dominate his will, and (ii) that he actually used that position for obtaining an unfair advantage for himself. Unfair advantage means gain, benefit or advantage obtained by unrighteous or undesirable means.

Presumptions as to persons deemed to be in a position to dominate the will of another. A person is deemed to be in a position dominate to the will of another in the following cases of relation or circumstances :

(i) Where he holds a *real or apparent authority* over the other e.g., the relationship between the *master and the servant, police officer and accused, income tax officer and assessee.*

(ii) Where he stands in a *fiduciary relationship* to the other. Fiduciary relationship means a relationship of mutual trust and confidence. Such a relationship is supposed to exist in the following cases: *parent and child (father and son), fiance & fiancee, guardian and ward, solicitor and client, trustee and beneficiary.*

(iii) Where he makes a contract with a person whose *mental capacity is temporarily or permanently affected by* reason of age, illness, mental or bodily distress etc. Such a relation exists between a medical attendant i.e. *doctor and his patient, spiritual guru and disciple, teacher and student.* The rule is not confined to the above relationships. It applies whenever the relationship between the parties is that one of them is, by reason of confidence reposed in him by the other, able to take unfair advantage over the other.

No presumptions : It has been held by judicial decisions that the existence of a power to dominate the will of another cannot be presumed in the case of *landlord and tenant, creditor and debtor, husband and wife, mother and daughter, grandfather and grandson, principal and agent.* In these cases, the party alleging undue influence must prove that undue influence existed.

Effect of Undue Influence : An agreement induced by undue influence is ***voidable*** at the option of the party whose consent was thus secured. While setting aside such a contract, the Court may impose conditions as to the return of any benefit received under the contract by the party at those instances it is set aside (Sec. 19A). The aggrieved party may, if he desires, treat the agreement as binding and enforce it against the other party.

Distinction between Coercion and Undue Influence

In both coercion and undue influence, the consent of one of the parties is not free, his freedom of will is impaired and he is under the influence of another. However, the difference between the two is as follows:

1. **Property :** In the case of coercion, the consent is obtained by the threat of an offence (i.e., committing or threatening to commit an act forbidden under the Indian Penal Code, or detaining or threatening to detain property unlawfully) and the person is forced to give his consent. But in the case of undue influence, consent is obtained by dominating the will of the giver, and consent is freely given under the belief that he is not to be put to any loss by giving such a consent.
2. **Crime :** Coercion includes criminal act and involves criminal liability but in undue influence there is no criminal act.
3. **Character or Force :** Coercion is mainly of a physical character. It involves mostly use of physical or violent forces. But on the other hand, undue influence is of moral or mental character. It involves the use of moral force or mental pressure. Hence it is known as *moral coercion.*
4. **Consent :** In the case of coercion, consent is destroyed whereas in the case of undue influence, consent is induced by improper means.
5. **Place :** An act of coercion may be committed outside India but undue influence exercised in India will be questioned by the law of the land/country once it is exposed.

6. **Presumption :** Coercion as an act has to be proved by the person who alleges it; in no case is coercion presumed by the law. But in certain types of relations of utmost confidence, and undue influence may be presumed by the law and the party against whom it is alleged must disprove it.
7. **Third Party :** An act of coercion may be directed against a third party whereas undue influence is exercised against the party to the agreement.

FRAUD

Definition of Fraud : Section 17 of the Indian Contract Act states that *Fraud* means and includes following acts committed by a party to a contract, or with his connivance, or by his agent, with intent to deceive another party thereto or his agent, or to induce him to enter into the contract :

(i) *False suggestion is the suggestion, as to a fact*, of that which is not true, by one who does not believe it to be true;

(ii) suppression of truth i.e., the *active concealment of a fact* by one having knowledge or belief of the fact;

(iii) *a promise made without any intent of performing it*;

(iv) *any other act fitted to deceive*;

(v) *any such act or omission* as the law specially declares to be fraudulent. To constitute fraud, the act complained of must be brought within any of the above five categories.

Essentials of Fraud

Section 17 also lays down the essential elements in the concept of fraud. They are the following :

(i) **Suggestions as to a fact :** There must be a representation or assertion and it must be false. Without a representation, there can be no fraud except in case (a) where silence may itself amount to fraud, or (b) where there is an active concealment of a fact.

(ii) **The active concealment of a fact :** If a person purposely and actively conceals a fact, which is his duty to disclose, it will be taken as a fraud, on his part. In *Peek Vs. Gurney (1874)* the prospectus of a company deliberately avoided reference to a particular document which would have disclosed certain liabilities. This was done to create an impression that the Company was prosperous though in fact it was not. It was held that this amounted to fraud and anyone who purchased shares on the faith of this prospectus could avoid the contract.

(iii) **The representation must relate to a fact :** A misstatement relating to law cannot amount to fraud, for ignorance of law is no excuse. Hence the misrepresentation must relate to a fact.

(iv) **Fraud by a party or his agent to the contract :** Fraud must be committed by a party to the contract or with his connivance or by his agent. It should not be committed by a stranger. That is when a person is induced by a stranger to subscribe towards shares of a company on false information, he cannot set side the contract on the basis of fraud.

(v) **The representation must in fact deceive :** If the person on whom the fraud was practised was not in reality deceived, then he is in just the same position as if no false representation had been made to him.

(vi) **Actually deceived or suffered damage :** The plaintiff must suffer some damage by relying upon eg., the presentation of the fact. The damage may consist of actual and temporal injury, i.e., some loss of money or some tangible detriment capable of assessment.

Silence amounting to Fraud

According to explanation to Section 17 "Mere silence as to facts likely to affect the willingness of a person to enter into a contract is not fraud, unless the circumstances of the case are such that, regard being had to them, it is the duty of the person keeping silence to speak, or unless his silence is, in itself equivalent to speech". From the above, the following rules can be deduced:

1. The general rule is that *mere silence is not fraud.*
2. Fradulent silence : Silence is fraudulent, "if the circumstances of the case are such that, regard being to them, it is the *duty* of the person, keeping silence, to speak". The *duty to speak* or putting expression or hearsay or flourishing description, does not amount to representation of fact. Traders and manufacturers are inclined to speak optimistically of their products, e.g., "X products are the best in the market". Such statements do not amount to fraud, unless a clear intention to deceive is proved.
3. Silence is fraudulent where the *circumstances* are such that, "silence is in itself equivalent to speech".

Effect of Fraud

(i) A contract induced by fraud is ***voidable*** at the option of the party whose consent was obtained by fraud. Such a party, however, has the option of insisting that the contract should be performed and he should be put in the position in which he would have been if the representation had been true.

(ii) The aggrieved party can ***sue for damages***. Fraud is a civil wrong or tort; hence, compensation is payable to the party affected.

(iii) In cases of fraudulent silence, the contract is not voidable if the party whose consent was so caused that it had the means of discovering the truth with ordinary diligence.

GOOD FAITH (*UBERRIEMAE FIDEI*) CONTRACTS

Mere silence is not fraud : The general rule is that a person need not disclose to the other party material facts which he knows but he must refrain from making active misstatement. This means mere silence is not fraud. Thus, silence does not amount to a representation and cannot amount to fraud. In ordinary contract of sale, for example, the buyer must take care of himself. The seller is under no obligation to disclose material facts.

Exception to the General Rule

It is fraud for one to conceal material facts which he is under an obligation to disclose when he is entering into a contract with another. This duty to disclose does not arise in cases of all contracts. It arises only in the following cases :

(i) **Statutory Obligation to disclose :** Certain statutory provisions requires parties to a contract to make disclosure of material facts. *Thus Sections 55 of the Transfer of Property* Act, 1882 requires a seller of real estate property to disclose all defects as to his title or property to the buyer. Therefore, if in contravention of this provision the seller conceals any defect in his title and tells the buyer that his property is free from all encumbrances, the buyer may treat the contracts as void even if he buys a property, in case the property turns out to be mortgaged or subject to similar encumbrances.

(ii) **Duty to disclose in Contracts of *Uberrimae fidei* (Utmost Good Faith):** Where parties to a contract stand in such a relationship that utmost good faith is required of them, they must disclose all material facts, e.g., a contract between father, mother and son just come of age. Nondisclosure in such a case would be treated as fraudulent. The following are a few *instances of contracts uberrimae fidei*:

(a) **Insurance Contracts :** An insurer contracts on a condition or understanding the basis that all material facts should be communicated to him. So non-disclosure would vitiate the contract. Thus in a life insurance contract, if the assured declares that he is not suffering from a particular disease while, though unknown to him he was in fact suffering from it, the insurance contract would be liable to be set-aside. Similarly, in a proposal for fire insurance, non-disclosure of the refusal of another insurance company would entitle the insuring company to repudiate the contract.

(b) **Contracts relating to Family Settlements :** Full disclosure of all material facts are necessary when family disputes are settled by mutual agreement. In *Gordan Vs. Gordan (1821)*, a secret marriage not disclosed by one of the parties to the family arrangement was held sufficient to entitle the other party to set-aside the family settlement.

(c) **Contracts for the allotment of Shares in Companies :** A Company inviting the public to subscribe to its share must disclose all information regarding itself in the prospectus with strict accuracy. The Companies Act, 1956 sets out certain items which must be contained in a *prospectus* and thus required a full disclosure of all material facts.

(d) **Contract of Agency :** The agent must disclose to his principal every information coming to his knowledge which may influence the principal in making the contract with the third person.

(e) **Contract of Partnership :** Mutual trust and confidence is the basis of a partnership. It requires utmost good faith between parties before and after its formation.

(f) **Contract of Suretyship or Guarantee:** Sec. 143 of the Contract Act lays down that any guarantee which the creditor has obtained by means of keeping silence as to material circumstances is invalid. A creditor must disclose all material circumstances to the surety.

(g) **Contracts in which Parties Stand in a Fiduciary Relation to each other :** Parties standing in a fiduciary relation to each other are duty bound to disclose all material facts to the other party which are likely to effect his willingness to enter into a contract, e.g., *solicitor and client, father and son, doctor and patient*. In all cases silence and non-disclosure of fact will itself amount to fraud.

(h) **Contract to Marry :** Strictly speaking, contracts of marriage are not contracts of utmost good faith. However, in *Ahmad Yarknan Vs. Abdul Garni Khan*, the Nagpur High Court observed that, "But contract to marry may also come under this category though the case law on the subject is meagre and conflicting". Nevertheless, since a marriage cannot be nullified on the ground of nondisclosure; when the contract is still in the executory stage, one partly may set aside the contract and defend the suit for damages, if the other party has failed to disclose the material facts in accordance with the decision in the case cited above.

(iii) **Silence is, in itself, equivalent to speech :** Silence will amount to fraud in all those cases where it shall be considered equivalent to speech.

MISREPRESENTATION

Misrepresentation is any untrue statement made by a party to the contract to another, which is a material statement of fact and not of law and which induced the other party to act upon the statement and enter into the contract. Misrepresentation arises when the representation or statement made is inaccurate but the inaccuracy is not due to any desire to defraud the other party i.e., *there is no intention to deceive.*

Definition : Sec. 18 defines "*Misrepresentation*" means and includes -

(1) The *positive assertion*, in a manner not warranted by the information of the person making it, of that which is not true, though he believes it to be true. Thus, in misrepresentation a person making a statement makes it without the knowledge of the statement being untrue and with an honest belief in its truth.

(2) Any *breach of duty* which, without an intent to deceive, gains an advantage to the person committing it, or anyone claiming under him, by misleading another to his prejudice or to the of prejudice anyone claiming under him.

(3) Causing, however, innocently, a party to an agreement to make a mistake as to the substance of the thing which is the subject of the agreement.

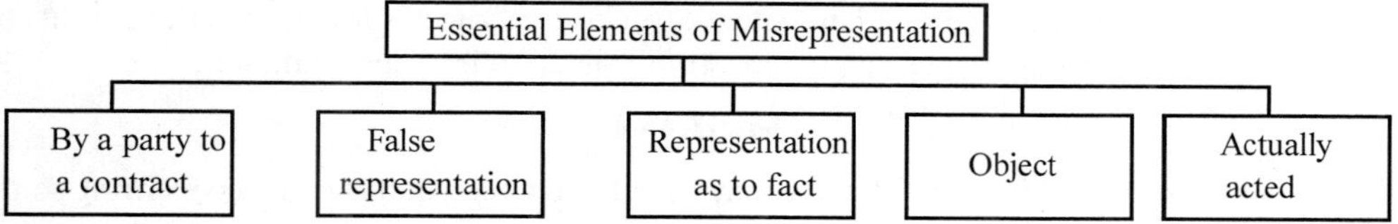

Effect of Misrepresentation

In case of misrepresentation, the contract becomes *voidable* and the aggrieved party can :

(i) avoid the agreement,

(ii) insist that the contract be performed and he shall be put in the position in which he would have been if the representation made had been true,

(iii) If the party to whom the innocent misrepresentation is made had the means of discovering the truth with ordinary diligence, the contract is not voidable (Sec. 19).

"*Ordinary diligence*" means such diligence as a reasonably prudent man would consider necessary, having regard to the nature of the transaction.

A person seeking to avoid a contract on the ground of misrepresentation must prove:

(i) that the representation related to a matter of fact;

(ii) that it was made before or at the time when the contract was entered into;

(iii) that it was untrue;

(iv) that it was made to induce the other party to enter into the contract; and

(v) that it, in fact, induced him to enter into the contract.

Distinction between Fraud and Misrepresentation

1. **Intention :** Both in fraud and misrepresentation, there is a statement which is false; but in fraud the statement is made with the knowledge that it is false or without believing in its truth. In innocent misrepresentation, however, the person making it honestly believes it to be true or does not know to be false.

2. **Damages :** The party aggrieved by fraud can sue the person guilty of the fraud for damages he may have suffered by reason of the fraud (the fraud having been successfully played on him) In the case of an innocent misrepresentations, the aggrieved party cannot sue for damages, but can only avoid the agreement.

3. **Rescission :** The remedy of rescission of the contract is available when the contract is vitiated by fraud as well as when it is vitiated by innocent misrepresentation. However, in the case of fraud, this right can be exercised even after the contract has been performed. Where it is an innocent misrepresentation the remedy of rescission cannot be exercised after the contract has thus been executed.

4. **Where truth can be discovered with ordinary diligence :** In case of misrepresentation, the aggrieved party cannot avoid the contract if it had the means of discovering the truth with ordinary diligence.

But in fraud, as a rule, the contract is voidable even though the aggrieved party had the means of discovering the truth with ordinary diligence.

5. **Criminal act :** Fraud, in certain cases, can be a criminal act and punishable under the Indian Penal Code. But misrepresentation of the facts does not show any criminal intent on the part of the maker of the statement and it is not criminally punishable.
6. **Silence :** In certain cases (fraudulent) silence can be construed as fraud, as in the case of contracts of *uberrimae fidei*, but silence cannot constitute an act of misrepresentation.

MISTAKE

Meaning and Definition of Mistake : Mistake may be defined as erroneous belief concerning something, consent cannot be said to be "free" when an agreement is entered into under a mistake. An agreement is valid as a contract only when the parties agree upon the same thing in the same sense. It often happens that one of the parties to a contract pleads mistake as a ground for setting it aside, because according to him, there was not genuine consent to the agreement which is the essence of every contract. With regard to this, it must be borne in mind that mistakes of every description could not be permitted to be used in such a manner without making it impossible for contracts to be entered into at all.

Examples

A agrees to buy from B a certain house. It turns out that the house had been destroyed by fire before the time of bargain though neither party was aware of the fact. The agreement is void. A cannot insist for possession of the house. The agreement is void as there is mistake on the part of both the parties about the existence of the subject matter.

A, who owns two Ford cars, offers to sell his 'White Ford' for ₹ 3,00,000. B accepts the offer thinking A is selling his 'Brown Ford'. There is a mistake as to the identity of the subject matter.

Types of Mistakes

The Indian Contract Act lays down the following rules regarding mistakes. Mistake may be of two types: (i) mistake of law and (ii) mistake of fact. Mistake of law may again be subdivided into (a) mistake as to law in India and (b) mistake as to a foreign law, i.e. a law not in force in India. Mistake of fact may be either (a) bilateral or (b) unilateral.

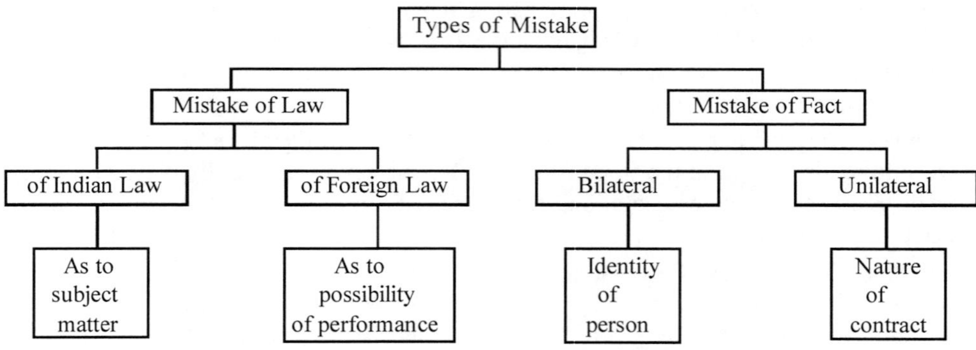

Mistake of law : If it is a mistake of law, the agreement cannot be avoided, except when mistake is with regard to a foreign law in which case it would be considered a question of fact, because one is not bound, in civil law, to know the law of a country other than his own, though he must know the law of his own country. In other words, it is a mistake of fact that the individual may avoid an agreement.

Mistake of fact : In order that a mistake of fact may be capable of avoiding the transaction it is necessary to show :

(i) that the mistake was bilateral and not unilateral, i.e., both the parties or all the parties to the contract are mistaken; and

(ii) that the mistake is as to a fact essential to the agreement. Section 20 also states the above position as, *"Where both the parties to an agreement are under a mistake as to a matter of fact essential to the agreement, the agreement is void"*. An erroneous opinion as to the value of the thing which forms the subject matter of the agreement is not to be deemed a mistake as to a matter of fact. The various cases falling under bilateral and unilateral mistakes are discussed below.

Instances and Cases falling under Bilateral Mistake

(i) **Mistake as to the subject matter :** Where both the parties to an agreement are working under a mistake relating to the subject-matter, i.e., they assume that a certain state of things exists which in fact does not exist, *the agreement is void.* Following are the cases which fall under this category:

(a) **Mistake as to the *existence of the subject-matter :***

Illustration : A agrees to buy from P a certain horse. It turns out that the horse was dead at the time of the bargain, though neither party was aware of the fact, the agreement is void.

(b) **Mistake as to the *identity of the subject-matter :*** Cases are there in both the parties are mistaken as to the identity of the property which is the subject matter of the contract. A mistake as to the quality of an article is not material unless it is a mutual mistake, regarding some attribute of the article, without which the article is of an essentially different character from the article in the minds of the parties. In such a case, the contract is *void.*

Illustration : A bought from B certain goods which were to arrive from Bombay through a ship named 'Peerless'. Two ships with the name 'Peerless' sailed from Bombay, one in October and the other in December. A had the first ship in his mind, and B had the second in his mind. The agreement was held to be void as there was no true consent of the parties. *v. [Raffles Wichelhans Exch., (1864) H & C 906)]*

(c) ***Mistake about the quality of the subject matter*** : A mistake about the quality of the subject-matter may not render the agreement void. But if the bilaterial mistake is about the quality of the subject -matter which makes the subject - matter different from that as wes believed to be, the agreement will be void.

Illustration : A offered to purchase a race horse from B, a horse dealer. B accepted the offer believing it to be for a cart horse. In this case, the agreement is void as both the parties are mistaken about the quality of subject-matter. Here, the mistake as to quality makes the subject-matter altogether different from the thing as it was believed to be.

(d) **Mistake as to the *quantity of the subject-matter* :** There may be a mistake as to the quantity or extent of the subject matter, which will render the contract void.

Illustration : A agreed to buy 200 sewing cotton reels each containing 400 metres of the thread. But unknown to both the parties, the length of the thread per reel was much less than 400 metres. The agreement was void as there was mistake of both the parties about the quantity of the subject-matter. *[Earnest beck & Co. vs. K.S. Owski & Co., (1924) AC 43]*

(e) **Mistake as to the *title to the subject matter* :** If the seller is selling a thing which he is not entitled to sell and both the parties are acting under a mistake, render the contract void.

Illustration : A agreed to sell to B all his rights in a land including the right to mine minerals. Subsequently, it was found that A's right did not include the right to mine the minerals. This fact was not known to both the parties at the time of agreement. The agreement was held to be void because without this right to mine, the land was worthless for B, whose only object was to work the mines. *[Ramchandra vs. B. Ganesh Chandra, 39 IC 78]*

(f) **Mistake as to the *price of the subject matter*** : There may sometimes be a genuine mistake as to the price of an article for sale in which case the contract will be void. Where a seller intending to write the figure of ₹ 2,500 as price of an article, wrote ₹ 250 and the buyer knowing the mistake accepted the offer, the court held the contract as void.

Illustration : A agreed to let out his house to B for a monthly rent of ₹ 450. But in the written agreement the figure of rent was put as 540 by mistake. The agreement was held to be void. *[Garrad vs. Frankel (1862) 54 ER 961]*

(ii) **Mistake as to the *possibility of performing the contract*** : Consent is nullified if both the parties believe, at the time of entering into contract, that the contract is capable of being performed when in fact this is not the case. Sometimes, both the parties believe that the agreement is capable of being performed, but in fact it is not possible to perform. In such case, the agreement is void as both the parties are mistaken about the possibility of performance of the agreement. In other words, where the agreement is impossible to perform but the fact of impossibility is unknown to both the parties, the agreement is void.

(a) ***Physical Impossibility*** : A contract for the hire of a room for witnessing the coronation procession was held to be void because, unknown to the parties, the procession had already been cancelled.

(b) ***Legal Impossibility*** : A contract is void if it provides that something shall be done which cannot, as a matter of law, be done.

Instances and Cases falling under Unilateral Mistake

Unilateral mistake does not generally affect the validity of a contract. But in the following cases, even though there is a unilateral mistake, *the agreement is void :*

(i) **Mistake as to the *identity of persons contracted with*** : This mistake is material only where the personality of the other party is of importance to the person making the error, and may arise out of either the negligence or the fraud of the other party.

(ii) **Mistakes as to the *nature of transaction*** : Where there is a mistake with regard to the nature of the transaction, there cannot be a contract. Where an old gentleman, not capable of reading, by reason of age, was asked to sign a document which he was told was a guarantee, thought it was really a bill of exchange, and he, believing it to be a guarantee and intending to sign a guarantee, signed the document, it was held that he was not liable even to a bona fide holder for value of the bill of exchange.

Effect of Unilateral Mistake

According to Sec. 22, "A contract is not voidable merely because it was caused by one of the parties to it being under a mistake as to a matter of fact". Thus, *unilateral mistake does not generally affect the validity of a contract.*

Remedies for Mistake

(i) If the consent is caused by mistake of both parties, then agreement is *void* (S. 20).

(ii) Where the contract is void on account of mistake, any person who has received any advantage under it, is *bound to restore it or make compensation for it to the person from whom he received it* (S. 65).

Note : Whether one party is playing fraud, and the other has been induced to enter into a contract under mistake, the case would be decided on the basis of mistake.

Rectification : When the parties are in fact agreed but the written instrument to which they have reduced their contract does not truly express the intention of both of them, then the terms of the instrument cannot be enforced, but the Court can rectify the instrument so as to make it express the true intentions of the parties and enforce it as rectified. The courts will not rectify an instrument on the ground of mistake unless it is shown that there was an actually concluded contract antecedent to the instrument sought to be rectified and that the contract is inaccurately described in the instrument.

REVIEW QUESTIONS

1. What is meant by consent to a contract?
2. When is a consent said to be free and genuine?
3. When is consent said to be not free?
4. Discuss the effect of flow in consent on the formation of a contract.
5. Define : (i) Coercion, (ii) Undue influence, (iii) Misrepresentation, (iv) Fraud and (v) Mistake.
6. What is coercion?
7. What are the characteristics of coercion?
8. 'Mere silence is not fraud'. Explain the statement and state exception to this rule.
9. On whom does the burden of proof lies in case of undue influence?
10. State the cases in which undue influence is (a) presumed and (b) not presumed.
11. What is meant by mistake a contract ? Discuss the elements of mistake.
12. What are the consequences of mistake on contract?
13. Can a person whose consent is caused by fraud claim damages under Indian Law?
14. What are the legal remedies available to a person who consent is caused by fraud?
15. A young widow was forced to adopt a boy under the threat of preventing her husband's corpse from being lifted to cremation grounds. Is the adoption valid?
16. A man by the name of N called at a jeweler's shop and chose a costly ring. He tendered in payment cheque which he signed in the name of G, a person of credit. He took the ring and pledged it to B, who had no notice of the fraud. Can the jeweler recover the ring from B?
17. A fraudulently informs B that A's house is free from encumbrances. B thereupon buys that house. The house is subject to a mortgage. What are the rights of B.
18. B is A's daughter and has just come of age. A sells to B a horse, A knows it to be unsound. A says nothing to B about the horse's unsoundness. Does A's silence amount to a fraud ? If so, why? If not, why not?

19. P purchased an electric fan thinking that it was powerful enough to keep his room cool. The fan turned out to be inadequate for the entire room. So he wanted to return the fan to the seller and get out of the contract on the ground of mistake. Can he succeed?

20. A agrees to buy a motor car from B for ₹ 15,000 and pays half the purchase price in advance. Unknown to both parties at the time of making the contract, the car had been destroyed by an accident. Advise A.

21. A inspected 10 rifles in a shop. Later, he telegraphed "Send three rifles". The telegraph clerk by mistake transcribed the message as "Send the rifles". The shopkeeper sent 10 rifles. Is A bound to accept them?

22. X, an old man of feeble sight, endorsed a bill of exchange for ₹ 3,000 when he was falsely told that it was a guarantee. Is he liable under the bill of exchange?

23. A agrees with B to sell his horse worth ₹ 1,000 for ₹ 10 only. Is this agreement valid?

❑ ❑ ❑

Chapter

OBJECT AND PUBLIC POLICY

Section 23 the Contract Act states that the object or consideration of an agreement is unlawful in the following cases : (a) Where it is forbidden by law, or (b) Where it defeats the provisions of any law, or (c) Where it its fraudulent, or (d) Where it is injurious to another person or his property, or (e) Where it is immoral, or (f) Where it is opposed to public policy.

1. Forbidden by Law

The term *'law'* means the law for the time being in force in India, and includes the personal laws i.e., Hindu Law, Muslim Law, Tax Laws etc.

Illustrations

A agreed to pay ₹ 600 to B if he steals C's scooter. This agreement is void as the consideration is unlawful. The theft is forbidden by law.

A promise B to drop a prosecution which he has instituted against B for robbery, and B promises to restore the value of the things taken. The agreement is void, as its object is unlawful. (*William Vs. Bayley*).

X granted a loan to the guardian of a minor to enable him to celebrate the minor's marriage. It was held that X could not recover back because agreement is void as its object (i.e. minor's marriage) is illegal. [*C. Srinivasa Vs. K. Raja Rama Mohana Rao*].

A promises to obtain for B an employment in the public service, and B promises to pay ₹ 2,00,000 to A. The agreement is void as the consideration for it is unlawful.

X, a Hindu already married and his wife alive, entered into a marriage agreement with 'Y' an unmarried girl. This agreement is void because the second marriage is forbidden by Hindu Law.

2. The Object and Consideration must not defeat the provisions of any law

Sometimes, the object or consideration of an agreement is not directly forbidden by the law. But it is of such a nature that, if permitted, it would defeat the provision of law. In such cases, the object or consideration is unlawful. The agreement with such an object or consideration is unlawful, and void. Here also the term 'law' means the law for the time being in force in India and includes Hindu Law, Muslim Law, Municipal Law, Tax Laws etc.

The following are held if permitted, it would defeat the provisions of any law :

(a) An insolvent debtor agreeing to pay in full any creditor in preference to the creditor (void under Insolvency Act).

(b) A person agreeing to give annuity to the natural father of the person who is taken in adoption by him (*void under Hindu Law*).

(c) A landlord agreement to pay consideration to a tenant to induce him to vacate possession of his premises. (*Illegal under Rent Restriction Control Act*).

(d) An agreement by a debtor not to raise the plea of limitation (*void under the Limitation Act*).

3. The Object and Consideration must not be Fraudulent

Sometimes, the object or consideration of an agreement is fraudulent. The word '*fraud*' means (i) the quality of being deceitful; (ii) criminal deception; (iii) using of false representation to obtain an unjust advantage or to injure the rights or interests of another party.In such cases, the object or the consideration and agreement is unlawful and void. The agreement based on such an object or consideration is unlawful, and void. If the two parties agree to practise fraud on a third party then the agreement between the first two parties is unlawful and void.

4. If it involves or implies injury to the person or property of another

The object or consideration of an agreement will be unlawful if it tends to injure any person or property of another. Thus, an agreement to pull down another's house is unlawful. The word '*injury*' means criminal or wrongful harm. Loss which ensues to a trader as a result of competition by a rival trader is not taken to be injury within the meaning of this clause.

W.H. Smith & Sons Vs. C. Clington (1909) : A requested B, an editor of a newspaper to publish a libel (defamatory article) against C and promised to indemnify B against the consequences arising from libel published. Held that the agreement is void as it involves injury to C and the editor cannot recover the amount form A.

5. The Object and Consideration must not be Immoral

Sometimes, the object or consideration of an agreement is such that it is regarded as immoral. In such cases, the object or the consideration is unlawful. The agreement with such an object or consideration is unlawful, and void. The term immoral depends upon the standard of 'morality' prevailing at a particular place and time. But certain acts have been regarded as immoral since times immemorial e.g., interference in marital relations.

6. The Object and Consideration must not be opposed to Public Policy

Sometimes, the object or consideration of an agreement is opposed to public policy, in such cases, the object or consideration is unlawful. The agreement based on such an object or consideration is *unlawful*, and *void*. An agreement is said to be opposed to public policy when it is against public interest i.e., when it is harmful to public welfare.

PUBLIC POLICY

Meaning of Public Policy or Interest

'*Public interest*' implies common good or general social welfare. The term '*public interest*' is, therefore, 'an elusive abstraction', yet it indicates a standard of goodness for judging private acts and conduct in the social context. Public interest is to be distinguished from private interest. According to *Dictionary of Sociology*, a thing may be said to be in the public interest where it is or can be made to appear to be contributive to the general welfare rather than to the special privilege of a class, group or individual. Anything which is not detrimental to public good shall be in public interest.

Agreement opposed to Public Policy

On the basis of decided cases on the subject, *the following agreements have been held to be void being against the public policy :*

1. Trading with an alien enemy.
2. Agreements to promote hostile action in a friendly State.

3. Agreements interfering with course of justice.
4. Agreements in restraint of legal proceedings.
5. Agreements for stifling criminal prosecution.
6. Agreements tending to an abuse of legal process.
7. Agreements to oust the jurisdiction of courts.
8. Agreements to vary periods of limitation.
9. Agreements for the sale or to influence of public offices/titles/honours.
10. Agreements to influence election to public offices.
11. Agreements tending to create interest opposed to duty
12. Agreements tending to create monopolies.
13. Agreements in restraint of parental rights.
14. Agreements restricting personal liberty.
15. Agreements in restraint of marriage.
16. Marriage brokerage agreements.
17. Agreements interfering with marital duties.
18. Agreements in fraud of creditors.
19. Agreements to defraud revenue authorities.
20. Agreements in restraint of profession.
21. Agreements tending to create monopolies.
22. Agreements in restraint of trade.

Agreements interfering with the course of justice : Agreements for stifling or hushing up prosecutions are bad in law. When an offence has been committed, the guilty party must be prosecuted and any agreement which seeks to prevent the prosecution of such a person is opposed to public policy and is void. But under the Indian criminal law there are certain cases which can be compromised or compounded. These are mostly minor offences like simple hurt. An agreement for the compromise of such a case is valid. In civil cases compromises and settlements are not only allowed but also are encouraged. An agreement to refer present or future disputes to arbitration is a valid agreement. But an agreement varying the statutory period of limitation is not valid.

AGREEMENT IN RESTRAINT OF TRADE

An agreement which interferes with an individual's right to engage himself in any lawful trade, occupation or profession is called an "*agreement in restraint of trade*". It is in the interest of the community that every man should be at liberty to work for himself, avail the fruit of his labour skill or talent by any contract that he enters into. He should also be at liberty to take up any trade or business and use his skill or talent by any contract that he enters into. He should also be at liberty to take up any trade or business and use his skill to the best of his capacity.

Section 27 of Indian Contract Act 1872 provides that *every agreement in restraint of trade is to that extent void.* The reason for this being that not only a person is restricted in his choice but the society as a whole suffers if the skills of individuals are permitted to go waste. In India, all restraints, whether partial or complete, qualified or unqualified, in point of time or place are void, unless the case falls within recognised exceptions. These **exceptions** are given below :

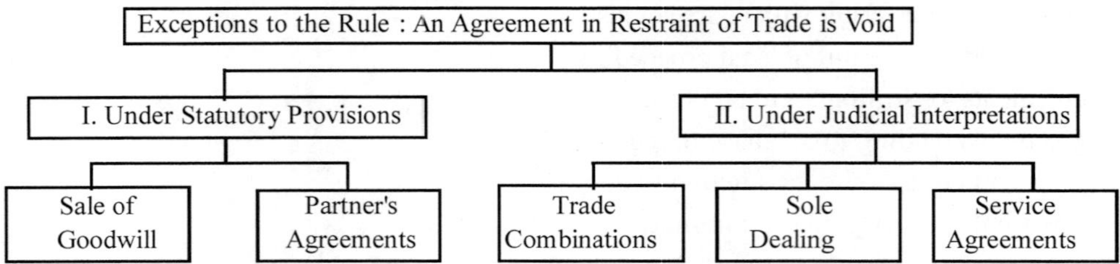

1. **Sale of Goodwill :** An agreement between seller and buyer of goodwill, that the seller will not carry on similar business within specified local limits so long as the buyer or his representatives carry on the business is a valid, provided in the opinion of the court, the limits are reasonable. Reasonableness of restrictions will depend on many factors e.g., (i) the area in which the goodwill effectively enjoyed, (ii) the price paid for it, (iii) the nature of the business, and (iv) the time of restrictions (*Section 27 Exception 1*).

2. **Exceptions under Partnership Act :** The Indian Partnership Act, 1932 also contains certain exceptions as follows :

   (i) **Existing partner's agreements :** An agreement between existing partners of a firm may provide that a partner shall not carry on any business other than that of the firm while he is a partner *(Section 11(2) of the Indian Partnership Act, 1932).*

   (ii) **Agreement with outgoing partners :** A partner may make an agreement with his partners that on ceasing to be a partner, he will not carry on any business similar to that of the firm within a specified period or local limits. Notwithstanding anything contained in Section 27 of the Contract Act, as such the agreement shall be valid if the restrictions imposed are reasonable *(Section 36(2) of the Indian Partnership Act, 1932).*

   (iii) **Agreement upon dissolution :** Partners may, upon or in anticipation of the dissolution of the firm, make an agreement that some or all of them will not carry on a business similar to that of the firm within a specified period or within specified local limits *(Section 54 of the Indian Partnership Act, 1932).*

   (iv) **Sale of firm's Goodwill :** Any partner may, upon the sale of the goodwill of a firm, make agreement that such partner will not carry on any business similar to that of the firm within a specific period or within specific local limits. Such agreement shall be valid if the restrictions imposed are reasonable *(Section 55(3) of the Indian Partnership Act, 1932).*

3. **Service contracts :** Agreements of service often contain *negative covenants* preventing the employees from working elsewhere during the period covered by the agreements. For instance, Doctors are usually barred from private practice during term of their fulltime employment in governing hospitals. But a restraint on a employee not to engage in a similar business, or not to accept a similar engagement, after the termination of service is taken to be void.

   It is important that in such a contract, the restraint imposed must be reasonable. Whether a restraint is reasonable or not depends on particular facts of each case.

4. **Trade combinations :** A voluntary agreement among the members of the Trade Associations or Chambers of Commerce etc., to regulate their areas of operation or to fix prices of goods and commodities is not void under Section 27. Nowadays, traders carry on their trade in an organised way. There are combinations of manufacturers, grain merchants etc. Such ground being to about standardised goods fixed prices

and certain extent eliminate cut throat competition. Thus regulations as to the opening and closing of business in a market, licensing of traders, mode of dealings etc., are valid, even if there is incidental diminution of freedom of trade. But a combination which tends to create monopoly and which is against public interest is declared void. Similarly, where the intention in such an agreement is to raise prices to an unreasonable extent, the agreement would be void under Section 27.

5. **Exclusive agency :** The principal may restrain his agent from dealing in goods of any other rival. For example, Reliance Textiles Co. Ltd., may grant a Selling Agency to Maharaja & Company on the condition that it will not deal in the goods of any other manufacturer.

VOID AGREEMENTS

A void agreement is one without any legal effects and does not create any legal rights and obligations. Following are the various types of void agreements. These are contained in Sections 11, 20, 23 to 30 and 56 of the Indian Contract Act.

1. Agreements by persons who are not competent to contract (Section 11).
2. Agreements under a mutual mistake of fact material to the agreement (Section 20).
3. Agreements with unlawful consideration or object (Section 23).
4. Agreements, the consideration or object of which is unlawful in part (Section 24).
5. Agreements without consideration (Section 25).
6. Agreements in restraint of marriage (Section 26).
7. Agreements in restraints of trade (Section 28).
8. Agreements in restraint of legal proceedings (Section 28).
9. Agreements the meaning of which is uncertain (Section 29).
10. Wagering agreements (Section 30).
11. Agreements to do impossible acts (Section 56).

A void agreement is *void ab initio* (i.e., void from the very beginning) and without any legal effect. "*An agreement not enforceable by law is said to be void*".

WAGERING AGREEMENT

According to Section 30 of the Indian Contract Act, 1872 "*agreements by way of wager are void*". The section does not define "wager".

Definition : *Sir William Anson* defines "wager as a promise to give money or money's worth upon the determination or ascertainment of an uncertain event.

Essentials of Wagering agreement : 1. Uncertain event, 2. Mutual chances of gain or loss, 3. Neither party to have control over the event, 4. No other interest in the event, and 5. The promise must be to pay money or money's worth.

The event in question need not necessarily be unlawfull. It may be also a lawful event.

Examples of Wagering Agreements

1. A and B agree that, if it rains on Monday, A will pay B ₹ 100, and if it does rain on that day, B will pay the same amount to A. It is a wagering agreement.
2. A promises to B to pay him ₹ 100 if Indian Hockey Team beats Pakistan Hockey Team; in consideration to which B promises to pay ₹ 100 to A if Pakistan Hockey Team beats Indian Hockey Team. This agreement is a wagering agreement.

3. *A bet on a horse race* carrying a prize is a wagering agreement, though horse race is permitted by some local laws.
4. A *lottery* is a game of chance. So, an agreement to buy a ticket for a lottery is a wagering agreement, even though it is authorised by the Government. *(Dorabji Vs. Lance)* The only effect of Government authorising a lottery is to exempt the person conducting the lottery and the buyer of the lottery ticket from criminal prosecutions.
5. A *share market transaction* in which there is no intention to give or to take delivery of the shares, and where the parties intend to deal only with the differences in prices is a wagering agreement. (*Manilal Vs. Alibhai, Sobhagmal Vs. Mukundchand*).
6. A *commercial transaction* (i.e., a transaction for the purchase and sale of commodities) in which there is no intention to give or take delivery of the commodities and where the parties intend to deal only with the differences in prices is a wagering transaction.
7. A *cross-word puzzle* in which prizes depend upon correspondence of the competitor's solution with a previously prepared solution kept with the editor of a newspaper is a lottery, and so, is a wagering transaction. (*Coles Vs. Odham's Press*).
8. A and B bet regarding the height of Kutab Minor in Delhi. It is a wagering agreement, if none of them knew its height, even though it is not an uncertain event.
9. A agrees with B that he will pay B ₹ 100, if C is elected president of some co-operative society. B agrees to pay A some amount, if C is defeated at the election. It is a wagering agreement.
10. In a *wrestling match*, A tells B that Wrestler No. 1 will win. B challenges the statement of A. They bet with each other over the result of the match. It is a wagering agreement.
11. An *insurance agreement* where the assured or the insured has no insurable interest in the subject-matter of insurance is a wagering agreement.
12. A agrees to sell to B his horse at ₹ 500, if it wins the race and at ₹ 50, if it does not. The horse wins and B refuses to pay. This is a case of wagering agreement. It is void. (*Brogden Vs. Mariatt*).

Effects of Wagering transactions : A wagering agreement being *void* cannot be enforced in any court of law. Section 30 expressly declares that "no suit shall be brought for recovering anything alleged to be won on any wager, or entrusted to any person to abide the result of any game of other uncertain event on which any wager is made". Thus the amount won on a wager cannot be recovered.

Babasaheb Vs. Rajaram (1931) : Two wrestlers agreed to enter into a wrestling competition subject to the condition that the person who failed to appear on the day fixed for the match should forfeit ₹ 500 to the other party, and that if the competition took place, the winner should receive ₹ 1,125 out of the gate collections. The defendant having failed to turn up, the plaintiff sued him for the recovery of ₹ 500. Rejecting the arguments of the defendant that the contract was a wager, the Court held that the amount was recoverable on the ground that, "the stakes did not come of the pockets of the parties but had to be paid from the gate money provided by the public."

Effects of Wagering Agreements

Sec. 30 of the Act clearly lays down that all wagering contracts are void. Wagering is equal to gambling. As a matter of fact, though a wagering agreement is void and unenforceable, but it is not forbidden by law.

Gherulal Parakh Vs. Mahadeodas Maiye (1959) : The appellant and the respondent entered into a partnership to carry on wagering contracts with two firms of Hapur. They agreed to make the contracts in the name of the respondents on behalf of the firms and to divide the profit and loss resulting from the transaction in equal shares. The respondent entered into such contracts. The net result of these contracts was a loss.

Since the respondent had to pay the full amount due to the merchant at Hapur, he wanted the appellant to bear his share of the loss. Since the appellant denied his liability, the firm was dissolved and the respondent sued the appellant.

The Court held that, "Though a wager is void and unforceable, it is not forbidden by law and, therefore the object of a collateral agreement is not unlawful under Section 23 of the Contract Act and partnership being an agreement within the meaning of Section 23, it is not unlawful, though its object is to carry on wagering transactions. We, therefore, hold that in the present case the partnership is not unlawful within the meaning of Section 23 of the Act. "Accordingly, while *a wagering agreement cannot be enforced between immediate parties, collateral transactions are enforceable.*

In the State of Maharashtra and Gujarat wagering agreements are, by a local statute, not only void but also illegal.

In the case of void agreements, collateral agreements, i.e., agreements which are subsidiary or incidental to the main agreement, are valid. Therefore, though wagering are void, transactions collateral to such agreements are valid.

Exceptions

1. **Horse Race :** The section does not render void a subscription or contribution, or an agreement to subscribe or contribute, toward any plate, prize or sum of money, of the value or amount of five hundred rupees or upwards to the winner or winners of any horse races. However any transaction connected with horse racing is declared illegal under section 294 A of the Indian Penal Code shall be invalid.

2. **Cross-word competitions and cross-word puzzle :** A crossword puzzle in which solution can be made by only one word is not a game of chance but it is a game of skill. But there are some cases, in which solution can be made by one or other of two or more alternative words. In such cases the prize is to be given to the competitor whose solution corresponds to the solution already made by the publisher or the editor. This is purely a wager.

3. **Sports competitions, Literary competitions etc., :** Competitions such as athletics, wrestling, indoor games of any type (Carom, Judo, Billiard, Table tennis, playing cards, etc.), Boxing, Football, Cricket, Hockey, etc., are not games of chance. It is decided by skill or judgement. Therefore, competition is not a wager.

4. **Picture Puzzle :** A picture puzzle competition is not a game of chance.

5. **Lottery or Raffle :** Lottery is a game of chance. In a lottery the event is wholly dependent on the drawing of lots. It is a game either of gain or loss of the absolute right to a prize. Lottery is, therefore, a wager. But the lottery is nowadays governed by the State Lottery Rules.

6. **Chit Fund :** It is a plan under which all subscribers are paid back their contribution of capital to the fund by a fixed date. Though in some cases it is determined by lots to get more than capital and sooner. Thus, it is not lottery.

7. **Flower show competition, Dog show competition, Beauty contest etc:** These types of contests or competitions are not matter of chance competitions-they require skill and judgement.

8. **Contract of Insurance :** Contract of insurance is not a wager. In this contract the insured has insurable interest in the property or life. The insurer promise to pay a certain sum of money on the death of insured provided the insured pays the premium regularly to the insurance company.

Distinction Between Wagering Agreement and Contract of Insurance

	Wagering Agreement	*Contract of Insurance*
1.	**Gambling :** It is a game of chance	It is not a game of chance
2.	**Intention :** In this case, the parties contemplate to get a certain sum of money on the happening of an uncertain future event.	There is no such intention.
3.	**Insurable interest :** The parties do not cover up their risk of future loss. There is no insurable interest.	One of the parties covers up his risk for future loss. He has insurable interest.
4.	**Indemnity :** It is not a contract of indemnity.	General (non-life) insurance is a contract of indemnity.
5.	**Legal effect :** It is void agreement *ab initio*.	It is a valid contract.
6.	**Parties interest :** Only one of the parties is interested in protecting the subject matter.	Both the contracting parties are interested.
7.	**Stakes :** There is the same stake for both the parties.	The stakes of the parties are not the same.
8.	**Risk :** Neither of the parties is subject to any particular risk before entering into a contract	The insured (subject matter) is subject to risk.

ILLEGAL AGREEMENTS

The term *'illegal agreement'* may be defined as the agreement which is expressly or impliedly prohibited by law e.g., by Indian Penal Code, or by some other special legislation etc. Thus, an agreement to commit a murder, or to publish a libel (a defamatory statement) is an illegal agreement. As a matter of fact, the illegal agreements are *void* and do not confer any rights and obligations on the parties concerned. As a result of this, they are *not enforceable* in a Court of Law.

Illustrations

(i) A, B, and C entered into an agreement to carry on the business of smuggling and agreed to divide the profits in equal shares. It is an illegal agreement as the smuggling is forbidden by law.

(ii) A agreed with B, a prostitute, to give her certain ornaments on hire. A knew that B had to use these ornaments in the furtherance of her trade. B failed to pay the hire charges, and A filed a suit for the recovery of the same. It was held that the agreement was illegal and void. Thus, A could not recover anything from B.

Effects of Illegal Agreements

The effects of illegal agreements may be discussed under two heads : (i) *Effects on main transaction* and (ii) *Effects on collateral transaction.*

(i) **Effects on main transaction :** We have already discussed that an illegal agreement is *void ab initio* (i.e., void from the very beginning) and without any legal effects. As a matter of fact, an illegal agreement is non-existent, and the law will not permit the parties to enforce any right under it. This is so because the law treats the illegal agreement as if it had not been made at all. Therefore, no remedy is available to either party. Thus, nothing can be recovered under the illegal treatment. If something has been paid by any party, that party cannot get it back from the other party.

The general principle of law that *no suit can be filed in respect of an illegal agreement* is based on the following two ***maxims*** :

(a) *From an illegal cause, no action arises*. Thus, the courts refuse to help either party. Moreover, the law discourage people from entering into an illegal agreement which arises from an illegal cause.

(b) *In case of equal guilt, the defendant is in a better position*. Thus the party, who has paid some money against an illegal agreement, cannot get it back. In other words, the defendant can keep whatever has been received by him against the illegal agreement. This is because of the fact, that the courts do not help either party.

(ii) **Effects on collateral transactions :** We know that 'collateral transaction' is an incidental or parallel transaction. In other words, it is the transaction which is subsidiary to the main transaction, e.g., the loan taken for the purpose of carrying an illegal business such as smuggling. The collateral transaction to an illegal agreement, also becomes illegal. Consequently, a collateral transaction is void and cannot be enforced in a Court of Law. It may be noted that even if the collateral transaction is lawful in itself, it will be treated as illegal and void.

(iii) **Plaintiff not relying on the illegal contract :** If the plaintiff has parted with possession of his property on an illegal contract, he can recover the property provided he relies upon his independent right of ownership. In case such as bailment or a lease in which only a limited interest is transferred, the owner can recover the property from the bailee or the lessee, if he relies upon his title to the same but does not establish his claim on the illegal contract.

Exceptions : The maxim, *From an illegal cause no action arises* subject to the following exceptions.

(a) **Illegal purposes not carried out :** Where the contract which is illegal remains executory, i.e., the illegal purpose has not been carried out in whole or in part, either party to its is allowed an opportunity for repentance and is permitted to recover money paid or goods delivered in respect of the contract. It is however necessary, that the party seeking to recover must withdraw from the transaction before the illegal purpose is executed and the withdrawal should be genuine.

(b) Where the parties to an illegal contract, the less guilty party may be able to recover money paid, or property transferred under the following circumstances:

(i) Where the plaintiff has been the victim of fraud or oppression at the hands of the defendant, he may, upon proof of such fraud or oppression, recover anything paid or delivered to the defendant under the contract.

(ii) Where the contract is rendered illegal by a statue in the interests of a particular class of persons of whom the plaintiff is one.

AGREEMENTS IN RESTRAINT OF LEGAL PROCEEDINGS

As a matter of fact,every person has a freedom to enforce his legal rights. Moreover, justice also requires that one should be free to go to 'Courts of Law for the enforcement of his legal rights. An agreement which interferes with the course of justice is void on account of its being opposed to public policy. It is a well known rule of English Law that "an agreement purporting to oust the jurisdiction of the courts is illegal and void on ground of public policy". This rule of English Law has been incorporated in Section 28 of the Indian Contract Act. This Section has been amended in 1996 by the Indian Contract (Amendment) Act, 1996 and the amended section reads as under :

"Every agreement, -

(a) *by which any party thereto is restricted absolutely from enforcing his rights under or in respect of any contract, by the usual legal proceedings is in the ordinary tribunals, or which limits the time within which he may thus enforce his rights; or*

(b) *which extinguishes the rights of any party thereto, or discharges any party thereto from any liability, under or in respect of any contract on the expiry of a specified period so as to restrict any party from enforcing his rights, is void to that extent".*

1. ***Restrictions from enforcing legal rights*** : An agreement which restrains a person form enforcing his legal rights, is void. It may be noted that the restriction must be absolute. In other words, a person must be wholly restrained from enforcing his legal remedies in the Courts of Law.

2. ***Agreement which cuts short the limitation period*** : An agreement which reduces the limitation period than that prescribed by the Law of Limitation, is void e.g., according to the Indian Limitation Act an action for breach of contract may be brought within three years from the date of breach. If an agreement provides that no action should be brought after two years, if void as it curtails the period of limitation.

3. ***An agreement which extinguishes the rights of a party*** : An agreement which extinguishes the rights of a party, is void. By entering into an agreement, the parties acquire certain rights under the agreement. Any agreement, which states that such rights would be extinguished after the expiry of a specified period, is void.

4. ***An agreement which discharges a party from liability*** : An agreement which discharges a party from liability, is void, By entering into an agreement, the parties also become liable to perform certain obligations. Any agreement, which states that a party would be discharged from his liability after the expiry of a specified period, is void.

Exceptions to the rule 'agreements in restraint of the legal proceedings is void' : (a) Restraints for referring future disputes to arbitration and (b) Restraints for referring the existing disputes to arbitration.

REVIEW QUESTIONS

1. What do you understand by the legality of object and consideration.
2. State essentials and legal rules for lawful objects and considerations.
3. All agreements are contracts if they are made for lawful consideration and with lawful object elucidate.
4. "Every agreement of which the object or consideration is unlawful, is void". Explain, and state the cases in which the object and consideration is unlawful.
5. Explain the doctrine of public policy.
6. Do you agree with the view that the heads of public policy are not closed?
7. 'An agreement in restraint of trade is void'. Discuss the statement giving exceptions to it, if any.
8. "A wagering agreement is void and unenforceable, but it is not forbidden by law". Critically examine the statement with suitable examples.
9. 'No action is allowed on an illegal agreement'. Explain the statement and state the exceptions to this rule.

❐ ❐ ❐

CONTINGENT AND QUASI CONTRACTS

Meaning of Contingent Contract : When the performance of a contract is not immediately due but it becomes so only after the happening or non-happening of some contingency (i.e., some uncertain event) it is known as *Contingent Contract*. The contract of insurance, contract of indemnity and guarantee are the examples of contingent contract. In simple words, it is a *conditional contract*.

Definition : A contingent contract is a contract indicating to do or not to do something, if some event, collateral to such contract, does or does not happen (Sec. 31).

Characteristics of Contingent Contract

There are three essential characteristics of a contingent contract, viz. :

1. Its performance depends upon the uncertainty of happening or non-happening in future of some event. It is this dependence on a future which distinguishes a contingent contract from other contracts.
2. The event must be collateral, i.e., incidental to the contract.
3. The contingent event should not be mere will of the promisor.

Impossible Events

According to Sec. 36, *"Contingent agreements to do or not to do anything if an impossible event happens, are void, whether the impossibility of the event is known or not to the parties, to the agreement at the time when it is made".*

Examples : 1. A agrees to pay B ₹ 1,000 if two straight lines should enclose a space. The agreement is void. 2. A agrees to pay B ₹ 1,000 if B will marry A's daughter C. C was dead at the time of the agreement. The agreement is void.

The event should not be the discretion of the promisor : We have already discussed that an event, upon which the contingent contract is dependent, also includes an '*act of the party*'. However, the '*mere will or discretion*' of the promisor is not an event for the purpose of a contingent contract. Thus, if the performance of a contract depends upon the good will or discretion of the promisor, the contract is not contingent contract. Such a contract is rendered void on the ground of uncertainty.

Difference between Contingent Contracts and Wagering Agreements

1. **Mutual Promise :** A wagering agreement consists of mutual promises each of which are conditional on the happening or non-happening of a certain event. A contingent contract may not consist of the mutual promise. It may be said that all wagers are contingent contracts but all contingent contracts are not wagers. For example, insurance contracts, contracts of indemnity and guarantee are contingent contracts but not wagers.

2. **Validity :** A wagering agreement is absolutely void. It is illegal in Maharashtra and England. But a contingent contract is a valid contract.

3. **Performance :** In a wagering agreement, neither party intends to perform the contract, but only to deal in differences. This is not so in contingent contracts.

4. **Interest in the subject matter :** In wagering agreement, the parties to the agreement have no other interests in the subject matter of the agreement, except for the stake. But in a contingent contract, parties do have some other interest in the subject matter. They are interested in the occurrence or non-occurrence of the event.

5. **Future Event :** In a wagering agreement the future event is the sole determining factor of the contract while in a contingent contract, the future event is merely collateral or incidental to the contract.

6. **Nature :** All contingent contracts are not of a wagering nature, because all the contingent contracts are not void. All wagering agreements are also contingent contracts because they are dependent on uncertain event.

QUASI-CONTRACTS

Certain obligations are imposed by law. These obligations are similar to those which are created by contract. When such obligations are imposed by law in the absence of any contract, it is called *quasi-contract*. The quasi-contracts are based on the maxim of no man must grow rich out of another person's costs. In other words, these are based on the equitable principle, that *a person shall not be allowed to enrich himself at the expense of another.*

Quasi-Contracts under Indian Contract Act

The Indian Contract Act refers the Quasi-contracts under the heading.

Certain relations resembling those created by contract, (Sections 68 to 72).

1. Claim for necessaries supplied to a person incapable of contracting on his account (Sec. 68).
2. Reimbursement of a person paying money due by another in payment of which he is interested (Sec. 69).
3. Obligation of person enjoying benefit of a non-gratuitous act (Sec. 70).
4. Rights and liabilities of the finder of lost goods (Sec. 71).
5. Liability of persons to whom money is paid or things delivered, by mistake or under coercion (Sec. 72).

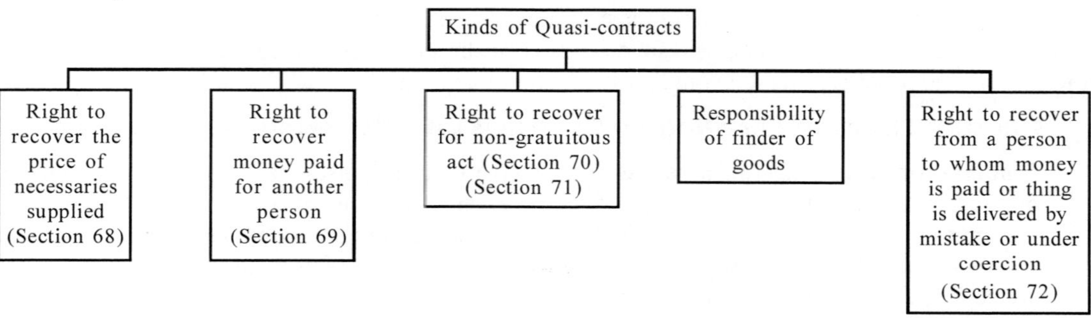

1. Necessaries Supplied to Person Incapable of Contracting

If a person, incapable of entering into a contract, or any one whom he is legally bound to support, is supplied by another person with necessaries suited to his condition in life, the person who has furnished such supplies is entitled to be reimbursed from the property of such incapable person (Sec. 68). Thus, though the contracts by minors, idiots, lunatics, etc., are void, but Section 68 provides that their estates are liable to reimburse the trader who supplies them with necessaries of life. This is on the basis of quasi-contracts.

2. Payment by an Interested Person

A person (i) who is interested in the payment of money, (ii) in which another is bound by law to pay, and (iii) who therefore pays it, is entitled to be reimbursed by the other (Sec. 69).

Illustration : B holds land in Chennai on a lease granted by A, the landlord. The revenue payable by A to the Government being in arrears towards his land is advertised for sale by the Government. Under the revenue law, the consequences of such a sale will be the annulment B's lease. B in order to prevent the sale and the consequent annulment of his own lease, pays to the Government the sum due from A. A is bound to make good to B the amount so paid.

The essentials of Sec. 69 are as follows : (i) The payments made should be bona fide for the protection of one's interest. (ii) The payment should not be a voluntary one. (iii) The payment must be such as the other party was bound by law to pay.

3. Liability for Non-Gratuitous Act

Where a person lawfully does anything for another person or delivers anything to him, not intending to do so gratuitously, and such other person enjoys the benefit thereof, the latter is bound to make compensation to the former in respect of, or to restore, the things so done or delivered (Sec. 70).

To establish a right of action under Sec. 70, the following conditions must be fulfilled : (i) The thing must have been done lawfully, i.e., the act must be lawful. (ii) It must have been done by a person not intending to act gratuitously. (iii) The person for whom the act is done must have enjoyed the benefit of the act.

Illustrations

(a) A, a tradesman, leaves good, at B's house by mistake. B treats the goods as his own. He is bound to pay for them.

(b) A saves B's property from fire. A is not entitled to compensation from B, if the circumstances show that he intended to act gratuitously.

Upendra Vs. Naba : In this case U and N were two co-owners of a sanitary tank. They were sued criminally for ignoring the order of the Municipal Corporation to fill up the tank. U filled up the tank and sued N for contribution. It was held that N was liable to pay the contribution as the tank was lawfully filled up by U without intending to do so gratuitously.

It should be noted that Section 70 does not apply to persons incompetent to contract and as such they are under no obligation to compensate the other person for any benefit received by them. Both the parties must be competent to contract. It should also be noted that a person is not bound to pay for which he had option of refusing.

4. Responsibility of Finder of lost goods

A person who finds goods belonging to another and takes them into his custody, it is subject to the same responsibility as a *bailee* (Sec. 71). He is bound to take as much care of the goods bailed to him as a man of ordinary prudence would under similar circumstances, take of his own goods of the same bulk quality and value. It is also the duty of the finder of lost goods to *trace the true owner*. He must take all necessary measures in this regard. If he does not take these measures, he will be guilty of wrongful conversion of property. Till the true owners is found out, the property in the goods will vest in the finder and he can *retain* it as his own against the whole world (except the true owner, of course).

Hollins Vs. Fowler. A picked up a diamond from the floor of B's shop and handed over to B to keep it till the owner is found. Inspite of best efforts, the true owner could not be searched. After some time, A tendered to B the lawful expenses incurred by him for finding the true owner and asked him (B) to return the diamond to him (A). B refused to do so. Held, B must return the diamond to A as A was entitled to retain it against the whole world, except the true owner.

The Finder, however, can sell the goods in the following cases :

(i) where the thing found is *in danger of perishing* or losing the greater part of its value;

(ii) where the *owner cannot*, with reasonable diligence, *be found out*;

(iii) where the owner is found out, but *refuses to pay lawful charges* of the finder; and

(iv) where the lawful charges of the finder, in respect of the thing found, *amount to two-thirds of the value of the thing found.*

5. Action for Money paid, or thing delivered, by Mistake or under Coercion

A person to whom money has been paid, or anything delivered by mistake or under coercion, must repay or return it (Sec. 72). Mistake must be as to the existence of the obligation and not merely as to some collateral matter which may form a motive for the payment.

6. Accounts Stated

This is a form of action known to English Law, where the obligation arises from an admission of indebtedness, from which the law may imply an undertaking to pay, e.g., an I.O.U. (I owe you). Thus, where the balance has been struck in an account, an action can be brought thereon without going into all the transactions which led up to it.

7. Claim for Quantum Meruit

In addition to the above types of quasi-contracts, a claim can also be made on the basis of Quantum Meruit. Where one person has rendered service to another in circumstances which indicate an understanding between them that it is to be paid for although no particular remuneration has been fixed, the law will infer a promise to pay Quantum Meruit i.e., *as much as the party doing the service has deserved.*

The *object* of allowing a claim on quantum meruit is to recompensate the party or person for value of work which he has done. Damages are compensatory in nature while quantum meruit is restitutory. It is but reasonable compensation awarded on implication of a contract to remunerate. Where a person orders from a wine merchant 12 bottles of whisky and he sends 10 bottles of whisky and 2 of brandy, and the purchaser accepts them, the purchaser must pay a reasonable price for the brandy.

The claim for quantum meruit arises in the following cases : (i) When an agreement is discovered to be *void*, or when a contract becomes *void.* (ii) When something is done *without any intention to do so gratuitously* (Sec. 70). (iii) When there is an express or implied contract to render services but there is *no agreement as to remuneration.* (iv) When one party abandons or prevents or even *refuses to perform the contract.* (v) When a contract is *divisible* and the party not in default has enjoyed the benefit of the part performance. (vi) When and *indivisible* contract for a lump sum is completely performed, but badly, the person who has performed the contract can claim the lump sum; but the other party can make a deduction for bad work.

(a) **In case of Void Agreement, or contract that becomes Void (Section 65)** :When an agreement is discovered to be void, or when a contract becomes void, any person who has received any advantage under such agreement or contract is bound to restore it, or to make compensation for it, to the person from whom he received it.

Example I : A pays B, ₹ 1,000 in consideration of B's promise to marry C, A's daughter, C is dead at the time of the promise. The agreement is void but B must repay A ₹ 1,000.

Example II : A contracts with B to deliver to him 250 maunds of rice before the 1st day of May. A delivers 130 maunds before that day, and none after. B retains the 130 maunds after the first of May. He is bound to pay A for them.

Example III : A, a singer contracts with B, the manager of a theatre, to sing at his theatre for two nights in every week during the next two months, and B engages to pay her ₹ 100 for each night's performance. On the sixth night, A wilfully absents herself from the theatre, and B, in consequence rescinds the contract. B must pay A for the five nights on which she had sung.

Example IV : A contracts to sing for B for ₹ 1,000 which are paid in advance. A is too ill to sing. A is not bound to make compensation to B for the loss of the profits which B would have made if A had been able to sing, but must refund to B ₹ 1,000 paid in advance.

(b) **In case of non-gratuitous act (Section 70)** : The obligation to pay arises if the following three conditions are satisfied :

(i) The thing must have done or delivered lawfully;

(ii) The person who had done or delivered the thing must not have intended to do so gratuitously; and

(iii) The person for whom the act is done must have enjoyed the benefit of the act.

Example : A, a tradesman leaves goods at B's shop by mistake. B treats the goods as his own. He is bound to pay A for them.

(c) **In case of act preventing the completion of contract** : If one party himself does not complete the contract or prevents the other party to complete the contract, the aggrieved party can sue on quantum meruit.

Example : C an owner of a magazine engaged P to write a book to be published as series in his magazine. After a few series were published, the publication of the magazine was stopped. It was held that P could claim payment on quantum meruit for the part already published. *(Planche Vs. Calburn).*

(d) **In case of divisible contract :** The party at default may sue on a quantum meruit if the following conditions are satisfied :

(i) if the contract is divisible; and

(ii) if the party not at default has enjoyed benefits of the part performance.

Example : S agreed to construct a house for H for ₹ 12 lakhs but he abandoned this contract after having done the work worth ₹ 9 lakhs. Afterwards, H got the work completed. It was held that S could not recover anything for the work done because he was entitled to the payment only on the completion of the work.

(e) **In case of indivisible contract performed completely but badly :** The party at default may claim the lumpsum less deduction for bad work if the following conditions are satisfied :

(i) if the contract is indivisble ;

(ii) if the contract is for lumpsum;

(iii) if the contract is completely performed; and

(iv) but the contract is performed badly.

Example: X agreed to decorate Y's flat for a lumpsum of ₹ 20,000. X did the complete work but Y complained of faulty workmanship. It costs Y another ₹ 3,000 to remedy the defect. It was held that X could recover only ₹ 17,000 from Y (Hoenig Vs.Issacs (1952)].

Planche Vs. Calburn, (1831) : C engaged P to write a book on ancient armoury to be published in instalments in a periodical called "The Juvenile Library" for the fee of £100. After a few issues of the periodical had appeared, it was abandoned. Held, P could recover on quantum meruit for the work he had done under the contract.

Distinction between Quasi-Contract and General Contract

Basis of distinction	*Quasi-contract*	*Contract*
1. Essentials for the formation of a valid contract	The essentials for the formation of a valid contract are absent	The essentials for the formation of a valid contract are present
2. Obligation	Obligation is imposed by law.	Obligation is created by the consent of the parties.

Similarity between Quasi-Contracts and Contracts

The outcome of quasi-contracts resemble that created by a contract. So far as *claim for damages* are concerned, there is a similarity between a quasi-contracts and contract because in case of breach of a quasi-contract, Section 73 provides for the same remedies as provided in case of breach of a contract.

Compensation for failure to discharge obligation created by quasi-contracts (Sec. 73) : When an obligation created by a quasi-contract has not been discharged, the injured party is entitled to receive the same compensation from the party in default, as if the sued person had contracted to discharge it and had broken his contract.

REVIEW QUESTIONS

1. What do you understand by a contingent contract?
2. What are the essentials and legal rules for a valid contingent contract?
3. Define quasi-contracts.
4. State the circumstances in which quasi-contractual obligations arise.
5. State the legal position of a finder of lost goods.
6. What is quantum meruit? Under what circumstances is quantum meruit granted?

❑ ❑ ❑

7

Chapter

DISCHARGE OF CONTRACT

A contract may be terminated or discharged in any one of the following ways: (i) Performance of the promise or tender, (ii) Mutual consent cancelling the agreement or substituting a new agreement in place of the old, (iii) Subsequent impossibility of performance. (iv) Operation of Law, and (v) Breach made by one party.

DISCHARGE OF CONTRACT BY PERFORMANCE

Performance may be (i) Actual Performance, or (ii) Attempted Performance. A party to contract is said to have actually performed his promise when he has fulfilled all his obligation under the contract. It then becomes a duty of the other party to do what he had undertaken to do. When both the parties perform their respective promises, a contract is said to have been actually performed. Actual performance brings the contract to an end.

Offer to perform is called *Tender of Performance*. When the parties to a contract offer to perform their respective promises it is a tender or offer of performance. Offer to perform or Tender may also be called *Attempted Performance*.

Essentials of a Valid Tender

Every offer of performance or tender must fulfil the following conditions :

1. *Tender must be unconditional*. A conditional offer of performance is not a good offer and the other party is entitled to reject it.
2. Tender must be made at a *proper time* and *place.*
3. Tender must be made under such *circumstances*, that the person to whom it is made may have a reasonable opportunity of ascertaining that the person by whom it is made is able and willing, to fulfil the whole of the promise.
4. If the offer is an offer to delivery anything to the promisee, the promisee must have a reasonable opportunity of seeing that the thing offered is the thing which the promisor is bound to deliver (Section 38).
5. The tender must be of *whole and not only of the part*. A tender of less than actually due is not a tender at all.
6. Tender must be made to the promisee or his duly authorised agent. Tender made to a stranger would be invalid.
7. Tender made to one of several promisees has the same effect as a tender to all of them.
8. If any promisee neglects or refuses to afford the promisor reasonable facilities for the performance of the promise, the promisor is excused by such neglect or refusal as to any non-performance caused thereby. (Section 67).

9. The tender must be in the *proper form*. Tender of money should be in the legal tender i.e., current coins/currency notes. A tender by cheque is valid when the person to whom it is tendered is willing to accept such payment.
10. The party making the tender must always be ready and willing to fulfil the obligation whenever called upon. If the tender is of cash payment, actual cash must be available in readiness for payment.
11. A mere *offer by post to pay the amount* is not a valid tender. There is no readiness and willingness in this case to pay the money then and there.
12. A tender may either be *tender of goods* or *tender of money*.

Effect of Refusal to accept offer of performance (Section 38)

Where a promisor has made an offer of performance to the promisee and the offer has not been accepted, the promisor is not responsible for non-performance, nor does he thereby lose his rights under the contract.

Effect of refusal of party to perform promise wholly (Section 39)

When a party to a contract has refused to perform or disabled himself from performing his promise in its entirety, the promisee may put an end to the contract, unless he had signified by words or conduct, his acquiescence in its continuance.

Persons entitled to Demand Performance

1. **Promisee :** The performance of a contract can only be demanded by the promisee. A third party cannot demand the performance of the contract, even though it was made for his benefit.
2. **Legal Representative:** In case of death of the promisee, his legal representative can demand performance, unless a contrary intention appears from the contract or the contract is of personal nature.
3. **Joint promisees:** Where a person has made promise to two or more persons jointly, the performance of the promise may be demanded either (i) by all the promisees jointly; or (ii) in case of death of any of the joint promisees, by the representatives of such deceased person jointly with the surviving promisee; or (iii) in case of death of all joint promisees, by the representatives of all of them jointly.
4. **Third party:** A third party can demand performance of a contract in the following cases : (i) *Trust* : Where a contract between A and B creates an express or implied trust in favour of C, C can demand performance. (ii) *Estoppel* : Where a party is estopped from denying his liability to pay or to do something to a third person, that third person can demand performance. (iii) *Contract for maintenance or marriage expenses of a female member* : Where on a partition of a joint Hindu family, a benefit is secured to female member of the family who was entitled to maintenance or marriage expenses such female member can demand performance. (iv) Where the money to be paid under the contract is *charged on some immovable property*. (v) Where the rights under a *contract have been assigned to a third person* by operation of law, or act of the parties.

Persons bound to perform the promise in a contract

1. **By the parties :** According to Section 37 of the Act, the parties to a contract must either perform or offer to perform, their respective promises, unless such performance is dispensed with or excused under the provisions of this Act, or of any other law. Thus as a general rule, the parties to the contract must perform or offer to perform their respective promises. When one party performs his promise, he can

enforce the performance of the promise of the other party. The parties may be excused from the performance either under the provisions of the Contract Act or under any other law e.g., an insolvent may be released from performing his part of the contract under the Insolvency law.

2. **Promisor (Section 40) :** If it appears from the nature of a case that was the intention of the parties to any contract that any promise contained in it should be performed by the promisor himself, such promise must be performed by the promisor.

3. **Representatives (Section 37) :** Promises bind the representative of the promisors in case of the *death* of such promisors before performance, unless a contrary intention appears from the contract. But performance of contracts involving personal service cannot be enforced by or against legal representatives.

4. **Agent (Section 40) :** Unless it appears from the nature of a case that it was the intention of the parties to any contract that any promise contained in it should be performed by the promisor himself, the promisor or his representative may employ a competent person (who may be an agent) to perform the promise. *Contracts which are not a personal nature may be performed through an agent or representative appointed by the promisor for this purpose.*

5. **Third person (Section 41) :** In certain cases, a promise may also be performed by a third person. When a promisee accepts performance of the promise from a third person, he cannot afterwards enforce it against the promisor.

It is clear that in a case, involving personal skill or volition, the promisor is himself bound to perform his promise. But if he dies, the personal cause of action also cease to exist. The rule is that the *personal cause of action dies with the person concerned.* In all other cases the promise may be performed either by the representatives, agents or legal heirs of the promisor.

DEVOLUTION OF JOINT LIABILITIES AND JOINT RIGHTS

Devolution of Joint Liabilities

When two or more persons make a joint promise, the promisee may, in the absence of an express agreement to the contrary, compel any (one or more) of such joint promisors to perform whole of the promise (section 43). Thus, in India the *liability of joint promisors is joint as well as several.*

Illustration : A, B and C jointly promise to pay D ₹ 30,000. D may compel either A or B or C or any two of them to pay him ₹ 30,000.

Right of contribution : Where a joint promisor has been compelled to perform the whole promise, he may compel every other promisor to contribute equally with himself to the performance of the promise (unless a contrary intention appears from the contract). If any one of the joint promisors make default in such contribution, the remaining joint promisors must bear the loss arising from such default in equal shares.

Release of a joint promisor (Section 44) : Where two or more persons have made a joint promise, a release of one of such joint promisors by the promisee does not discharge the other joint promisor or promisors, neither does it free him from responsibility to the other joint promisor or promisors.

Devolution of Joint Rights

When a person has made a promise to two or more persons jointly, then, unless a contrary intention appears from the contract, the right to claim performance rests with all the joint promisees and after the death of any of them with the representatives of such deceased promisee jointly with the survivor or survivors and after the death of the survivors also, with the representatives of all jointly. Thus, unlike the case of joint promisors whose liability is joint as well as several, *the right of the joint promisees is only joint and thus any of them cannot enforce performance unless so agreed.* (Section 45).

Illustration : A in consideration of ₹ 5,000 lent to him by B and C promises B and C jointly to repay them that sum with interest on a day specified. B dies. The right to claim performance rests with B's representative jointly with C during C's life, and after C's death with the representatives of B and C jointly.

TIME FOR PERFORMANCE

1. **Where no time is specified (Section 46) :** Where by a contract, a promisor is to perform his promise without 'application by the promisee, and no time for performance is specified, the engagement must be performed within a reasonable time'.
2. **When time is specified (Section 47) :** Where a promise is to be performed on a certain day and the promisor has undertaken to perform it without application by the promisee, the promisor may perform it at any time during the usual hours of business of such day and at the place at which the promise ought to be performed.
3. **On Application for performance by promisee (Section 48) :** Where a promise is to be performed on a certain day and the promisor has undertaken to perform it only on application by the promisee, it is the duty of the promisee to apply for performance at a proper place and within the usual hours of business. The question "What is a proper time and place?" is, in each particular case, a question of fact.

Time Fixed for Performance as Essence of the Contract

Sometimes the contracting parties regard the time fixed for performance as of the essence of the contract, so that if the performance is not made at the stipulated time, the other party can treat the whole contract as broken and claim damages on that footing.

1. **Effect of failure to perform at fixed time contract in which time is essential :** When a party to a contract promises to do a certain thing at or before a specified time, and fails to do any such thing at or before the specified time the contract, or so much of it as has not been performed, becomes *voidable* at the option of the promisee, if the intention of the parties was that time should be of the essence of the contract. Thus, whenever time is of the essence of the promise, failure to perform the whole of the promise at the stipulated time entitles the other party to avoid the agreement
2. **Effect of such failure when time is not essential :** If it was not the intention of the parties that time should be of the essence of the contract, the contract does not become voidable by the failure to do such thing at or before the specified time. But the promisee is entitled to compensation from the promisor for any loss occasioned to him by such failure.
3. **Effect of acceptance of performance at time other than that agreed upon :** If in case of a contract voidable on account of the promisor's failure to perform his promise at the time agreed, the promisee accepts performance of such promise at any time other than that agreed, the promisee cannot claim compensation for any loss occasioned by the non-performance of the promise at the time agreed, unless at the time of such acceptance, he gives notices to the promisor of his intention to do so.

PLACE FOR PERFORMANCE OF A CONTRACT

Without application for performance by promisee (Section 49)

When a promise is to be performed, without application by the promisee, and no place is fixed for the performance of it, is the duty of the promisor to apply to the promisee to appoint a reasonable place for the performance of the promise, and to perform it at such place. If, however, a place for performance is fixed by the contract, the promisor is bound to perform at that place only. Place to be fixed should be reasonable to both the parties. *Place for performance applies both to delivery of goods as well as to payment of money.*

Manner of Performance (Section 50)

The performance of any promise may be made in any manner or at any time, which the promisee prescribes or sanctions.

Performance of Reciprocal Promises

'*Reciprocal promises*' means a promise in return for a promise. Thus, where a contract consists of promises by one party (to do or not to do something in future) in consideration of a similar promise by other party, it will be called a case of reciprocal promises. Reciprocal promises may be divided into three groups. 1.Mutual and Dependent, 2. Mutual and Independent, and 3. Mutual and Concurrent.

1. **Mutual and Dependent :** In such a case, the performance of one party depends upon the prior performance of the other party. In such a case, if the promisor who must perform fails to perform it, he cannot claim the performance of the reciprocal promise. On the other hand, he must make compensation to the other party to the contract for any loss which such other party may sustain by the non-performance of the contract.

2. **Mutual and Independent :** In such cases, each party must perform his promise without waiting for the performance or readiness to perform of the other.

3. **Mutual and Concurrent :** In such cases, the promise has to be simultaneously performed. According to Section 51, when a contract consists of reciprocal promises to be simultaneously performed, no promisor need perform his promise unless the promisee is ready and willing to perform his reciprocal promise.

Reciprocal promise to do things legal and also other things illegal (Section 57): Where persons reciprocally promise, firstly, to do certain things which are legal and secondly, under specified circumstances, to do certain things which are illegal, the first set of promises is a contract but second is a void agreement.

Alternative promises (Section 58) : In the case of an alternative promise, one branch of which is legal and other illegal, the legal branch alone can be enforced. The rule also applies to cases where the alternative promises are severable. The legal part is enforceable but the illegal part is void. In case the promises are inseparable, the whole contract is void.

Order of performance (Section 52) : (i) Where the order in which reciprocal promises are to be performed is expressly fixed by the contract, they shall be performed in that order; (ii) Where the order is not expressly fixed by the contract, they shall be performed in that order which the nature of the transaction requires.

Consequences of Preventing Performance (Section 53)

When a contract contains reciprocal promises, and one party to the contract prevents other from performing his promise, the contract becomes voidable at the option of the party so they prevented, and he is entitled to compensation from the other party for any loss which he may sustain in consequence of the non-performance of the contract.

Effect of default (Section 54) : When a contract consists of reciprocal promises, such that one of them cannot be performed, or that its performance cannot be claimed till the other has been performed, such promisor cannot claim the performance of reciprocal promise and must make compensation for any loss which such other party may sustain by the non-performance of the contract.

APPROPRIATION OF PAYMENTS

Appropriation means application of payments. The question of appropriation of payment is closely connected with the question of time and place of performance as to several debts owing by one party to another. When a debtor (customer) owes several distinct debts to the same creditor (banker) and make a payment without instruction to the creditor, the question may arise against which debt the payment is to be appropriated. The principles are incorporated in Sections 59-61 of the Indian Contract Act, 1872. In England the law on the subject was paid down in *Clayton's Case* (1816).

1. **Express appropriation by Debtor :** According to Sec. 59 of the Indian Contract Act, the debtor has the right to instruct expressly which debt, if he owes more than one, shall be cancelled by the money he tenders to the creditor.

   Example : A owes to B among other debts the sum of 567 rupees. B writes to A and demands payment of this sum. A sends to B 567 rupees. This payment is to be applied to the discharge of the debt of which B had demanded payment.

2. **Implied Appropriation by Debtor :** If there is no express instruction as to the appropriation, there may be circumstances which imply that the debtor intended appropriation to a particular debt, the debtor's intention must be followed if money is accepted. If the creditor does not agree to the specific directions of the debtor as to the appropriation, he must refuse to accept the payment.

   Examples :

   (i) A owes B among other debts, ₹ 1,000 upon a promisory note which falls due on Ist June. He owes no other debt of that amount. On the 1st June A pays to B 1,000 rupees. The payment is to be applied to the discharge of the promissory note.

   (ii) A owes to B among other debts, the sum of ₹ 5670. B writes to A and demands the payment of this sum. A sends to B ₹ 5670. This payment is to be applied to the discharge of the debt of which B had demanded payment

3. **Principal and Interest when both due :** The general rule is that in absence of any appropriation by the debtor at the time of payment, the payment should be attributed in the first instance to interest and then to the principal. *Harishchandra and another Vs. Kailashchandra and another.* When both principal and interest are due, the debtor can stipulate that a particular payment made by him is to be appropriated to the principal, the interest remaining due. If the creditor accepts the payment he must also accept the debtor's appropriation. If he does not like to do so he must refuse to accept the payment.

4. **Appropriation by Creditor :** According to Sec. 60 of the Indian Contract Act, where the customer has failed or omitted to intimate and there are no other circumstances indicating to which debt the payment is to be applied, the creditor has the right to appropriate it, at his discretion to any *lawful debt* actually due and payable to him from the debtor. *He may even apply it to liquidate either a time-barred debt or an unenforceable debt.* Appropriation, under this section cannot be made towards an illegal debt.

   Example : A owes several debts to B, one of them of ₹ 5,000 is time barred. A sends ₹ 10,000 to B without indicating to which debt the amount is to be appropriated. B may appropriate ₹ 5000 against the time barred debt if he so chooses.

5. **Appropriation by Law (Where neither party appropriates) Section 61:** Creditor can make his appropriation at any time even when he is being examined at the trial of the case. Entries in the books of account are not binding on the creditor if he has not communicated them to the debtor. Section 61 of the Indian Contract Act reads, where neither party makes any appropriation, *the payment shall be applied in discharge of the debts in order of time*, whether they are or are not barred by the law in force for the

time being as to the limitation of suits. *If the debts are of equal standing* (i.e., of the same date) *the payment shall be applied in discharge of each proportionately*

Example : A owes two debts of ₹ 2000 each which are time barred and another debt of ₹ 4,000 to B. A sends ₹ 2000. Neither party makes any appropriation. ₹ 2000 would be appropriated ratably against the two debts of ₹ 2000 each which are time barred i.e., ₹ 1000 would be appropriated against each debt.

In case of a *running or current account*, according to this section, the first item on the debit side is discharged or reduced by the first item on the credit side. In other words, it is the *sum first-paid-in is that first-paid-out*. This is known as the *Rule in Clayton's case*. Sometimes, all three rules under sections 59-61 are also referred as the Rule in Clayton's case.

6. **The rule in re Hallett's estate :** Suppose that a man has an account in a bank in which he keps his own money as well as some money's of which he is a trustee. He makes a series of deposits and withdrawals, in the course of which some trust funds are misappropriated. In this case, the withdrawals are to be debited first to his own moneys and then to the trust funds; and the deposits are to be credited first to the trust fund and next to his own fund, whatever be the order of withdrawals and deposits. *In re Hallett's Estate.*

CONTRACTS WHICH NEED NOT BE PERFORMED

Sections 62 to 67 of the Indian Contract Act mention the contracts which need not be performed.

(i) If the parties to a contract agree to *substitute a new contract* for it or to rescind or alter it, the original contract need not be performed. (Section 62);

(ii) Promisee may *dispense with or remit, wholly or in part*, the performance of a promise made to him, or may extend the time for such performance, or may accept instead of it any satisfaction which he thinks fit (Section 63);

(iii) When a person at whose option a contract is *voidable* rescinds it, the other party thereto need not perform any promise contained therein in which he is a promisor. (Section 64);

(iv) If any promisee *neglects or refuses to afford* the promisor, reasonable facilities for the performance of his promise, the promisor is excused from performance of the contract thereby (Section 67);

(v) When a contract becomes *void because of supervening impossibility or illegality*. (Sec.56);

(vi) When a person has the right to rescind a contract (Sec. 75);

(vii) When a promisor is excused by any other law e.g., the *Limitation Act*, or a company is not liable to fulfil a contract under the *doctrine of ultra vires.*

DISCHARGE OF CONTRACT BY NEW AGREEMENT

The rights and obligations created by an agreement can be discharged without their performance by means of another agreement between the parties which provides for the extinguishment of the earlier rights and obligations. The parties may agree to terminate the existence of the contract by any of the following ways.

(i) **Novation or Substitution (Section 62) :** It means that there being a contract in existence some new contract is substituted for it, either between the same parties or between different parties; the consideration mutually being the discharge of the old contract. It is a transaction by which, with the consent of all the parties concerned, the old contract is revoked and substituted by a new contract. Since novation implies a fresh contract in place of the original one, all the parties to the old contract must agree to it. The new agreement should be valid and made before the breach of the original promise. If the new agreement is unenforceable, then the old contract revives.

(ii) **Alteration :** The term '*alteration*' may be defined as change in one or more terms of the contract. The alteration is valid when it is made with the consent of all the parties. The valid alteration discharges the original contract, and the parties become bound by the new contract (i.e., contract with altered terms).

(iii) **Rescission :** If the parties to a contract agree to rescind it, the original contract need not be performed.

The recession of a contract may occur under various circumstances : (a) It may be done by *mutual consent* (Sec. 62). (b) Where a party to a contract fails to perform his obligations, the other party can *rescind* the contract without prejudice to his rights to receive compensation for breach of contract. (c) In a *voidable* contract, one of the parties has the option of rescinding it.

(iv) **Remission (Sec. 63) :** It is the acceptance of a lesser sum than that was contracted for or a lesser fulfilment of the promise made. It is a unilateral act of the promisee discharging, at his will and pleasure, the obligation of another. A promisee may remit or give up a part of his claim and a promise to do so is binding even though there is no consideration for doing so. The effect of the provision is that the party who has the right to demand the performance of a contract may:

(a) remit or dispense with it, wholly or in part; or (b) extend the time for performance; or (c) accept any other satisfaction instead of performance.

(v) **Waiver :** It means to "*dispense with*" or the abandonment of a right which a person is entitled to. A party to a contract may waive his rights under the contract, whereupon the other party is released from his obligation.

(vi) **Merger :** When a superior right and an inferior right coincide and meet in one and the same person, the inferior right vanishes into the superior right. This is known as *merger*. A man holding property under lease buys the property. His rights as a lessee vanish. They are merged into the rights of ownership which he was now acquired.

Illustration : A is a tenant of B's flat. A purchases the flat from B. A's tenancy is inferior right to B's ownership. As the ownership (superior right) vests in A on purchase, the tenancy of A merges and is extinguished in ownership. A becomes owner and ceases to be a tenant.

DISCHARGE OF CONTRACT BY OPERATION OF LAW

In the following cases, the rights and liabilities arising out of the existence of a contract are discharged by operation of law.

(a) **Insolvency :** The insolvency of the promisor discharges the contract. The promisor is discharged from all liabilities incurred prior to his adjudication.

(b) **Merger :** It occurs when there is acceptance of a higher right or security in the place of the lower. It is an operation of law which extinguishes a right by virtue of its coinciding with another and greater right in the same person.

(c) **Death :** Where performance of a contract is required to be made in person and the personal qualification of the promisor are the consideration for the contract, the death of the promisor discharges the contract. In other contracts the rights and liabilities of the deceased person pass to his legal representatives.

(d) **Lapse of time :** The Limitation Act, 1963 provides that a contract should be performed within a specified period. Such a period is called *period of limitation*. If the contract is not performed, and if no legal action is taken by the promisee within the period of limitation, he is deprived of his remedy at law. In other word, the contract in such a case is terminated.

(e) **Material alteration or unauthorised alteration :** It means a change in one or more of the material terms of a contract. Any alteration if made in writing without other party's consent, the contract is discharged provided that the alteration is in a material part. Where the alteration is immaterial, the deed is not vitiated. It matters not if such alteration was made by a stranger or by a party to the deed. A party of to a contract is not discharged by an alteration which he has authorised

DISCHARGE OF CONTRACT BY IMPOSSIBILITY

Meaning : According to Sec. 56, impossibility of performance may fall into (i) impossibility existing at the time of contract known as *pre-contractual* or *initial impossibility*, and (ii) subsequent or supervening impossibility also known as *post-contractual impossibility*. The agreement in the first case is *void ab initio* due to absolute impossibility.

Section 56 of the Contract Act says that "*an agreement to do an act impossible in itself is void*". It further lays down that even though the act was not impossible, or unlawful at the moment of time the agreement was made, but becomes impossible or unlawful afterwards, the contract becomes void when the act becomes impossible or unlawful.

INSTANCES/CASES COVERED UNDER SUPERVENING IMPOSSIBILITY

1. **Destruction of the object necessary for the performance of the contract:** If the subject matter of the contract known as pre-contractual or initial impossibility, and (ii) subsequent or supervening impossibility also known as post-contractual impossibility. The agreement in the first case is void ab initio due to absolute impossibility.

Illustrations

(a) In ***Taylor Vs Caldwell (1863)*** a music hall was let for a series of concerts on certain days. The hall was burnt down before the date of the first concert. The contract in this case becomes void.

(b) In ***V.L. Narsn Vs PSV Iyer (1953)*** there was an agreement between the owner of a theatre and a producer, to exhibit a picture. The municipal authorities issued orders to demolish the theatre because it was unsafe. Neither of the parties knew that the building was defective. Held that the contract was discharged.

(c) A person contracted to deliver a part of a specific crop of potatoes. The potatoes were destroyed by pests though no fault of the party. The contract was held to be discharged.

2. **Change of Law :** The performance of a contract may become unlawful by a subsequent change of law. In such cases, the original contract becomes void.

Re Shipton, Anderson & Co. (1915) : A agreed to sell to B a specific quantity of wheat lying in his godown. Before the delivery could be made, the godown was sealed by the Government and it requisitioned the whole quantity of wheat under statutory powers. It was held that the contract is discharged as the delivery of the wheat became impossible.

3. **Personal Incapacity :** Where the performance of a contract depends on the personal skill or qualification of a party, the contract is discharged on the illness, incapacity or death of that party.

Robinson Vs. Davison (1871) : An artist undertook to sing at a theatre on a particular day. On the day in question, the defendant was unable to perform owing to illness. It was held that the artist was not liable to damages.

4. **Non-existence or non-occurrence of an event or a state of things necessary for performance :** If a contract is made on the basis of continued existence of certain state of circumstances, the contract stands discharged if the state of things changes or ceases to exist.

Krell Vs. Henry (1903) : A contract was to hire a flat for viewing the coronation procession of the King. The procession had to be cancelled on account of king's illness.In a suit for the recovery of the rent, it was held that the contract become impossible of performance and that the hirer need not pay the rent.

5. **Outbreak of war :** A contract entered into during war with an alien enemy is *void ab initio*. A contract entered into before the war commenced between citizens of countries subsequently at war, remains suspended during the tendency of the war. After the termination of the war, the contract revives and may be enforced.

Example : A contracts to take in cargo for B at a foreign port. A's Government afterwards declares war against the country in which the port is situated. The contract becomes void when the war is declared.

Cases not covered by Supervening Impossibility

Ordinarily when a person undertakes to do something, he must do it unless his performance becomes absolutely impossible due to any of the circumstances discussed above. Therefore, in the following cases, a contract is not discharged on the ground of supervening impossibility. :

1. **Difficulty of performance :** Sometimes some uncomtemplated events or delays occur and they make the performance of the contract more cumbersome or expensive. In such a case, the contract is not discharged by the mere fact that it has become more difficult for performance.

Blackburn Bobbin Co. Vs.Allen & Sons (1918) : A sold B a certain quantity of Finland timber to be supplied between July and September. Before any timber was supplied war broke out in the month of August and transport was disorganised so that A could not bring any timber from Finland. It was held that the difficulty in getting the timber from Finland did not excuse A from performance.

2. **Commercial impossibility :** A party to the contract cannot be discharged from performing his part of the contract simply on the ground that it will be non-profitable for him to perform the contract.

Karl Ettlinger Vs. Chagandas & Co. (1915) : The defendant agreed to supply goods to the plaintiff, to be sent from Bombay to Antwerp. Owing to the outbreak of war before the shipment there was a sharp increase in the shipping rates. When the defendant contended frustration, it was held that the increase in freight rates did not excuse performance.

Disappointed expectations do not lead to frustrated contracts : By a contract in writing, the plaintiffs bought of the defendants a number of dhotis to be manufactured by specified mills and to be delivered as and when the same may be received from the mills. The sellers delivered only part of the goods owing to the mills failing to perform their contract with the defendants as they were engaged in fulfilling certain Government contracts. The defendants pleaded frustration. It was held that the bargain was not frustrated, as the stipulation as to delivery did not make delivery by the mills a condition precedent. It was a simple case of breach. "The closing or even the destruction of the mills would not affect a contract between third parties, which is in terms absolute".

3. **Impossibility due to the behaviour of a third party :** The doctrine of supervening impossibility does not cover the cases where a contract could not be performed because of the default by a third person on whose word the promisor relied.

Ganga Saran Vs. Ram Charan R Gopal (1952) : The respondent agreed to supply to the appellant 61 bales of cloth to be manufactured by the New Victoria Mills, Kanpur, "as soon as they are supplied to him by the said Mill". In a suit for damages for non-delivery of goods the defendant pleaded impossibility on the ground that the goods were not supplied to him by the Mill. Held, that the words "as soon as they are supplied to him by the Mill" simply indicate the process of delivery and did not convey the meaning that the delivery was contingent on their being supplied by the Mill. Hence the case did not fall within the provisions of Sections 32 and 56 as the default was due to the fault of the defendant.

4. **Self Induced Impossibility :** When the impossibility is due to the default of the contracting party himself. Section 56 would not apply. In such cases, the contract is not discharged on the ground of frustration. That is, a contract is not discharged in case of self-induced impossibility.

5. **Strikes, Lock-outs, and Civil Disturbances :** Strikes, lock-outs and civil disturbances also do not discharge a contract unless the parties have specifically agreed in this regard at the time of formation of the contract.

6. **Partial impossibility or Failure of one of the objects :** Where a contract is made for several purposes, failure of one of the objects does not discharge the contract.

7. **Rights and obligations under a transfer of property under a case :** Doctrine of frustration does not apply to leases including those of agricultural land.

8. **Temporary interruption or intervention :** A temporary interruption in the performance of a contract does not discharge the contract.

9. **Matters with the contemplation of parties :** When the parties have the knowledge or the reasonable source to contemplate the event, the doctrine of frustration as a rule is not applicable. The doctrine of frustration is applicable only when the frustrating event is outside the contemplation of the contracting parties.

In India the leading case is ***Satya brata Vs. Mangiram Bangur & Co. (1954)*** where the Supreme Court has clarified that the doctrine of frustration is really an aspect of part of law of discharge of contract by reason of supervening impossibility.

Effects of Supervening Impossibility

1. Section 56 provides that when the performance of a contract becomes subsequently impossible or illegal, the contract becomes *void.*

2. Section 64 of the Contract Act further provides that when a contract becomes void, any person who has received any advantage under it must *restore* it, or make *compensation* for it, to the person whom he received it.

3. Sec. 56 (para 3) provides that, "where one person has promised to do something which he knows, or with reasonable diligence, might have known, and which the promisee did not know to be impossible or unlawful, such promisor must make compensation to such promisee for any loss which such promisee sustains through the non-performance of the promise".

Example : P contracts to marry B being already married to C, and being forbidden by the law to which he is subject to practice polygamy. P must make compensation to B for any loss caused to her by the non-performance of his promise.

THE DOCTRINE OF FRUSTRATION

Definition : When the common object of a contract can no longer be carried out, the court may declare the contract to be at an end. This is known as the *Doctrine of Frustration. Anson* says, "Most legal systems make provision for the discharge of a contract where, subsequent to its formation, a change of circumstances renders the contract legally or physically impossible of performance". The law relating to this subject, as in England and India respectively, is stated below.

EIndian Law : In *Satyabrata Ghosh Vs. Mugniram Bangur and Co. and Another,* (1954) the Supreme Court of India discussed the English cases relating to frustration and came to the following conclusions :

The doctrine of frustration of contract comes into play when a contract becomes impossible of performance, after it is made, on account of circumstances beyond the control of the parties. It comes within the purview of Sec. 56 of the Indian Contract Act. The word *'impossible'* in this section has not been used in the sense of physical or literal impossibility. The performance of an act may not be literally impossible but it may be impracticable and useless from the point of view of the object and purpose which the parties had in view; and if an untoward event or change of circumstances totally upsets the very foundation upon which the parties rested their bargain, it can be said that the promisor finds it impossible to do the act which he promised to do.

REVIEW QUESTIONS

1. What do you understand by discharge of contract?
2. State different ways in which a contract may be discharged.
3. What do you understand by performance of a contract?
4. What contracts need not be performed?
5. State the persons by whom the contract should be performed.
6. In what circumstances performance by a third party is effective?
7. What do you understand by time and place of performance of a contract? Are they always mentioned in the contract?
8. Summarise the rules laid down in the Act as to the appropriation of payments made by a debtor.
9. Explain how substitution of a new agreement is a mode of discharging a contract.
10. Discuss the different ways in which a contract may be discharged by operation of law.
11. Discuss the impossibility of performance as a mode of discharge of contract, stating differently the effect of 'initial' and supervening impossibility.
12. What do you understand by the doctrine of frustration of contract?
13. Does the frustration discharge the contract in all cases?

❐ ❐ ❐

BREACH OF CONTRACT AND REMEDIES

Parties to a contract are expected to perform their respective promises. If a party breaks his obligation which the contract imposes, there takes place "breach of contract". If the contract is unilateral, the only remedy available to the party who suffers by breach is to claim relief for the breach. If the contract is bilateral, the party who suffers, by breach has two remedies: (i) he can claim relief for breach, and (ii) in certain circumstances, he can be absolved from the further performance of the contract. Breach of contract may be (i) *actual breach of contract*, or (ii) *anticipatory breach of contract.*

1. Actual Breach of Contract

(a) **At the time when the Performance is due :** Actual breach of contract occurs when, at the time when the performance is due, one party fails or refuses to perform his obligation under the contract.

(b) **During the Performance of the Contract :** Actual breach of contract also occurs when during the performance of the contract, one party fails or refuses to perform his obligation under the contract. This may be discussed under the following two heads:

(i) *Express Repudiation (by word or act) :* Where there has been some performance of the contract and one party by his word or act refuses to continue to perform his obligation in some essential respect, the other party can treat the contract as no longer binding on him and sue the former party for breach of contract.

(ii) *Implied Repudiation or Impossibility created by the act of party to the contract :* If a party, during the performance, makes by his own act the complete performance of the contract impossible, the effect is as if he has breached the contract, and the other party is discharged from the further performance of the contract.

2. Anticipatory Breach of Contract

Anticipatory breach of contract occurs when a party repudiates his liability or obligation under the contract before the time for performance arrives. This may happen in one of the following ways :

(a) **By Renunciation (Express repudiation) :** Anticipatry breach of contract takes place when one party expresses his inability to perform or renounces his liabilities under the contract expressly, before the performance is due. This is known as *express anticipatory breach of contract.*

(b) **By creating some Impossibility (Implied repudiation) :** A promisor may, before the time for performance arrives, by doing some act make the performance of his promise impossible. The effect in such a case is the same as though he had renounced the contract at that time. This is known as *implied anticipatory breach of contract.*

Rights of the Promisee in case of Anticipatory Breach

(i) He can treat the contract as discharged so that he is absolved from the performance of his part of the promise.

(ii) He can immediately take a legal action for breach of contract, i.e., file a suit for damages, specific performance, or injunction. Anticipatory breach does not necessarily discharge the contract. It, however, discharge the promisee (the aggrieved) if he so chooses, and entitles him to sue for a breach at once.

Now, the question arises whether the other party may treat the renunciation as a breach and file a suit immediately or wait till the date of performance and then file the suit. This was answered in the case of ***Hochester Vs. D' La' tour (1853).***

On April 12th the defendant touring company engaged the services of the plaintiff the tour to commence from June 1st. On May 11th, the defendant informed the plaintiff that his services were no longer required. The plaintiff filed a suit against the defendant immediately after May 11th. The defendant contended that the plaintiff ought to have waited till June 1st i.e. the due date of performance and then filed the suit. The court negatived the contention and observed as follows :

A contract is a contract from the time it is made and not when performance is due. The contractual relationship arises from the date of the agreement itself and not from the date of performance. When parties enter into a contract they have two rights:-

(1) To enforce the performance on the due date.

(2) To keep the relationship alive till the due date.

So, if one party renounces the contract before the due date of performance, he snaps the contractual relationship. The other party *may* treat the renunciation as a breach and file a suit immediately. He need not wait till the due date of performance. However, it is only an option. If he waits till the due date of performance, he keeps the contract alive for the benefit of both the parties. The other party may change his mind and perform the contract on the due date. But, he may suffer a disadvantage. If a supervening impossibility occurs between the date of renunciation and the date of performance, the contract will be discharged. The other party will be excused from performing his obligation on the due date of performance.

Frost Vs. Knight : A promised to marry B after the life time of B's father. During the life time of B's father A refused to marry B. B filed a suit against A for breach of promise. A contended that she ought to have waited till the life time of her father and then filed the suit. Court also accepted this contention.

Measure of Damages in Anticipatory Breach of Contract

(i) **If the contract is ended at once :** If the promisee elects to end the contract at once, he can sue the promisor for damages. The amount of damages will be measured by the difference between the price prevailing on the date of breach and the contract price (anticipatory repudiation).

(ii) **If the contract is kept alive till the date of performance of the contract :** If the promisee keeps the contract alive till the date of performance, the measure of damages will be the difference between the price prevailing on the date of the performance and the contract price. The aggrieved party may, after putting an end to the contract, bring an action for damages for breach, but he will be bound under Section 64 to restore to the other party the benefits he might have received under the contract.

REMEDIES IN CASE OF BREACH OF CONTRACT

Where a breach of a contract has been committed by a party, there are several courses of action which the aggrieved party is entitled to pursue. (i) Suit for damages, (ii) Bring an action for specific performance, (iii) Suit for injunction, (iv) Claim for quantum meruit, (v) Restitution and (vi) He can also sue to declare that the contract is no longer binding on him. i.e., cancellation or recission. He can proceed for one or more of the above mentioned reliefs. The remedies by way of specific performance, injunction and declaration are dealt with by the Specific Relief Act, 1963.

Note : The Indian Contract Act deals only with the remedy of damages.

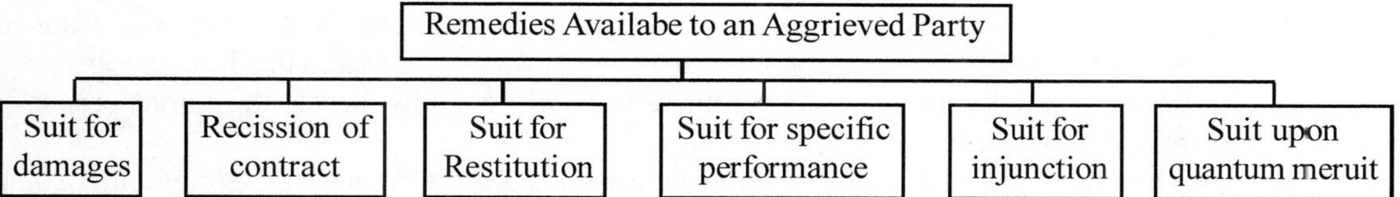

Suit for Recission of Contract (Sec. 39) : Rescission means a right not to perform obligation.

In case of breach of a contract, the promisee may put an end to the contract. In such a case, the aggrieved party is discharged from all the obligations under the contract and is entitled to claim compensation for the damage which he has sustained because of the non-performance of the contract.

Example : X agrees to supply 10 tons of wheat to Y on 20th October. Y promises to pay for the goods on its receipt. X does not supply the goods on the due date. Here, Y is discharged from the liability of paying the price. Y is entitled to rescind the contract and to claim compensation for the damage which he has sustained because of non-supply of goods on the due date.

SUIT FOR DAMAGES

The word *damages* compensation in money, The word *damage* means loss, injury, or deterioration is to be distinguished from its plural *damages*, for a loss or damage, which the party who suffers by a breach of contract is entitled to receive from the party who has broken the contract. The fundamental principle underlying damages is not punishment but compensation i.e, restitution by pecuniary compensation.

Where two parties have made a contract which one of them has broken, the damages which the other party ought to receive in respect of such breach of contract should be such as may fairly and reasonably be considered either arising naturally i.e., according to the usual course of things, from such breach of contract itself, or such as may reasonably be supposed to have been in the contemplation of both parties, at the time they made the contract, as the probable result of the breach of it.

Compensation for Loss or Damage caused by Breach of Contract (Section 73) : Section 73, of the Indian Contract Act which deals with compensation for loss or damage caused by breach of contract is based on the judgement in the above case. It states that the aggrieved party may claim the damages as follows :

(a) Such damages which naturally arose in the usual course of things from such breach. This relates to *ordinary damages* arising in the usual course of things.

(b) Such damages which the parties knew, when they made the contract, to be likely to result from the breach. This relates to *special damages.*

(c) The aforesaid compensation is not to be given for any remote or indirect loss or damage sustained by reason of the breach, and

(d) Such compensation for damages arising from breach of quasi contract shall be same as in any other contract.

Kinds of Damages : Damages are of four kinds : 1. Ordinary or general damages, 2. Special damages, 3. Exemplary damages, 4. Nominal damages.

1. **Ordinary or General Damages :** Ordinary damages are those which flow as a natural consequence is the usual course of things from the breach; i.e., damages which the parties may be deemed to have known as likely to arise on a breach, even at the time of entering into a contract. It is compensatory in nature.

   Example : A agreed to sell B two bales of cotton at Rs. 1,000 per bale, the delivery to be given on 15th January. A failed to give delivery. The remedy for B would be to claim the difference between the market price and the contract price for the same quality of cotton in case the market price is higher than the contract price.
2. **Special Damages :** Special damages are those resulting from a breach of contract under some *special circumstances*. The special circumstances must have been known to both the parties. They ought to have known the loss that is likely to result from out of the breach of the contract, by taking the special circumstances into account. In such circumstances, special damages are awarded.

   Pinnock Bros. Vs. Lewis & Peat Ltd. (1923) : P bought from L some copra cake. P sold the cake to B, who sold it to various dealers who in turn sold it to farmers, who used it for feeding cattle. The copra cake was poisonous and the cattle fed on it died. The various buyers filed suits against P and obtained damages. P claimed from L damages and costs he had to pay. Held, as it was within the contemplation of the parties that the copra cake was to be used for feeding cattle. L was liable to pay damages.

3. **Exemplary Damages :** These damages are intended to show the Court's strong disapproval of the conduct of the defendant in committing the wrong. (i) In cases of breach of promise to marry; and (ii) Where a banker refuses to honour the cheque in spite of having enough funds with him belonging to the person issuing the cheque. The smaller the amount for which the cheque is dishonoured, the greater the insult done, and so more are the damages awarded. Exemplary damages are known as *vindictive* or *punitive damages.*

4. **Nominal Damages :** This means a sum of money which may be token of, but which has no existence in point of quantity. In other words, the breach involved may have been only technical in character and so, some nominal damages of one rupee may be awarded. *Contemptuous damages*, is synonymous to nominal damages.

5. **Remote Damages :** "Such compensation is not to be given for any remote and indirect loss or damage sustained by reason of the breach". The remote or indirect damages are not due to natural and probable consequences of the breach of the contract. In other words, these are the damages which arise indirectly from the breach. The injured party is not entitled to any remote or indirect loss (Sec. 73).

Hobbs Vs. London & S.W. Railway Co. (1875) : Mr. Hobbs and family travelled from Hampden to Wimbledon. But the train went in wrong direction and the family had to get down at a place, where there was no conveyance and no place to stay. The result that they had to walk home several miles at midnight on drizzling night. Mrs. Hobbs got ill. Mr. Hobbs filed a suit (i) for damages for inconvenience and (ii) also damages for wife's illness. The court awarded damages in respect of the first claim. But the second claim did not arise in the usual course of things and was to remote a consequence.

Restitution and Compensation : Damages are paid as restitution and compensation and not as punishment. In fact through damages, efforts are made to put the party back into the same position as if the contract had been performed. In other words, if a contract is broken, law will endeavour, so far as money can do it, to place the injured party in the same position as if the contract had been performed.

Example : In a contract of sale of goods, the damages are measured equal to the profits, i.e., the difference between the contract price and market price of such goods on the date of breach.

Mental Pain and Suffering : In ordinary cases damages for mental pain and suffering caused by the breach are not allowed. But they may be allowed in special cases. Similarly, a photographer who had agreed to take photographs at a wedding, failed in breach of his contract to appear there. As a result the bride had no photographs of her wedding. She was allowed damages for resulting injury to her feelings.

Mitigation of Loss : The injured party has to take all reasonable steps to minimise the loss caused by the breach. Explanation to Section 73 of the Indian Contract Act reads as under :

"In estimating the loss or damage arising from a breach of contract, the means which existed of remedying the inconvenience caused by the non-performance of the contract must be taken into account".

The loss caused by the breach must be kept to the minimum. The damages which results due to the negligence of the aggrieved party, are not recoverable.

Neki Vs. Prabhu : The plaintiff took a shop on lease and paid an advance. The defendant could not give him possession and the plaintiff chose to do no business for 8 months though there were other shops available in the vicinity. Held, he was entitled only to a refund of his advance, and nothing more, as he had failed in his duty to minimise the loss by not taking another shop in the neighbourhood.

Liquidated and Unliquidated damages : The term *liquidated damages* means the sum which has been fixed by the parties as a genuine pre-estimate of the damage likely to be caused by the breach of the contract. The parties may try to avoid the delay and the expense involved in litigation and hence decided that amount to be paid as damages also. Where such a sum is fixed by the parties, the court never tries to interfere with it, provided it is reasonable (Sec. 74).

Example : A contract with B to pay B Rs. 1,000 if he fails to pay B Rs. 500 on a given day. A fails to pay B Rs. 500 on that day. B is entitled to recover from A such compensation not exceeding Rs. 1,000 as the Court considers reasonable.

Interest by way of Penalty : Several times, in bonds and other instruments standing as securities for money, provision for enhanced rates of interest in case of default will be provided. (a) If the stipulation for payment of higher rate of interest is from the date of default, it is a question depending on the facts of each case whether it is a penalty or not. (b) If the enhancement is from the date of the bond or security it is always a penalty. (c) Where compound interest is payable on default, if it is at the same rate, it is not a penalty. If it is at a higher rate it is a penalty; whether they amount to penalty or not depends on the facts of each case.

Rules Regarding Determination of Amount of Damages (Sec 73)

The purpose of awarding damages is to restore the parties to a position where they would have been if the contract had been performed and not where they would have been if they never made the contract. Further,when parties enter into a contract, they contemplate the performance and not the breach of it. Hence, damages are assessed as on the date of the performance.

The foundation for the modern law of damages was laid down in the case of *Hadley Vs. Baxendale (1854).*

The plaintiff was the owner of a mill. The defendant was a carrier. The plaintiff's mill stopped owing to the breakage of a crank-shaft. He entrusted the broken shaft with the defendant to be delivered to the maker as a pattern for a new one. The only information given to him was that the plaintiff was the owner of the mill and the broken shaft was a part of the machinery.

Due to some neglect on the part of the defendant, the delivery of the shaft was delayed. With the result, the mill remained idle. The plaintiff lost profit which he would otherwise have made. The question before the court was whether the plaintiff was entitled for the loss of profit also?

The court laid down two rules. This statement of the law is generally known as the rule in *Hadley Vs. Baxendale*. This rule is incorporated in Section 73 of The Indian Contract Act.

Damages are recoverable in two cases :

Rule 1 **:** When they arise naturally in the usual course of things, and

Rule 2 : When they are such as may reasonably be supposed to have been in the contemplation of both parties, at the time they made the contract, as the probable result of the breach of it.

Applying the two rules mentioned above, the court held in the above case, that the plaintiff could not recover the loss of profit. The first rule speaks of compensation for any loss or damage caused to the aggrieved party, which naturally arose in the usual course of things from such breach. This is the actual loss caused to the plaintiff. The test is an *objective test*.

The second rule speaks of loss or damage which the parties *knew*, when they made the contract, is likely to result from the breach of it. Here, the test is *subjective*.

According to Sir William Anson both branches of the rule is the same. "*Recovery depends on foreseeability*".

(i) *Damages for loss arising naturally :* When a party sustains a loss by reason of contract, he is entitled to, so far as money can do it, to be put in the same situation with regards to damages, as if the contract has been performed, subject to the qualification that the *loss or damage* is such : as (a) has *arisen naturally in the usual course of things:* or (b) as the *parties knew*, when they made the contract, to be likely to result from the breach of it; and (c) which is *not remote and indirect*.

(ii) *Mitigation of loss :* In estimating the loss or damage that means which existed for remedying the inconvenience caused by the breach must be taken into account. Thus, when a breach of contract has occurred it is the duty of the party who suffers by such breach to lessen the injurious consequences of the breach.i.e. *mitigation of loss*. If he does not do so, it means that his own neglect has contributed to the damage and to that extent damages will be disallowed.

(iii) Special damages only under special circumstances : When a party claims *special damages* (which would not ordinarily flow from the breach), he must prove it to have been *in the contemplation of both the parties* and expressly provided for.

(iv) When no loss arises from the breach of contract, only *nominal damages* are to be given.

(v) Damages are given by way of *restitution* and *compensation* only and not by way of punishment.

(vi) Compensation for *quasi-contracts* as damages is the same as for a contract.

(vii) The measure of damages in the contract of sale and purchase of goods shall be the *difference between the price agreed upon and the market price*. i.e., actual loss or damage only.

(viii)Regarding damages for the breach of contracts for the payment of money on a particular date, *interest on the principal* sum from the date on which sum was agreed to be paid, is to be paid to the aggrieved party, i.e., creditor, and this will be regarded as sufficient compensation.

(ix) *Difficulty of calculating damages* is not ground for refusing damages. The court must make an assessment of loss due to damage and pass a decree for it.

Chaplin Vs. Hicks (1911) : H organised a beauty competition in which 50 ladies were to be selected by votes of the readers of certain newspapers. H would select 12 out of the 50 and secured theatrical jobs for them. C was one of the 50 and by H's breach of contract. C was prevented from being present when the final selection was made. It was held that C was entitled to damages even though it was difficult to calculate them. The fact that damages are difficult to assess does not prevent the injured party from recovering them.

(x) ***Damages for Loss of Reputation :*** Generally, such damages are not recoverable. An exception to this rule arises in case of a banker, who wrongfully refuses to honour a customer's cheques. If the customer is a businessman, he can recover damages in respect of any loss to his business reputation by such breach.

(xi) ***Cost of Decree :*** The aggrieved party is entitled, in addition to the damages, to get the cost of getting the decree for damages. However, the cost of suit for damages is at the discretion of the court.

Liquidated Damages and Penalty

A contract sometimes mentions that is case of breach of contract, a particular sum is payable by the party committing the breach. The sum so stipulated or agreed upon, may either be liquidated damage or penalty. Liquidated damage is a sum fixed or ascertained by the parties to the contract, which is a fair and genuine pre-estimate of the probable loss that might occur as a result of breach of contract. Thus, liquidated damages are an assessment of loss, which in the opinion of the parties, will occur due to breach. Such damages are effective and recoverable by the aggrieved party from the other.

Penalty is the sum mentioned in the contract at the time of its formation which is disproportionate to the damage likely to occur as a result of the breach of the contract. Penalty is fixed with a view to getting the contract performed, but it has no concern with the probable loss likely to occur to the parties due to the brach of the contract. Thus the liquidated damages are the fair assessment of the amount which will compensate the aggrieved party for the loss suffered due to breach of the contract. Whereas, the penalty is not a fair assessment of the loss for breach It is fixed with a view to prevent the party from committing the breach of the contract, that is, to compel the other party to perform the contract.

Distinction between Liquidate Damages and Penalty

The following are the differences between liquidated damages and penalty.

Liquidated Damages	*Penalty*
1. Reasonable and Proportionate:	
The amount of liquidated damages is reasonable and is proportionate to the loss of the aggrieved party.	The amount of damages is unreasonable and is disproportionate to the loss of the aggrieved party. It is extravagant and unconscionable.
2. Fair and Genuine:	
The damage is a fair and genuine pre-estimate of the probable loss that may result in the event of a default.	It is not based on a fair estimate of the probable loss arising from a default.

3. Object:

The object of liquidated damages is to secure compensation to the aggrieved party in the event of a default.	The object of penalty is to terrorise the parties so as to compel the performance as per the terms of the contract.

4. Recoverability through Court:

Liquidated damages are permitted by the court. So they are recoverable by the injured party through a court of law.	Penalty is not permitted by the court. It is not recoverable through a court of law.

CANCELLATION OR RECISSION

Recission is the revocation of a contract. It is the way by which a contract may be discharged. Where one of the parties to a contract commits breach, the other party may treat the contract as rescinded. He is freed from all the obligations under the contract. Under section 64 the party rescinding a voidable contract shall if he has received any benefit thereunder from another party to such contract restore such benefit to the person from whom it was received. Further under section 75 a person who rightfully rescinds a contract is entitled to compensation for any damage which he has sustained through the non-fulfilment of the contract.

Example : A singer contract with B, the manager of theatre to sing at his theatre for two nights in every week during the next two months and B engages to pay her Rs. 1000 for each night performance. On the sixth night A wilfully absents herself from the theatre and B in consequence rescinds the contract. B is entitled to claim compensation for the damage which he has sustained through the non-fulfilment of the contract.

When is recission granted? Under section 27(1) of the Specific Relief Act, the court may grant rescission in the following two cases.

(i) Where the contract is voidable at the option of the plaintiff the court grants recission to the plaintiff.

(ii) Where the contract is unlawful for causes not apparent on its face and defendant is more to blame than the plaintiff, the court may grant recission.

When may rescission be refused?

The court may, however, refuse to rescind the contract.

(a) Where the plaintiff has expressly or impliedly ratified the contract; or

(b) Where owing to the change of circumstances, the parties cannot be restored to their original positions; or

(c) Where third parties have, during the subsistence of the contract acquired rights in good faith and for value; or

(d) Where only a part of the contract is sought to be rescinded and such part is not severable from the rest of the contract.

SUIT FOR RESTITUTION OF BENEFIT

Restitution means an act restoration. According to Anson, a person who has been unjustly enriched at the expense of another must compensate the other. It means return of the benefit received by one party to the contract from the other under a void contract. When a contract becomes void it need not be performed by either party.

This principle of restitution applies in the following circumstances.

(i) In case of voidable contracts (sec. 64) : contracts become voidable at the option of the party whose consent is obtained fraud etc. The party rescinding, under such circumstances, to restore the benefits received to the other party

(ii) In case of contract becoming void (sec. 65)

Section 65 provides that when an agreement is discovered to be void or when a contract becomes void any person who has received any advantage under such agreement or contract is bound to restore it or to make compensation for it to the person from whom he received it.

This section applies to contracts 'discovered to be void' and contracts which become void. It does not apply to contracts which are known to be void. Thus, if A pays Rs. 200 to B to beat C, the money is not recoverable.

Example : A pays B Rs. 1000 in consideration of B's promising to marry C, A's daughter. C is dead at the time of promise. The agreement is void but B must repay A Rs. 1000.

(b) A, a singer contracts with B, the manager of a theatre to sing at his theatre for two nights in every week during the next two months and B engages to pay her Rs. 1000 for each night's performance. On the sixth night A wilfully absents herself from the theatre and B in consequence rescinds the contract. B must pay A for the five nights on which she had sung. (B can of course claim damages against A for breach of contract).

SUIT FOR SPECIFIC PERFORMANCE

Generally speaking, specific performance is directed only in certain cases like where monetary compensation is not an adequate remedy and when there exists no standard for ascertaining the actual damages caused by the non-performance of the act. This remedy is, however discretionary, and will not be granted in the following cases :

(i) where *monetary compensation is an adequate remedy*;

(ii) where the *court cannot supervise the execution* of the contract, e.g., a building contract;

(iii) where the contract is for personal service, i.e., a contract to paint a picture;

(iv) where one of the parties is incompetent to contract, e.g., minor;

(v) where the contract is *ultra vires*, e.g., where the contract is made by a company in excess of its powers as laid down in its memorandum of association or against the Companies Act;

(vi) where the contract is made by trustees in *breach of trust*;

(vii) where a material part of the subject-matter of the *contract has ceased to exist*, e.g., where a contract is for the purchase and sale of a ship which is sunk after the contract had been entered or into, where a contract is for the purchase and sale of a building destroyed by fire after it had been entered into.

(viii)Where the contract is *inequitable* to either party. The remedy of specific relief unlike that of damages cannot be obtained as a matter of right but rests entirely on the discretion of the Court.

The contracts which may be specifically enforced are as follows : 1. Agreement to sell or transfer immovable property, 2. Sale with a condition to repurchase, 3. Agreement for exchange of immovable property, 4. Agreement to lease, 5. Contract by limited owner to sell or lease.

SUIT FOR INJUNCTION

An injunction is preventive relief. An aggrieved party can sue for an injunction, i.e., an injunction is an order of the court restraining the wrongdoer from doing, or continuing, the wrongful act complained of. Injunction is usually granted to enforce negative stipulations in cases where damages are not adequate relief. It is particularly appropriate in cases of anticipatory breach of contract. Injunction may be *temporary* or *perpetual*. Injunction may also be either *mandatory* or *prohibitory*. When, to prevent the breach of an obligation, it is necessary to compel the performance of certain acts which the court is capable of enforcing, the court may in its discretion grant an injunction to prevent the breach complained of, and also to compel performance of the requisite acts. A prohibitory injunction is negative. Other remedies under Specific Relief Act, 1963 includes *Declaratory Right, Rectification, Restitution, Recision, etc.*

SUIT FOR QUANTUM MERUIT

Quantum Meruit means as much as is earned. Right to Quantum Meruit means a right to claim the compensation for the work already done.

Example : C an owner of a magazine engaged P to write a novel to be published by instalments in his magazine. After a few instalments were published, the publication of the magazine was stopped. It was held that P could claim payment for the part already published [Planche Vs. Calburn].

Distinction between Quantum Meruit and Damages

	Quantum Merit	***Damages***
1.	This right does not arise out of any contract but it is of quasi-contractual nature.	This right arises out of a contract (when it is broken).
2.	This right arises out of some past performance (a) some work is done, or (b) some services are rendered.	This right arises when there is non-performance i.e., breach of a contract.
3.	It is by nature restitutory.	It is by nature compensatory.
4.	It arises when a quasi-contract is in existence	It arises only when a contract is broken.

REVIEW QUESTIONS

1. What do you understand by 'breach of contract?'
2. Distinguish between actual breach and anticipatory breach.
3. What remedies are available to an aggrieved party for a breach of contract?
4. What are the different types of damages which can be awarded by the court?
5. Explain the principles governing the assessment and award of damages for breach of contract.
6. Discuss as to when an aggrieved party can file a suit for specific performance and for an injunction.
7. Write short notes on (a) Suit for Restitution of benefit, (b) Suit for Quantum meruit, (c) Suit for Recession
8. X agreed to marry B, a minor girl. X, later on, marries C, B claims compensation for breach of contract. Decide.
9. A applies to a banker for a loan at a time when there is stringency in the money market. The banker declines to make the loan except at an unusually high rate of interest. A accepts the loan on these terms. Is the transaction enforceable ?

❐ ❐ ❐

9 Chapter

CONTRACT OF GUARANTEE

Definition of Contract of Indemnity

Sections 124, 125 and the 127 of the Indian Contract Act deal with contract of indemnity.

A contract by which one party promises to save the other from any loss caused to him by the conduct of the promisor himself, or by the conduct of any other person is called ***Contract of Indemnity****. The promisor in such a contract is called* ***indemnifier*** *while the promisee who is to be protected is called the* ***indemnity holder or Indemnified*** (Sec.124).

ESSENTIALS OF A CONTRACT OF INDEMNITY

1. There must be *two parties* in a contract of Indemnity viz., Indemnifier and Indemnified.
2. A contract of Indemnity may be *express or implied.*
3. This contract being a *species of contract*, is subject to all the rules of contract, such as free consent,
   legality of object, etc.
4. A contract of indemnity is enforceable only when the promisee suffers a loss the happening of which is unknown and against which the Indemnity holder was promised to be protected.
5. *Consideration* in the case of Contract of indemnity is essential to enable the indemnity holder to make claim to be compensated.

CONTRACT OF GUARANTEE

Definition of Contract of Guarantee

It is a contract to perform the promise or discharge the liability of a third person in case of his default (S.126). Surety is a person who gives the guarantee. The person in respect of whose default the guarantee is given is called *'Principal Debtor'*. The person to whom the guarantee is given called the *'Creditor'*.

Essential of Contract of Guarantee

1. **Form:** A Contract of guarantee is just like any other contract which may be either oral or in writing.
2. **Tripartite agreement:** Every contract of guarantee involves three agreements between (i) the creditor and principal debtor, (ii) the surety and the creditor, and (iii) the surety and the principal debtor.

   Consent of the Parties : There must be consent and concurrence of all the three parties.

   Example : X sells and delivers goods to Y. X afterwards requests Z to pay in default of Y. Z agrees to do so. Here, Z cannot become surety without the consent of Y.

3. **Secondary Liability:** The test which applied to determine whether the contract is one of guarantee or indemnity is whether the obligation has been undertaken at the debtor's request in which case the contract is one of guarantee. If the obligation is undertaken without any request of the debtor, the contract is one of indemnity. The intention of the parties is also important whether making himself primarily or collaterally liable. Hence, the promise to be primarily and independently liable is not a guarantee, though it may be an indemnity. Hence in a contract of guarantee, the primary liability is with the principal debtor.

4. **Existing liability:** It is not necessary that the principal contract must be in existence at the time the contract of guarantee is made; the original contract by which the principal debtor undertakes to repay the money to the creditor may be about to come into existence.

   Example : X took a loan of ₹ 10,000 from Y on 1st Jan. 2005 and paid nothing on account of interest and principal. On 2nd Jan. 2008, Z gave the guarantee to Y for the payment of ₹ 10,000 due from X. This is not a valid contract of guarantee because the primary liability between X and Y is a time barred debt which is not enforceable by law.

5. **The promise to pay must be conditional:** In other words, the liability of the surety should arise only when the principal debtor makes a default.

6. **Consideration :** Something done for the benefit of the principal debtor is considered as consideration for the guarantee to make the contract valid. The legal detriment incurred by the promisee at the promisor's request is sufficient to constitute the element of consideration.

7. **Competency:** The principal debtor, surety and creditor must be a person competent to contract. However, under certain circumstances, a surety is liable though the principal debtor is not i.e., the original contract is void as is the case of a contract with a minor in which the surety is liable not only as surety but also as principal debtor *Kashiba Vs. Shripat, (1894)*. A person of unsound mind or an undischarged insolvent cannot give a valid guarantee.

8. **Consent:** There must be free consent, otherwise the contract of guarantee may become void or voidable. Generally a contract of guarantee is not contract of the utmost good faith i.e., *uberrimae fidei*, but it is sometimes a first cousin to it. Mere non-disclosure will not effect the contract of surety unless there is an intentional concealment.

Example I : A engages B as clerk to collect money for him. B fails to account for some of his receipts, and A in consequence calls upon him to furnish security for his duty accounting. C gives his guarantee for B's duty accounting. A does not acquaint C with B's previous conduct. B afterwards makes a default. The guarantee is invalid.

Example II : A guarantees to C payment for iron to be supplied by him to B to the amount of 2,000 tons. B and C have privately agreed that B should pay ₹ 500 per ton beyond the market price, such excess to be applied on liquidation of an old debt. This agreement is concealed from A. A is not liable as a surety.

KINDS OF GUARANTEE

A contract of guarantee may be either '*Retrospective*' e.g., for an existing debt or '*Prospective*' i.e., for a future debt. Guarantee are further divided into '*Specific*' also known as simple or single guarantee and '*Continuing*'. When the guarantee is given for a single or particular debt, it is called a *specific guarantee* and it comes to an end when the debt guaranteed has been paid. A guarantee which extends to a series of transactions is called a *continuing guarantee* (Sec. 129 of the Indian Contract Act).

Guarantee may be for a part of a whole debt or for the whole debt subject to a limit: When the intention of the parties is not explicit it will be presumed that where a portion of a floating balance is guaranteed it is for a part of it only. When portion of a fixed and ascertained debt is guaranteed the guarantee applied to the whole debt subject to the limit.

CONTINUING GUARANTEE

Definition of Continuing Guarantee: A guarantee which extends to a series transactions is called *Continuing Guarantee* (Sec.129). A guarantee may be ordinary guarantee or a continuing guarantee. In the former, the guarantee is in respect of one single transaction while in the case of continue guarantee, the guarantee extends to a series of transactions.

Illustration : A in consideration that B will employ C in collecting the rents of B's shopping complex promises B to be responsible, to the amount of 3,000 rupees, for the due collection of payments by C of those rents. This is a continuing guarantee.

1. **Notice of Revocation :** A continuing guarantee is revoked when the surety gives a notice to the creditor for the revocation of guarantee. Notice will be applicable only for future transactions and not for those transactions which had already taken place. (Sec. 130)
2. **Death :** The continuing guarantee is revoked by the death of the surety provided such a notice had been received by the creditor. (Section 131)
3. **Variation in Contract:** If any variation has been made in the terms of contract of guarantee between the creditor and the principal debtor without the knowledge or concurrence of the surety, the contract of guarantee is revoked. (Sec. 133)
4. **Creditor's act of Omission:** Any act or omission by the creditor which impairs the eventual remedy of the surety against the debtor amounts to revocation of the contract of guarantee (See. 139).
5. **Novation:** When the parties agree to substitute a new contract for the old contract or rescind or alter the old contract of guarantee, it will amount to revocation. (Sec. 62)
6. Release or discharge of principal debtor (Section 134)
7. When the creditors enter into an arrangement with the principal debtor (Section 135).
8. Loss of security (Section 141).

RIGHTS OF SURETY

A. Rights of Surety against the Creditor

1. **Ask the creditor to sue the debtor:** On the guaranteed debt having fallen due for payment, the surety may ask the creditor to sue the debtor to collect the due amount, but he cannot compel him to do so. But he must then indemnify the creditor against any risk or delay arising as a consequence.
2. **Require the creditor to terminate the debtor's services:** In the case of the fidelity guarantee, if the principal debtor's dishonesty comes to light, the surety can require the creditor to terminate the principal debtor's services so as to save him from further loss.
3. **Claim to any set off :** The surety on being called upon to pay, can claim any set-off to which the principal debtor is entitled from the creditor.

4. **Access to the securities of the debtor with the creditor :** The surety can, after paying the guaranteed debt, compel the creditor to assign to him all the securities taken by the creditor either before or at the time of the contract of guarantee, whether the surety was aware of them or not.

5. **Right to share reduction :** On debtor's insolvency the surety is entitled to claim the proportionate reduction of his liability by the amount of dividend claimed by the creditor (from the Official Receiver of the Principal debtor). Similarly, debtor's debt obligation is scaled down by subsequent legislation, the surety is entitled to claim proportionate reduction in his liability.

B. Against the Principal Debtor

6. **Right of suborgation :** After paying the guaranteed debt, the surety steps into the shoes of the creditor and acquires all the rights which the latter had against the principal debtor (i.e., he gets subrogated to all the rights and remedies available to the creditor) (Sec. 140). If the creditor has the right to stop goods in transit or has a lien, the surety, on payment of all he is liable for, will be entitled to exercise these rights.

7. **Right as to securities with the creditor :** The surety has the right to proceed against such securities of the principal debtor, as the creditor could himself proceed.

8. **Right of indemnity :** The surety is entitled to be indemnified by the principal debtor for all payments rightfully made by him (Sec. 145).

9. **Compel the principal debtor to perform the promise :** The surety has also the right to insist the principal debtor to perform the promise. The surety can, before making payment, compel the debtor to relieve him from liability by paying of the debt, provided that liability is an ascertained and subsisting one.

10. **Prove the debt in bankruptcy of the debtor :** In case of the bankruptcy of the principal debtor, the surety may prove the debt in respect of contingent ability even if he has not been called upon to pay a definite amount.

C. Against Co-sureties

When two or more persons guarantee the same debt jointly or severally, whether under the same or different contracts, they are known as *co-sureties*. As the co-sureties share the liabilities, they have in equity also the right to share the means of recovery.

11. **Right to share the securities rateably (proportionately):** If they are liable in equal amounts, they will be entitled to share equally the securities belonging to the principal debtor in possession of the creditor. In case their liabilities are unequal, they will share the securities rateably/proportionately.

12. **Right to contributions :** If any one of the sureties has to pay more than his share, he has a right to call upon his co-sureties for such contribution as will enable him to recoup himself to the extent of excess amount paid by him over and above his proportionate liability.

13. **Right to counter-security :** Co-surety has also the right to benefit of a counter-security given to another surety by the principal debtor.

14. **Right to plead the co-sureties and debtor in one suit :** It is open to a surety to implead the co-sureties as well as the principal debtor in one suit. Where one surety has paid more than his proportionate share the proper procedure is to file a suit for contribution against his co-surety making the principle debtor also a party thereto.

Rights of the Creditor against Surety

1. **Demand payment when due:** As the liability of the surety arises, the creditors is entitled to demand payments from the surety although the debt is time-barred against the principal debtor (*Bombay Dyeing and Manufacturing Co. Ltd. Vs. State of Bombay, 1985*) or principal debtor has been adjudged as bankrupt or the principal debtor's contract is void or voidable. He can file a suit against the surety without suing the principal debtor even if the principal debtor is solvent. The liability of the surety is immediate and not be deferred until the creditor has exhausted his remedies against the principal debtor.

2. **Proceed against surety before resorting to debtor's securities**: A creditor can directly proceed against the surety before resorting to the securities deposited by the principal debtor. This is feasible although the liability of the surety becomes the primary one along with the principal debtor. Of course, a contract may specifically provide that the creditor must exhaust his remedies against the principal debtor or give notice of default or proceed against the securities.

3. **Claim for legal expenses:** A creditor can claim the cost of baseless legal suit against the principal debtor, sued at the request of the surety i.e., *the right of indemnity*.

4. **Prove against the Official receiver in case of surety's insolvency:** If the surety becomes insolvent, the creditor has the right to recover the dues from the estate of the insolvent party.

5. **Proceed against any one surety in the case of co-sureties:** In case of co-sureties, the creditor will be at liberty to proceed against any one of the sureties for the whole debt because the liability of sureties is joint and several.

6. **Concurrent remedy:** A creditor may also pursue his remedy concurrently against both the principal debtor and the surety , and obtain a degree against both in the same suit.

Rights of Co-sureties among themselves

1. **Co-sureties have liabilities among themselves under Sec.132:** Where two persons contract with a third person to undertake a certain liability, and also contract with each other that one of them shall be liable only on the default of the other, the third party not being a party to such a contract, the liability of each of such two persons to the third person under the first contract is not affected by the existence of the second contract, although such third person may have been aware of its existence.

2. **Release:** Where there are co-sureties, a release by the creditor of one of them does not discharge the other neither does it free surety so released from responsibility to other sureties (Sec. 138).

3. **Contribution:** Co-sureties are liable to contribute equally if there is more than one surety in respect of one debt, though contracted on different dates unless contracted otherwise (Sec. 146).

4. **Equality:** Where the sureties are bound in different sum, they are bound to pay equally as far as the limits of their respective obligations permit (Sec. 147).

Liabilities of Co-sureties

Co-sureties are jointly and severally liable in India. The discharge of one co-surety from his liability does not release the other co-sureties from their liability. *They are liable to bear the loss equally, subject to the limit of the debt guaranteed by him.* As mentioned earlier, if one of them has paid more than his share, he can claim contribution from others. Where the co-sureties have limited their liabilities to different sums, they should contribute equally and not exceeding their respective limits.

Illustration: A, B and C are sureties for D guaranteeing different sums namely, A₹ 10,000 B. ₹ 20,000 and C ₹ 40,000. In case of default by D the liabilities of the co-sureties would be as under:

(i) D Makes default in payment to the extent to of ₹ 30,000. Liabilities of A, B and C is ₹ 10,000 each.

(ii) D makes default to the extent to ₹ 40,000. Liability shall be as of A's 10,000 (maximum obligation), as of B and C, ₹ 15,000 each being equal contribution.

(iii) D makes default of ₹ 70,000. A, B and C will pay the full amount of guarantee.

DISCHARGE OF SURETY

Discharge of surety means he is freed from his obligations. This can happen in various ways, either by the action of the surety himself or by the creditor or by the principal debtor or by both or by operation of law.

A. From the Side of the Principal

1. *By Revocation.* A surety may revoke his liability by giving a notice to the creditor (Sec. 130). This section refers to continuing guarantee but by implication is equally applicable to a specific guarantee too.

2. *By Death.* By the death of the surety the contract of guarantee comes to an end unless there is different intention in the contract (Sec. 131). This section refers to continuing guarantee but by implication is equally applicable to a specific guarantee too.

3. *By general rules of contract.* A contract of guarantee is discharged by all the different ways as the cases of a contract in general and the surety is discharged as a party to the contract.

4. *By payment by debtor.* Surety is also discharge from his liability when the principal debtor has paid the debt himself.

B. From the Side by the Creditor

1. ***Variation in the term of the contract*** : When a variation is made in the terms of the contract of guarantee between the principal debtor and the creditor without the consent of the surety, the latter is dicharged from his liability. Variation must be such which materially affects the interest of the surety. If a person stood surety for different distinct debts and consequently there were different contracts and if a variation was made in one of those contracts, he (surety) is not discharged from his liability in the case of other contracts (Sec.133).

   Exception : However, there is one exception to the rule is discharge of surety by variance in the terms of contract. It is where guarantee is for the performance of several distinct debts or obligations. A variation in the nature of one of them will not discharge surety as to the rest. Again the surety will not be discharged by a variation to which he has assented, but in such a case the creditor has to show that the surety assented to the alteration. Where variation is not material, there also a surety is not discharged.

2. ***Release or discharge of debtor by creditor*** : The surety is discharged by any contract between the creditor and the debtor by which the principal debtor is released. When the creditor is guilty of any act of omission or commission, the legal consequence of which is the discharge of the principal debtor, the surety is discharged from his liability. (S.134).

Illustrations

(i) 'A' gives a guarantee to 'C' for goods to be supplied by 'C' to 'B', 'C' supplied goods to 'B' and afterwards 'B' becomes embarrassed and contract with his creditors (including 'C') to assign to them his property in consideration of their releasing him from their demands. Here 'B' is released from his debt by the contract with 'C', and 'A' is discharged from his suretyship.

(ii) 'A' contracts with 'B' to grow a crop of Indigo on A's land and to deliver it to 'B' at a fixed rate, and 'C' guarantees A's performance of this contract. 'B' diverts a stream of water which si necessary for irrigation of A's land the thereby prevents him from raising the indigo. 'C' is no longer liable on his guarantee.

(iii) 'A' contracts with 'B' for a fixed price to build a house for 'A' within a stipulated time, 'B' supplying the necessary timber. 'C' guarantees A's performance of the contract. 'B' omits to supply the timber. 'C' is discharged from his suretyship.

Thus, under this clause, the surety is discharged in the following two circumstances;

(a) If the creditor makes a fresh contract with the principal debtor by which the latter is released from his liability;

(b) If the creditor does any act or omission which has the effect of discharging the principal debtor from his liability.

Hewison v. Ricketts (1894)

The plaintiff sold some goods to a person on a hire-purchase agreement, and the defendant guaranteed the instalments payable. On the debtor's failure to pay the instalments, the plaintiff terminated the contract and seized the goods. Subsequently, he sued the defendant and seized the goods. It was held that since the plaintiff had put an end to the contract, he could not recover from the surety.

3. ***Compounding by the Principal debtor by Creditor or extending time for payment :*** Where a creditor compounds with, or gives time to agrees not to sue the principal debtor, the surety is discharged unless the surety assents to such a contract (S.135). However, it must be remembered that if the contract to extend time is not given to the principal debtor but is given to a third person, the surety is not discharged (S.136).

***Midland Motor Showrooms v. Newman* (1929) 2 KB 256.**

'A' purchased a car from 'B'. The price of the car was to be paid in instalment. The payment of the instalments was guaranted by 'C'. The amount of the instalments fell in arrears. 'B' settled with 'A' that he should pay certain sum immediately and the balance by the end of the month. It was held that the settlement amounted to giving time to the principal debtor (A) and the surety (C) was discharged from liability under the guarantee.

4. ***Agreement not to sue debtor* :** An agreement by the creditor not to sue the principal debtor without the consent of the surety, discharge the surety from his liability (S.137). It may be pointed out here that if the creditor did not sue the principal debtor or did not enforce any other remedy against the debtor, the surety is not discharged unless provided otherwise in the contract of guarantee.

5. ***Creditor's Act or Omission Impairing Surety's Remedy* :** If the creditors does any which is inconsistent with the right of the surety, or omits to do any act which his duty to the surety requires him to do, and the eventual remedy of the surety himself against the principal debtor is thereby impaired, the surety

is discharged (S.139). The term "impairing the surety's remedy" means damaging or diminishing the rights of the surety.

The following acts committed by the creditor will not discharge the surety:

1. When the creditor contracts with a third to give time to the principal debtor for the payment of the debt or the performance of the promise, surenty is not discharged.

2. When the creditor does not sue i.e., mere forbearance or enforce any other remedy against the principal debtor for the payment of the money or the performance of the terms, the surety is not discharged from his liability to the creditor (S.137).

3. Release by the creditor of one co-surety does not dischargee the other co-sureties from their liability to the creditor (Sec. 138).

4. Release of any security/securities by the creditor which he had received from the debtor subsequent to the contract of guarantee.

It is the duty of the creditor not to do anything inconsistent with the rights of the surety. A surety is entitled after paying off of the creditor to his indemnity from the principal debtor. If the act or omission of the creditor deprives the surety of the benefit of this remedy, the surety is discharged. Thus, where the servant whose honesty was guaranteed is continued in the employment after his act of dishonesty, the surety is discharged.

***Re darwen v. Pearch* (1927) ICH 176**

In this case the principal debtor was a shareholder in a company.His shares were party paid and the payment of the unpaid calls was guaranteed by the surety. On default by the principal debtor in the payment of calls, the company forfeited the shares. Held, the surety was discharged because the forfeiture of shares deprived the surety of his right to the shares after making payment of the outstanding calls.

6. ***By Loss of Security (Section 141)*** **:** In the creditor loses or without the consent of the surety, parts with any security given to him at the time of the contract of guarantee, the surety is discharged from liability to the extent of the value of security. This has already been discussed under the heading "rights of surety against creditor".

From the Side of the Contract itself

The surety is liable under the guarantee only if the contract of guarantee is valid. If the contract of guarantee is in valid then the surety will not be liable i.e. he will be discharged from his liabilities. Thus, where a guarantee is obtained by coercion, undue influence, fraud etc., then it will not be valid and the surety is not liable under such a guarantee.

The following are the ways in which a contract of guarantee becomes invalid:

1. ***Guarantee obtained by Misrepresentation*** **:** When a guarantee has been obtained by the creditor by misrepresenting the facts or such a misrepresentation had been made with his knowledge and assent, concerning a material part of the transaction (S.142).

2. ***Guarantee obtined by Concealment*** **:** Any guarantee obtained by means of keeping silent by the creditor with regard to a material fact which had the surety known about such a material fact would not have entered into the contract of guarantee (S.143).

3. ***Failure of the Consurety to join*** : Where a person gives a guarantee upon a contract that the creditor shall not act upon it until another person has jointed in it as co-surety, the guarantee is not val:d if that other person does not join (S.144).

4. ***Failure of Consideration*** : Failure of consideration is a good ground for the discharge of a surety. But there must be substantial failure of consideration in order to make or operate as discharge invalid.

Since there is a common consideration between the creditor the principal debtor and the surety (Sec.127) any failure of consideration between the creditor and the principal debtor, makes the contract void and the surety is discharged.

London General Omnibus v. Hollowy **(1921) 2 KD 72.**

In that case 'A' was invited to give a guarantee for the fidelity of B's servant. The employer had earlier dismissed him for dishonesty but did not disclose this fact to the surety. The servant committed embezzlement. Held, the surety was not liable because, "he would have presumed to have made himself answerable for an honoured man and not a known thief".

Distinction Between Indemnity and Guarantee

Indemnity	*Guarantee*
1. **Number of parties** : There are two parties: Indemnifier and Indemnified.	There are three parties to it viz., the principal debtor, the surety and the creditor.
2. **Number of Contracts :** There is only *one* contract between the indemnified and indemnifier.	*Three contracts* : (i) between the principal debtor and the creditor, (ii) between the surety and the creditor
3. **Form :** May be *written or oral* in both Indian and English Law.	According to Section 4, of the Stature of Frauds (in England) it should be in writing : in Indian law it may be *written or oral.*
4. **Interest in the transaction :** The indemnifier has one interest in the transaction apart from the indemnity i.e., apart from hyis promise to pay	The guarantee is totally unconnected with the contract but the only interest in the contract is his promise to the loss.
5. **Nature of risk :** It is possibility of risk of any loss happening in future against which the indemnifier undertakes to indemnify i.e., *continuing risk.*	There is an existing debt the discharge or performance of which is guaranteed by the surety i.e., it is the *absolute and subsisting risk.*
6. **Nature of liability :** The indemnifier is primarily and independently liable.	In a guarantee the liability of the surety is co-extensive with that of the principal debtor (ancillary liability). The guarantor is *secondarily liable* except where the principal debtor is incapable of contracting.
7. **Subrogation :** An indemnifier cannot have subrogation unless there is an assignment. Otherwise he must bring the suit in the name	If a surety pays the debt or performs the obligation he can file a suit in his own name against the Principal debtor to reimburse the amount so paid.
8. **Request :** It is not necessary for the indemnifier to act at the request of the indemnified.	It is necessary for the surety to give his guarantee at the request of the debtor.

REVIEW QUESTIONS

1. Define a contract of indemnity
2. What is a contract of guarantee?
3. In a contract of guarantee there is a triangular relationship. How?
4. Is a contract of guarantee a contract of *uberrimae fidei*?
5. What is the nature of surety's liability?
6. What are different kinds of guarantee?
7. Is a contract of guarantee revoked on the death of surety?
8. On being sued by the creditor, can the surety rely on any set-off or counter-claim which the debtor possess against the creditor?
9. The liability of a surety is co-existensive with that of the principal debtor. Explain the satement.
10. When is a contract of guarantee held to be invalid?
11. List the rights of the surety against the co-sureties.
12. When can a surety revoke his guarantee?
13. Does the death of a surety operate in the absence of any contract to the contrary, as a revocation of a continuing guarantee, so far as regards future transactions?
14. Does a creditor's omission to sue the principal debtor within the period of limitation discharge the surety?
15. Is the surety discharged if without his knowledge the creditor accepts interest in advance from the principal debtor?
16. Why is a surety undoubtedly and not unjustly an object of some favour both at law and at equity?
17. Define a contract of guarantee. What are the essentials and legal rules for a valid contract of guarantee?
18. Define a continuing guarantee and state how it can be revoked.
19. State the nature and extent of surety's liability. How and in what circumstances the surety is discharged from his liability?
20. " The liability of surety is secondary; it is co-extensive with that of the principal debtor unless it is otherwise provided by the contract". Discuss.
21. "A surety is a favoured debtor". Comment.
22. Explain the difference between a contract of indemnity and contract of guarantee.
23. Write short notes on: (a)Cosurety (b) Continuing guarntee.

❐ ❐ ❐

CONTRACT OF BAILMENT AND PLEDGE

Definition of Bailment

Section 148 of the Indian Contract Act defines a Bailment thus, *A Bailment is the delivery of goods, by one person to another, for some specified purpose, and upon a contract that they shall, when the purpose is accomplished, be returned or otherwise disposed of according to the directions of the person delivering them. The person delivering the goods is called* the ***Bailor***. *The person to whom they are delivered is called the* ***Bailee***.

CHARACTERISTICS OF BAILMENT

1. A bailment is normally *based upon a contract* either express or implied between the bailor and the bailee. However, the finder of goods is an exception to this rule i.e., a finder of goods becomes a bailee though there is no contract between the finder and the true owner. A person already in possession of goods may become a bailee by a subsequent agreement, express or implied.
2. A bailment necessarily involves *delivery of goods* by one person (called the *bailor*) to another person (called the *bailee*) for some purpose upon a contract. Delivery, however, may be actual or constructive.
3. In bailment, the *possession of goods* must change, though temporarily.
4. In bailment, *ownership of the goods* is retained by the bailor. It is not transferred.
5. The delivery of goods in bailment is *for some specified purpose*. The purpose may be the lending, giving or depositing the goods for (i) safe custody, or (ii) as a security for a debt, or (iii) for repair, or (iv) for conversion of form etc.
6. When the purpose for which the bailment is created, is accomplished, *the goods are to be returned or disposed* according to the instructions of the bailor, The goods returned should be the same ones which were bailed.
7. Bailment is possible only of *goods* i.e., of movable property and chattels and not of immovable property.

This money paid into a bank to the credit of a current (or any type of) account does not constitute bailment. *Money and actionable claims are not goods*. However, the deposit of government promissory notes, promissory notes, with the bank for safe custody is treated as bailment. But if they are sent for collection, it is not bailment.

Bailment with Reward and Without Reward

Gratuitous and Non-gratuitous bailment: A *gratuitous bailment* is that in which neither the bailor nor the bailee is entitled to any remuneration e.g., lending of a book to a friend . On the other hand, a *non-gratuitous bailment* is that in which either the bailor or the bailee gets remuneration e.g., giving of a watch or scooter for repair or clothes for stitching. It is also called as *bailment for reward*. Cases of bailments for reward are divided into two classes , viz., (i) those in which a reward is received by the bailor, and (ii) those in respect of which the reward is to be received by the bailee.

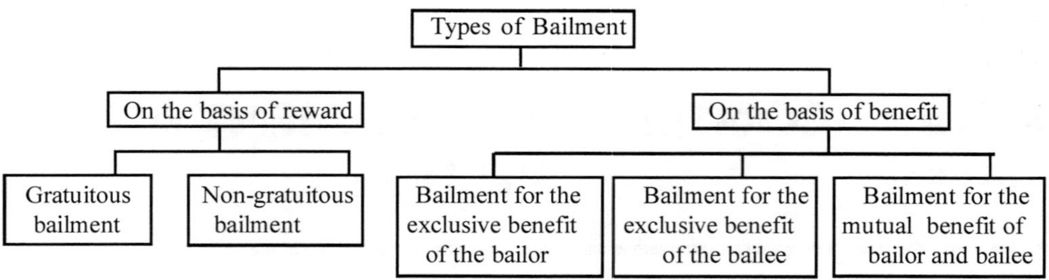

Rights of Bailor

1. ***Restoration of goods lent grautiously (Section 159)*** **:** The lender of a thing for use may at any time even before the expiry of the time or accomplishment of the purpose require its return if the loan was gratuitous (i.e. without reward), even though he lent it for a specified time or purpose. But if, on the faith of such loan made for a specified time or purpose, the borrower has acted in such a manner that the return of the thing lent before the time agreed upon would cause him loss exceeding the benefit derived by him from the article. The lender must if the compels return, indemnify the borrower for the amount in which the loss occasioned exceeds the benefit so derived. In the case of non gratuitous bailment the bailee can claim back after the expiry of the time or the accomplishment of the purpose.

2. ***Entitled to increase of profits to goods bailed (Section 163)*** **:** In the absence of any contract to the contrary, the bailee is bound to deliver to the Bailor, or according to his directions, any increase or profits which may have accrued from the goods bailed.

Illustration

'A' leaves a pregnant cow in the custody of 'B' to be taken care of. The cow gives birth a calf. 'B' is bound to deliver the calf as well as the cow to 'A'.

3. ***Enforcement of rights*** **:** The bailor can enforce by suit all the liabilities or duties of the Bailee.

4. ***Claim for Compensation*** **:** The bailee can claim compensation damage for the loss of the goods occasioned due to bailee's negligence like unauthorised use, unauthorise mixture, destruction or refuses to return or even deterioration of the goods bailed.

5. ***Right of Termination (Section 153)*** **:** A contract bailment is voidable at the option of the bailor, if the bailee does any act with regard to the goods bailed, inconsistent with the conditions of the bailment. In such a case, the bailor can terminate the bailment.

Illustration

'A' lets to 'B' for hire, a horse for his own riding. 'B' drives the horse in his carriage. This is, at the option of 'A', a termination of the bailment.

6. ***Right to have his share in the compensation received in any such suit.***

Duties of Bailor

1. ***To disclose faults in goods bailed (Section 150)*** **-** The bailor in gratuitous bailment, is bound to disclose to the bailee, faults in goods bailed, of which he (the bailor) is aware and which are likely to interfere with the use of them or expose the bailee to extraordinary risks. If the bailor does not make such disclosure, he is responsible for damages arising to the bailee directly from such faults.

The above Section makes a distinction between gratuitous and non-gratuitous bailment. In case of gratuitous bailment, the bailor is bound to disclose only the defects or faults known to him. He is not liable for defects of which he is not aware. But in case of non-gratuitous bailment, the Bailor is responsible for all defects whether known to him or not. Igorance of defects is no defence for him. Where the goods bailed are of dangerous nature, the bailor is bound to disclose the fact to the bailee, otherwise he will be liable for all the resulting damages.

2. ***Repayment of (Extraordinary) Expenses (Section 158)*** : In a gratuitous bailment, where the goods are to be kept or are to be carried, or to have work done upon them by the bailee for the bailor, the bailor shall repay to the bailee all the necessary expenses incurred by him for the purpose of the bailment. But incase of non-gratutious bailment, it is the duty of the bailor only to bear extraordinary expenses, if any, incurred by the bailee in relation to the things bailed. In such a bailment, the bailor is not to bear ordinary or usual expenses.

Illustration

'A' lends a horse to 'B' for safe custody. The horse falls ill and 'B' has to incurmedical expenses on it. If the bailment is gratutious (without reward). 'A' must reimburse 'B' for usual feeding expenses as well as medical expenses. But if the bailment is non-gratutious, (with reward)., 'A' must repay 'B' the medical expenses only, these being extraordinary expenses.

3. ***Responsibility for lack of title (Section 164)***: The bailor is responsible to the bailee for any loss which the bailee may sustain by reason that the bailor was not entitled to make the bailment, or to receive back the goods or to give directions regarding them.

4. ***To receive back the goods*** : It is a right as well as a duty of the bailor to receive back the goods after the expiry of the term or the accomplishment of the purpose of bailment or when the bailee returns them. If bailor refuses to receive them back, the bailee becomes entitled to receive compensation from him for necessary expenses incurred by him (bailee).

Rights of Bailee

The duties of the bailor are the rights of the bailee. These rights include :

1. ***Right to Compensation (Sections 164 & 166)*** : If bailor has no right to bail the goods or to receive them back or to give directions regarding them and consequently the bailee is exposed to some loss, the bailor is responsible for the same. If the bailor has not title to the goods, and the bailee, in good faith delivers them back to or according to the directions the Bailor, the Bailee shall not be responsible to the owner in respect of such delivery.

2. ***Right to Remuneration (by gratuitous bailee)*** : The bailee is entitled to lawful charges for providing services. But where the goods are bailed and work is to be carried on them by the bailee, and the bailee is to receive no remuneration, the bailee is entitled to claim the necessary expenses incurred by him. It may be noted that this right can be claimed by gratutious bailee only.

3. ***Right of Particular Lien (Section 170)*** : Where the bailee has, in accordance with the purpose of the bailment, rendered any services involving the exercise of labour or skill in respect of the goods bailed, he has, in the absence of a contract to the contrary, a right to retain such goods until he receives due remuneration for the services he has rendered in respect of them. The right is restricted only to retain the goods and does not include the right to sell them. It is necessary that the services relating to the goods must have been entirely performed and the remuneration must have become due.

4. ***Right of General Lien (Section 171) :*** Bankers, factors, wharfingers, attorneys of a High Court and policy brokers are entitled to retain, as a security for a general balance of amount, any goods bailed to them in the absence of a contract to the contrary. Even the other types of bailees may also be given this right of general lien to retain the goods as a security for such balance of account, by entering into an agreement to this effect.

5. ***Right to Claim Compensation in case of Faulty Goods (Section 150) :*** The bailee has a right to know the faults in the goods bailed to him, them of which the bailor is aware and which materially interfere with the use of them, or expose the bailee to extraordinary risks. A bailee is entitled to receive compensation from the bailor for any loss or damages arising directly from such faults in the goods bailed.

6. ***Right to Inter Plead (Section 167) :*** If a person, other than the bailor, claims goods bailed, the bailee may apply to the Court to stop the delivery of the goods to the bailor, and to decide the title to the goods.

7. ***Right to Bailment by Several Joint Owners :*** If serveral Joint Owners of goods bail them, the bailee may deliver them back to, or according to the directions of one Joint Owner without the consent of all, in the absence of any agreement to the contrary. In such a case delivery of goods to nay one of the serveral Joint Bailors of goods will amount to delivery of goods to all of them, in the absence of any agreement to the contrary.

8. ***Right to Sue (Section 180) :*** Bailee can use any person who has wrongfully deprived him of the use of possession of the goods bailed or has done them an injury. His remedies against wrong-doers are the same as those of the owner. An action may, therefore, be brought by the bailee or the bailor.

Duties of Bailee

1. ***Duty of Reasonable Care of Goods Bailed (Section 151 and 152) :*** In all cases of bailment, the bailee is bound to take as much care of the goods bailed to him as a man of ordinary prudence would, under similar circumstances take of his own goods of the same bulk, quality and value as the goods bailed. If the bailee has taken reasonable amount of care which a man of ordinary prudence would take, then in the absence of any special contract, he will not be responsible to the loss, destruction or deterioration of the goods bailed.

Houghland v. R.R Low (Luxury) Coaches Ltd (1962) 1 QB 694 CA.

'H' was a passenger in one of 'R's luxury coaches. 'H' put her suit case in the boot of the coach from where it was lost. It was held the 'R' was liable for damages. In this case it 'R's duty to take reasonable care for the safety of customer's luggage.

Martin v. London Country Council, (1947) K.B. 628

'M' was admitted in a hospital as a patient. On her entry, the hospital officials took charge of her jewellery for safe custody. The jewellery was stolen from a room where it was kept. It was held that the hospital officials were bailee for reward and were liable for the loss of jewellery. In this case, the bailee had failed to exercise a care which the nature and quality of the articles required.

There may be a special contract between the bailor and the bailee by which the bailee may be required to take a higher degree of care or under which he may be responsible for compensating the bailor for any loss, destruction or deterioration of the goods. Such special terms are usually incorporated in contracts of carriage etc.

2. ***Not to make unauthorised Use of Goods Bailee (Sections 153 of 154)*** **:** Bailee must use the goods according to the conditions of the contract of bailment or the directions of the Bailor. He must not use the goods in a manner inconsistent with the terms of bailment. If he does so, the bailor can terminate the bailment and recover any loss that might have been caused due to such unauthorised use. According to Section 153 of the Indian Contrat Act "A Contract of bailment is voidable at the option of the bailor if the bailee does any act with regard to the goods bailed, inconsistent with the conditions of the bailment."

   Further according to Section 154 of the Indian Contrat Act, "If the bailee makes any use of the goods bailed, which is not according to the conditions of the bailment, he is liable to make compensation to the bailor for any damage arising both the goods from or during such use of them. If the goods are used for some unauthorised purposes and are damaged or lost during use, he bailee will be held responsible, even though he has exercised reasonable care, because while making an unauthorised use, the became liable as an insurer.

3. ***Duty Not to Mix Goods Bailed with Other Goods (Section 155 to 157)*** **:** The Bailee sound to mix the goods bailed with othe goods of his own, without the consent of the bailor. He must maintain separate indentity of bailor goods. Section 155 to 157's contain rules regarding blending or mixing of the goods:

   (a) *Mixture with Bailor's Consent* : If the bailee, with the consent of the bailor, mixes the goods of the bailor with his own goods, the bailor and the bailee shall have an interest, in proportion to their respective shares, in the mixture thus produced.

   (b) *Mixture without Bailor's Consent when goods cannot be separated* : If the bailee, without the consent of the bailor, mixes with his own goods, and the goods can be separated or divided, the property in the goods remains in the parties respectively, but the bailee is bound to bear the expenses of separation or division, and any damages arising from the mixture.

   (c) *Mixture without Bailor's Consent when goods cannot be separated* : If the bailee, without the consent of the bailor, mixes the goods of the bailor with his own goods, in such a manner that it is impossible to separate the goods bailed from the other goods and deliver them back, the bailor is entitled to be compensated by the bailee for the loss of the goods.

4. ***Duty to Return Goods (Sections 160 and 161)*** **:** As soon as the purpose of bailment is accomplished, the bailee should return the goods bailed to the bailor, otherwise he will be liable in damages for loss destruction or deterioration occasioned by the delay, and will also be liable during such period as an insurer. Section 160 of the Act provides that "It is the duty of the Bailee to return or deliver the goods bailed, according to the Bailor's directions, without demand, as soon as the time for which they were bailed has expired or the purpose for which they were bailed has been accomplished". If by the default of the Bailee, the goods are not returned, delivered or tendered at the proper time, he is responsible to the Bailor for any loss, destruction or deterioration of the goods from that time.

Bontex Knitting Works Ltd. v. St. John Garage

'G' agreed to carry certain goods of 'B' expeditiously. The driver of the van which was carrying the goods, left the van unattended for one hour for lunch. During that time the goods were stolen. 'B' filed a suit for damages against 'G'. Held, carrier has a duty van., to deliver the goods or return them. The carrier could not do so. The van driver's departure constitutes a fundamental breach of the contract to carry the goods forth with to the destination, damages were awarded.

5. ***Duty not to set up adverse title*** **:** Bailee cannot set up as against the bailor, a title over goods bailed in favour of anyone (including himself) other than the bailor. He is also stopped from denying the right of the bailor to bail the goods and to receive them back. It is the duty of the bailee to return the goods only to the bailor even though any third person is claiming the title over them.

TERMINATION OF BAILMENT

Under the following circumstances, a contract of bailment is terminated :

1. **Lapse of time:** When the contract of bailment is for a specified period it is terminated on the expiry of such period.
2. **Accomplishment of the purpose:** A bailment is terminated on the accomplishment of the purpose for which it was made.
3. **Inconsistent use of goods (Section 153):** A contract of bailment may be terminated by the bailor if the bailee does any act with regard to the goods bailed, inconsistent with the conditions of bailment.
4. **Death (Section 162):** A gratuitous bailment is terminated by the death of either the bailor or the bailee.
5. **Gratuitous bailment (Section 159):** The lender of a thing for use may at any time terminate the bailment, even if it was lent gratuitously for a specified time or purpose. But if any losses caused to the bailee because of such premature termination, it must be made good by the bailor.

FINDER OF LOST GOODS

Section 71 lays down that " *A person who finds goods belonging to another and takes them into his custody is subject to the same responsibility as a bailee*". He is bound to take as much care of the goods as a man of ordinary prudence would, under similar circumstances, take of its own goods of the same bulk, quality and value as the goods found.

The rules relating to the rights of the Finder of Goods are given below:

1. **Right of possession:** The finder is entitled to retain possession of the goods against every one except the true owner.
2. **Right of particular or special lien:** When the true owner is found, the finder can exercise (possessory) Particular lien over the goods against the owner until he receives compensation for expenses, etc., incurred in connection with preservation of the goods found. But he cannot sue the owner for the compensation, or trouble and expenses voluntarily incurred by him to preserve the goods and to find out the owner.
3. **Right to reward:** Where the owner has offered a specific reward for the return of the goods lost, the finder may sue for such a reward, and may retain the goods until he receives it (Section 168).
4. **Right of sale:** When a thing which is commonly the subject of sale is lost, the finder may sell it when (i) the owner cannot with reasonable diligence be found, or (ii) if found , the owner refuse to compensate the finder for his lawful charges, or (iii) the thing found is in danger of perishing or of losing the greater part of its value, or (iv) the lawful charges of the finder in respect of the thing found, amount to two-thirds of its value.

Illustration: F picks up a diamond on the floor of S's shop. He hands it over to S to keep it till the true owner is found. No one appeared to claim it for quite some weeks in spite of the wide advertisements in the newspapers. F claims the diamonds from S who refuses to return. S is bound to return the diamond to F who is entitled to retain the diamond against the whole world except the true owner.

Obligations of Finder of lost goods: The duties and liabilities of a finder is treated at par with the bailee. The finder's position, therefore, has been considered along with bailment. The main obligation (duties and liabilities) are: (1) He must take reasonable care of the goods and if, inspite of this, the goods are destroyed, he is not responsible for any loss. (2) He must not use the goods for his own purpose. (3) He must not mix the goods with his own goods. (4) He must try to find out the owner of the goods. If he does not do that, he will be liable as a trespasser.

POSSESSORY LIEN

Lien is the right to retain debtor's property until the charges due in respect of the property are paid. A lien is right of a person in possession of goods belonging to another, to retain or detain the goods, until certain demands are satisfied. Possession is essential to create a right to lien. This right is sometimes called as *Possessory Lien*.

Particular Lien and General Lien

Lien is of two kinds- *Particular Lien* and *General Lien*. 'Particular Lien', also called as '*Special Lien*'. It is right to retain goods belonging to debtor for the discharge of a debt or liability incurred in their connection. Persons entitled to a particular lien are carriers, mechanics, repairers, unpaid seller of goods, finder of lost goods, pawnee and agent, etc. A bailee is also entitled to particular lien only i.e., he has a right to retain that a particular property in respect of which he has extended some skill or services and his charges are due.

General Lien is the right to hold goods bailed belonging to another, not only for the discharge of a debt or liability incurred in respect of those goods, but also as a security for the general balance of account. Section 171 provides for general lien only in case of bankers, factors, wharfingers, attorneys of High courts, policy brokers etc.

Termination of Lien

In the following circumstances, the right of lien can be terminated: (1) The right of lien is a personal right, which continues so long as the bailee is in possession of the goods. It is lost as soon as the *possession of the goods is surrendered* by the bailee. (2) The right of lien is terminated as soon as the *amount due to the bailee is paid* to him. The tender (offer) of the amount also terminates the lien. (3) The bailee may *give up his right (waiver) of lien* by entering into an agreement. In such cases, the lien is also terminated.

PLEDGE

According to Section 172 for the Indian Contract Act, 1872 *a pledge is a bailment of goods as security for payment of debt or performance of promise.* The person who offers the security (i.e., the bailor) is called the '*pawnor*' or '*pledgor*', and the person who receives the goods as security (i.e., bailee) is called the '*pawnee*' or '*pledgee*'.

From this it is clear that in the case of pawn or pledge (i) there should be bailment of goods, and (ii) the object of such bailment should be to hold the goods as a security for the payment of a debt or performance of promise and not for safe custody or any other purpose.

Since pledge is a branch of bailment, it must satisfy the essential requirements of a bailment viz., (i) there must be delivery of goods, (ii) the delivery must be made for some specific purpose, (iii) the delivery must be made on condition that the goods shall be returned in specific time when the purpose is over, or disposed of according to the directions of the bailor, and (iv) only possession, but not the ownership of the goods, is transferred.

Rights of Pledgee

1. ***Rights of Retainer :*** The pledgee has a right to retain the possession of the goods pledged till be recovers the debt, interest and other necessary expenses incidental to possession or preservation of the goods.
2. ***Security for other debts :*** He cannot retain the goods for debts other than those for which pledge is made. Unless the parties contract then they shall be security also for any other subsequent debts.
3. ***To recover any extraordinary expenses :*** The pledge is also entitled to receive any extraordinary expenses incurred for the preservation of goods pledged. He is entitled to this right of the pawnee even if the (pawnor) has violated some provisions of the law in respect of the goods pledged. This point is well stressed by the Supreme Court recently in the *Bank of Bihar v. The State of Bihar and other A.I.R. (1971).*
4. ***To bring civil suit for amount due :*** In the case of default by the pledger to make payment of the debt, the pledgee has the right either (a) to bring a Civil suit against the pledgor for the amount due, and retain the goods pledged as collateral security; or (b) to sell the goods pledged himself after giving the pledgor reasonable notice of sale ; (e) to ask the court to put the pledged articles to sale.
5. **Sale after Notice :** The notice of sale should be clear and specific in language indicating the intention of the pledge to sell the security. It should be noted that this duty of the pledgee to give notice of sale cannot be dispensed with even if the Agreement of pledge authorises the pledgee to sell the security without notice to the pledgor. Further, it is not obligatory for pledgee to sell the goods within reasonable time after the notice of sale is served. If the proceeds of such sale are insufficient to meet claim of the pledgee, the pledgor is still liable to pay the balance. If the sale proceeds are greater than the amount so due, the pledgee has to return the excess or surplus to the pledgor.
6. ***Right to compensation :*** The pledgee has a right to be compensated for any damage which he suffers as a result of non-disclosure of any defects or faults it the goods pledged which are within the knowledge of the pledgor.
7. ***Right to claim damager:*** The pledgee has a right to claim any damages suffered because of the defective title of the pledgor.
8. ***Remedies as owner of the goods:*** In case of injury to the goods or their deprivation by a third party the pledgee would have all such remedies that the owner of the goods would have against them. In *Morvi Mercantile Bank Ltd v. Union of India*, the Supreme Court held that the bank (pledgee) was entitled to recover not only Rs. 20,000 the amount due to it, but he full value of the consignment i.e. Rs. 35,000. However the amount over and above his interest is to be held by him in trust for the pledgor.

Duties of a Pledgee/ Pawnee

1. ***Take reasonable care :*** The pledgee must take that much care which an ordinary prudent man would take of his own goods under similar circumstances.
2. ***Not to make any unauthorised use :*** The pledgee must make use of goods pledged according to the agreement between the two parties. If he makes any unauthorised use, the pledgor is entitled to terminate a the contract and claim damages, if any.

3. ***Return on Repayment :*** The pledgee must return the goods pledged on payment of the debt. If the goods are not returned by the pledgee at the proper time, he is responsible to the pledgor for any loss destruction or deterioration of the goods pledged.

4. ***Return any increase :*** The pledge must return to the pledger any increase or profit which have accrued from the goods pledged, e.g., dividends, bonus shares, etc., in respect of pledged shares.

5. ***Not to set up adverse title :*** The pledgee should not deny the pledger's title. He should not set up his own title or that of a third party.

Duties of a Pledgor/Pawnor

1. ***Right of Redemption :*** Even after the exprity of a stipulated period, or if there has been a default by the pawnor, he may redeem the goods pledged at any subsequent time before the actual sale of the goods pledged. But he must pay expenses which may have arisen from his default. The period of limitation in the case of loan on a pledge is three years to run from the date of the loan. In the case of a promise, however, for the keeping of which the pledge is made, three years to run from the date of the breach of the promise.

2. ***Right to receive Notice of Sale :*** The pledgor has a right to receive a reasonable notice of sale, under Sec. 176 of the Indian Contract Act, from the pledgee.

3. ***Right to receive the surplus :*** The pledgor has right to receive the surplus sale proceeds after meeting the claims of the pledgee.

4. ***Right to take action for conversion :*** If the sale is effected without giving a reasonable notice by the pledgee to the pledgor, the latter has got a right to ask for damages on the ground of conversion. But he cannot sue for a declaration that the sale is contrary to law. *(Narasayyamma v. Andhra Bank Ltd. (1960) A.P. 273.)*

5. ***Receive any increase or profit :*** The pledgor has a right to receive any increase or profit which may have accrued from the goods pledged.

PLEDGE BY NON-OWNER

Generally, *no person can pledge the goods except when he is the legal owner of the goods*. But under certain circumstances a pledge by a non-owners is also valid. (1) Pledge by a *mercantile agent* (Section 178); (2) Pledge by person in *possession under voidable contract* (Sec.178.A); (3) Pledge by *pawnee* who has only a limited interest (Sec.179); (4) Pledge of *co-owner*: A Joint owner who is in sole possession of the goods, with the consent of others, can make a valid pledge. (5*) Seller* in possession after sale: A seller, left in possession of goods sold, is no more owner of the goods but a pledge created by him is valid, provided the pawnee acts in good faith and has no notice of the sale of goods to the buyer. (6) Where a *buyer* or person who has agreed to buy, obtains possession of goods with the seller's consent , before the payment of price, pledges these goods to a pawnee who takes them in goodfaith and without notice of the seller's right of lien or any other right of the seller pledge in valid.

REVIEW QUESTIONS

1. Define bailment.
2. A contract of bailment may be without consideration. Why?
3. Explain how a bailment may result without the owner actually delivering the goods to the bailee.
4. What is the duty of a bailee as regards care of goods bailed?
5. What are the rules regarding return of goods by the bailee?
6. What happens if a bailor does not disclose the known faults in the goods to the bailee?
7. To what extent is a bailee responsible for loss arising from defective title of the bailor?
8. Who is a gratuitous bailee?
9. Explain a bailee's duty of care towards the goods bailed.
10. Where the title of a bailor to the goods is defective and the bailee suffers as a consequence, what is the liability of the bailor?
11. What do you understand by bailee's lien? Is it the same thing as particular lien?
12. Distinguish between a general lien and a particular lien.
13. Who are entitled to general lien?
14. If a third person wrongfully deprives a bailee of the use or possession of the goods bailed, or does them any injury, who can take action against that third party?
15. What is the legal position of a finder of lost goods?
16. "The position of a finder of goods is exactly that of a bailee in the case of a deposit" Explain.
17. When can a finder of goods sell them?
18. When does a contract of bailment terminate?
19 What is a pledge? What is the object of a contract of pledge?
20. How does a pledge differ from a bailment?
21. What is the right of a pawnee against the true owner, when the pawnor's title is defective?
22. Where a pawner fails to redeem his pledge, what are the rights of the pawnee?
23. When is a pledge created by a co-owner valid?
24. Define bailment and state its characteristic features. Discuss the various kinds of bailment.
25. Discuss the rights and duties of bailor and bailee.
26. What are the circumstances in which the contract of bailment stands terminated?
27. What are the rights and duties of the finder of lost goods?
28. Define a pledge. Discuss the rights of the pledgee and pledgor.
29. When will a pledge made by a non-owner of the goods be valid?
30. What is a lien? State its kinds.
31. Distinguish between (a) Particular lien and General lien; (b) Bailment and Pledge; (c) Pledge and Lien.

❒ ❒ ❒

11

Chapter

CONTRACT OF AGENCY

Law relating Agency is contained in chapter X of the Indian Contract Act, 1872 (Sections 182 to 238). *Agency is a contractual relation between two parties created by agreement express or implied.* The relationship of agency arises wherever one person called the *agent* has authority to act on behalf of another called the *principal*.

Essentials of Contract of Agency

1. The relationship of an agency is based upon a contract.
2. The contract may be either express or implied.
3. There should be the appointment of an agent by the principal.
4. The person employing the agent must himself have legal capacity or be competent to do the act for which he employs the agent
5. The Principal should confer authority on the agent to act for him.
6. The authority conferred should be such as will make the principal answerable to third parties.
7. The object of the appointment must to establish relationship between principal and their parties.
8. The relationship of the agency is based on confidence (goodfaith) between the principal and the agent.
9. A contract of Agency requires no consideration (sec 185).
10. An agent is neither a servant nor a bailee.

Anyone may be an Agent

Section 184 of the Contract Act provides that any person may become an agent. In other words, *even a minor can be employed as agent and the principal shall be bound by the acts of such an agent*. But no person who is not of the age of majority and of sound mind can become an agent so as to be responsible to his principal. Thus, if an agent is to be held liable to the principal, he must be a major and of sound mind.

A person who is *major* and who is of *sound mind* can employ another person as an agent. Section 183 states that person who is the age of majority and is sound mind can become a principal. Thus, *a minor cannot act as principal*. It may be noted that consideration is an essential element for the validity of every contract, but, Section 185 lays down that "*No consideration is necessary to create an agency*". A contract of agency is one of *good faith*; the agent must disclose to the principal in the making of the contract with the third parties.

CLASSIFICATION OF AGENTS

1. Express or Implied agents: 2. General, Special or Universal agents; 3. Agent or Sub-agent. Another broad classification of agents is *mercantile (or commercial) agents and non-mercantile (or non-commercial) agents*. The following are some of the important mercantile agents. Banker, Factor, Broker, Auctioneer, Commission Agent and *Del Credere* Agent.

1. **Banker :** Banker acts as an agent of the customer when he collects cheques or drafts or bills or buys or sells securities on behalf of his customers. He has a *general lien* in respect of the general balance of account.

2. **Factor :** A factor is one who is entrusted with the possession of goods and who has the authority to buy, sell or otherwise deal with the goods or to raise money on their security. He has a *general lien* on the goods.

3. **Broker :** A broker is one who negotiates and makes contracts between the principal and the third party. He is not entrusted with the possession of goods and hence he has *no lien* on the goods.

4. **Auctioneer :** An auctioneer is one who is entrusted with the possession of goods for sale at a public auction. He has only a *particular lien* on the goods for his charges.

5. **Commission Agent :** The term 'commission agent' is a general term which is used in practice even for a factor or broker.

6. **Del credere agent :** An agent who in consideration of an extra remuneration guarantees to his principal the performance of the contract by the other party. The *del credere* commission is a higher reward than is usually given in the form of a commission. He occupies the position of a guarantor as well as of an agent. But his liability is secondary and arises only on the insolvency or failure of the party. A *del credere* agent is appointed generally when the principal deals with a person about whom he knows nothing.

Non-mercantile agents include counsel, solicitor, guardian, promoter, wife, receiver, clearing and forwarding agent; they are always engaged by merchants to conduct their suits in connection with mercantile disputes.

Difference between a Commission Agent and a Del Credere Agent

1. A commission agent undertakes only the function of sale of goods on behalf of his principal. But a del credere agent not only undertakes to sell goods on behalf of his principal, but also guarantees the payment of the price of the goods which he sells on credit. In other words, a del credere agent serves both as an agent and a guarantor.

2. A commission agent may buy or sell goods on behalf of his principal. But a del credere agent comes into picture only in the context of sale of goods on behalf of the principal.

3. A commission agent comes into picture in the case of cash sales as well as credit sales of goods. But a del credere agent comes into picture only in the case of credit sales of goods.

4. The ordinary selling commission payable to a commission agent is based on total sales. But the extra del credere commission payable to a del credere agent may be based either on total sales or only on credit sales.

5. A commission agent does not protect the principal against the risk of bad debts involved in credit sales. But a del credere agent protects the principal against the risk of bad debts involved in credit sales.
6. The duties and responsibilities of a del credere agent are more than those of a commission agent.

Universal Agents : A universal agent is an agent whose authority to act for the principal is universal or unlimited. In other words, a universal agent is an agent who is authorised to do any legal act on behalf of his princpal. A universal agent is, usually, appointed by a principal (i.e., businessman) who, because of his physical conditions, wants to retire from business, giving a blanket power of attorney to the agent. A universal agent has unlimited authority to do all such acts as could be delegated, and which the principal himself could lawfully perform. In short, he has authority to bind the principal by any legal act.

CREATION OF AGENCY

An agency may arise in different ways. It need not be always created expressly by any writing and may be inferred from the circumstances and conduct of the parties. An agency may be constituted in following ways: (1) by *express agreement*; (2) by *implication* or *law*, i.e., from the conduct of the parties or from the necessity of the case, (3) by *ratification,* (4) *by operation of law.*

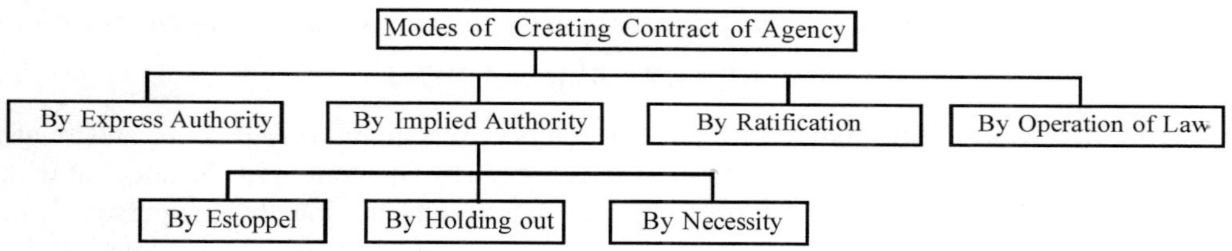

Implied Agency

Implied agency includes: (a) Agency by estoppel, (b) Agency by holding out, (c) Agency by necessity.

Agency by Estoppel (Sec. 237) : In many cases, an agency may be implied from the conduct of the parties, though no express authority has been given. Thus. where the principal knowingly permits a person to act in certain business in his name or on his behalf, such a principal is estopped from denying the authority of the supposed agent to bind him.

Illustration : If a railway company holds out that its parcel clerk can accept consignments for despatch, it cannot afterwards say, that had no such legal authority. There are *three possible cases of agency by estoppel*: (a) A person can be held out as an agent although he is actually he is actually not so, (b) A person acting as agent may be held out as having more authority than he actually has, (c) A person may be held agent after he has ceased to be so.

Agency by Holding out : Where a person permits another by a long course of conduct to pledge his credit for certain purposes, he is bound by the act of such person in pledging his credit for similar purposes, though in some cases without the previous permission of his master. This is a case of agency by '*holding out*'. Similarly where a husband holds out his wife as having his authority by words or conduct and a third party advances money to the wife on the faith of such conduct, the husband is liable for such debts.

Agency by Operation of law : Sometimes, an agency arises by operation of law. When a company is first formed, its *promoters* and its agents are recruited and implied by operation of law. A *partner* is the agent of the firm for the purposes of the business of the firm, and the act of a partner, which is done to carry on in the usual way, business of the kind carried on by the firm, binds the firm (Secs.18 and 19 of the Indian Partnership Act, 1932). In all these cases the agency is implied by operation of law.

Agency by Necessity: Sometimes extraordinary circumstances require that a person who is not really an agent should act as an agent of another. In such a case, though there might not have been an express or implied authority to do an act, the law implies such an authority in favour of that person on account of the necessity that had arisen. Before an agency of necessity can be inferred, the following conditions should be fulfilled; There should have been actual and definite commercial necessity to agent to act promptly.

(a) There should be a real and definite necessity for the creation of the agency,

(b) It should be impossible to obtain the principal's instructions, The agent should not be in position or have any opportunity to communicate with his principal within the time available

(c) The person acting as an agent should act *bona fide* and in the interest of parties concerned.

Agency of Husband and Wife: The wife has authority to pledge her husband's credit for the necessaries because there exists a relationship of principal and agent between spouses so long as they are living together.

Agency by Precedent and Subsequent Authority: A contract of agency may be formed either precedent authority or by subsequent authority. Agency by subsequent authority is known as *agency by ratification.*

AGENCY BY RATIFICATION

Ratification is a kind of affirmation or approval of a previous unauthorised act or acts relating to a contract. It implies the adopting by the principal of an act made by an agent in his behalf, but without his authority. Section 196 of the Contract Act provides that "where acts are done by one person on behalf of another, but without his knowledge or authority, he may elect to ratify or to disown such acts. If he ratifies them, the same effects will follow as if they had been performed by his authority".

Illustration: A without having any authority of B acts as B's agent and enters into a contract with C. The contract will be binding on B, if he ratifies or approves of the same.

Mode of Ratification (Section 197)

Ratification may be express or implied by the conduct of the person on whose behalf the acts are done.

***Example I* :** A, without authority, buys goods for B. Afterwards B sells them to C on his own account; B's conduct implies a ratification of the purchases made for him by A.

***Example II* :** A, without B's authority, lends B's money to C. Afterwards B accepts interest on the money due from C. B's conduct implies a ratification of the loan.

Effect of Ratification

Ratification relates back to the date when the act was done by the agent. It is the adoption of the contract. It only endorses the unauthorised act of the agent as authorised. *It is authorisation retrospectively*. In other words, it is equivalent to previous authority. It is cure of the lack of authorisation or a substitute for authorisation. This is known as '*Doctrine of Relation Back*'.

Essentials of a Valid Ratification

To make a ratification valid, the following conditions must be fulfilled.

1. **Act must have been done *on behalf* of the person ratifying** : A person can ratify only that which is purported to have been done for him and cannot ratify that which is purported to have been done for somebody else. Act done by a person on his own account cannot be ratified. Only when an act is done on behalf of the ratifier, such act can be ratified. Thus, where the act of the President of a municipality was not on behalf of the committee, but in his own right, the municipal committee cannot ratify it. *[Harsarn Das Vs. Executive Officer, Municipal Board, Hapur, 1966 All L.J. 678].*

2. **The principal must be *in existence* at the time of the act that is to be ratified :** For a valid ratification it is essential that the principal must have been in existence at the time when the act was done. No body as an agent can bind by contract a principal who does not exist at the date of the contract. Thus, a company cannot ratify or adopt a contract which was entered into by the promoters on its behalf before its incorporation. Similarly, a contract made on behalf of a child in the womb cannot be ratified by him when the child attains the age of majority.

3. **Ratifier should be *competent* to ratify the act :** The person on whose behalf the act was done should have contractual capacity at the time both when it was done and also when it was ratified. One who is not competent to authorise an act, cannot give it validity by ratifying it. Thus, when the minor was not in a position to give authority at the date when acts were performed, he cannot subsequently ratify these acts.

4. **The transaction must have been *subsisting* at the time when it is ratified :** Before any act can be ratified, it must exist at date of ratification. To constitute ratification the approval of a transaction must occur before the other party had withdrawn from it and before the agreement has been terminated or discharged.

5. **The principal must have signified his *unconditional acceptance* of the act :** The principal must accept the act of the agent unconditionally. Where the acceptance is qualified or conditional ratification is invalid.

6. **Ratification may be *express* or *implied* :** Ratification may be in express words or in writing and it can also be implied from the conduct of the person on whose behalf the act was done.

7. **Ratification must have been made *with full knowledge* of all the materials facts :** Valid ratification involves knowledge of all material facts on the part of the ratifier. No valid ratification can be made by a person whose knowledge of the facts of the case is materially defective. It is the actual knowledge and not mere opportunity for acquiring actual knowledge which is essential for valid ratification.

8. ***Whole transaction* must be ratified :** A contract cannot be ratified in parts and repudiated in part. If ratified, the whole transaction must be ratified. Once a part is accepted, it is an implied acceptance of the whole. Either you ratify or you do not. For instance if an agent purchases without authority 20 bags of paddy, it is not open to the principal to ratify 12 of them, without approving of the other 8 bags of paddy.

9. Ratification may be of ***one act or of a series of acts*;**

10. **Ratification must be made *within a reasonable time* :** The ratification of a contract must be made within a reasonable time after the contract is made. Where a time is expressly limited, a ratification after the time has expired will not serve. The time of commencement of performance of the contract was September but the Board ratified the tender in October, when the defendent had already withdrawn his tender. Ratification was held to be too late.

11. **Act to be ratified should *not be void or illegal* :** A contract which is void in law cannot be ratified. An act which is void from the very beginning cannot be ratified. An act considering a criminal offence is incapable of ratification. A voidable contract however, can be ratified. Payment of dividend out of capital is void and cannot be ratified. Similarly, a forgery of signatures being a crime cannot be ratified.

12. **Ratification must *communicated* :** There can be no valid ratification of an act unless it is communicated to the other party. Ratifier cannot keep his thoughts to himself.

13. **Ratification must *not injure their person* :** Ratification is equivalent to previous authority. An exception to this rule is provided in Section 200, which says that when interest of third parties are likely to be affected, the principle of ratification does not apply. Ratification cannot relate back to the date of contact if third parties have, in the intervening time acquired rights.

14. **Ratification *relates back to the date of the act of the agent*** : Ratification relates back to the original dating or making of the act or contract. It has a retrospective effect. It tantamounts to previous authority. It places all the parties in exactly the same position as they would have occupied in the case of a precedent authority.

NATURE AND EXTENT OF AUTHORITY OF AN AGENT

An agent is appointed with some authority by which he can bind the principal with third persons. In general , acts of an agent done with his authority, bind the principal (Sec.225). The authority, however, is not unlimited.

Express and Implied authority: The authority of an agent may be express or implied (Sec.186). An authority is said to be expressed when it is given by words spoken or written. An authority is said to implied when it is to be inferred from the circumstances of the cases; and things spoken and written or the ordinary course of dealing, may be accounted as circumstances of the case (Sec.187.)

Ostensible or apparent authority: Ostensible or Apparent Authority is the authority of an agent as it appears to others. When an agent is employed for a particular business, the persons dealing with him can presume that he has authority to do all such lawful acts as are necessary or incidental to such business (Sec 188).

Emergency authority: An agent has authority, in emergency, to all such acts for the purpose of protecting his principal from loss as would be done by person of ordinary prudence, in his own case, under similar circumstances (Sec.189).

Distinction between Agent and Servant

	Agent	*Servant*
1.	An agent is authorised to act on behalf of his principal and has power to create legal relations between the principal and third persons.	A servant has no representative character. He has no authority to make contract on behalf of his master.
2.	An agent is not subject to the direct control and supervision of the principal.	A servant acts under the direct control and supervision of his employer.
3.	An agent may work for several principals.	A whole time servant serves only one master.
4.	The principal directs an agent "as to what is to be done".	The master has the right to direct not only "what work is to be done" but also "how the work is to be done".
5.	An agent may be paid by way of commission on the basis of work done.	A servant is paid by way of salary or wages.
6.	The principal is liable for only those acts of his agent which are done within the scope of authority and is not liable for those acts of the agent which are done outside the scope of such authority.	An employer is liable for the wrongful acts of the servant, if such acts are committed in the course of employment.

Distinction between Agent and Independent Contractor

Agent	*Independent Contractor*
1. An agent represents his principal and has the authority to create contractual relationship between his principal and third parties.	An independent contractor does not represent his employer. And no authority to create contractual relationship between his master and third parties.
2. An agent is not personally liable in ordinary cases.	Independent contractor is personally liable for all acts done by him.
3. The question of authority arises in case of agency.	The question of authority does not arise in the case of independent contractor.
4. An agent is bound to act in the matter of agency subject to the directions and control of his principal.	An independent contractor undertake a to perform a certain specified work, the manner and means of performances being left to his discretion.

Delegation of Agent's Authority

Sub-Agent and Substituted Agent

Definition of Sub-Agent: Section 191 defines a sub-agent as "*person employed by and acting under the control of the original agent in the business of the agency*".

Appointment of Sub-agent: The ordinary rule of the law is that *an agent cannot delegate his powers or duties to another without the express authority of the principal*. To this rule, there are certain *exceptions* where an agent can appoint a sub-agent;

(a) where the ordinary custom or usage of trade permits employment of sub-agents;

(b) where it is necessary because of the nature of the agency;

(c) where the act to be done is purely ministerial and does not involve any confidence or require any skill;

(d) where the agent has express authority to appoint sub-agent;

(e) where in the course of the agent's employment unforeseen emergencies arise which render it necessary to delegate his authority;

(f) where the principal knows that the agent intends to appoint a sub-agent;

(g) where the authority of the agent to appoint a sub-agent can be inferred from the conduct of the parties.

Substituted Agent

A substituted agent is a person appointed by the agent to act for principal in the business of the agency with the knowledge and consent of the latter.

Illustration: A directs B, his solicitor to sell his estate by auction and to employ an auctioneer, for the purpose. B names C as an auctioneer to conduct the sale . C is not a sub-agent but is A's agent for the conduct of the sale.

A substituted agent is deemed to be an agent to the principal and not his sub-agent. A privity of contract is established between the principal and the substituted agent. The agent is not concerned about the work of substitute. A duty, however, is implied on the original agent to choose a proper substituted agent with reasonable care. The agent selecting such an agent must use direction and prudence. But he is not to guarantee solvency, skill or integrity of the person selected. If he fails to exercise such care, he comes liable for damages to the principals for his negligence.

Difference between Sub-Agent and Substituted Agent

Both a sub-agent and substituted agent are appointed by the agent. But, however, the following are the points of the distinction between the two.

1. The agent not only appoints a sub-agent but also delegates to him a part of his own duties. The agent does not delegate any part of his task to the substituted agent.
2. A sub-agent does his work under the control of the agent but a substituted agent works under the instructions of the principal.
3. Privity of contract is established between a principal and a substituted agent. But there is no privity of contract between the principal and the sub-agent.
4. The sub-agent is responsible to the agent alone and is not generally responsible to the principal. But a substituted agent is responsible to the principal and not to the original agent who appointed him.
5. In the case of a substituted agent, the agent's duty ends once he has named him, but in the case of a sub-agent, the agent remains answerable for the acts of the sub-agent as long as sub-agency continues.

RIGHTS, DUTIES AND LIABILITIES OF AN AGENT

Rights of an Agent

1. An agent is entitled to receive agreed *remuneration*. In the absence of any special contract, payment for the performance of any act is not due to the agent until the completion of such act (Sec.219).
2. A agent may *retain out of any sums received* on account of the principal in the business of the agency, or all moneys due to himself respect of advances made or expenses properly incurred by him in conducting such business and also such remuneration as may be payable to him for acting as agent (Sec.217).
3. In the absence of any contract to the contrary, the agent is entitled to *particular lien* i.e., right to retain goods, papers (documents) and other property, whether movable or immovable, of the principal *received by him,* until the amount due to himself for commission, disbursements and services in respect of the same has been paid or accounted for him (Sec. 221).
4. Under certain circumstances, an agent can *stop the goods in transit.*
5. The employer of an agent is bound *to indemnify* him against the consequences of all lawful acts done by such agent in exercise of authority conferred upon him. (Sec.222).
6. The principal must *pay compensation* to his agent in respect of injury caused to such agent by the principal's neglect or want of skill (Sec.225).

DUTIES OF AN AGENT

1. To follow the instructions of the principal : An agent is bound to conduct the business of his principal according to the direction given by the principal, or in the absence of any such directions, according to the custom which prevails in doing business of the same kind at the place where the agent conducts such business. When the agent acts otherwise, if any loss be sustained, he must make it good to his principal and if any profit accrues, he must account for it. (Sec. 211) Where there are no express instructions, the agent has to perform his duty according to the custom of the business in the particular locality he works. An agent is not bound to obey the unlawful instructions of the principal. (Bexwell v. Christies).

2. ***To work with reasonable skill and diligence*** : An agent is bound to conduct the business of the agency with as much skill as is generally possessed by persons engaged in similar business, unless the principal has notice of his want of skill. The agent is always bound to act with reasonable diligence and to use such skill as he possesses and to make compensation to his principal in respect of the direct consequences of his own neglect, want of skill or misconduct, but not in respect of loss or damage which are indirectly or remotely caused by such neglect, want of skill of misconduct (Sec. 212)/ A del credere agent stands at a different footing. He is liable for breach of his duties even without any proof of want of skill or neglect.

3. ***To render proper accounts*** : An agent is bound to render proper accounts to his principal on demand. *(Sec. 213)*. Rendering accounts does not mean the showing of the accounts, but of the accounts supported by vouchers. The agent is *answerable for any secret profit* which he had earned from his agency work.

4. ***To communicate with the principal in difficult situations*** : It is the duty of an agent, in case of difficulty, to use all reasonable diligence in communicating with this principal, and in seeking to obtain his instructions. *(Sec. 214)*

5. ***No to deal on his own account*** : It is a duty of an agent not to deal on his own account. If an agent deals on his own account in the business of the agency, without first obtaining the consent of his principal and acquainting him with all material circumstances which have come to his own knowledge on the subject, the principal may repudiate the transaction, if the case shows either that any material fact has been dishonestly concealed from him by the agent or that the dealings of the agent have been disadvantageous to him. *(Sec.215)*.

   That part, if an agent, without the knowledge of his principal, deals in the business of the agency on his own account instead of an account of his principal, the principal is entitled to claim from the agent any benefit which may have resulted to him from the transaction *(Sec. 216)*.

6. ***To pay all sums*** : It is a duty of an agent to pay all sums to his principal, which are received for principal *(Sec. 218)*. He is entitled to deduct his lawful charges. Where an agent receives money on behalf of the principal, under an illegal or void contract, the agent must account to the principal.

   Illustration

   An agent entered into a number of wagering conracts with third parties. Agent earned good profits and refused to pay in to his principal on the plea of illegality. Held : Principal can recover the money *(Bhola Nath v. Mul Chand)*.

7. ***Not to set up adverse title*** : It is a duty of an agent not to set up adverse title. If he acts otherwise, the principal can prohibit him from doing so. But he can set up superior title of his principal against third parties.

8. ***Not to delegate his authority*** : With a few exceptions, it is a duty of an agent not to delegate his authority.

9. ***Not to use agency informations against Principal*** **:** It is a duty of an agent not to use informations obtained in the course of agency against the principal. If he does so, the principle can restrain him from doing so by an injunction from the court.

10. ***Agent's duty on termination of agency by principal's death or insanity*** **:** When an agency is terminated by the principal's death or becoming of unsound mind, the agent is bound to take, on behalf of the representatives of his late principal, all reasonable steps for the protection and preservation of the interest entrusted to him *(Sec. 209).*

11. ***Not to put himself in position where interest and duty conflict*** **:** An agent is under a duty, in all cases, to act in the interest of the principal. He must not put himself in a position where his duty to the principal and his personal interest conflict unless he has made full disclosure of his interest to his principal, specifying its exact nature and obtained his assent.

    Illustration

    'P' employed 'A', a stock-broker, to buy some shares for him. 'A' sold his own shares to 'P' without disclosing that the shares belonged to him. Held 'P' could rescind the contract. [*Armstrong v. Jackson,* (1977) K.B. 822].

PRINCIPAL AND THIRD PARTIES

The rights and liabilities of principal in relation to third parties under contracts made by his agent depend upon whether (a) an agent contracts as agent for a named principal: (b) an agent expressly contracts as an agent for an unnamed principal (c) an agent contracts for a principal whose existence he does not disclose.

Agent Acting for a Named Principal

1. **When the agent acts within the scope of his authority (Section 226):** Where an act is done by an agent within the scope of his authority, his acts are binding on the principal. The principal will also be bound by the acts of the agent provided (a) the act is lawful and (b)it is within the scope of agent's authority. Thus, where an agent is authorised to receive payment on behalf of the principal, a payment to the agent discharges the debtor from liability to the principal and the fact that the agent embezzled the money is immaterial.

2. **When the agent exceeds his authority (Section 227 and 228):** Ordinarily, the principal is liable for those acts of the agent which are within the scope of his authority. According to Section 227, where an agent has done more than what he is authorised to do and it is separable, the principal is bound by that part which is within his authority.

3. **Principal bound by notice given to agent (Section 229):** A notice given to the agent is as effectual as notice given to principal as otherwise notice might be avoided in every case by employing agents. Thus, the knowledge of a manager of a bank is knowledge of the bank. Similarly, knowledge of one partner in firm is a knowledge of all the partners. The principal is bound by notice given to the agent in the course of the business. *Knowledge of the agent is the knowledge of the principal.* But where knowledge is not acquired by the agent in course of his employment, it cannot be imputed to the principal. However, the rule contained in this section will not apply if the agent had committed a fraud on the principal.

4. **Liability of principal by estoppel (Section 237):** A principal is liable where he has, by words or conduct, induced a belief in the contracting party that the act of the agent was within the scope of

his authority. The liability of the principal under Section 237 is not based on any real authority, but is by estoppel.

5. **Liability for misrepresentation or fraud by an agent (Section 238):** The principal is liable for the fraud of his agent acting within the scope of his authority, and whether the fraud is committed for the benefit of the principal or that of the agent.

Agent acting for an Unnamed Principal

Where an agent disclosed the fact, that he is an agent, but at the same time does not disclose his principal's name , the contract made by the agent is binding on the principal. But the unnamed principal should be in existence at the time of the contract. Where an agent signed the contract as a broker, "to my principal's", but did not disclose the name of the principal, it was held that the broker was not personally liable.

Agent acting for an Undisclosed Principal

The doctrine of the undisclosed principal comes into operating when an agent enters into a contract with a person without disclosing the name and the existence of his principal. Where the agent does not disclose the existence of his principal he is personally liable for the contract. On such contracts he can sue and be sued in his own name because he is then in the eyes of law the real contracting party. But the agent's right to action comes to an end with the intervention of the undisclosed principal. Once the third party knows of the existence of the principal as well as of the agent, he has right to sue both or either of them. Once he elects to sue one and other, it would appear that he exhausts his cause of action.

PERSONAL LIABILITY OF AN AGENT

General Rule (Section 230) : In the absence of any contract to that effect, an agent cannot personally enforce contract entered into by him on behalf of his principal, nor is he personally bound by them.

When the Agent becomes Personally Liable

The circumstances under which an agent becomes personally liable are shown below:

(a) **In case of foreign principal** (Section 230) : Where the contract is made by an agent for the sale or purchase of goods for a merchant residing abroad, in the absence of any contract to the contrary, it is presumed that the agent is personally liable for such contracts.

(b) **In case of undisclosed principal** (Section 230) : Where the contract is made by an agent for an undisclosed principal, in the absence of any contract to the contrary, it is presumed that the agent is personally liable.

(c) **In case of incompetent principal** (Section 230) : Where a contract is made by an agent for a person who cannot be sued. (e.g. minor, lunatic, foreign ambassador), in the absence of any contract to the contrary, it is presumed that the agent is personally liable.

(d) **In case of principal not in existence (Nonexistent principal) :** Where a contract is made by the promoter for a company not yet incorporated, the promoters are personally liable.

(e) **In case of acts not ratified** (Section 235) : A person untruly representing himself to be the authorised agent of another, and thereby inducing a third person to deal with him as such agent, is liable, if his alleged employer does not ratify his acts, to make compensation to the other in respect of any loss or damage which he has incurred by so dealing.

(f) **In case of acts in his own name** : Where a contract is made by an agent without disclosing that he is contracting as an agent, the agent is personally liable.

Example : X took a loan from Y by executing a hundi in Y's favour. X did not sign the hundi as agent of the firm nor did he disclose to Y the name of his principal. The agent was held personally liable. (*Trilok Chand Vs. Rameshwar Lal*).

(g) **In case of express agreement :** Where a contract made by an agent specifically provides for the personal liability of the agent, the agent will be personally liable.

(h) **In case of custom or usage of trade :** Where there is a custom or usage of trade making the agent personally liable, in the absence of any contract to the contrary, the agent is personally liable.

Example : X, a share broker purchased 100 shares @ ₹ 100 per share and sold the same shares @ ₹ 90 per share on behalf of Y who refused to give the difference. X is personally liable because it is a custom that a share broker is personally liable for the contracts entered into by him.

(i) Where an agent *acts beyond his authority*.

(j) Agency coupled with interest

(k) Where the agent *signs negotiable instruments in his own name.*

(l) When the agent *appoints sub-agent without authority*.

(m) Where the *agent is an unauthorised one.*

(n) Where agent acts, *receives or pays money by fraud or by mistake*.

Misrepresentation and Fraud by Agents: Misrepresentation made or frauds committed, by agents acting in the course of their business for their principals have the same effect on agreements made by such agents as if such misrepresentations or frauds had been made or committed by the principals. But misrepresentation made, or frauds committed, by agents, in matters which do not fall within the scope of authority, do not affect their principal (Sec.238).

Money received by agent by playing fraud on third person : Where an agent received the money from the third person by fraud and paid it to the principal, the third person cannot sue the principal unless the latter was aware of the fraud or had means of knowing that it was the third person's money.

TERMINATION OF AGENCY

Agency may be terminated in the same manner as any other contract, viz., by the *operation of law or by the acts of the parties*. In certain cases, the agency is *irrevocable*, i.e., it cannot be terminated.

Termination of Agency by Acts of the Parties

1. By *agreement* between principal and agent;
2. By *revocation* of the agent's authority by the principal;
3. By *renunciation* of business by the agent.

Termination of Agency by Operating of Law

4. By *performance* of the contract of agency;
5. By *efflux of time*;

6. By *death or insanity* of the agent or principal;
7. By the *insolvency* of the principal and in some cases that of the agent;
8. By the *destruction of the subject matter* of agency;
9. Where the principal or agent is an incorporated company, by its *dissolution*;
10. By the principal becoming an *alien enemy*.

Effect of Termination (Section 208): As between the principal and the agent, termination of agency is effective only when it becomes known to the agent, but so far as third parties are concerned, termination of agency takes effect when it is known to them.

IRREVOCABLE AGENCY

When a agency (i.e., the relationships between the principal and agent) cannot be terminated is said to be an irrevocable agency.

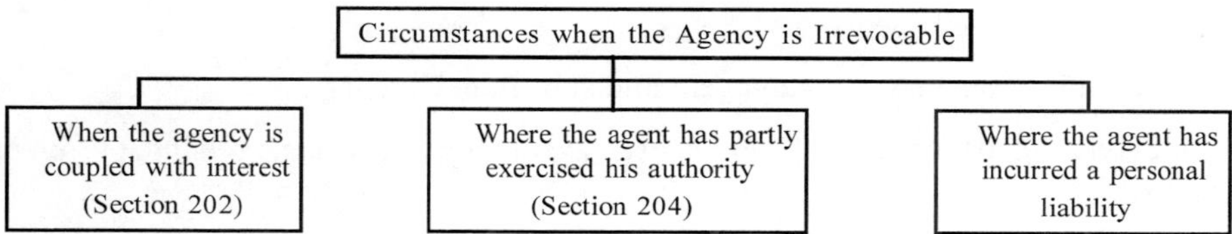

1. **Where the Agency is Coupled With Interest (Sec 202) :** An agency is said to be coupled with an interest when the agency is created for the purpose of securing some benefit over and above his remuneration as an agent. Thus, an agency is coupled with interest when the agent has an interest in the authority granted to him or when the agent has an interest in the subject-matter with which he is authorised to deal. Such an agency cannot, in the absence of any contracts to the contrary, be terminated to the prejudice of such interest.

Illustration : A gives authority to B to sell A's land and to pay himself out of the proceeds the debts due to him from A. A cannot revoke this authority nor can it be terminated by his insanity or death.

Illustration : A consigns certain wheat to B for sale. Subsequently B advanced some money to A the principal. Held the subsequent advance could not convert the agency into one coupled with interest.

This rule, will not apply to cases where the interest of the agent arises after the creation of agency. The interest of the agent should have arisen interior to the authority. It is important that the agency is created with the object of securing a benefit or gain to the agent and is not sufficient that it does so incidentally.

2. **Where the agent has incurred a personal liability:** When an agent has incurred personal liability, the agency becomes irrevocable, for the principal cannot be permitted to withdraw, leaving the agency exposed to risk or liability he has incurred.

3. **Where the agent had partly exercised the authority:** Section 204 of the Act lays down that the principal cannot revoke the authority given to agent after the authority has partly exercised so far as regards such acts and obligations as arise from acts already done in the agency.

Illustration: A authorises B to buy 1,000 bags of paddy on account of A and to pay for it out A's money remaining in B's hands. B buys 1,000 bags of paddy eg., in his own name, so as to make himself personally liable for the price. A cannot revoke B's authority so far as regards payment for the paddy.

REVIEW QUESTIONS

1. Define the term 'agency'.
2. What are the essentials and legal rules for a valid agency?
3. Briefly explain the various modes by which an agency may be created.
4. What is agency by estoppel? In what way does it differ from an agency by holding out?
5. Who are important mercantile agents? What are their functions?
6. 'Ratification is tantamount to prior authority'. Comment and explain the requisites of a valid ratification.
7. What are the different kinds of agents? How they can be classified?
8. State briefly the duties and rights of an agent. What is the degree of skill required of an agent?
9. Discuss the duties of an agent under the Indian Contract Act.
10. Define the term 'substituted agent'.
11. "What are the differences between sub-agent and substituted agent.
12. State the rules relating to the personal liability of an agent for a contract entered into by him on behalf of his principal.
13. Discuss briefly the different modes in which the agency can be terminated.
14. When does the termination take effect?
15. Explain (a) Irrevocable Agency (b) Agency coupled with interest.

❑ ❑ ❑

12 Chapter

CONTRACT OF SALE OF GOODS

The Sale of Goods Act, 1930 codifies the law relating to the sale of goods in a separate enactment. Prior to the passing of this Act, provisions of Indian Contract, 1872 (Chapter VII, Sections 76-123) were made applicable to the sale of goods. The Act came into force on 1st July, 1930. It contains 66 sections and extends to the whole of India except the State of Jammu and Kashmir.

Contract of Sale of Goods

Section 4 (1) of the Sale of Goods Act, 1930 defines *"A contract of sale of goods is contract whereby the seller transfers or agrees to transfer the property in goods to the buyer for a price".*

Essential Characteristics of a Contract of Sale of Goods

1. There must be two parties to a contract of sale viz., a *buyer* and *a seller*.
2. The object of the contract of sale must be *transfer of property* in the goods by one person to another. *'Property'* here means *'ownership'*.
3. The subject matter of the contract of sale must be *'Goods'*. The term Goods and includes every kind of movable property other than actionable claims and money, and includes stock and share, growing crops, grass and things attached to or forming part of the land which are agreed to be severed before sale or under the contract of sale.
4. Consideration for a sale of goods must be money consideration, called the *'Price'*; when goods are exchanged for other goods, the transaction is not 'sale, but an 'exchange' or 'barter'. However, there is nothing to prevent the consideration being partly in money and partly in goods.
5. A contract of sale may be writing or by words of month, or partly in writing and partly by words of month, or may be implied from the conduct of the parties.
6. A contract of sale includes both an actual sale and agreement to sell.

Illustration : Where an old car is exchanged for a new one and the difference is paid in cash, the contract is one of sale.

Delivery and Payment : The contract of sale may provide for any of the following combination.

Option	*Delivery*	*Payment*
1.	Immediate	Immediate
2.	Immediate	By instalments
3.	Immediate	At some future date
4.	By instalments	By instalments
5.	By instalments	Immediate

6.	By instalments	At some future date
7.	At some future date	At some future date
8.	At some future date	Immediate
9.	At some future date	By instalments

Agreement to Sell (Section 4(3)): Where under a contract of sale, the transfer of property in goods is to take place at a future date or subject to some conditions thereafter to be fulfilled, the contract is called an '*Agreement to Sell*'. Thus, whereby a contract of sale, a seller purports to effect a present sale of future goods, the agreement operates as an executory contract.

Illustration : A agrees to buy B's car and pay for it, if his wife approves. It is an 'agreement to sell' for B and 'an agreement to buy' for A.

DISTINCTION BETWEEN SALE AND AGREEMENT TO SELL

The distinction between a sale and an agreement to sell depends upon the crucial point whether the property (ownership) in the goods has passed or is yet to pass from the seller to his buyer. All other points of distinction follow from this basic point.

(i) **Transfer of property:** In a sale, the property in the goods passes from the seller to his buyer immediately so that the seller is no more the owner of his goods sold. In an agreement to sell, the transfer of property in the goods is to take place at a future date or subject to certain conditions being fulfilled so that the seller continues to be owner until the agreement to sell becomes an actual sale.

(ii) **Risk of loss:** In a sale, in the event of the goods being destroyed, the loss falls on the buyer even though the possession of the goods was with the seller. In an agreement to sell, if the goods are destroyed, the loss falls on the seller even though the goods were in the possession of his buyer.

(iii) **Nature of contract:** A sale is an *executed* contract whereas an agreement to sell is an *executory* contract.

(iv) **Consequences of breach:** In a sale, if there is a breach of contract by the buyer, the seller can sue for his price, even though the goods are still in his possession. In an agreement to sell, the seller can sue only for damages and not for his payment of the price.

(v) **Right to resell:** In a sale, the seller cannot resell the goods and if he does so, the subsequent buyer does not acquire a good title to his goods. In an agreement to sell, in case of resale, the bona fide buyer for value, without notice of the prior agreement to sell, the seller is not bound to part with the goods until he is paid for.

(vi) **Insolvency of buyer:** In a sale, if the buyer becomes insolvent before he pays for the goods, the seller must return them to the Official Receiver or Assignee, he will be entitled to a rateable dividend only for the price of the goods. In an agreement to sell, the seller is not bound to part with the goods until he is paid for.

(vii) **Insolvency of seller:** In sale, upon insolvency of the seller, since the ownership has passed to the buyer, he (buyer) can recover identical goods from the Official Receiver or Assignee of the seller. In an 'agreement to sell', if the buyer has paid for the goods, he can only claim a rateable dividend from the seller's estate.

(viii) **Nature of rights :** The buyer acquires a *jus in rem* i.e., right against the whole world. On the other hand, an agreement to sell is a mere contract which secures to the buyer, only *jus in personam* i.e., right against a particular individual.

Difference between Sale and Bailment

	Sale	Bailment and Pledge
1.	*Ownership* in goods is transferred from the seller to the buyer.	There is transfer of possession and not of ownership from the bailor to the bailee.
2.	The buyer may *use the goods* in any way he likes.	A bailee can use the goods only according to the directions of the bailor.
3.	There is *no return of goods* from the buyer to the seller, unless there is breach.	The goods are necessarily returned after the specified time or accomplishment of the purpose.
4.	The *consideration* is the price in terms of money.	The consideration is an undertaking to return the goods after the accomplishment of purpose.
5.	The question of *any charges to be paid* by the seller to buyer or *vice versa* does not a rise	The bailor has to repay the charges which the bailee has incurred in keeping the goods safe.

GOODS – the subject-matter of Contract of Sale

The term '*subject matter*' means the things for which a contract of sale can be made. Only the goods can be the subject matter of contract of sale. The term '*goods*' means every kind of movable property and includes (a) stocks and shares, (b) growing crops, grass (c) the things attached to or forming part of the land which can be severed (i.e., separated) from the land. It may however, be noted that the things attached to or forming part of the land may be the subject-matter of the contract of sale only if it is agreed that they shall be removed from the earth, e.g., standing crops or trees may be sold if agreed to be removed from the earth.

However, the term *'goods' does not include money and actionable claims*. The term '*money*' means the legal tender (i.e., currency) and not old or rare coins. The terms *actionable claim*, means claim which can be enforced through the court of law e.g., debt due from one person to another is an actionable claim, and cannot be the subject-matter of contract of sale. The goods forming subject-matter of the contract of sale may be classified as under: (i) existing goods, (ii) future goods, (iii) contingent goods. Existing goods may be (a) specific goods (b) ascertained goods and (c) unascertained goods.

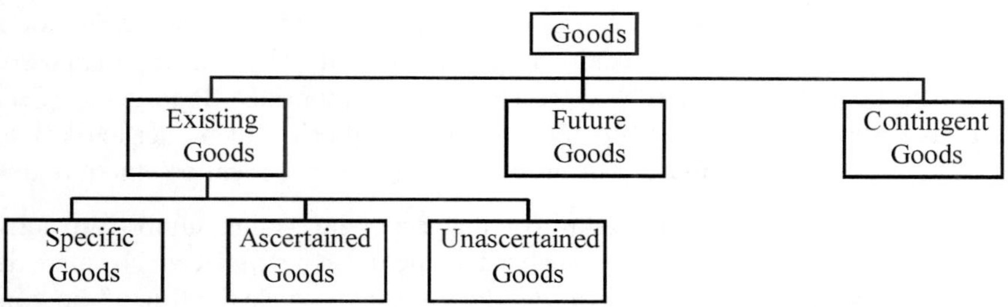

Difference between Future Goods and Contingent Goods

1. **Possession or Acquisition :** Future goods are goods which are not possessed by the seller at the time of making the contract of sale, but which will be manufactured, produced or acquired by the seller after the contract of sale is made. On the other hand, contingent goods are goods the acquisition of which by the seller depends upon an uncertain contingency which may or may not happen.

2. **Certainty :** Future goods are more certain about their coming into existence, whereas contingent goods are less certain about their coming into existence.

3. **Control over factors of Production :** In the case of future goods, the factors of production are within human control. But in the case of contingent goods, the factors of production are not within the control of human beings.

PRICE

Section 2 (10) of the Act defines '*price*' as *the money consideration for a sale of goods*. The price may be 'money' actually paid or promised to be paid depending on whether the agreement is for a cash or credit sale. If other consideration than money is to be given, it is not a sale. However, where goods are sold for a fixed sum and the price is paid partly in term of cash and partly in terms of valued goods, it is a sale.

Modes of fixing price: Sections 9 and 10 lay down how price is to be fixed at law. Accordingly, there are *five methods of fixing price*, which are given below: 1. Price expressly stated in the contract; 2. Price to be fixed in manner provided by the contract; 3. Price to be determined by the course of dealings between the parties; 4. Reasonable price; 5. Price fixation by third party e.g valuer. A valuer is a person who is appointed to value a thing because of his special skill, aptitude or knowledge.

Earnest money or deposit: Sometimes, it happens that the buyer pays part of the price in advance as a token of good faith or as a security for the due performance of the contract. If such amount is not given as a part payment of the purchase money, it is called *earnest money* or *deposit*. If the contract is duly performed, the earnest money is adjusted against the purchase price and only the balance of the price is required to be paid. But if the contract is not perfomed or cannot be performed through the fault of the buyer, the earnest money is forfeited by the seller. If the contract is not performed or cannot be performed through the fault of the seller, the seller must return the earnest money. Thus, *earnest money is security for the fulfillment prompt performance of the agreement*.

Stipulation as Time: Section 11 of the Act states that where a different intention appears from the terms of the contract, stipulation as to time of payment is not deemed to be of the essence of a contract of sale. Whether any stipulation as to time is of the essence of the contract or not depends on the terms of the contract. However, stipulation as to time, except as regards the time of payment, are usually of the essence of the contract.

DOCUMENT OF TITLE OF GOODS

Any document which is used in the ordinary course of business as proof of the possession or control of goods, or authorising or purporting to authorise, either by endorsement or by delivery, the possessor of the document to transfer or receive goods thereby represented is document of title to goods (Sec.2(4)). Thus a document of title is a proof of the ownership of the goods. It authorises its holder to receive goods mentioned therein or to further transfer such right to another person by proper endorsement or delivery.

A document of title to goods contains an undertaking on the part of the issuing authority to deliver the goods to the holder thereof unconditionally. Although such a document can be transferred by mere delivery or by endorsement, yet it is regarded as '*quasi negotiable instrument*' because the title of the transferee (even if bona fide) will not be superior to that of the transferor in the case of transfer of such document.

Bill of lading, dock-warrant, warehouse keeper's certificate, wharfinger's certificate, railway receipt, delivery order, etc., are popular examples of the documents of title to goods.

(a) **Bill of lading :** A bill of lading is a receipt given by the ship owner acknowledging the receipt of goods for carriage. It has been defined as a "receipt for goods shipped on board a ship, signed by the person who contracts to carry them, or his agent, and stating the terms on which the goods were delivered to and received by the ship".

(b) **Dock warrant :** A dock warrant is document which is issued by a dock owner. It contains the details of the goods; certifying that the goods are held on behalf of the person whose name is appeared in it or his assignee by endorsement. It authorises the person holding it to receive the possession of the goods.

(c) **Warehouse keeper's certificate :** Warehouse is a building in which goods are stored. Warehouse keeper's certificate is a document issued by the warehouse keeper stating that the goods specified in the document are in the warehouse or wharf. Warehousing (Development & Regulation) Bill 2007 gives legal validity to warehouse receipt and makes a fully negotiable instrument.

(d) **Railway receipt :** A railway receipt is a document which issued by the railway as the acknowledgement of the receipt of goods. It provides that on surrender of the receipt at the destinatin of the goods by the consignee the goods mentioned therein will be delivered to him.

(e) **Delivery Order :** A delivery order is an order which is given by the owner of goods directing a person who holds the goods on his behalf to deliver them to a person named therein.

Charter Party is an agreement by which a shipowner agrees to place an entire ship or a part of it, at the disposal of a merchant for the conveyance of goods to the agreed port of destination for a sum of money which the merchant undertakes to pay for the carriage. *It is not a document of title to goods.*

CONDITIONS AND WARRANTIES

A contract of sale of goods contains various terms of stipulations with reference to goods which are the subject matter of sale, e.g., regarding the nature and quality of the goods, the price and the mode of its payment, the delivery of goods and its time and place. But every such term is not likely to be of equal importance. Some of these terms are essential to the contract and their non-fulfillment may seem to frustrate the very basis of the contract. They may be so vital to the contract that their breach may seem to be a breach of the contract as a whole. Such terms are known as *Conditions of the contract of sale goods.* On the other hand, there may be certain terms which are not so vital to the contract that their breach may seem to be a breach of the contract as such. Such terms are known as *Warranties of the contract of sale.* Thus, conditions are more important terms (i.e., major terms) and warranties are less important terms. (i.e., minor terms) in the contract of sale.

Section 12(2) of the Sale of Goods Act, 1930 has defined a *condition* thus :

"*A condition is a stipulation essential to the main purpose of the contract, the breach of which gives rise to a right to treat the contract as repudiated*". From this definition, it is clear that a condition is a stipulation essential to the main purpose of the contract and the breach of which gives the aggrieved party a right to treat the contract as repudiated.

A *warranty* is defined by Section 12(3) of the Sale of Goods Act, 1930 thus:

"A warranty is a stipulation collateral to the main purpose of the contract, the breach of which gives rise to only claim for damages but not to a right to reject the goods and treat the contract as repudiated". From this definition, one can say that a warranty is a stipulation which is only collateral or incidental to the main purpose of the contract, and the breach of which gives the aggrieved party only a right to sue for damages, and not the right to treat the contract as repudiated.

Characteristic Features of a Conditions

1. A condition is a stipulation or term regarding goods forming part of the contract of sale, and it is not a mere expression of opinion or commendatory statement (i.e., statement of praise).

2. A condition is a stipulation in a contract of sale essential to the main purpose of the contract. It goes to the very root of the contract and forms the very foundation of it.

3. The breach of a condition gives the aggrieved party the right to treat the contract as repudiated, and also entitles him to claim damages.

4. If a condition in a contract of sale is broken, no doubt, the aggrieved party can treat the contract as repudiated and reject the goods. But he has also an alternative option. That is, he can treat the breach of condition as a breach of warranty and can claim only damages without rejecting the goods.

Characteristic Features of a Warranty

1. A warranty is a stipulation or term regarding goods forming part of the contract of sale, and is not a mere expression of opinion or statement of commendation or praise.

2. A warranty is a stipulation or term which is not essential to the main purpose of the contract and is only collateral (i.e., incidental, subsidiary or minor) to the main purpose of the contract. In short, it is only of secondary importance.

3. The breach of a warranty gives the aggrieved party only the right to sue for damages, and not the right to repudiate the contract. It may be noted that the measure of damages for breach of warranty is the estimated loss directly or naturally resulting in the ordinary course of events from the breach. *(Bostock & Co. Vs. Nicholson & Sons).*

Normally a statement is made after the contract does not become a warranty unless it is supported by fresh consideration (*Roscorla Vs. Thomas*). Nothing however prevents a buyer from *treating the breach of condition as a breach of warranty*, opting to claim damages instead of enforcing his rights to avoid the contract in toto.

Test to determine whether a stipulation in a contract of sale is a condition or a warranty : There is no hard and fast rule as to which stipulation is a condition, and which one is a warranty. Section 12(4) of the Sale of Goods Act, 1930 lays down to the same effect thus :

Whether a stipulation in a contract of sale is a condition or a warranty depends in each case on the construction of the contract. A stipulation may be a condition, though called a warranty in the contract. The court is not to be guided by the terminology of the parties, but has to look to the intention of the parties of referring to the terms of the contract, its construction and the surrounding circumstances to judge whether a stipulation is a condition or a warranty.

The most suitable test to distinguish between the terms '*condition*' and '*warranty*' is that, if the stipulation is such that its breach would be fatal to the rights of the aggrieved party (i.e., its breach would cause irreparable damage to the aggrieved party) and entitle him to repudiate the contract, it would be a condition, and if the stipulation is such that its breach would not be fatal to the rights of the aggrieved party and would not entitle him to repudiate the contract, it would be only a warranty.

Examples of Conditions and Warranties

1. A says to B, a horse dealer, "I want a horse which runs at a speed of 60 kilometres per hour". B points out a particular horse and says that it runs at 60 kilometres per hour. A buys the horse. Later, A finds that the horse runs only at a speed of 45 kilometres per hour. Here, there is a breach of condition, because the stipulation made by the seller regarding the horse is a condition forming the very basis of the contract.

2. A goes to B, a horse dealer, and says, "I want a good horse". B shows a particular horse and says, "It can run at a speed of 60 kilometres per hour. A buys the horse. Later, he finds that the horse can run at a speed of only 45 kilometres per hour. Here, there is only a breach of warranty, because the stipulation made by the seller is only a collateral term, constituting only a warranty.

3. X sells certain quantity of foodstuffs to Y. (In the case of sale of foodstuffs, there is an implied condition that the foodstuffs will be fit for human consumption, even if it is not expressly stated in the contract of sale). It is found that the foodstuffs are not fit for human consumption. In this case, there is breach of condition, and so,Y has the right to repudiate (i.e., set aside) the contract.

Cases of treating the breach of condition as breach of warranty: A buyer can treat the breach of a conditions as a breach of warranty. This option has been given to him under Section 13(1) of the Act. According to it, in the following cases, a breach of condition would be treated as a breach of warranty only.

Voluntary waiver : (i) Where the buyer elects to treat the breach of condition as a breach of warranty. For example, where he claims damages instead of repudiating the contract. (ii) Where the buyer waives the 'condition'. Waiver may be express or implied. Once the buyer has waived a condition, he is estopped from insisting on its fulfillment.

Acceptance of Goods : "Where, a contract of sale is not severable and the buyer has accepted the goods or part thereof, the buyer breach of any condition to be fulfilled by the seller can only be treated as a breach of warranty". In such case, the buyer would be deprived of his right of rejecting the goods and treating the contract as repudiated, unless there is a term in the contract, express or implied, to that effect.

Thus, where the buyer has accepted the goods and thereafter discovers that some condition was not fulfilled, he cannot reject the goods. He must keep them and can only recover damages for his loss.

Difference between Condition and Warranty

Condition	Warranty
1. **Relation to main purpose** It is an essential to the main purpose of the contract.	It is subsidiary to the main purpose of the of the contract.
2. **Rights of aggrieved party** Breach of condition gives the aggrieved party a right to repudiate the contract and to get damages.	Breach of warranty entiles the aggrieved party to claim damages only.
3. **Treating condition as warranty.** Under certain circumstances a breach of condition may be treated as a breach of warranty.	A warranty cannot become a condition.
4. **Legal effect of breach** Breach of condition will affect the legality of the contract.	Breach of warranty will not affect the legality of the contract.
5. **Discharge on breach** In case of breach of condition the aggrieved party is free to discharge his promise.	In case of breach of warranty the aggrieved party is not free to discharge his promise.

Express and Implied Conditions and Warranties

Conditions and Warranties may be either express or implied. They are express, when they are expressly provided by the parties. On the other hand, there are certain conditions and warranties which are implied by law.

Implied Conditions

Implied conditions are those conditions which the law incorporates into a contract of sale of goods unless the parties stipulate to the contrary. Section 14 to 17 lay down implied conditions which are discussed below:

1. **Conditions as the title {Section 14 (a)}**: In a contract of sale, there is an implied condition on the part of the seller that: (a) in the case of a sale, he has a right to sell the goods; (b) in the case of an agreement to sell, he will have a right to sell the goods at the time when the property is to pass.

2. **Sale by description (Section 15):** Where there is a contract for the sale of goods by description, there is an implied condition that the goods shall correspond with the description.

3. **Sale by sample (Section 17):** In the case of a contact for sale by sample, there is an implied condition:

   (a) that the bulk shall correspond with the sample in quality;

   (b) that the buyer shall have a reasonable opportunity of comparing the bulk with the sample;

   (c) that the goods shall be free from any defect, rendering them unmerchantable, which would not be apparent on reasonable examination of the sample. This applies only to *latent defect* i.e., those which are not discoverable on reasonable examination. But if the *defect is patent* i.e., apparent and visible, the seller is not responsible.

   Where the *contract is severable*, the buyer can retain those goods which corresponds with the sample and reject the other part. But where the *contract is not severable*, the buyer may either reject the whole or accept the whole and claim damages for the portion which is inferior to the given sample. But he cannot retain one part and reject the other part.

4. **Sale by Sample as well as by description (Section 15) :** If the sale is by sample as well as description, there is an implied condition that the bulk of the goods shall correspond both with the sample and with the description.

5. **Condition as to fitness or quality (Section 15)**

   Priest Vs. Last (1903) : P, a draper, purchased a hot water bottle from a retail chemist. P asked the chemist whether it will withstand boiling water. Chemist told him that the bottle was meant to hold hot water. The bottle burst when water poured into it and injured his wife. It was held that the chemist shall be liable to pay damages to P, as he knew that the bottle was purchased for the purpose of being used as a hot water bottle.

   Where the article can be used for only one particular purpose, the buyer need not tell the seller the purpose, for which he requires the goods. But where the article can be used for a number of purposes, the buyer should tell the purpose for which he requires the goods, if he wants to make the seller responsible

   Sale under patent or trade name : In the case of a contract for the sale implied condition as to its fitness for any particular purpose. It is so because in such a case, the buyer is not relying on the skill and judgement of the seller but relies on the good reputation of the trade name.

6. **Condition as to merchantability – (Section 16(2)) :** This condition is implied only where the sale is by description. Where goods are bought by description from a seller be of a merchantable quality i.e., the goods are of merchantable quality if: (i) they are reasonably saleable under the description by which they are known in the market; (ii) they are purchased for personal use, they must be reasonably fit for the purpose for which they are generally used.

Morelli Vs. Fitch Gibbons (1928) : Morelli asked for a bottle of Stone's ginger wine in a restaurant. When he was trying to open the cork, the bottle broke and he was injured. Held, since the bottle was unmerchantable, Morelli was entitled to recover damages.

In ***Jackson Vs. Rotax Motor and Cycle Co. (1910)*** where the first instalment of supply of goods was accepted and the further supplies of horns were found dented and scratched owing to defective packing, it was held, that by acceptance of the first instalment, the buyer was not precluded from rejecting the further supplies on the ground that they were unmerchantable eventhough they could be set right at a triffling cost.

7. **Condition as to wholesomes :** In the case of eatables and provisions, in addition to the condition of the merchantable quality, there is an added obligation on the part of the seller that the goods shall be wholesome.

   Chaproniere Vs. Mason (1905) : C bought a bread from a store. It contained a stone which broke one of C's teeth. Held, C could recover damages.

   Frost Vs. Aylsbury Dairy Company Ltd. (1905) : F purchased milk from A, a dairy owner. The milk was contaminated with germs of typhoid fever. F's wife on taking the milk, got infection and died. Held, F was entitled to get damages.

8. **Condition implied by custom or usage of trade – Section 16 (3) :** An implied warranty or condition as to quality or fitness a particular purpose may be annexed by custom or usage of trade. It is clear that a usage would override the law provided it is reasonable and just. If usage is given effects, it necessarily changes the rule of law applicable to the case. The usage is relied on to show the intention of the parties. If a well recognised usage exists, they may properly take it for granted instead of expressing their intention. Usage can be admitted to explain the meaning of the language used by the parties but it is not allowed to contradict it, because an agreement of the parties always overrides usage.

Implied Warranties

Unless a contrary intention is expressed in a contract, the following are the warranties which are implied in every contract of the sale goods.

1. **Quiet possession – {Section 14(b)}:** In a contract of sale, unless the circumstances of the contract are such as to show different intention, there is implied warranty that the buyer shall have and enjoy quiet possession of the goods.
2. **Freedom from encumbrance – {Section 14(c)} :** In contract of sale, there is implied warranty that the goods shall be free from any charge or encumbrance, in favour of any third party not declared or not known on the part of the buyer before or at the time when the contract was made or he has been given notice of them.
3. **Royality of fitness by usage of trade :**
4. **Disclosure of dangerous nature of goods :** There is another implied warranty on the part of the seller, that in case the goods sold are inherently dangerous or they are likey to be dangerous to the buyer, the seller must warn the buyer about the probable danger. If there is a breach of his warranty, the seller will be liable in damages.

Exclusion of implied conditions and warranties (Section 62) : Implied conditions and warranties in a contract of sale may be negatived or varied by (i) express agreement between the paties; (ii) the course of dealings between the parties; (iii) the custom or usage of trade, if usage is such as to bind both the parties to the contract.

DOCTRINE OF *CAVEAT EMPTOR*

The term '*caveat emptor*' is Latin word which means '*let the buyer beware*' i.e., a buyer purchases the goods at his own risk provided the seller is acting within the law. As a matter of fact, it is the buyer's duty to select goods of his requirement. The seller is not bound to supply the goods which shall be fit for any particular quality. This rule is known as the '*doctrine of caveat emptor*'. It is contained in the opening words of Section 16 of the Sale of Goods Act, which reads under:

Subject to the provisions of this Act and any other law for the time being in force, there is no implied warranty or conditions as the quality or fitness for any particular purpose of goods supplied under a contract of sale.

In other words, it is not the seller's duty to give to the buyer the goods which are suitable for a particular purpose of the buyer. The buyer must take care of his own purpose while purchasing the goods i.e., *it is his duty to purchase the goods of his requirement.* As such, the buyer must take care while purchasing the goods. If the buyer makes a wrong choice of the goods, he cannot blame the seller if the goods turn out to be defective or do not serve his purpose. The seller is not supposed to know the particular purpose for which the buyer is purchasing the goods.

Exceptions to the Doctrine of *Caveat Emptor* (Section 16)

The doctrine of caveat emptor is subject to the following exceptions showing in fig.

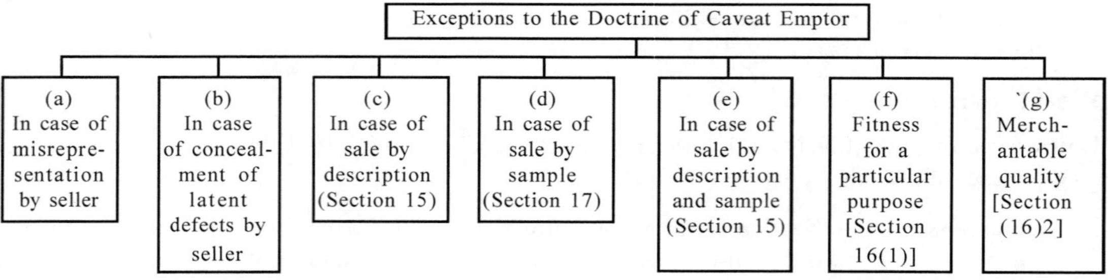

1. **Conditions as to quality of fitness for buyer's purpose:** Ordinarily, there is no implied condition that the goods shall be fit for the particulat purpose of the buyer. But in certain circumstances, if the buyer makes his purpose clear to seller and buys the goods relying upon his skill and judgement, then there is an implied condition that the goods shall be fit for the buyer's specific purpose. In such cases, the doctrine of caveat emptor does not apply.

2. **Condition as to merchantability:** Sometimes, the goods are sold by description. In such cases, there is an implied condition that the goods shall be of merchantable quantity. Thus, in case of sale by description the seller is bound to deliver the goods of merchantable quantity and in such cases, the doctrine of caveat emptor does not apply.

3. **Conditions as to wholesomeness :** It is a part of the condition as to merchantability. This condition is applicable in cases of eatables i.e., foodstuffs and other goods which are used for human consumption. In such cases, in addition to the principal condition as to merchantability, another implied condition is that the goods must be wholesome i.e., sound, pure and fit for consumption at the time of sale.

4. **Conditions implied by customs :** The implied conditions as to '*fitness*' and '*merchantability*' are applicable only if certain requirements are fulfilled. However, the implied condition as quality or fitness for a particular purpose may be attached by the *custom or usage of trade* {section 16 (3)}. This is so because the parties enter into an agreement with reference to those known usages. A custom may provide that a particular defect will amount to unfitness and the buyer can reject the goods. But the customs must not be unreasonable and also not be inconsistent with the express terms of the contract.

5. **Sale under a patent or trade name :** In the case of a contract for the sale of a specified article under its patent or other trade name, there is no implied condition that the goods shall be reasonably fit for any particular purpose{(provsio to Sec. 16(1)}.

6. **Consent obtained by fraud:** Where the consent of the buyer, in a contract of sale, is obtained by the seller by fraud or where the seller knowingly conceals a defect which could not be discovered on a reasonable examination i.e., where there is latent defect in the goods, the doctrine of caveat emptor does not hold good.

REVIEW QUESTIONS

1. Define the term 'contract of sale'.
2. State the essentials and legal rules for a valid contract of sale.
3. Explain the difference between a contract of sale and an agreement to sell.
4. When does an agreement to sell ripen into sale?
5. Explain (a) Goods (b) Price (c) Document of title to goods.
6. How is contract of sale made? State briefly the necessary formalities of such a contract with examples.
7. Define the term 'condition'. Explain the implied conditions in a contract of sale as provided in the Sale of Goods Act, 1930.
8. Define the term 'warranty '. Explain and illustrate the implied warranties in a contract of sale as provided in the Sale of Goods Act, 1930.
9. Explain the rule of 'caveat emptor'. Discuss the cases in which the rule of caveat emptor does not apply.
10. Distinguish between (a) condition and warranty (b) Sale and pledge (c) Sale and bailment (d) Sale and Hire purchase (e) Future goods and contingent goods.

❒ ❒ ❒

13

Chapter

PERFORMANCE OF CONTRACT OF SALE

The term '*performance of the contract of sale*' may be defined as the performance of the respective duties of the seller and the buyer as per the terms of the contract. Thus, the performance of the contract of sale comprises the two parts, namely: (i) Seller's duty to deliver the goods , (ii) Buyer's duty to accept the goods and pay the price.

DELIVERY OF GOODS

Definition of Delivery

'*Delivery*' means voluntary transfer of possession from one person to another {Sec.2(2)}.

"Delivery of goods sold may be made by doing anything which the parties agree shall be treated as delivery or which has the effect of putting the goods in the possession of the buyer or any person authorised to hold them on his behalf" (Sec.33).

Delivery of goods may be *actual*, *symbolic*, *constructive*. Where the goods are handed over by the seller to the buyer or his duly authorised agent, the delivery is actual. Where goods are bulky and incapable of actual delivery, e.g., hay stack in a meadow, the delivery may be symbolic. Handing over of the key of warehouse to the buyer is symbolic delivery of the goods to the buyer and is as effective as actual delivery, even though there is no change in the possession of the goods. When a third person (e.g., bailee), who is in possession of the goods of the seller at the time of the sale, acknowledges to the buyer that he holds the goods on his behalf, there place a delivery by attornment or constructive delivery {Section .36(3)}.

RULES AS TO DELIVERY OF GOODS

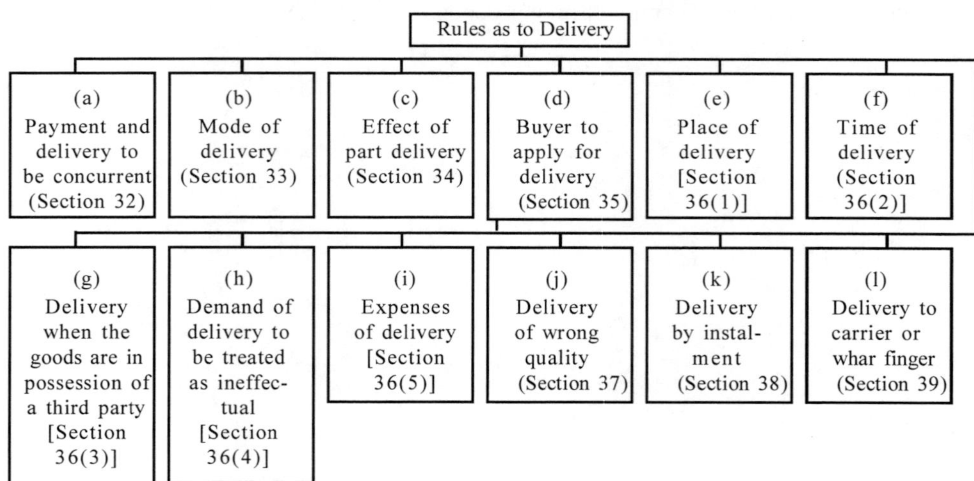

1. **Mode of delivery (Section 33) :** Delivery should have the effect of putting the goods in the possession of the buyer or his duly authorised agent. Delivery of goods, as already observed, may be actual, constructive, or symbolic.

2. **Delivery and payment—Concurrent conditions:** Delivery of the goods and payment of the price must be according to the terms of the contract. Unless otherwise agreed, delivery of the goods and payment of the price are concurrent conditions (sec. 32).

3. **Effect of part delivery:** A delivery of part of the goods in process of the delivery of the whole, has the same effect, for the purpose of passing the property in such goods, as a delivery of the whole. But a delivery of the goods, with an intention of severing it from the whole, does not operates as delivery of the remainder (Sec.34).

4. **Buyer to apply for delivery:** Apart from any express contract, the seller of goods is not bound to deliver them until the buyer applies for delivery (Sec.35). Where the goods are subsequently acquired by the seller, he should intimate this to the buyer and the buyer should then apply for delivery.

5. **Place of delivery:** Where the place at which delivery of the goods is to take place is specified in the contract, the goods must be delivered at that place during business hours on a working day. Where there is no specific agreement as to place, the goods sold are to be delivered at the place at which they are at the time of sale. As regards the goods agreed to be sold, they are to be delivered at the place at which they are at the time of agreement of sell, or if not, then in existence, at the place at which they are manufactured or produced [Sec.36(1)].

6. **Time of delivery:** Where under the contract of sale, the seller is bound to send the goods to the buyer, but no time for sending them is fixed, the seller, is bound to send them within a reasonable time [Sec. 36 (2)].

7. **Demand of delivery to be treated ineffectual :** Demand or tender of delivery may be treated as ineffectual unless made at a reasonable hour. Whar is a reasonable hour is a question of fact [Section 36 (4)].

8. **Goods in possession of a third party:** When at the time of sale goods are with a third party, there is no delivery by the seller to the buyer until such third party acknolwedges to the buyer that he holds them on his behalf. But where the goods have been sold by the issue or transfer of any document of title to goods, e.g., railway receipt or bill of lading, such third party's consent is not required [Sec. 36 (3)].

9. **Cost of delivery :** Unless otherwise agreed, all expenses of and incidental to the *making of delivery* are borne by the seller, and all expenses of and incidental to *obtaining of delivery* are borne by the buyer [Sec.36 (5)].

10. **Delivery of wrong quantity (Section 37) :** The delivery of quantity of goods contracted for should be stricly according to the terms of the contract. A wrong delivery entitles the buyer to reject the goods. The three different contingencies which may arise in case of a wrong delivery i.e., delivery of a wrong quantity by : (i) *Shortages*, (ii) *Excess delivery* and (iii) *Mixed delivery*.

    (a) **Delivery of goods less than contracted for:** Where the seller delivers to the buyer a quantity of goods less than he contracted to sell, the buyer may reject the goods. If the goods have been rejected for short delivery, the seller can make,within the time limit, another delivery in accordance with their terms of the contract.

    (b) **Delivery of goods in excess of the quantity contracted for :** Where the seller delivers to the buyer a quantity of goods larger than the contrat signed to sell, the buyer may (i) accept the whole; or (ii) reject the whole; or (iii)accept the quantity he ordered and reject the rest. If the buyer accepts the whole of the goods so delivered, he must pay for them at the contract rate [Sec.37(2)].

(c) **Delivery of goods contracted for mixed with other goods:** Where the seller delivers to the buyer the goods he contracted to sell mixed with goods of a different description, the buyer may accept the goods which are in accordance with the contract and reject the rest, or may reject the whole consignment [Sec.37(3)].

11. **Instalment deliveries [Section 38]:** Unless otherwise agreed, the seller is not entiled to deliver the goods by instalments and if he does so, the buyer is not bound to accept the goods [Sec.38 (1)]. The parties may, however, agree that the goods are to be or may be delivered by instalments.

12. **Delivery to carrier or wharfinger [Section 39]:** Where, in pursuance of a contract of sale, goods are delivered to a carrier for the purpose of transmission to the buyer or to a wharfinger for safe custody, delivery of goods to them is *prima facie* deemed to be a delivery of the goods to the buyer [Sec.39(1)].

RULES REGARDING DELIVERY OF GOODS

1. ***Mode of delivery (Sec. 33) :*** Delivery should have the effect of putting the goods, in the possession of the buyer or his duly authorised agent. Delivery of goods, as already observed, may be either actual, or constructive, or symbolic.

2. ***Delivery and Payment-concurrent conditions :*** Delivery of the goods and payment of the price must be according to the terms of the contract. Unless otherwise agreed, delivery of the goods and payment of the price are concurrent conditions, that is to say, the seller shall be ready and willing to give possession of the goods to the buyer in exchange for the price and the buyer shall be ready and willing to pay the price in exchange for possession of the goods (Sec. 32).

3. ***Effect of part delivery :*** A delivery of part of the goods in process of the delivery of the whole, has the same effect, for the purpose of passing the property in such goods, as a delivery of the whole. But a delivery of the goods, with an intention of severing it from the whole, does not operate as delivery of the remainder (Sec. 34).

Illustrations

(a) 'S' directed the wharfinger to deliver his goods lying at the wharf to 'B' to whom these goods had been sold. 'B' weighted the goods and took way a part of them. Held, the delivery of a part of the goods had the same effect as a delivery of the whole *[Hammond Vs Anderson, (1803) RR 763]*.

(b) 'S' sold five bales of certain goods to 'B'. 'B' received one bale, said for it and refused to accept the other four. Held this amounted to cart delivery *[Mitchell reid Co. Vs Baldev Dass, (1888) 15 Cal. 1]*

4. ***Buyer to apply for delivery :*** Apart from any express contract, the seller of goods is not bound to deliver them until the buyer applies for delivery (Sec. 35). Where the goods are subsequently acquired by the seller, he should intimate this to the buyer and the buyer should then apply for delivery. Unless otherwise agreed, the buyer has no cause of action against the seller if he does not apply for delivery.

5. ***Place of delivery :*** Where the place at which delivery of the goods is to take place is specified in the contract, the goods must be delivered at that place during business hours on a working day. Where there is no specific agreement as to place, the goods sold are to be delivered at the place at which they are at the time of sale. As regards the goods agreed to be sold, they are to be delivered at the place at which they are at the time of agreement. to sell, or, if not then in existence, at the place a which they are manufactured or produced Sec. 36 (1).

6. ***Time of delivery :*** Where under the contract of sale the seller is bound to send the goods to the buyer, but not time for sending them is fixed, the seller, is bound to send them within a reasonable time Sec. 36(2). But where the contract uses words like "directly", "without loss of time", or "forthwith", quick and immediate delivery is contemplated. Demand or tender of delivery should be made at reasonable hour. What is a reasonable hour is a question of fact [Section 36(4)].

7. ***Goods in possession of a third party :*** When at the time of sale goods are with a third party, there is no delivery by the seller to the buyer until such third party acknowledge to the buyer that the holds them on his behalf. But where the goods have been sold by the issue or transfer of any document of title to goods, e.g., railway receipt or bill of lading, such third party's consent is not required [Sec. 36(3)].

8. ***Cost of delivery :*** Unless otherwise agreed, all expenses of and incidental to making of delivery are borne by the seller, but all expenses of and incidental to obtaining of delivery are borne by the buyer [Sec. 36(5)].

9. ***Delivery of wrong quantity (Sec. 37) :*** The delivery of quantity of goods contracted for should be strictly according to the terms of the contract. A defective delivery entails the buyer to reject the goods. The three different contingencies which may arise in case of a defective delivery, i.e., delivery of a wrong quantity, are :

   (a) *Delivery of goods less than contracted for :* Where the seller delivers to the buyer a quantity of goods less that he contracted to sell, the buyer may reject the goods. If he accepts them, he shall pay for them at the contract rate [Sec. 37(1)]

Illustrations

'A' sells to 'B' 2,000 gross of "200 yards reels" of sewing cotton. After taking delivery 'B' finds that the length of the cotton per reel is less than 200 yards, the average being shortage of about 6 per cent. 'B' may reject the goods. If he waives the right of rejection, he is liable to pay the price of the goods at the contract rate *[Beck etc. Vs Syzmanoski, (1924) A.C. 43]*.

If the goods have been rejected for short delivery, the seller can make, within the time limit, another delivery in accordance with the terms of the contract.

   (b) *Delivery of goods in excess of the quantity contracted for :* Where the seller delivers to the buyer a quantity of goods larger than the contracted to sell, the buyer may (i) accept the whole ; or (ii) reject the whole ; or (iii) accept the quantity he ordered and reject the rest. If the buyer accepts the whole of the goods so delivered, he must pay for them at the contract rate [Sec. 37(2)].

Illustrations

(a) A places an order with B to supply two dozen bottles of syrup. B sends five dozen. A is entitled to reject the whole, or he may accept two dozen and reject the rest. If he accepts all the five dozen, he must pay for them at the contract rate.

(b) Where the contract is for the sale of "liquor" so much quantity or so much quantity "more or less", the seller is allowed a reasonable margin. If this margin exceeds, the buyer cannot be compelled to accept the goods if, however, the deficiency or excess is so small as to be negliable, the Court applies the maxim *de minimis mon curatlex* (Law does not take account of trifles).

The right to reject the goods is not equivalent to the right to cancel the contract. If the buyer rejects the goods (either because they are less than or in excess of the quantity contracted for), the seller has a right to tender again the contract quantity and the buyer is bound to accept the same *[Vilas Udyog Ltd. Vs Prag Vanaspati Products, A.I.R. (1975) Guj. 112]*.

(c) *Delivery of goods contracted for mixed with other goods :* Where the seller delivers to the buyer the goods he contracted to sell mixed with goods of a different description, the buyer may accept the goods which are in accordance with the contract and reject the rest, or may reject the whole [Sec. 37(3)].

Illustrations

'A' contracts with 'B' to buy 100 tons of cane sugar. 'A' delivers to 'B' 75 tons of cane sugar and 25 tons of beet sugar. 'A' may either accept 75 tons of cane sugar which in accordance with the contract, and reject 25 tons of beet sugar which is of a different description, or reject the whole sugar.

The provisions of Sec. 37 are subject to any of trade, special agreement, or course of dealing between the parties (Sec. 37(4)).

10. ***Instalment deliveries (Sec. 38) :*** Unless otherwise agreed the seller is not entitled to deliver the goods by instalment and if he does so, the buyer is not bound to accept the goods (Sec. 38(1)). The parties may, however, agree that the goods are to be or may be delivered by instalments.

Illustrations

'X' bought from 'Y' 25 tons of pepper for October-November shipment. 'Y' shipped 20 tons in November and 5 in December. Held, the case was governed by Sec. 38 under which the buyer of goods is not bound to accept delivery thereof by instalments, unless otherwise agreed 'X' could, therefor, reject the entire lot *[Renter v. Sale, (1879) 48 L.J. 492]*.

When there is a contract for the sale of goods to be delivered by instalments, the delivery should be installments as stipulated in the contract. Such a contract may be express or may be inferred from the circumstances of the case, or from the nature of the contract. In a contract for delivery by instalments which are to be separately paid for, the seller may sometimes make no delivery or make defective delivery in respect of one or more instalments, or the buyer may neglect or refuse to take delivery of, or pay for, one or more installments. In such a case, it is a question in each case depending on the terms of the contract and the circumstances of the case, whether the breach giving rise to a claim for compensation [Sec. 38(2)].

11. ***Delivery to a carrier or Wharfinger (Sec. 39) :*** Where, in pursuance of a contract of sale, goods are delivered to a carrier for the purpose of transmission to the buyer or to a wharfinger for safe custody, delivery of goods to them is *prima facie* deemed to be a delivery of the goods to the buyer (Sec. 39(1)). In such a case, the seller must enter into a reasonable contract with the carrier or wharfinger on behalf of the buyer for the safe transmission or custody of the goods, otherwise, if the goods are destroyed, the buyer may decline to treat the delivery to the carrier or wharfinger as a delivery to himself, or may hold the seller responsible in damages [Sec. 39(2)]. Unless otherwise agreed, where goods are sent by the seller to the buyer by a route involving sea transit, the seller must inform the buyer in time to get the goods insured otherwise the goods will be at the seller's risk during such sea transit [Sec. 39(3)].

TRANSFER OF PROPERTY, POSSESSION AND RISK

There are three stages in the performance of a contract of sale of goods by seller, viz., (a) the transfer of property in the goods, (b) the transfer of possession of the goods (i.e., delivery), and (c) the passing of the risk.

Significance of Transfer of Ownership/Property

It is important to know the precise moment of time at which the property in goods passes from the seller to the buyer for the following reasons:

1. **Risk follows ownership:** Unless otherwise agreed, risk follows ownership whether delivery has been made or not and whether price has been paid or not. Thus the risk of loss as a rule lies on the owner. But if delivery has been delayed through the fault of either the buyer or the seller, the goods are at the risk of the party at fault. Thus '*risk*' and '*property*' go together.

2. **Owner to take action against third parties:** When the goods are in any way damaged or destroyed by the action of third parties, it is only the owner of the goods who can take action against them.

3. **Insolvency of the seller or the buyer:** In the event of insolvency of either the seller or the buyer, the question whether the Official Receiver or Assignee can take over the goods or not depends on whether the property in the goods has passed from the seller to the buyer.

4. **Seller's right to suit for price:** The seller can sue for the price, unless otherwise agreed only if the goods have become the property of the buyer.

Passing of Property

1. **Goods must be ascertained :** Where there is a contract for the sale of unascertained goods, no . property in the goods is transferred to the buyer unless and until the goods are ascertained.

2. **Intention of the parties:** Where there is a contract for the sale of specific or ascertained goods, the property in them passes to the buyer at the time parties intend it to pass [Sec. 19(1)]. For the purpose of ascertaining the intention of the parties, regard shall be had to the terms of the contract, the conduct of the parties and the circumstances of the cases [Sec.19(2)].

Where the intention of the parties as to the time when the property in the goods is to pass to the buyer cannot be ascertained from the contract, the rules contained in Secs. 20 to 24 apply [See. 19(3)]. These rules are as follows:

Specific Goods (Sections 20 to 22)

The rules relating to transfer of property in specific goods are as follows:

1. **Passing of property at the time of contract :** When there is an unconditional contract for the sale of specific goods in a deliverable state, the property in the goods passes to the buyer when the contract is made. Deliverable state means such a state that the buyer woud under the contract be bound to take delivery of them.
2. **Passing of property delayed beyond the date of contract:**

   (i) **Goods not in a deliverable state:** Where there is a contract for the sale of specific goods not in a deliverable state i.e., the seller has to do something to the goods to put them into a deliverable state, the property does not pass until such thing is done and the buyer has notice of it (Sec. 21).

   (ii) **When the price of goods is to be ascertained by weighing, etc. :** Where there is a contract for the sale of specific goods in a deliverable state, but the seller is bound to weigh, measure, test or do some other act or thing with reference to the goods for the purpose of ascertaining the price. The property does not pass until such act or thing is done and the buyer has notice thereof (Sec.22).

Unascertained goods (Sections 23) : Where there is contract for the sale of unascertained goods, the property in the goods does not pass to the buyer until goods are ascertained (Sec. 18). Until goods are ascertained there is merely an agreement to sell.

Delivery to Carrier

A seller is deemed to have unconditionally appropriated the goods to the contract where he delivers them to buyer or to a carrier or other bailee (whether named by the buyer or not) for the purpose of transmission to the buyer, and does not reserve the right of disposal [Sec.23(2)}: The delivery to the carrier may be absolutely for the buyer or seller.

1. **Absolutely for the buyer:** Where the bill of lading or railway receipt is made out in the name of the buyer and is sent to him, the presumption is that no right of disposal has been reserved by the seller in respect of those goods. The ownership in such a case passes from the seller to the buyer.
2. **Absolutely for the seller:** Where the bill of lading or railway receipt is taken in the seller's or his agent's name and is sent to the agent of the seller to be delivered to the buyer on the fulfilment of certain conditions, the seller is deemed to have reserved the right of disposal of the goods. In such a case the ownership does not pass to the buyer until the necessary conditions are fulfilled and the documents of title are delivered to the buyer.

Goods sent on Approval or 'on Sale or Return' (Section 24)

Where goods are delivered to the buyer on approval or 'on sale or return' or other similar term, the property there in passes to the buyer :

(i) When he signifies his approval or acceptance to the seller;

(ii) When he does any other act adopting the transaction. If the seller delivers the goods to the buyer 'on sale or return' on the terms that the goods were to remain his property until settled or paid for, the property would not pass to the buyer until these terms are complied with.

(iii) If he does not signify his approval or acceptance to the seller but retain the goods without giving notice of rejection, beyond the time fixed for the return of the goods, or if no time has been fixed, beyond a reasonable time (Sec. 24). The question as to what is a 'reasonable time' is a question of fact.

TRANSFER OF TITLE BY NON-OWNERS

The general rules as to transfer of title is that only the owner of goods can transfer a good title. The rule is expressed by the maxim " *Nemo dat quod non habet*", which means that "*no one can give what he himself has not*".

A. Exceptions Under the Sale of Goods Act, 1930

1. **Estoppel:** Section 27 provides that by his conduct the owner of the goods may be precluded from denying the seller's authority to sell.

   Illustration: Where A, who had unlawfully acquired the goods of B, sells them to C in the presence of B. Here B remains silent, then he will be precluded from denying A's authority to sell the said goods.

2. **Sale by a Mercantile Agent (Section 27) :** As a rule, a mercantile agent having an authority to sell goods conveys a good title to the buyer provided the following conditions are fulfilled:

(a) The sale must be made by a mercantile agent.

(b) He must be in possession of the goods or a document of title to goods.

(c) He must be in possession of the goods or a document of title to the goods with the consent of the owner.

(d) He must be acting in the ordinary course of business of a mercantile agent, and

(e) The buyer must have acted in good faith and had not at the time of the contract of sale notice that the seller had no authority to sell.

3. **Sale by one of several joint owners (Section 28):** Section 28 of the Sale of Goods Act recognises yet another exception i.e., sale by one of several joint owners with the permission of the other co-owners.

4. **Sale by a person in possession of goods under a voidable contract (Section 29):** When the seller of goods has obtained their possession under a voidable contract, but the contract has not been rescinded at the time of the sale, the buyer acquires a good title to the goods, provided he buys them in good without notice of the seller's defect of title.

5. **Sale by seller in possession after sale [Section 30(1)]:** Where a seller, having sold goods, continues to be possession are of the goods or of the documents of title to the goods and sells them either himself or through a mercantile agent to a person who buys them in good faith and without notice of the previous sale, the buyer gets a good title. It is important to note, however, that the possession of the seller must be as seller and not as hirer or bailee.

6. **Sale by an unpaid seller [Section 54 (3)] :** Where an unpaid seller who had exercised his right of lien or stoppage in transit resells the goods, the buyer acquires a good title to the goods as against the original buyer.

B. Exceptions as provided in Other Laws

7. Sale by a *Finder of lost goods* (Sec.71 of the Indian Contract Act).
8. Sale by a *Pawanee* pledge in case where pawnor pledger makes default in payment.
9. Sale by a *Official Assignee* or *Official Receiver* in case of insolvency of an individual.
10. Sale by any liquidator of a company.
11. *Execution Sales*: Under Order 21 of Civil Procedure Code, *Officers of Court* can sell goods and convey the title to the buyer.
12. Sale by *Executors* and *Administrators*
13. *Purchase in Market Overt* : Market-Overt means "open public and legally constituted market". Where goods are sold in market overt, the buyer acquires good title to them though the seller may not be having a good title, the goods are sold in accordance with the custom of the market, and the buyer acts in good faith and has no reason to believe that the ownership of the seller to goods was whatsoever defective or non-existent.
14. Under the Negotiable Instruments Act, a *holder in due course* gets a better title than what his endorser had.

RIGHTS OF THE BUYER

1. ***Right to have delivery (Sec. 37) :*** The first right of the buyer is to have delivery of hte goods as per the term of the contract.

2. ***Right to reject the goods*** for defective delivery short/excess supply [Sec. 37(1)(2)].

3. ***Right to repudiate (Sec. 38(1)) :*** The buyer of goods is not bound to accept delivery of the goods in installments and can repudiate the contract, unless otherwise agreed.

4. ***Right to notice of insurance :*** [Sec. 39(3)]

5. ***Right to examine (Sec. 41) :*** The buyer has a right to examine the goods before he accepts them and the seller must afford a reasonable opportunity to the buyer for examining the goods. This is necessary to ascertain whether the goods are in conformity with the contract.

6. ***Right to sue of breach of contract :***

   (a) Suit for Damages (Sec. 57) : Where the seller wrongfully neglects or refuses to deliver the goods to the buyer, he may sue the seller for damages for not delivering the goods.

   (b) *Suit for Price :* If the buyer has paid the price and the goods are not delivered, he can recover the amount paid.

   (c) *Right to a suit for specific performance : (Sec. 58) :* The buyer may sue the seller for specific performance of the contract to sell. In a suit for breach of contract to deliver specific or ascertained goods, the Court may, if it thinks fit, on the application of the plaintiff, direct that the contract shall be performed specially without giving the defendant the option of retaining the goods on payment of damages.

   (d) *Repudiating of contract before due date (Sec. 60) :* Where the seller repudiates the contract before the date of delivery, the buyer may either wait will date of delivery, or he may treat the contract as rescinded and sue for damages for the breach. This is called the *rule of anticipatory breach of contract.*

   (e) *Suit for interest (Sec. 61(2)(b)). :* Where there is breach of contract on the part of the seller and consequentially the price has to be refunded to the buyer, the buyer has a right to claim interest on the amount of the price.

   (f) *Suit for breach of warranty (Sec. 59) :* Where there is a breach of warranty by the seller, or where the buyer elects or is compelled to treat any branch of condition on the part of the seller as a branch of warranty, the buyer is not only by reason of such breach of warranty entitled to reject the goods but he may, (a) set up against the seller the breach of warranty in diminution or extinction of the price l or (b) sue the seller for damages for breach of warranty (Sec. 59(1)).

The fact that a buyer has set up a breach of warranty in diminution or extinction of the price does not prevent him from suing for the same breach of warranty if he has suffered further damage (Sec. 59(2)). The measure of damages for breach of warranty is the estimated loss arising directly and naturally from the breach, which is *prima facie* the difference between the value of the goods as delivered and the value they would have had if the goods were according to the warranty.

DUTIES OF THE BUYER

1. ***To take delivery of and pay for the goods (Sec. 31) :*** It is the duty of the buyer that he must accept the goods and pay for them in accordance with the terms of hte contract of sale.

Delivery and payment - concurrent conditions : Delivery of the goods and payment of the price must be according to the terms of the contract. Unless otherwise agreed, delivery of the goods and payment of the price are concurrent conditions, that is to say, the seller shall be ready and willing to give possession of the goods to the buyer in exchange for the price and the buyer shall be ready to accept the same.

2. ***To apply for delivery (Sec. 35) :*** Unless otherwise agreed, the seller of goods is not bound to deliver them until the buyer applies for delivery.

3. ***To demand delivery at a reasonable hour [Sec. 36(41)].***

4. ***To take risk of deterioration (Sec. 40) :*** The seller of goods may, in some cases, agree to deliver them at his own risk at a place other than that where the goods are when sold. But the buyer shall, unless otherwise agreed, take the risk of deterioration of the goods necessarily incident to the course of transit.

5. ***Liability of buyer for neglecting to refusing delivery of goods (Sec. 44) :*** When the seller is ready and willing to deliver the goods and requests the buyer to take delivery, and the buyer does not, within a reasonable time after such request take delivery of the goods, he is liable to the seller for any loss occasioned by his neglect or refusal to take delivery and also for reasonable charge for the care and custody of the goods.

6. ***Duty to accept instalment delivery and pay for it. [Section 38(2)].***

7. ***Duty to intimate the seller where he reject the goods [Section 43.]***

8. ***Duty to pay damages for non-acceptance (Sec. 56) :*** Where the buyer wrongfully neglects or refuses to accept and pay for the goods, he will have to compensate the seller, in a suit by him, for damages form on-acceptance.

9. *Delivery to carrier or wharfinger :* Where the seller is to send the goods to the buyer, delivery of the goods to a carrier for transmission to the buyer or the delivery to a wharfinger for safe custody is *prima facie* delivery to the buyer. The seller must, however, make such contract with the carrier or wharfinger as may be reasonable; otherwise the buyer may decline to treat such delivery as delivery to himself or may hold the seller responsible for damages in case of loss or damages. In case the goods are sent by a route involving sea transit, the seller shall give such notice to the buyer as may enable the buyer to insure them. (Sec. 39).

10. *Buyer's right of examining the goods :* The buyer has a right to examine the goods and cannot be deemed to have accepted the goods delivered, unless he has a reasonable opportunity of examining them. Similarly when the seller tenders delivery of goods, the seller must afford the buyer a reasonable opportunity of examining the goods. (Sec. 41).

11. *Acceptance of goods delivered :* The buyer is deemed to have accepted the goods when he intimates to the seller that he has accepted them, or he does any act in relation to the goods which is inconsistent with the ownership of the seller e.g., when the buyer sells them to another person or when the buyer does not intimate to the seller within a reasonable time that he has rejected them. When the buyer rejects the goods, it is enough that he intimates to the seller that he rejects them and the buyer need not return the goods (Sec. 42-43).

12. *Liability of buyer for refusing delivery :* If the buyer neglects or refuses to take delivery within a reasonable time, he is liable to the seller for loss and charges for the care and custody of the goods (Sec. 44).

Buyer's liability in case of rejection of goods (Sec. 43) : Unless otherwise agreed where goods are delivered to the buyer and he rejects them, he is not bound to return them to the seller. It is sufficient if he intimates to the seller that he has rejected the goods. If the seller refuses to take away the goods, the buyer becomes the bailee of the goods, and he may charge for keeping them.

Where the neglect or refusal of the buyer to take delivery amounts to repudiation of the contract, the seller may sue for price and for damages.

Buyer's Liability in case Rejection of Goods (Section 43)

Unless otherwise agreed where goods are delivered to the buyer and he rejects them, he is not bound to return them to the seller. It is sufficient if he intimates to the seller that he has rejected the goods, and he may charge for keeping them. Where the neglect or refusal of the buyer to take delivery amounts to repudiation of the contract, the seller may sue for price and for damages.

MEANING OF UNPAID-SELLER

A seller is deemed to be an 'unpaid seller' : (a) When the whole of the price has not been paid or tendered ; (b) When a bill of exchange or other negotiable instrument has been received as conditional payment and the condition has not been fulfilled by reason of the dishonour of the instrument, or otherwise (Sec. 45).

The Sale of Goods Act has expressly given two kinds of rights to an unpaid seller of goods, namely.

1. Against the Goods

(a) When the property in the goods has passed	* Right of lien * Right of stoppage in transit * Right of resale
(b) When the property in the goods has not passed	* Right of withholding delivery * Right of lien * Right of stoppage in transit * Right of resale

2. Against the Buyer Personally

(i) Right to sue for Price, (ii) Right to sue for damages, (iii) Right to sue for interest

Right of Unpaid Seller

- Against the Goods
  - In case Property in Goods has not Passed
    - (i) Withholding Delivery
    - (ii) Stoppage in Transit
  - In case Property in Goods has Passed
    - (i) Lien
    - (ii) Stoppage in Transit
    - (iii) Resale
- Against the Buyer (Personally)
  - (i) Suit for Price
  - (ii) Suit for Damages
  - (iii) Repudation of Contract
  - (iv) Suit for Interest

Unpaid Seller's Right Against the Goods

The unpaid seller has right (i) against the goods and (ii) against the buyer personally. The unpaid seller had right against the goods whether the property in the goods has passed to the buyer or not.

- **(a) Unpaid seller's lien:** The unpaid seller had a particular or special lien on the goods for the price while he is in possession of such goods.
- **(b) Stoppage in transit:** The unpaid seller had right of stopping the goods in transit after he has parted with the possession of them in case of the insolvency of the buyer.
- **(c) Right of resale:** The unpaid seller had a right of resale under certain conditions.
- **(d) Right of witholding delivery:** Where the property in goods has not passed to the buyer, the unpaid seller has, besides his other remedies, a right of withoholding delivery of the goods.

Unpaid Seller's Lien

'*Lien*' means a right in which a creditor has to retain possession of goods until payment of the price. Lien depends on actual possession and not on title. '*Unpaid seller's lien' is possessory lien as well as a particular lien.* The unpaid seller is entitled to a lien in the following three cases:

- **(i) No stipulation as to credit:** The unpaid seller has a lien where the goods have been sold without any stipulation as to credit.
- **(ii) Sale on credit :** The unpaid seller has a lien where the goods have been sold on credit but the term of credit has expired.
- **(iii) Insolvency of buyer:** The unpaid seller has a lien where the buyer becomes insolvent.

The unpaid seller may exercise his right of lien not withstanding that he is possession of the goods as an agent or bailee for the buyer (Sec.47). Where the unpaid seller has made a part delivery, he may exercise his right of lien on the remainder, unless he has waived the lien (Sec.48).

Sec. 49(2) makes it clear that the lien is not lost even if the seller obtains a decree for the payment of a price.

Termination of lien: The unpaid seller of goods loses his lien in the following cases:

- (i) **Delivery to carrier:** The unpaid seller loses his lien when he delivers the goods to a carrier for the purpose of transmission to the buyer without reserving the right of disposal of the goods. The ordinary rule is that a delivery to common carrier for conveyance is delivery of possession to the buyer, the carrier being the buyer's agent. But the seller may reserve the right of disposal of the goods.
- (ii) **Lawful possession by buyer:** The unpaid seller loses his lien where the buyer or his agent lawfully obtains possession of the goods.
- (iii) **Waiver:** The unpaid seller loses his lien, when he waives his lien expressly or impliedly (Sec.49).

Right of Stoppages in Transit

When the buyer becomes insolvent, the unpaid seller who has parted with the possession of the goods has the right of stopping them in transit i.e., he may resume possession of the goods so long as they are in course of transit and may retain them until payment or tender of the price (Sec.50). Thus the right of stoppage in transit can be exercised by the unpaid seller, when the buyer becomes insolvent, the seller has parted with the possession and the buyer has not obtained possession.

Duration of transit: The right of stoppage in transit can be exercised by the unpaid seller while the goods are in transit. The Sale of Goods Act lays down the following rules for determining whether the goods are in transit or the transit is at an end:

1. Goods are deemed to be in course of transit from the time when they are delivered to a carrier or other bailee for the purpose of transmission to the buyer, until the buyer or his agent in that bahalf takes delivery of them from such carrier or other bailee.
2. If the buyer or his agent in that behalf obtains delivery of the goods before their arrival at the appointed destination, the transit is at an end.
3. If, after the arrival of the goods at the appointed destination, the carrier or other bailee acknowledges to the buyer or his agent that he holds the goods on his behalf and continues in possession of them as bailee for the buyer or his agent, the transit is at an end and it is immaterial that a further destination for the goods may have been indicated by the buyer.
4. If the goods are rejected by the buyer and the carrier or other bailee continues in possession of them, the transit is not deemed to be at an end even if the seller has refused to receive them back.
5. When goods are delivered to a ship chartered by the buyer, it is a question depending on the circumstances of the particular case whether they are in the possession of the master as a carrier or an agent of the buyer.
6. Where the carrier or other bailee wrongfully, refuses to deliver the goods to the buyer or his agent in that behalf, the transit is deemed to be at an end.
7. Where part delivery of the goods has been made to the buyer or his agent in that behalf, the remainder of goods may be stopped in transit, unless such part delivery has given in such circumstances as to show an agreement to give up possession of the whole of the goods (Sec.51.)

The unpaid seller may exercise his right of stoppage in transit either by taking actual possession of the goods or by giving notice of his claim to the carrier or other bailee in whose possession the goods are lying. (Sec.52).

Such notice may be given either to the person in actual possession of the goods or to his principal. In the latter case, the notice to be effectual shall be given at such time and in such circumstances that the principal, by the exercise of reasonable diligence, may communicate it to his servant or agent in time to prevent a delivery to the buyer.

Distinction between Right of Lien and Right of Stoppage in Transit

1. **Nature of right:** The right of lien is to retain possession, while the right of stoppage in transit is to regain or resume possession.
2. **Possession of goods:** The right of lien can be exercised on goods which are in actual or constructive possession of the seller, while right of stoppage in transit can be exercised when the goods are in the possession of a middleman between the seller who had parted with the possession of the goods and the buyer who has not yet acquired the possession.
3. **Commencement and end:** The right of lien comes to an end when the possession of the goods is surrended by the seller, but the right of stoppage in transit commences when the goods have left the possession of the seller and continues until the buyer had acquired their possession.
4. **Insolvency of the buyer:** The unpaid seller's right to stop the goods in transit arises only when the buyer is insolvent but the right of lien can be exercised even when the buyer is able to pay but does not pay. This right remains in force till the right of stoppage in transit starts. Possession is the test of this right.
5. **Mode of exercising :** Right of Lien can be exercised by the seller himself. Right of stoppage in transit can be exercised by the seller through the carrier or the other bailee.

Effect of Sub-sale or pledge by buyer (Section 53): The unpaid seller's right of lien or stoppage in transit is not affected by any sale or pledge of the goods which the buyer may have made, unless the seller has assented to it. But this right is defeated if he has transferred a document of title to goods (e.g., a bill of lading or a railway receipt) to the buyer and the buyer transfers it by way of sale to a person who takes it in good faith and for consideration.

Right of Resale

The unpaid seller has the right of resale of the goods. When the goods are of a *perishable nature*, the unpaid seller may resell the goods without any notice to the buyer. When the unpaid seller has exercised his right of lien or stoppage in transit, he has to give *notice to the buyer* of his intention to resell. Thereupon, the buyer may pay the price within a reasonable time. If the buyer does not pay, the unpaid seller can resell the goods and recover from the original buyer, damages for any loss occasioned by his breach of contract. *The original buyer shall not be entitled to any profit which may occur on the sale*. If however, the unpaid seller resells the goods without notice to the buyer, the unpaid seller shall not be entitled to recover damages and the buyer shall be entitled to the profit, if any, on the resale. Where an unpaid seller who has exercised his right of lien or stoppage in transit, resells the goods, the buyer acquires a good title there to as against the original buyer (Sec.54).

Unpaid Seller's Rights against the Buyer Personally

These rights refer to those, which an unpaid seller may enforce against the buyer personally, called *rights in personam*.

1. Suit for price (Section 55): When property in the goods has passed to the buyer and the buyer wrongfully refuses to pay for the goods, the seller may sue him for the price of the goods [Sec.55 (1)]. Where property in the goods has not passed to his buyer and the goods have not been appropriated to the contract, if the price is payable on a certain day irrespective of delivery, the seller may sue buyer on his wrongful refusal to pay for the price [Sec.55 (2)].

2. Suit for damages for non-acceptance (Section 56): Where the buyer wrongfully neglects or refuses to accept and pay for the goods the seller may sue him for damages for non-acceptance. Where there is no default of the seller and the buyer wrongfully refuses to take delivery of the goods within reasonable time, the seller is entitled to recover from the buyer: (i) any loss caused by the buyer's refusal to take delivery; and (ii) any reasonable charge for the care and custody of the goods (Sec.44).

3. Repudiation of contract before due date: Where the buyer repudiates the contract before the due date of delivery, the seller may wait till the due date of delivery or may treat the contract as rescinded and sue for damages for this breach under Section 60 of the Act. This rule is called '*rule of anticipatory breach of contract*'.

4. Suit for interest: Where there is specific agreement between the seller and the buyer about payment of interest of the price of the goods from the date on which the payment becomes due, the seller may charge interest from the buyer. In the absence of any such agreement, the seller may recover interest from such date as the seller may notify to the buyer. In the absence of a contract to the contrary, *the court may award interest as such rate as it thinks fit*, on the amount of the price to the seller in a suit by him for the price from the date on which the goods are supplied or from the date on which the price is payable.

SALE BY AUCTION

The term 'auction sale' may be defined as a public sale. A person may himself sell his own goods by auction, or he may appoint an agent, known as auctioneer, to sell the goods by auction on his behalf.

Normally, in an auction sale, the goods are sold on behalf of the owner by an auctioneer; and the agency relationship between the auctioneer and the owner is disclosed to the public. In this chapter, we shall discuss the procedure of auction sale, and other legal provisions relating thereto.

Procedure of Auction Sale

The auction sale is usually organised by giving advertisements about the goods to be sold along with other terms and conditions of the sale by auction. The auctioneer gives wide publicity for the sale of the goods by auction, and fixes the time and place for it. The intending buyers, known as bidders, can inspect the goods, during the time fixed by the auctioneer, before or at the time of sale. On the time and place fixed for auction, the bidders are invited to compete for the purchase of the goods. The bidders offer their respective prices for which they are willing to purchase the goods. The auctioneer loudly speaks the prices offered by the bidders so that the other bidders may have an opportunity to offer higher price, if they want, and purchase the goods. In this way, the bidders go on offering more and more prices, and goods are generally sold to the highest bidder, i.e., to the person who pays or is ready to pay the highest price.

The highest bid constitutes an offer to buy, and the fall of hammer or any other customary announcement constitutes an acceptance of the offer by the auctioneer. It may, however, be noted that the auctioneer is not bound to accept the highest bid. He may reserve his right to refuse any bid or to accept a lower bid in preference to a higher one. [*M. Lachia sany v. Coffee Board* (1980) 4 SCC 636]

LEGAL RULES REGARDING AUCTION SALE

The legal rules regarding the auction sale are contained in various provisions of Section 64 of the Sale of Goods Act, which may be discussed under the following heads:

1. Completion of auction sale. 2. Retraction of bid. 3. Transfer of ownership. 4. Seller's right to bid 5. Fraudulent sale. 6. Auction sale with reserve or upset price.

Completion of Auction Sale

We know that, in an auction sale, at an appointed time and place, the auctioneer puts up the goods for sale to the intending buyers (bidders) by inviting bidding from them. The bidders offer to pay the price by showing their willingness to pay the price. The auctioneer then accepts the highest bid by a tap with his hammer, or by any other customary manner. On such acceptance, the auction sale is complete This rule is contained in Section 64(2) of the Sale of Goods Act, which provides that, the sale by auction is complete as soon as the auctioneer announces its completion (i.e., the acceptance of the bid) by the fall of the hammer, or in any other customary manner, e.g., by shouting one, two, three; or by shouting going, going, gone, etc.

On the fall of then hammer or any other customary manner of acceptance, the contract of sale comes into existence. It may however be noted that on the fall of the hammer, etc., the ownership does not transfer to the buyer. Only the contract of sale is completed. [*Consolidated Coffee Ltd. v. Coffee Board,* AIR 1981 SC 162]

A bid by an intending buyer is construed as an offer. As an offer, it can be withdrawn any time before acceptance, which in this case occurs by the fall of the hammer, or any other customary manner. It has been held that it is customary in this country to repeat the offer three times. [*Agra Bank v. Hamin* (1890) 14 Mad 235]

Retraction of Bid

We have already discussed that the sale is complete as soon as the bid is accepted by the auctioneer. Before the completion of the sale, the bidder has the right to retract (i.e., withdraw) his bid. This rule is also contained in Section 64(2) of the Sales of Goods Act, which provides that, before the sale is completed by the fall of the hammer, any bidder may withdraw his bid, i.e., he has the right to say that he is not ready and willing to purchase the goods. This is based on the principle that a bid is an offer, and it can be revoked before it is accepted by the fall of the hammer.

Transfer of Ownership

On the completion of sale by the fall of hammer, the ownership of the goods is immediately transferred to the buyer (i.e., highest bidder) if the auction is of specific goods in a deliverable state. Thus, once the hammer falls for the sale of specific goods in a deliverable state, the highest bidder becomes the owner of the goods, and he can deal with the goods as his own.

Seller's Right to Bid

Sometimes, in an auction sale, the seller apprehends that the bidders may enter into a knockout agreement. (It is an agreement between the bidders not to bid against each other, with a view to prevent competition among themselves). In such eases, the seller has the right to bid in the auction, or to appoint a person to bid on his behalf. However, the seller can do so only if he has expressly reserved his right to do so, and the sale has been notified subject to such a right of the seller. This rule is contained in Section 64(3) of the Sale of Goods Act, which provides that, the seller or any one person of his behalf may bid at the auction if seller's right to bid is expressly reserved. It may, however, be noted that the seller can appoint only one bidder to bid on his behalf. If he appoints more than one bidder the sale is voidable, because in such cases the intention of the seller is not to protect his interest, but to enhance the price. [*Thornett v. Names* (1846) 15 M & W 367]

As a matter of fact, if the seller makes use of pretended bidding to raise the price, the sale is voidable at the option of the buyer, and he can put an end to the contract of sale if he so chooses. [Section 64(6)].

Fraudulent Sale

We have discussed in the last article, that the seller or any one person on his behalf may bid at the auction if the sale is notified to be subject to such a right of the seller. If the seller has not reserved' his right to bid at the auction, he cannot bid at the auction. Moreover, then he cannot appoint any person to bid on his behalf. If he does so, the buyer may treat the sale as fraudulent. This rule is contained in Section 64(4) of the Sale of Goods Act, which provides that, where the seller's right to bid at the auction is not notified, the buyer may treat the sale as fraudulent if the seller or any person on his behalf bids at the auction. And the buyer may refuse to take the goods sold to him. In such cases, the sale is also fraudulent if the auctioneer knowingly takes any bid from the seller or any person on his behalf.

Auction Sale with 'Reserve or Upset' Price

The term 'reserve' or 'upset' price may be defined as the minimum price below which the auctioneer will not sell the goods put up for auction sale. In an auction sale, the seller has the right to make the sale subject to a reserve or upset price. And the sale may be notified subject to such price [Section64 (5)]. Normally, the reserve price is fixed by the seller to protect himself against the knockout agreements. Where the reserve price is fixed, the auction is known as 'with reserve'. In such cases, the auctioneer is not bound to accept the highest bid if it is below the reserve price. Even when, by mistake, the auctioneer knocks down (i.e., completes the sale by striking of hammer or any other customary manner) the goods for less than the reserve price, he can refuse to deliver the goods to the buyer (i.e., the bidder whose bid was accepted). And the buyer will have no remedy against the auctioneer. [*Rainbow v. Howkins* (1904) 2 KB. 3221.

It may also be noted that where a reserve price has been fixed then, even if the goods are specific, the ownership will not pass if the highest bid falls short of the reserve price. [*Consolidated Coffee Ltd. v. Coffee Board* AIR 1981 sc 162]

Sometimes, no minimum price is fixed by the seller, and the auction is notified without any reserve price. In such cases, the auction is known as 'without reserve'. In case of auction 'without reserve' the auctioneer is bound to deliver the goods to a bidder whose bid is accepted by him. And he cannot refuse to deliver the goods on the ground that the real value of the goods is more that the amount of the bid accepted by him. It may, however, be noted that a valid contract of sale results only when the highest bid is accepted. But the auctioneer in not bound to accept the highest bid. And the refusal of the auctioneer to accept the highest bid gives no cause of action to the bidder at all. As the bidder is free to withdraw his bid before acceptance, the auctioneer is also free to refuse to accept the highest bid. [*Fenwick v. Macdonald* (1904)6 F. (court of Section) 850].

The auctioneer also has the right to make the auction subject to any conditions he likes.

Important Terms in Auction Sale

The following terms are important in an auction sale:

1. ***Knock-out agreement:*** The term 'knock-out agreement' may be defined as an agreement between the bidders not to bid against each other at an auction ale. Such agreements are made by the bidders with a view to prevent competition among themselves. By a knockout agreement, the various bidders agree that only one of them shall bid, and anything obtained by him shall afterwards be shared privately among themselves. It may be noted that knock-out agreements are not illegal. [*Jai Bhagwani Timber v. State*, AIR 1992 MP 250]

   The seller may protect his interest against such agreements by reserving his right to bid at the auction or by fixing a reserve price. However, if a knock-out agreement is made with the intention of defrauding the seller, the auction sale is voidable at the option of the seller.

2. ***Damping:*** The term 'damping' may be defined as an unlawful act by which an intending purchaser is prevented from bidding or raising the price at an auction sale. The damping is usually done in any of the following ways

   (a) By pointing out defects in the goods put up for auction sale.

   (b) By taking the intending buyers away from the place of auction by some other device.

   It may be noted that the damping is illegal and the auctioneer can withdraw the goods from auction.

3. ***Puffers:*** The term 'puffer' may be defined as a person who is employed by the seller to raise the price by ficticious bids. A puffer has no intention to purchase the goods. Such persons are also known as 'by-bidders', 'white bonnets', or 'decoy ducks'.

4. ***Sale of goods in lots:*** Sometimes, the goods are put up in lots for sale by auction. In such cases, each lot is, prima facie considered to be a separate subject for sale.

Implied Warranties in Auction Sale

In an auction sale, the auctioneer impliedly gives the following warranties:

1. He warrants his authority to sell the goods on behalf of his principal. [*Anderson v. Croall & Sons* (1904) 6 F. 153 C S].
2. He warrants that he knows of no defects in his principal's title. [*Benton v. Campbell Parker & Co.* (1925) 2 K.B.410]
3. He warrants that possession of the goods would be given to purchaser against the payment of price. [*Benton 's case*]
4. He warrants the quiet possession of goods by the purchaser. [*Benton 's case*]

Liabilities and Duties of an Auctioneer

The Sale of Goods Act does not deal with the liabilities of an auctioneer in case of sale by auction. However, it has been held by courts that in an auction sale, the auctioneer incurs certain liabilities, though the extent of those liabilities depends upon the facts of each particular case. The liabilities of an auctioneer may be summer up as under:

1. The auctioneer warrants his authority to sell the goods on behalf of his principal. And if it is discovered that the auctioneer had no authority to sell the goods, he may be held liable for damages.
2. The auctioneer warrants that he knows of no defects in his principal's title. And in case of defect in principal's title, he nay be held liable for damages.
3. The auctioneer warrants that the possession of the goods would be given to the purchaser on the payment of the price, to him. And if the auctioneer refuses to give the possession on the payment of the price, he may be held liable for damages.
4. The auctioneer also warrants that the passion of the purchaser shall not be disturbed by his principal or himself. And if subsequently, purchaser's possession is so disturbed, the auctioneer may be held liable for damages.

PASSING OF PROPERTY IN SEA CARRIAGE FOR., CF., CIF., FOB., CONTRACTS

International commerce which involves transportation of goods from far away countries is largely depedent on Sea carriage. As various merits are associated with carriage of goods by sea, the question of ownership and risk have arisen quite often. As passing of property is dependent on the terms of contract, parties to such contracts have evolved definite models for carriage of goods, such as F.O.B., F.O.R., C.I.F., and C. & F. etc. each of which have definite and internationally accepted meaning assigned for them.

F.O.R. Contracts : The word F.O.R. stands for Free on Rail. Where the seller agrees to sell the goods on FOR basis he is required to bear all expenses prior to the putting of the goods on rail. As soon as the goods are put on rail the responsibility of the seller ceases and the risk as well as property vests in the buyer as held in under *Wood Ltd. Vs.Burgh Castle Brick and Cement Syndicate (1922) 1. K B 343*. In India, the F.O.R. contracts do not imply an undertaking on behalf of the seller to procure wagons : *National Coal Co. Ltd. Vs. G.P. Park 86 Cal. L J 220.*

A Contract was made for sale of goods on "F.O.R." at the place of despatch. Purchaser complains of short delivery of goods by Railways. What are the responsibilities of the Seller?

(Ref. : to *M/s. Marwar Tent Factory Vs. Union of India Ors. AIR 1990 SC 1751.* "Seller's liability to place the goods free on rail at the place of delivery. Once that is done the risk belongs to the buyer")

Sometimes, the goods are to be delivered to the buyer through sea routes. In all such cases, the parties may enter into certain contracts, which govern the delivery of the goods through sea routes. Following are the three important and usual forms of contracts of sale which involve the carriage of goods by sea:

C & F Contracts : In a C & F contract, the insurance is paid by the purchaser. In such a contract the buyer undertakes to insure the goods upon receipt of particulars of shipment while the goods are in transit. This contract is for all practical purposes an F.O.B. contract. Madras High Court held in Commissioner of Income Tax Vs. Burugh Vishwanatha Rao (Case No. 61/46) that in the case of such contracts property in the goods passed not when the goods are ascertained but subsequently. The time of shipment is the time of passing of property to the buyer as held by *Madras High Court in India C & T Distributing Co. Vs. State of Madras, AIR 1954, Mad. 1030.*

C.I.F. Contracts: The term '*C.I.F.*' means '*cost, insurance and freight*'. such a contract is a contract for the sale of goods at a price which inculdes the cost of goods, insurance and freight charges. Thus, in such contracts, the charges of insurance during transit and the freight charges are paid by the buyer. Where the buyer orders the goods from a seller, residing abroad, under a C.I.F. contract, the seller will insure the goods and deliver them to a shipping company for transmission to the buyer; the insurance policy on the goods and the bill of lading to be delivered to the buyer along with the invoice of the goods. It may be noted that in C.I.F contracts, the seller is bound to perform the following duties:

1. To load the sold goods safely on the ship named by the buyer.
2. To meet the expenses of loading the goods.
3. To enter into contract with the shipping company or ship owners for the transportation of goods and obtain a bill of lading. Such a contract should be upon reasonable terms.
4. To deliver the bill of lading to the buyer.

On the performance of the above duties, the contractual liability of the seller ceases, and the delivery of goods to the buyer is complete as far as he (i.e., seller) is concerned. Therefore, the buyer is bound to pay the price of the goods when the shipping documents are presented to him even if the goods have been lost by that time. It is also the buyer's duty to name a ship upon which the goods are to be delivered; if he fails to name a ship, he is guilty of breach of contract,and the seller can file a suit against him for the recovery of the damages.

REVIEW QUESTIONS

1. What do you mean by performance of a contract of sale?
2. What is meant by delivery of goods?
3. What are the rules as to delivery of goods under the Sale of Goods Act? Explain in detail.
4. Enumerate the remedies open to the buyer for breach of contract by the seller.
5. Is the buyer liable for rejecting, neglecting or refusing to accept delivery of goods?
6. What is the exact moment at which the transfer of property takes place? What is its importance?
7. 'No one can convey a better title than he himself has'. Explain the statement and state the exceptions to it.
8. What are the rights and duties of a buyer in a contract of sale?
9. What are the remedies for a breach of contract of sale (a) by the buyer and (b) by the seller?
10. Who is an unpaid seller?
11. State and explain the rights of an unpaid seller against (a) the goods and (b) the buyer (personally).
12. Distinguish between unpaid seller's right of lien and stoppage in transit.
13. Write short notes on :

    (a) Right of resale (b) Auction sales (c) Right of stoppage in transit (d) CIF contract (e) FOB Contract.
14. Write a detailed note on sale by action

❐ ❐ ❐

MODULE - II

ECONOMIC LAWS

14

Chapter THE COMPETITION ACT, 2002

After a half century of strongly inward oriented policies, India began opening itself to foreign trade and investment in 1991. The New Industrial Policy sought to prepare Indian industry for meeting the challenges of globalisation. The reforms aim at generating a market orientation for the erstwhile highly regulated domestic economy by deregulating the domestic economy and thus synergising the domestic economy and Indian industry with greater flexibility to respond to competitive pressure.

Last decade of 20th century witnessed a drastic change in the economic policies of India due to the advent of globalisation and progressive integration of world economy. The importance of globalisation is the free flow of trade, finance and information, which is expected to produce best outcomes for growth and human welfare. No doubt, in the initial period, such globalisation policy may end up with few gainers and more loosers, particularly amongst the developing and under developed countries.

Competition as one of the major by-products of globalisation casts upon the corporate sector an onerous responsibility for continuous improvement in the quality of products, competitive pricing, consumer satisfaction and social welfare. It also requires the government to provide conducive atmosphere by devising appropriate competition policy and adopting comprehensive legislation and independent regulatory authority for its effective implementation.

Meaning of Competition

A free enterprise economy implies competition. Competition is the great regulative force which establishes control over economic activities. Competition encourages enterprises to be innovative and bring out new goods and services for the benefit of consumers. It helps the consumers to widen their choice. It enables consumers to buy the goods they want at, the best possible price. Competition is likely to place each productive service in the precise position where it makes the right impact. Competition is an excellent institution which helps the matching of consumer needs to producers resources. It is competition which can ensure availability of goods or services in abundance of acceptable quality at affordable price.

Competition Policy

The competition policy focuses on two aspects viz, the protection of consumer interest and promotion of economic efficiency. Competition policy concerns itself with both restrictive business practices employed by the enterprises and also the government policies affecting competition. The competition policy also acts as supplement to industrial and trade policy and should be applied with flexibility taking into consideration the national interest and global economic and trade environment.

Despite many efforts made by the Government towards unshackling of the Indian economy, competition in the true sense still eludes India. Unlike advanced countries where competition has reached a certain level of maturation, India presents a sordid picture of either unequal competition in some sectors or total lack of competition in other sectors. It is true that the economists have us believe that free competition is a myth and is not present anywhere. However, one cannot deny the importance of even a modicum of competition in enthroning consumer interests and reducing economic costs to the nation.

Committee on Competition Law and Policy

The committee on Competition Law and Policy, 2000 headed by Mr. S.V.S. Raghavan, has shown commendable interest placing an acceptable competition legislation in the statute books. With the gradual but certain ascendance of the market economy in all economic spheres and with globalisation a reality, the need to frame an effective and coherent law on competition that would drive policy has become obvious. For the average Indian mindset, conditioned as it is by five decades of planned economic growth, competition has until recently mattered only to the extent of say checking private monopolies. A major difficulty therefore lies in understanding competition even in conceptual terms, leave alone in suggesting legislative and other measures to foster it.

Recommendations of the Committee

Since the essence and the spirit of competition need to be preserved while harmonising the competition policy with the Government policy, the Committee has made far-reaching recommendations, which it terms pre-requisites for achieving the desired results. These include repealing of the Industries Development and Regulation Act, 1951, BIFR under the Sick Industries Act and the Urban Ceiling Act. Favouring a large-scale divestment by the Government in State-owned enterprises; the Committee feels that any form of discrimination in favour of Government-owned enterprises should be removed. The Committee also favoured a progressive reduction and ultimate elimination of reservation of products for the small scale industrial and handloom sector that would in any case lose its rationale in an era of free imports. Simultaneously, however, the Committee has recommended that these sectors should be provided with cheaper bank credit linked to inflation rate to make them more competitive. On the equally sensitive labour reforms, the Committee has recommended easy exit to "non-viable ill-managed and inefficient units".

The existing laws on the subject -the MRTP Act (1969) and the Consumer Protection Act (1986) -are not sufficient to deal with anti-competitive practices. The Competition Commission of India (CCI) is to preside over the Competition Act and hear competition cases and also play the role of competition advocacy. The MRTP Act is repealed and the MRTP Commission is wound up.

All cases pertaining to monopolies trade practices or restrictive trade practices pending before the Monopolies and Restrictive Trade Practices Commission before the commencement of Competition Act, 2002, including such cases in which any unfair trade practice and giving false or misleading facts disparaging the goods, services or trade of another person [Section36A(1)(x) of Monopolies and Restrictive Trade Practices Act, 1969) has also been alleged, shall stand transferred to the Competition Commission of India and shall be adjudicated by the Commission in accordance with the provisions of the repealed Act as if that Act had not been repealed.

All cases pertaining to unfair trade practices pending before the Monopolies and Restrictive Trade Practices Commission before the commencement of this Act, shall on such commencement, stand transferred to the National Commission constituted under the Consumer Protection Act, 1986. The National Commission shall dispose of such cases as if they were cases filed under the Consumer Protection Act, 1986. The National Commission may, if it considers appropriate, transfer any such case to the concerned State Commission established under the Consumer Protection Act, 1986. The State Commission shall dispose of such case as if it was filed under that Act.

All investigations or proceedings, other than those relating to unfair trade practices shall stand transferred to the Competition Commission of India. All investigations or proceedings relating to unfair trade practices including proceedings relating to false or misleading facts disparaging the goods, services of another person shall stand transferred to the National Commission.

The Competition Act 2000 provides keeping in view of the economic development of the country, for the establishment of a Commission to prevent practices having adverse effect on competition, to promote and sustain competition in markets; to protect the interests of consumers and to ensure freedom of trade carried on by other participants in markets, in India, and for matters connected therewith or incidental thereto.

DEFINITIONS (Section 2)

(a) ***Acquisition*** means, directly or indirectly, acquiring or agreeing to acquire

(i) shares, voting rights or assets of any enterprise; or

(ii) control over management or control over assets of any enterprise;

(b) ***Agreement*** includes any arrangement or understanding or action in concert,

(i) whether or not, such arrangement, understanding or action is formal or in writing; or

(ii) whether or not such arrangement, understanding or action is intended to be enforceable by legal proceedings;

(c) ***Cartel*** includes an association of producers, sellers, distributors, traders or service providers who, by agreement amongst themselves, limit control or attempt to control the production, distribution, sale or price of, or, trade in goods or provision of services;

(d) ***Chairperson*** means the Chairperson of the Commission appointed under Sub-section (i) of Section 8;

(e) ***Commission*** means the Competition Commission of India established under sub-section (1) of Section 7;

(f) ***Consumer*** means any person who-

(i) buys any goods for a consideration which has been paid or promised or partly paid and partly promised, or under any system of deferred payment and includes any user of such goods other than the person who buys such goods for consideration paid or promised or partly paid or partly promised, or under any system of deferred payment when such use is made with the approval of such person, whether such purchase of goods is for resale or for any commercial purpose or for personal use;

(ii) hires or avails of any services for a consideration which has been paid or promised or partly paid and partly promised, or under any system of deferred payment and includes any beneficiary of such services other than the person who hires or avails of the services for consideration paid or promised, or partly paid and partly promised, or under any system of deferred payment, when such services are availed of with the approval ob the first-mentioned person whether such hiring or availing of services is for any commercial purpose or for personal use;

(g) ***Director General*** means the Director General appointed under Sub-section (1) of Section 16 and includes any Additional, Joint, Deputy or Assistant Directors General appointed under that section;

(h) Enterprise means a person or a department of the Government, who or which is, or has been, engaged in any activity, relating to the production, storage, supply, distribution, acquisition or control of articles or goods, or the provisions of services, of any kind, or in investment, or in the business of acquiring, holding, underwriting or dealing with shares, debentures or other securities of any other body corporate, either directly or through one or more of its units or divisions or subsidiaries, whether such unit or division or subsidiary is located at the same place where the enterprise is located or at a different place or at different places, but does not include any activity of the Government relatable to the sovereign functions of the Government including all activities carried on by the departments of the Central, Government dealing with atomic energy, currency, defence and space.

Explanation: For the purposes of this clause,-

(a) "activity" includes profession or occupation;

(b) "article" includes a new article and "service" includes a new service;

(c) "unit" or "division", in relation to an enterprise, includes

(i) a plant or factory established for the production, storage, supply, distribution, acquisition or control of any article or goods;

(ii) any branch or office established for the provision of any service;

(i) Goods means goods as defined In the Sale of Goods Act, 1930 and includes-

(a) products manufactured, processed or mined;

(b) debentures, stocks and shares after allotment;

(c) in relation to goods supplied, distributed or controlled in India, goods imported into India;

(j) Member means a Member of the Commission appointed under Sub-section (1) of sections and includes the Chairperson;

(k) Notification means a notification published in the Official Gazette;

(l) person includes -

(i) an individual;

(ii) a Hindu undivided family;

(iii) a company;

(iv) a firm;

(v) an association of persons or a body of individuals, whether incorporated or not, in India or outside India;

(vi) any corporation established by or under any Central, State or Provincial Act or a Government company as defined in Section 617 of the Companies Act, 1956 (1 of 1956);

(vii) any body corporate incorporated by or under the laws of a country outside India; (viii) a co-operative society registered under any law relating to co-operative societies; (ix) a local authority;

(x) every artificial juridical person, not falling within any of the preceding sub-clauses;

(m) Practice includes any practice relating to the carrying on of any trade by a person or an enterprise;

(n) Prescribed means prescribed by rules made under this Act;

(o) Price, in relation to the sale of any goods or to the performance of any services, includes every valuable consideration, whether direct or indirect, or deferred, and includes any consideration which in effect relates to the sale of any goods or to the performance of any services although ostensibly relating to any other matter or thing;

(p) ***Public financial institution*** means a public financial institution specified under Section 4A of the Companies Act, 1956 (1 of 1956) and includes a State Financial, Industrial or Investment Corporation;

(q) ***Regulations*** means the regulations made by the Commission under Section 64;

(r) ***Relevant market*** means the market which may be determined by the commission with reference to the relevant product market or the relevant geographic market or with reference to both the markets;

(s) ***Relevant geographic market*** means a market comprising the area in which the conditions of competition for supply of goods or provision of services or demand of goods or services are distinctly homogenous and can be distinguished from the conditions prevailing in the neighboring areas;

(t) ***Relevant product market*** means a market comprising all those products or services which are regarded as interchangeable or substitutable by the consumer, by reason of characteristics of the products or services, their prices and intended use;

(u) ***Service*** means service of any description which is made available to potential users and includes the provision of services in connection with business of any industrial or commercial matters such as banking, communication, education, financing, insurance, chit funds, real estate, transport, storage, material treatment, processing, supply of electrical or other energy, boarding, lodging, entertainment; amusement, construction, repair, conveying of news or information and advertising;

(v) ***Shares*** means shares in the share capital of a company carrying voting rights and includes -

(i) any security, which entitles the holder to receive shares with voting rights;

(ii) stock except where a distinction between stock and share is expressed or implied;

(w) ***Statutory authority*** means any authority, board, corporation, council, institute, university or any other body corporate, established by or under any Central, State or Provincial Act for the purposes of regulating production or supply of goods or provision of any services or markets therefore or any matter connected therewith or incidental thereto;

(x) ***Trade*** means any trade, business, industry, profession or occupation relating to the production, supply, distribution, storage or control of goods and includes the provision of any services;

(y) ***Turnover*** includes value of sale of goods or services;

(z) Words and expressions used but not defined in this Act and defined in the Companies Act, 1956 (1 of 1956) shall have the same meanings respectively assigned to them in that Act.

PROHIBITION OF CERTAIN AGREEMENTS

Anti-competitive Agreements (Section 3)

1. No enterprise or association of enterprises or person or association of persons shall enter into any agreement in respect of production, supply, distribution, storage, acquisition or control of goods or provision of services, which causes or is likely to cause an appreciable adverse effect on competition within India.

2. Any agreement entered into in contravention of the provisions shall be void.

3. Any agreement entered into between enterprises or associations of enterprises of persons or associations of persons or between any person and enterprise or practice carried on, or decision taken by,

any association of enterprises or association of persons, including cartels, engaged in identical or similar trade of goods or provision of services, which-

(a) directly or indirectly determines purchase or sale prices;

(b) limits or controls production, supply, markets, technical development, investment or provision of services;

(c) shares the market or source of production or provision of services by way of allocation of geographical area of market, or type of goods or services, or number of customers in the market or any other similar way;

(d) directly or indirectly results in bid rigging or collusive bidding, shall be presumed to have an appreciable adverse effect on competition:

This will not apply to any agreement entered into by way of joint ventures if such agreement increases efficiency in production, supply, distribution, storage, acquisition or control of goods or provision of services.

Explanation: "bid rigging" means any agreement, between enterprises or persons referred to in sub-section(3) engaged in identical or similar production or trading of goods or provision of services, which has the effect of eliminating or reducing competition for bids or adversely affecting or manipulating the process for bidding.

4. Any agreement amongst enterprises or persons at different stages or levels of the production chain in different markets, in respect of production, supply, distribution, storage, sale or price of, or trade in goods or provision of services, including

(i) tie-in-arrangement,

(ii) exclusive supply agreement,

(iii) exclusive distribution agreement,

(iv) refusal to deal, and

(v) resale price maintenance shall be an agreement in contravention if such agreement causes or is likely to cause an appreciable adverse effect on competition in India.

Explanation

(a) ***"tie-in arrangements"*** includes any agreement requiring a purchaser of goods, as a condition of such purchase, to purchase some other good

(b) ***"exclusive supply agreement"*** includes any agreement restricting in any manner the purchaser in the course of his trade from acquiring or otherwise dealing in any goods other than those of the seller or any other person;

(c) ***"exclusive distribution agreement"*** includes any agreement to limit, restrict or withhold the output or supply of any goods or allocate any area or market for the disposal or sale of the goods;

(d) ***"refusal to deal"*** includes any agreement which restricts, or is likely to restrict, by any method the persons or classes of persons to whom goods are sold or from whom goods are bought;

(e) ***"resale price maintenance"*** includes any agreement to sell goods on condition that the prices to be charged on the resale by the purchaser shall be the prices stipulated by the seller unless it is clearly stated that prices lower than those prices may be charged;

5. Nothing contained in this section shall restrict

(i) the right of any person to restrain any infringement of or to impose reasonable conditions, as may be necessary for protecting any of his rights which have been or may be conferred upon him under

  (a) the Copy Right Act, 1957,

  (b) the Patents Act, 1970,

  (c) the Trade and Merchandise Marks Act or the Trade Marks Act, 1999,

  (d) the Geographical Indications of Goods Registration and Protection) Act, 1999,

  (e) the Designs Act, 2000,

  (f) the Semi-Conductor Integrated Circuits Layout-Design Act, 2000.

(ii) the right of any person to export goods from India to the extent to which the agreement relates exclusively to the production, supply, distribution or control of goods or provision of service for such export.

Comments: Competition means striking against each other for settling something desired or doing something desired or doing something in the best manner possible a trial of ability. It is a contest between two rivals, or the answering all requirements; having sufficient capacity, ability or authority; possessing the requisite physical, mental, natural or legal qualifications.

Combination in restraint of trade is an effort of two or more parties, acting independently, to secure the business of a third party by the offer of the most favourable terms; also the relations between different buyers or different sellers which result from this effort. It is the struggle between rivals for the same trade at the same time; the act of seeking or endeavouring to gain what another is endeavouring to gain at ii same time. The term implies the idea of endeavouring by two or more to obtain the same object or result.

Agreement or understanding between two or more persons, in the form of a contract, trust, pool, holding company, or other form of association, for the purpose of unduly restricting competition. Monopolising trade and commerce in a certain commodity, controlling its production, distribution, and price, or otherwise interfering with freedom of trade without statutory authority.

A combination formed for the purpose of and with the effect of raising, depressing, fixing, pegging, or stabilising the price of a commodity is called "price-fixing ". It is a co-operative setting of price levels or range by competing firms, which would otherwise be set by natural market forces. Such agreements are prohibited in the US by the Sherman Anti-trust Act. Price-fixing within intent of Sherman Act is either horizontal (dealing with arrangements among competitors, as between competing retailers) or vertical (attempting to control resale price, as agreements between manufacturer and retailer).

Section 3 of the Competition Act, 2002, provides for prohibition of entering into anti-competitive agreements. It shall not be lawful for any enterprise or association of enterprises or person or association of persons to enter into an agreement in respect of production, supply, storage, distribution, acquisition or control of goods or provision of service which causes or Is likely to cause an appreciable adverse effect on competition within India. All such agreements entered into in contravention of the aforesaid prohibition shall be void. This clause also specifies certain activities which shall be presumed to have an appreciable adverse effect on competition and also specifies certain agreements when shall be in contravention if such agreement causes appreciable adverse effect on competition.

PROHIBITION OF ABUSE OF DOMINANT POSITION (SECTION 4)

No enterprise shall abuse its dominant position. There shall be an abuse of dominant position under sub-section (1), if an enterprise,-

(a) directly or indirectly, imposes unfair or discriminatory

(i) condition in purchase or sale of goods or services; or

(ii) price in purchase or sale (including predatory price) of goods or service; or

Explanation: the unfair or discriminatory condition in purchase or sale of goods or services and unfair or discriminatory price in purchase or sale of goods (including predatory price) or service shall not include such discriminatory conditions or prices which may be adopted to meet the competition; or

(b) limits or restricts-

(i) production of goods or provision of services or market there for; or

(ii) technical or scientific development relating to goods or services to the prejudice of consumers; or

(c) indulges in practice or practices resulting in denial of market access; or

(d) makes conclusion of contracts subject to acceptance by other parties of supplementary obligations which, by their nature or according to commercial usage, have no connection with the subject of such contracts; or

(e) uses its dominant position in one relevant market to enter into, or protect, other relevant market.

Explanation

(a) "dominant position" means a position of strength, enjoyed by an enterprise, in the relevant market, in India, which enables it to-

(i) operate independently of competitive forces prevailing in the relevant market; or

(ii) affect its competitors or consumers or the relevant market in its favour;

(b) "predatory price" means the sale of goods or provision of services, at a price which is below the cost, as may be determined by regulations, of production of the goods or provision of services, with a view to reduce competition or eliminate the competitors.

Comments: Sec 4, prohibits abuse of dominant position by any enterprise. Such abuse of dominant position, inter alia, includes imposition, either directly or indirectly, of unfair or discriminatory purchase or selling prices or conditions, including predatory prices of goods or service, limiting production or restricting of goods or provision of service, indulging in practices resulting in denial of market access, making the conclusion of contracts subject to acceptance by other parties of supplementary obligations and using dominant position in one market to enter into or protect other market.

COMBINATION (Section 5)

The acquisition of one or more enterprises by one or more persons or merger or amalgamation of enterprises shall be a combination of such enterprises and persons or enterprises, if-

(a) *Acquisition :* If *any acquisition* where

(i) the parties to the acquisition, being the acquirer and the enterprise, whose control, shares, voting rights or assets have been acquired or are being acquired jointly have,-

- either, in India, the assets of the value of more than rupees one thousand crores or turnover more than rupees three thousand crores; or
- in India or outside India, in aggregate, the assets of the value of more than five hundred million US dollars or turnover more than fifteen hundred million US dollars; or

(ii) the group, to which the enterprise whose control, shares, assets or voting rights have been acquired or are being acquired, would belong after the acquisition jointly have or would jointly have,-

- either in India, the assets of the value of more than rupees four thousand crores or turnover more thin rupees twelve thousand crores; or
- in India or outside India, in aggregate, the assets of the value of more than two billion US dollars or turnover more than six billion US dollars; or

(b) *Acquiring of Control :* If *acquiring of control* by a person over an enterprise when such person has already direct or indirect control over another enterprise engaged in production, distribution or trading of a similar or identical or substitutable goons or provision of a similar or identical or substitutable service, if

(i) the enterprise over which control has been acquired along with the enterprise over which the acquirer already has direct or indirect control jointly have,-

- either in India. assets of the value of more than rupees one thousand crores or turnover more than rupees three thousand crores; or -
- in India or outside India, in aggregate, the assets of the value of more than five hundred million US dollars or turnover more than fifteen hundred million US dollars; or

(ii) the group, to which enterprise whose control has been acquired, or is being acquired would belong after the acquisition, jointly have or would jointly have,-

- either in India the assets of the value of more than rupees four thousand crores or turnover more than rupees twelve thousand crores; or
- in India or outside India, in aggregate, the assets of the value of more than two billion US dollars or turnover more than six billion US dollars; or

(c) *Merger of Amalgamation :* If any *merger or amalgamation* in which

(i) the enterprise remaining after merger or the enterprise created as a result of the amalgamation, as the ease may b, have,-

- either in India, the assets of the value of more than rupees one thousand crores or turnover more than rupees three thousand crores; or
- in India or outside India, in aggregate, the assets of the value of more than five hundred million US dollars or turnover more than fifteen hundred million US dollars; or

(ii) the group, or its constituent enterprise remaining after the merger or the enterprise created as a result of the amalgamation, would belong after the merger or the amalgamation, as the case may be, have or would have,-

- either in India, the assets of the value of more than rupees four thousand crores or turnover more than rupees twelve thousand crores; or

- in India or outside India, the assets of the value of more than two billion US dollars or turnover more than six billion US dollars.

Explanation: For the purposes of this section,-

(a) **"control"** includes controlling the affairs or management by -

(i) one or more enterprises. Either jointly or singly, over another enterprise or group;

(ii) one or more groups, either jointly or singly, over another group or enterprise;

(b) **"group"** means two or more enterprises which, directly or indirectly, are in a position to

(i) exercise twenty-six per cent or more of the voting rights in the other enterprise; or

(ii) appoint more than fifty per cent of the members of the Board of Directors in the other enterprise; or

(iii) control the management or affairs of the other enterprise;

(c) **Determination of Value assets:** The value of assets shall be determined by taking the book value of the assets as shown, in the audited books of account of the enterprise, in the financial year immediately preceding the financial year in which the date of proposed merger falls, as reduced by any depreciation, and the value of assets shall include the brand value, value of goodwill, or value of copyright, patent, permitted use, collective mark, registered proprietor, registered trade mark, registered user, homonymous geographical indication, geographical indications, design or layout-design or similar other commercial rights, if any.

The Central Government shall, on the expiry of a period of two years from the date of commencement of this Act and thereafter every two years, in consultation with the Commission by notification, enhance or reduce on the basis of the wholesale price index or fluctuations in exchange rate of foreign currencies, the value of assets or the value of turnover [Section 20(3)]

Comments: Sec. 5 of the Act, deals with combination of enterprises and persons. The acquisition of one or more enterprises by one or more persons or acquiring of control or merger or amalgamation of enterprises under certain circumstances specified in the said clause shall be construed as combination.

REGULATION OF COMBINATIONS (Section 6)

1. No person or enterprise shall enter into a combination which causes or is likely to cause an appreciable adverse effect on competition within the relevant mar and such a combination shall be void.

2. Any person or enterprise, who or which proposes to enter into a combination, may, at his or its option, give notice to the Commission, in the form as may be specified, and the fee which may be determined, by regulations, disclosing the details of the proposed combination, within seven days of-.

(a) approval of the proposal relating to merger or amalgamation, referred to in clause (c) of Section 5, by the Board of Directors of the enterprises concerned with such merger or amalgamation, as the case may be;

(b) execution of any agreement or other document for acquisition referred to in clause (a) of Section 5 or acquiring of control referred to in clause (b) of that Section.

3. The Commission shall, after receipt of notice deal with such notice in accordance with the provisions contained in Sections 29,30 and 31.

4. The provisions of this Section shall not apply to share subscription or financing facility or any acquisition, by a public financial institution, foreign institutional investor, bank or venture capital fund, pursuant to any covenant of a loan agreement or investment agreement.

5. The public financial institution, foreign institutional investor, bank or venture capital fund, shall, within seven days from the date of the acquisition, file, in the form as may be specified by regulations, with the Commission the details of the acquisition including the details of control, the circumstances for exercise of such control and the consequences of default arising out of such loan agreement or investment agreement, as the case may be.

Comments: Under Section 6, no person or enterprise shall enter into a combination which is likely to cause or causes an appreciable adverse effect on competition within the relevant market in India. It further provides exemption from the provisions of this clause to certain institutions.

COMPETITION COMMISSION OF INDIA (Sections 7 to 17)

Establishment of Commission (Section 7)

The Act provides for the establishment of the Competition Commission of India. The Commission shall be a body corporate by the aforesaid name having perpetual succession and a common seal with power to acquire, hold and dispose of property. The place of head office of the Commission shall be decided by the Central Government. However, the Commission can establish offices at other places in India.

Composition of Commission (Section 8)

The Commission shall consist of a Chairperson and not less than two and not more than ten other Members to be appointed by the Central Government. The Central Government shall appoint the Chairperson and a Member during the first year of the establishment of the Commission. A person who is or has been or is qualified to be a judge of a High Court or is having special knowledge of, and professional experience in, not less than fifteen years in International trade, economics, business, commerce, law, finance, accountancy, management, industry, public affairs, administration or in any other matter which, in the opinion of the Central Government, be useful to the Commission shall be eligible for appointment as the Chairperson or as a Member.

Selection of Chairperson and other Members (Section 9)

The Chairperson and other Members shall be selected in the manner as may be prescribed.

Term of office of Chairperson and other Members (Section 10)

The Chairperson and every other Member shall hold office as such for a term of five years from the date on which he enters upon his office and shall be eligible for reappointment:

No Chairperson shall hold office after he attains the age of seventy years and no other member shall hold office after he attains the age of sixty-five years. This section also provides for discharge of functions of the Chairperson by the senior-most Member in case the Chairperson is unable to discharge his functions.

Resignation, removal and suspension of Chairperson and other Members (Section 11)

Resignation: The Chairperson or any other Member may, by notice in writing under his hand addressed to the Central Government. Resign his office: The Chairperson or a Member shall, unless he is permitted by the Central Government to relinquish his office sooner, continue to hold office until the expiry of three months from the date of receipt of such notice or until a person duly appointed as his successor enters upon his office or until the expiry of his term of office whichever is the earliest.

Removal: The Central Government may, by order, remove the Chairperson or any other Member from his office if such Chairperson or Member, as the case may be,-

(a) is, or at any time has been, adjudged as an insolvent; or,

(b) has engaged at any time, during his term of office, in any paid employment; or

(c) has been convicted of an offence which, in the opinion of the Central Government involves moral turpitude; or

(d) has acquired such financial or other interest as is likely to affect prejudicially his functions as a Member; or

(e) has so abused his position as-to render his continuance in office prejudicial to the public interest; or

(f) has become physically or mentally incapable of acting as a Member.

No Member shall be removed from his office on the ground specified unless the Supreme Court, on a reference being made to it in this behalf by the Central Government, has, on an inquiry, held by it in accordance with such procedure as may be prescribed in this behalf by the Supreme Court, reported that the member, ought on such ground or grounds to be removed.

Restriction on employment of Chairperson and other Members in certain cases (Section 12)

The Chairperson and other Members shall not, for a period of one year from the date on which they cease to hold office, accept any employment in, or connected with the management or administration of, any enterprise which has been a party to a proceeding before the Commission under this Act:

Financial and administrative powers of Member Administration (Section 13)

The Central Government shall designate any Member as Member Administration who shall exercise such financial administrative powers as may be vested in him under the rules made by the Central Government. The Member Administration shall have authority to delegate such of his financial and administrative powers as he may think fit to any other officer of the commission subject to the condition, that ,such officer shall, while exercising such delegated powers continue to act under the direction, superintendence and control of the Member Administration.

Salary and Allowances : The Salary, and the other terms and conditions of service of the Chairperson and other Members including travelling expenses shall not be varied to his disadvantage after appointment. (Section 14)

Vacancy, etc., not to invalidate proceedings of Commission (Section 15)

No act or proceeding of the Commission shall be invalid merely by reason of

(a) any vacancy in, or any defect in the constitution of, the Commission; or

(b) any defect in the appointment of a person acting as a Chairperson or as a Member; or

(c) any irregularity in the procedure of the Commission not affecting the merits of the case.

Appointment of Director General, etc. (Section 16)

1. The Central Government may, by notification, appoint a Director General and as many Additional, Joint, Deputy or Assistant Directors General or such other advisers, consultants or officer as it may think fit,

for the purposes of assisting the Commission in conducting inquiry into contravention of any of the provisions of this Act and for the conduct of cases before the Commission and for performing such other functions as are, or may be, provided by or under this Act.

2. Every Additional, Joint, Deputy and Assistant Directors General or such other advisers, consultants or officers, shall exercise his powers, and discharge his functions, subject to the general control, supervision and direction of the Director General.

3. The salary, allowances and other terms and conditions of service of the Director General and Additional, Joint, Deputy and Assistant Directors General or such other advisers, consultants or officers, shall be such as may be prescribed.

4. The Director General, and Additional, Joint, Deputy and Assistant Directors General or such other advisers, consultants or officers, shall be appointed from amongst persons of integrity and outstanding ability and who have experience in investigation; and knowledge of accountancy management, business, public administration, international trade, law or economics and such other qualifications as may be prescribed.

Registrar and Officers and Other Employees of Commission (Section 17)

The Commission may appoint a Registrar and such officers and other employees, as it considers necessary for the efficient performance of its functions under this Act. The salaries and allowances payable to and other terms and conditions of service of the Registrar and officers and other employees of the Commission and the number of such officers and employees shall be such as may be prescribed.

DUTIES, POWERS AND FUNCTIONS OF COMMISSION

(Sections 18 to 40)

Duties of Commission (Section 18)

Subject to the provisions of this Act, it shall be the duty of the Commission to eliminate practices having adverse effect on competition, promote and sustain competition, protect the interests of consumers, and ensure freedom of trade carried on by other participants, in markets in India: The Commission may, for the purpose of discharging its duties or performing its functions under this Act, enter into any memorandum or arrangement, with the prior approval of the Central Government, with any agency of any foreign country.

Inquiry into certain agreements and dominant position of enterprise (Section 19)

1. The Commission may inquire into any alleged contravention of the provisions either on its own notion or on -

(a) receipt of a complaint, accompanied by such fee as may be determined by regulations, from any person, consumer or their association or trade association; or

(b) a reference made to it by the Central Government or a State Government or a statutory authority.

2. The powers and functions of the commission shall include the powers and functions specified in subsections given below :

3. Inquiry in to Anti Competitive Agreements : The Commission shall, white determining whether an agreement has an appreciable adverse effect on competition, have due regard to all or any of the following factors, namely:

(a) certain of barriers to new entrants in the market;

(b) driving existing competitors out of the market;

(c) foreclosure of competition by hindering entry into the market;

(d) accrual of benefits of consumers;

(e) improvements in production or distribution of goods or provision of services; or

(f) promotion of technical, scientific and economic development by means, of production or distribution of goods or provision of services.

4. Inquiry into above of dominant position : The Commission shall, while inquiring whether an enterprise enjoys a dominant position or not have due regard to all or any of the following factors, namely:

(a) market share of the enterprise;

(b) size and resources of the enterprise;

(c) size and importance of the competitors;

(d) economic power of the enterprise including commercial advantages over competitors;

(e) vertical integration of the enterprises or sale or service network of such enterprises;

(f) dependence of consumers on the enterprise;

(g) monopoly or dominant position whether acquired as a result of any statute or by virtue of being a Government company or a public sector undertaking or otherwise;

(h) entry barriers including barriers such as regulatory barriers, financial risk, high capital cost of entry, marketing entry barriers, technical entry barriers, economies of scale, high cost of substitutable goods or service for consumers;

(i) countervailing buying power;

(j) market structure and size of market;

(k) social obligations and social costs;

(l) relative advantage, by way of the contribution to the economic development, by the enterprise enjoying a dominant position having or likely to have appreciable adverse effect on competition;

(m) any other factor which the Commission may consider relevant for the inquiry.

5. For determining whether a market constitutes a "relevant market" for the purposes of this Act, the Commission shall have due regard to the "relevant geographic market" or "relevant product market". The Commission shall, while determining the 'relevant geographic market", have due regard to an or any of the following factors, namely:-

(a) regulatory trade barriers;

(b) local specification requirements;

(c) national procurement policies;

(d) adequate distribution facilities;

(e) transport costs;

(f) language;

(g) consumer preferences;

(h) need for secure or regular supplies or rapid after- services.

6. The Commission shall, while determining the "relevant product market", have due regard to all or any of the following factors, namely:-

(a) physical characteristics or end-use of goods;

(b) price of goods or services;

(c) consumer preference;

(d) exclusion of in-house production;

(e) existence of specialized production;

(f) classification of specialized producers;

INQUIRY INTO COMBINATION BY COMMISSION (Section 20)

1. The Commission may, upon its own knowledge or information relating to acquisition referred to or acquiring of control referred to or merger or amalgamation referred to inquire into whether such a combination (acquiring of control or merger or amalgamation) has caused or is likely to cause an appreciable adverse effect on competition in India:

The Commission shall not initiate any inquiry after the expiry of one year from the date on which such combination has taken effect.

2. The Commission shall, on receipt of a notice or upon receipt of a reference, inquire whether a combination referred to in that notice or reference has caused or is likely to cause an appreciable adverse effect on competition in India.

3. The Central Government shall, on the expiry of a period of two years from the date of commencement of this Act and thereafter every two years, in consultation with the Commission, by notification, enhance or reduce, on the basis of the wholesale price index or fluctuations in exchange rate of rupee or foreign currencies, the value of assets or the value of turnover, for the purposes of that section.

4. For the purposes of determining whether a combination would have the effect of or is likely to have an appreciable adverse effect on competition in the relevant market, the Commission shall have due regard to all or a y of the following factors, namely:

(a) actual and potential level of competition through imports in the market;

(b) extent of barriers to entry to the market;

(c) level of combination in the market;

(d) degree of countervailing power in the market;

(e) likelihood that the combination would result in the parties to the combination being able to significantly and sustainably increase prices or profit margins;

(f) extent of effective competition likely to sustain in a market;

(g) extent to which substitutes are available or are likely to be available in the market;

(h) market share, in the relevant market, of the persons or enterprise in a combination, individually and as a combination;

(i) likelihood that the combination would result in the removal of a vigorous and effective competitor or competitors in the market;

(j) nature and extent of vertical integration in the market;

(k) possibility of a failing business;

(l) nature and extent of innovation:

(m) relative advantage, by way of the contribution to the economic development, by any combination having or likely to have appreciable adverse effect on competition;

(n) whether the benefits of the combination outweigh the adverse impact of the combination, if any.

Reference by Statutory Authority (Section 21)

If in the course of a proceeding before any statutory authority, entrusted with the responsibility of regulating any goods or service or market there for, a party has raised an issue that the decision taken by the statutory authority would be contrary to the provision of the Act, then the statutory authority shall be bound to make a reference to the Commission, The Commission will, after hearing parties to the proceedings shall, give to the statutory authority its opinion and the statutory authority shall thereafter pass its orders.

Benches of Commission (Section 22)

The jurisdiction, powers and authority of the Commission may be exercised by Benches there of, The Benches shall be constituted by the Chairperson and each Bench shall consist of not less than two Members. Every Bench shall consist of at least one Judicial Member.

Explanation: For the purposes of this sub-section, "Judicial Member" means a Member who is, or has been, or is qualified to be, a Judge of a High Court.

The Bench over which the Chairperson presides shall be the Principal Bench and the other Benches shall be known as the Additional Benches. There shall be constituted by the Chairperson one or more Benches to be called the Mergers Bench or Mergers Benches, as the case may be, exclusively to deal with matters referred to in Sections 5 and 6. The places as which the Principal Bench, other Additional Bench or Mergers Bench shall ordinarily sit shall be such as the Central Government may, by notification, specify.

Distribution of Business amongst Commission Benches (Section 23)

Where any Benches are constituted, the Chairperson may, from time to time, by order, make provisions as to the distribution of the business of the Commission amongst the Benches and specify the matters, which may be dealt with by each Bench.

If any question arises as to whether any matter falls within the purview of the business allocated to a Bench, the decision of the Chairperson thereon shall be final.

The Chairperson, may transfer a Member from one Bench to another Bench; or authorise the Members of one Bench to discharge also the functions of the Members of other Bench:

The Chairperson shall transfer, with the prior approval of the Central Government, a Member from one Bench situated in one city to another Bench situated in another city-

The Chairperson may, for the purpose of securing that any case or matter which having regard to the nature of the questions involved, requires or is required in his opinion or under the rules made by the Central Government in this behalf, to be decided by a Bench composed of more than two Members, issue such general or special orders as he may deem fit.

Procedure for Deciding a Case where Members of Bench differ in Opinion (Section 24)

If the Members of a Bench differ in opinion on any point, they shall state the point or points on which they differ, and make a reference to the Chairperson who shall either near the point or points himself or refer the case for hearing on such point or points by one or more of the other Members and such point or points shall be decided according the opinion of the majority of the Members who have heard the case, including those who first heard it.

Jurisdiction of Bench (Section 25)

An inquiry shall be initiated or a complaint be instituted or a reference be made under this Act before a Bench within the local limits of whose jurisdiction-

(a) the respondent, or each of the respondents, where there are more than one, at the time of the initiation of inquiry or institution of the complaint or making of reference, as the case may b actually and voluntarily resides, or carries on business, or personally works for gain; or

(b) any of the respondents, where there are more than one, at the time of the initiation of the inquiry or institution of complaint or making of reference, as the case may be. Actually and voluntarily resides or carries on business or personally works for gain provided that in such case either the leave of the Bench is given, or the respondents who do not reside, or carry on business, or personally works for gain, as aforesaid, acquiesce, in such institution; or

(c) the cause of action, wholly or in part, arises,

Procedure for Inquiry on Complaints (Section 26)

1. On receipt of a complaint or a reference from the Central Government or a State Government or a statutory authority or on its own knowledge or information, under Section 19, if the Commission is of the opinion that there exists a prima facie case, it shall direct the Director General to cause an investigation to be made into the matter.

2. The Director General shall, submit a report on his findings within such period as m y be specified by the Commission.

3. Where on receipt of a complaint the Commission is of the opinion that there exists no prima fade case, it shall dismiss the complaint and may pass such orders as it deems fit, including imposition of costs, If necessary.

4. The commission shall forward a copy of the report to the parties concerned or to the Central Government or the State Government or the statutory authority, as the case may be,

5. If the report of the Director General relates on a complaint and such report recommends that there is no contravention of any of the provisions of this Act, the complainant shall be given an opportunity to rebut the findings of the Director General.

6. If, after hearing the complainant, the Commission agrees with the recommendation of the Director General, it shall dismiss the complaint.

7. If, after hearing the complainant, the Commission is of the opinion that further inquiry is called for, it shall direct the complainant to proceed with the complaint.

8. If the report of the Director General relates on a reference made and such report recommends that there is no contravention of the provisions of this Act, the Commission shall invite comments of the Central Government or the State Government or the statutory authority, as the case may be, on such report and on

receipt of such comments, the Commission shall return the reference if there is no prima facie case or proceed with the reference as a complaint if there is a prima fade case,

9. If the report of the Director General recommends that there is contravention of any of the provisions of this Act, and the Commission is of the opinion that further inquiry is called for, it shall inquire into such contravention in accordance with the provisions of this Act.

Comments: In case, the report of the Director General recommends that there is no contravention of the provisions of the Act, the complainant shall be given an opportunity to rebut the findings of the Director General. If, after hearing the complainant, the Commission agrees with the recommendations of the Director General, the Commission shall dismiss the complaint, In case, the Commission, after hearing the complainant is of the opinion that further inquiry is required to be conducted, it shall direct the complainant to proceed with the complaint, if the report of the Director General relates to a reference and such report recommends that there is contravention of any of the provisions of the Act the Commission shall invite the comments from the Central Government or the State Government or the statutory authority, as the case may be, and it shall return the reference if there is no prima-fade case or the Commission may proceed with the reference as a complaint If there is a prima-facie case.

Orders by Commission after Inquiry into Agreements or Abuse of Dominant Position (Section 27)

Where after inquiry the Commission finds that any agreement or action of an enterprise in a dominant position, is in contravention, as the case may be, it may pass all or any of the following orders, namely:

(a) **direct any enterprise** or association of enterprises or person or association of persons, as the case may be, involved in such agreement, or abuse of dominant position, to discontinue and not to re-enter such agreement or discontinue such abuse of dominant position, as the case may be;

(b) **impose such penalty**, as it may deem fit which shall be not more than ten per cent, of the average of the turnover for the last three preceding financial years, upon each of such person or enterprises which are parties to such agreements or abuse:

Any agreement has been entered into by any cartel, the Commission shall impose upon each producer. Seller, distributor, trader or service provider included in that cartel, a penalty equivalent to three times of the amount of profits made out of such agreement by the cartel or ten per cent of the average of the turnover of the cartel for the last preceding three financial years, whichever is higher;

(c) **award compensation** to parties in accordance with the provisions contained in section 34;

(d) **direct that the agreements shall stand modified** to the extent and in the manner as may be specified in the order by the Commission;

(e) **direct the enterprises concerned** to abide by such other orders as the Commission may pass and comply with the directions, including payment of costs, if any;

(f) **recommend, to the Central Government** for the division of an enterprise enjoying dominant position.

(g) **pass such other** order as it may deem fit.

Division of Enterprise Enjoying Dominant Position (Section 28)

1. The Central Government, on recommendation may, notwithstanding anything contained in any other law for the time being in force, order in writing, direct division of an enterprise enjoying dominant position to ensure that such enterprise does not abuse its dominant position.

2. In particular, and without prejudice to the generality of the foregoing powers, may order referred may provide for all or any of the following matters, namely:

(a) the transfer or vesting of property, rights, liabilities or obligations;

(b) the adjustment of contracts either by discharge or reduction of any liability or obligation or otherwise;

(c) the creation, allotment, surrender or cancellation of any shares, stocks or securities;

(d) the payment of compensation to any person who suffered any loss due to dominant position of such enterprise;

(e) the formation or winding up of an enterprise or the amendment of the Memorandum of Association or Articles of Association or any other instruments regulating the business of any enterprise;

(f) the extent to which and the circumstances in which, provisions of the order affecting an enterprise may be altered by the enterprise and the registration thereof;

(g) any other matter which may be necessary to give effect to the division of the enterprise.

3. Notwithstanding anything contained in any other law for the time being in force or in any contract or in any Memorandum or Articles of Association, an officer of a company who ceases to hold office as such in consequence of the division of an enterprise shall not be entitled to claim any compensation for such cesser.

Procedure for Investigation of Combinations (Section 29)

1. Where the commission is of the opinion that a combination is likely to cause, or has caused an appreciable adverse effect on competition within the relevant market in India, it shall issue to notice to show cause to the parties to combination calling upon them to respond within thirty days of the receipt of the notice, as to why investigation in respect of such combination should not be conducted.

2. The Commission, if it is prima fade of the opinion that the combination has, or is likely to have, an appreciable adverse effect on competition, it shall, within seven working days from the date of receipt of the response of the parties to the combination, direct the parties to the said combination to publish details of the combination within ten working days of such direction, in such manner, as it thinks appropriate, the combination to the knowledge or information of the public and persons affected or likely to be affected by such combination.

3. The Commission may invite any person or member of the public, affected or likely to be affected by the said combination, to file his written objections, if any, before the Commission within fifteen working days from the date on which the details of the combination were published.

4. The Commission may, within fifteen working days from the expiry of the period specified, call for such additional or other information as it may deem fit from the parties to the said combination.

5. The additional or other information called for by the Commission shall be furnished by the parties within fifteen days from the expiry of the period specified.

6. After receipt of all information and within a period of forty-five working days from the expiry of the period specified as above, the Commission shall proceed to deal with the case in accordance with the provisions contained in this Act.

Comments: This section lays down the detailed procedure for investigation of Combinations if the commission is of the opinion that any combination is likely to cause or has caused an appreciable adverse effect on competition within the relevant market in India.

Inquiry into Disclosures (Section 30)

Where any person or enterprise has given a notice under Sub-section (2) of Section 6. The Commission shall inquire -

(a) whether the disclosure made in the notice is correct;

(b) whether the combination has, or is likely to have, an appreciable adverse effect on competition.

Orders of Commission on certain combinations (Section 31)

1. Where the Commission is of the opinion that any combination does not, or is not likely to, have an appreciable adverse effect on competition, it shall, by order, approve that combination including the combination in respect of which a notice has been given.

2. Where the Commission is of the opinion that the combination has, or is likely to have, an appreciable adverse effect on competition, it shall direct that the combination shall not take effect.

3. Where the Commission is of the opinion that the combination has, or is likely to have, an appreciable adverse effect on competition but such adverse effect can be dominated by suitable modification to such combination, it may propose appropriate modification to the combination, to the parties to such combination.

4. The panics, who accept the modification proposed by the Commission, shall carry out such modification within the period specified by the commission.

5. If the parties to the combination, who have accepted the modification, fail to carry out the modification within the period specified by the commission, such combination shall be deemed to have an appreciable adverse effect on competition and the Commission shall deal with such combination in accordance with the provisions of this Act.

6. If the parties to the combination do not accept the modification proposed by the Commission, such parties may, within thirty working days of the modification proposed by the Commission, submit amendment to the modification proposed by the Commission,

7. If the Commission agrees with the amendment submitted by the parties, it shall, by order, approve the combination.

8. If the Commission does not accept the amendment submitted then, the parties shall be allowed a further period of thirty working days within which such parties shall accept the modification proposed by the Commission.

9. If the parties fail to accept the modification proposed by the Commission within thirty working days or within a further period of thirty working days the combination shall be deemed to have an appreciable adverse effect on competition and the dealt with in accordance with the provisions of this Act.

10. Where the Commission has directed that the combination shall not take effect or the combination is deemed to have an appreciable adverse effect on competition, then, without prejudice to any penalty which may be imposed or any prosecution which may be initiated under this Act, the Commission may order that-

(a) the acquisition or

(b) the acquiring of control or

(c) the merger or amalgamation shall not be given effect to:

The Commission may, if it considers appropriate, frame a scheme to implement its order.

11. If the Commission does not, on the expiry of a period of ninety working days from the date of publication pass an order or issue direction the combination shall be deemed to have been approved by the commission.

Explanation: For the purposes of determining the period of ninety working days specified, the period of thirty working days and a further period of thirty working days specified shall be excluded.

12. Where any extension of time is sought by the parties to the combination, the period of ninety working days shall be reckoned after deducting the extended time granted at the request of the parties.

13. Where the Commission has ordered a combination to be void, the acquisition or acquiring of control or merger or amalgamation shall be dealt with by the authorities under any other law for the time being in force as if such acquisition or acquiring of control or merger or amalgamation had not taken place and the parties to the combination shall be dealt with accordingly.

Inquiry into acts taking place outside India but having an effect on competition in India: (Section 32)

The Commission shall have power to inquire into anti-competitive agreement or abuse of dominant position or combination even if -

(a) an agreement has been entered into outside India; or

(b) any party to such agreement is outside India; or

(c) any enterprise abusing the dominant position is outside India; or

(d) a combination has taken place outside India; or

(e) any party to combination is outside India; or

(f) any other matter or practice or action arising out of such agreement or dominant position is outside India;

if such agreement or dominant position or combination has, or is likely to have an appreciable adverse effect on competition in the relevant market in India.

Orders by Commission : (Sections. 27, 28, 31, 33, 34, 37, 38 and 39)

(Sections. 27. 28, 31, 33, 34, 37, 38 and 39 have yet not come into effect)

1. On anti-competitive agreements or abuse of dominant position: (Section 27)

Where after inquiry, the Commission finds that any agreement is an anti-competitive agreement or action of an enterprise is in abuse of dominant position, it may pass all or any of the following orders, namely-

(a) direct any enterprise or association of enterprises or person or association of persons, as the case may be, involved in such anti-competitive agreement, or abuse of dominant position, to discontinue and not to re-enter such agreement or discontinue such abuse of dominant position, as the case may be;

(b) impose such penalty, as it may deem fit, which shall be not more than ten per cent of the average of the turnover for the last three preceding financial years. Upon each of such person or enterprises which are parties to such agreements or abuse:

If any anti-competitive agreement has been entered into by any cartel, the Commission shall impose upon each producer, seller, distributor, trader or service provider included in that cartel, a penalty equivalent to three times of the amount of profits made out of such agreement by the cartel or ten per cent of the average of the turnover of the cartel for the last preceding three financial years, whichever is higher.

(c) award compensation to parties;

(d) direct that the agreements shall stand modified to the extent and in the manner as may be specified in the order by the Commission;

(e) direct the enterprises concerned to abide by such other orders as the Commission may pass and comply with the directions, including payment of costs, if any;

(f) recommend to the Central Government for the division of an enterprise enjoying dominant position;

(g) pass such other order as it may deem fit,

Power to award compensation (Section 34)

Any person may make an application to the Commission for an order for the recovery of compensation from any enterprise for any loss or damage shown to have been suffered by such person as a result of any contravention committed by such enterprise. After inquiry, the Commission may pass an order directing the enterprise to make payment to the applicant of the amount determined by it as realisable from the enterprise as compensation for the loss or damage caused to the applicant as a result of any contravention.

Division of enterprise enjoying dominant position: (Section 28)

The Central Government may, on recommendation by the Commission, by order in writing, direct division of an enterprise enjoying dominant position to ensure that such enterprise does not abuse its dominant position. The order may provide for all or any of the following matters, namely:

(a) the transfer or vesting of property, rights, liabilities or obligations;

(b) the adjustment of contracts either by discharge or reduction of any liability or obligation or otherwise;

(c) the creation, allotment, surrender or cancellation of any shares, stocks or securities;

(d) the payment of compensation to any person who suffered any loss due to dominant position of such enterprise;

(e) the formation or winding up of an enterprise or the amendment of the memorandum of association or articles of association or any other instrument regulating the business of any enterprise;

(f) the extent to which, and the circumstances in which, provisions of the order affecting an enterprise may be altered by the enterprise and the registration thereof;

(g) any other matter which may be necessary to give effect to the division of the enterprise,

An officer of a company who ceases to hold office as such in consequence of the division of an enterprise shall not be entitled to claim any compensation for such cesser.

2. On certain combination: (Section 31)

Where the Commission is of the opinion that any combination does not, or is not likely to, have an appreciable adverse effect on competition, it shall, by order, approve that combination including the combination in respect of which a notice has been given.

Where the Commission is of the opinion that the combination has, or is likely to have, an appreciable adverse effect on competition, it shall direct that the combination shall not take effect.

Where the Commission is of the opinion that the combination has, or is likely to have, an appreciable adverse effect on competition but such adverse effect can be eliminated by suitable modification to the combination, it may propose to the parties to such combination, appropriate modification to the combination.

The parties, who accept the modification proposed by the Commission shall carry out such modification within the period specified by the Commission. If the parties to the combination, who have accepted the modification, fail to carry out the modification within the specified period by the Commission, such combination shall be deemed to have an appreciable adverse effect on competition and the Commission shall deal with such combination in accordance with the provisions of this Act.

If the parties to the combination do not accept the modification proposed by the Commission, such parties may, within thirty working days of the modification proposed by the Commission, submit amendment to the modification proposed by the Commission. If the Commission agrees with the amendment submitted by the parties, it shall, by order, approve the combination. If the Commission does not accept the amendment submitted, then the parties shall be allowed a further period of thirty working days within which such parties shall accept the modification proposed by the Commission.

If the parties fail to accept the modification proposed by the Commission within thirty working days or within a further period of thirty working days, the combination shall be deemed to have an appreciable adverse effect on competition and be dealt with in accordance with the provisions of this Act.

Where the Commission has directed that the combination shall not take effect or the combination is deemed to have an appreciable adverse effect on competition, then, without prejudice to any penalty which may be imposed or any prosecution which may be initiated under this Act, the Commission may order that-

(a) the acquisition;

(b) the acquiring of control;

(c) the merger or amalgamation;

shall not be given effect to.

The Commission may, if it considers appropriate, frame a scheme to implement its order.

If the Commission does not, on the expiry of a period of ninety working days from the date of publication of details of the combination, pass order or issue direction, the combination shall be deemed to have been approved by the Commission.

Where any extension of time is sought by the parties to the combination, the period of ninety working days shall be reckoned after deducting the extended time granted at the request of the parties.

Where the Commission has ordered a combination to be void, the acquisition or acquiring of control or merger or amalgamation shall be dealt with by the authorities under any other law for the time being in force as if such acquisition or acquiring of control or merger or amalgamation had not taken place and the parties to the combination shall be dealt with accordingly,

Nothing shall effect any proceeding initiated or which may be initiated under any other law for the time being in force.

3. Grant interim relief: (Section 33)

Where during an inquiry before the Commission, it is proved to the satisfaction of the Commission that following acts are committed -

(a) anti-competitive agreement is entered into; or

(b) there is an abuse of dominant position; or

(c) that a combination causes an appreciable adverse effect on competition; or

(d) that the import of any goods is likely to affect the above;

The Commission may, without giving notice to the opposite party, where it deems it necessary, by order grant a temporary injunction restraining any party from carrying on such act or restrain any party from importing such goods until the conclusion of such inquiry or until further orders.

4. Review of orders: (Section 37)

Any person aggrieved by an order of the Commission from which an appeal is allowed by this Act but no appeal has been preferred, may, within thirty days from the date of the order, apply to the Commission for review of its order and the Commission may make such order thereon as it thinks fit. The Commission may entertain a review application after the expiry of the said period of thirty days, if it is satisfied that the applicant was prevented by sufficient cause from preferring the application in time. However, no order shall be modified or set aside without giving an opportunity of being heard to the person in whose favour the order is given and the Director General where he was a party to the proceedings.

5. Rectification of orders: (Section 38)

With a view to rectifying any mistake apparent from the record, the Commission may amend any order passed by it under the provisions of this Act. Commission may make -

(a) an amendment of its own motion;

(b) an amendment for rectifying any such mistake which has been brought to its notice by any party to the order.

Commission shall not, while rectifying any mistake apparent from record, amend substantive part of its order passed under the provisions of this Act.

Execution of orders of Commission: (Sec. 39)

Every order passed by the Commission under this Act shall be enforced by the Commission in the same manner as if it were a decree or order made by a High Court or the principal civil court in a suit pending therein. It shall be lawful for the Commission to send, in the event of its inability to execute it, such order to the High Court or the principal civil court. As the case may be, within the local limits of whose jurisdiction-

(a) in the case of an order against a company or a corporation or any other body corporate the registered office or the sole or principal place of business of the person in India, or where the person has also a subordinate office, that subordinate office, is situated;

(b) in the case of an order against any other person, the place where the person concerned voluntarily resides or carries on business or personally works for gain, is situated.

Thereupon the court to which the order is so sent shall execute the order as if it were a decree or order sent to it for execution.

Appeal (Section 40)

Any person aggrieved by any decision or order of the Commission may file an appeal to the Supreme Court within sixty days from the date of communication of the decision or order of the Commission to him on one or more of the grounds specified in section 100 of the Code of Civil Procedure, 1908. Supreme Court may, if it is satisfied that the appellant was prevented by sufficient cause from filing the appeal within the said period, allow it to be filed within a further period not exceeding sixty days. No appeal shall lie against any decision or order of the Commission made with the consent of the parties.

(Sec. 40 has yet not come into effect)

Exclusion of jurisdiction of civil courts: (Section 61)

No civil court shall have jurisdiction to entertain any suit or proceeding in respect of any matter which the Commission is empowered by or under this Act to determine and no injunction shall be granted by any court or other authority in respect of any action taken in pursuance of any power conferred by or under this Act.

PENALTIES

For contravention of orders of Commission : (Section. 42)

If any person contravenes any order or direction of the Commission or contravenes any condition or restriction of any approval, sanction, direction or exemption accorded or fails to pay the penalty imposed, he shall be liable to be detained in civil prison for a term which may extend to one year and he shall also be liable to a penalty not exceeding ₹ 10 lacs.

For failure to comply with direction of Commission and Director General: (Section 43)

If any person fails to comply with a direction given by the Commission or the Director General, the Commission shall impose on such person a penalty of ₹ 1 lac for each day during which such failure continues.

For making false statement or omission to furnish material information: (Section 44)

If any person being a party to a combination makes a false statement or omits to state any material particular, such person shall be liable to a penalty which shall not be less than ₹ 50 lacs but which may extend to ₹ 1 crore.

For offences in relation to furnishing of information: (Section 45)

If any person, who furnishes any particulars, documents or any information or makes any statement which is false, or omits to state any material fact or willfully alters, suppresses or destroys any document, the Commission shall impose on such person a penalty which may extend to ₹ 10 lacs.

When the Commission may impose lesser penalty? (Section 46)

When any person who is alleged to have entered into anti-competitive agreement, has made a full and true disclosure in respect of the alleged violations, the Commission may impose a lesser penalty as it may deem fit than leviable under the Act. However, lesser penalty shall not be imposed in cases where proceedings for the violation of any provision of the Act or rules or regulations have been instituted or any investigation has been directed to be made before making of such disclosure. The lesser penalty shall be imposed by the Commission only in respect of a producer, seller, distributor, trader or service provider included in the cartel who first made the full, true and vital disclosure.

In cases where the Commission is satisfied that in the course of proceedings, such person on whom lesser penalty had been imposed -

(a) did not comply with the condition on which lesser penalty was imposed; or

(b) had given false evidence; or

(c) the disclosure made is not vital;

such a person, thereupon, may be tried for the offence with respect which the lesser penalty was imposed and shall also be liable to the imposition of penalty to which such person would have been liable, had lesser penalty not been imposed.

Contravention by companies: (Section 48)

Where any person charged with any offence is a company, every person, who was in charge of, and was responsible to the company for the conduct of the business of the company, such a person, as well as the company, shall be deemed to be guilty of the contravention and shall be liable to be proceeded against and punished accordingly.

Such a person however, shall not be liable to any punishment, if he proves that the contravention was committed without his knowledge or that he had exercised all due diligence to prevent the Commission of such contravention.

Where a contravention is committed by a company and it is proved that the contravention had taken place with the consent or connivance of, or is attributable to any neglect on the part of any director, manager, secretary or other officer of the company, such director, manager, secretary or other officer shall also be deemed to be guilty of that contravention and shall be liable to be proceeded and punished accordingly.

(Sections42 to 48 have yet not come into effect)

Duties of Director General to Investigate Contravention (Section 41)

The Director General shall, when so directed by the Commission, assist the Commission in investigating into any contravention of the provisions of this Act or any rules or regulations made there under. The Director General shall have all the powers as are conferred upon the Commission.

Without prejudice to the provisions of sub-section (2), sections 240 and 240A of the Companies Act. 1956. So far as maybe, shall apply to an investigation made by the Director General or any other person investigating under is authority, as they apply in inspector appointed under that Act.

COMPETITION ADVOCACY (Section 49)

In formatting policy, the Central Government may make a reference to the Commission for its opinion on possible effects of such policy on competition. The Commission is required to give its opinion to the Central Government within sixty days from the date of such reference. Such opinion shall not be binding upon the Central Government, The Commission is also required to take suitable measures for the promotion of competition advocacy creating awareness and imparting training about the competition issues as may be prescribed.

REVIEW QUESTIONS

1. What are the recommendation of the Committee on Competition Law (2000)?

2 Define the following (under the Competition Act 2002). (a) Acquisition; (b) Agreement; (c) Cartel; (d) Consumer; (e) Services; (f) Goods; (g) Relevant market; (h) Relevant geographic market.

3. Enumerate the objectives and describe the extent of the competition Act, 2002

4. Explain the provisions of the Competition Act 2002 relating to prohibition of certain agreements and prohibition of abuse of dominant position.

5. Explain the provisions relating to regulation of combinations under the Competition Act,

6. Describe the provisions as regards prohibition of anti-competitive agreements.

7. Specify certain activities which are presumed to have an appreciable adverse effect on competition.

8. Explain the following expressions: (i) Bid-rigging (ii) Tie-in arrangement (iii) Exclusive Supply Agreement (iv) Exclusive distribution agreement (v) Refusal to deal (vi) Resale Price Maintenance

9. Describe the provision as regards prohibition of abuse of dominant position.

10. Explain the following terms: (i) Predatory price (ii) Dominant position

11. What are the circumstances under which combination is construed?

12. Explain the following terms in relation to the provisions relating to combinations:

    (i) Control (iii) group (iii) value of assets.

13. Explain the provisions relating to regulation of Combinations.

14. Explain the following terms:

    (i) Foreign Institutional Investor (ii) Venture Capital Fund.

15. State and explain the procedure to establish and composition of the Competition Commission of India.

16. What are the duties, powers and functions of the Competition Commission of India?

17. Describe the provisions as regards appointment of: (i) Director General and (ii) Registrar and other employees of the Commission.

18. Describe the provisions as regards 'Benches of Commission' and 'Distribution of business of Commission amongst Benches'.

    Inquiry into Certain Agreement and Abuse of dominant Position of Enterprises and Combinations

19. Explain the powers of the Competition Commission to inquire into anti- competition agreements and dominant position of enterprises.

20. What are the factors to considered while inquiring the Competition Commission, whether an enterprise enjoys a dominant position or not?

21. Explain the procedure to be followed by the Commission for inquiry into complaints regarding anti-competition agreements or abuse of dominant position.

22. What orders can be passed by the combination where it finds that an agreement is anti-competitive or that dominant position is being abused?

23. State factors to be considered by the Competition Commission, while determing whether an agreement has adverse effect on competition or not.

24. What factors are to considered by the Competition Commission, while determining the relevant geographic market.

25. Under what situations, the Central Government can order division of enterprise enjoying dominant position?

26. What type of matters may be provided by the Central Government in the order for division of enterprise enjoying dominant position?

27. Give the provisions as regards procedure to be adopted by the Commission for investigation of combination.
28. What type of orders can be passed after the Commission has conducted an investigation into combinations?
29. Does the Commission have power to inquire into such acts taking place outside India but have an adverse effect on Competition in India?
30. What factors are to be considered, by the Competition Commission of India while determining the relevant product market?
31. What factors are to be considered by the Competition Commission of India to determine whether a combination would have appreciable adverse effect on Competition in the relevant market?
32. Describe the power of the Commission to (i) grant interim relief, (ii) regulate its own procedure, (iii) review its own orders, (iv) rectify its orders, (v) execute its orders.
33. Can a person aggrieved by any decision or order of the Commission file an appeal? If so, with whom?
34. What are the powers of the Commission to give its opinion on possible effect of any competition policy formulated by the Central Government? Also mention its duties in this regard.
35. Explain the role of Competition Advocacy under the Competition Act, 2002.
36. What agreements, according to the competition Act, 2002, cause an adverse effect on Competition?
37. What agreements, according to the competition Act, 2002, do not cause adverse effect on Competition?

❏ ❏ ❏

15

Chapter

THE CONSUMER PROTECTION ACT, 1986

Need for Consumer Legislation : Most of the manufacturers and traders have been adopting unfair trade practices for the purpose of promoting sale, use or supply of any goods, or for the provision of any services. Unfair practices like false and misleading descriptions about the nature and quality of the goods, exaggerated statements about their power and potency, false weights and measurements etc., have been causing loss or injury to consumers of such goods and services. A number of Acts were enacted by the Government to protect the interests of consumers. For instance,

The Sales of Goods Act, 1930

The Adricultural Products Grading and Marketing Act, (AGMARK) 1937

The Prevention of Food Adulteration Act, 1954,

The Essential Commodities Act, 1955

The Standards of Weights and Measures Act, 1956

The Monopolies and Restrictive Trade Practices Act, 1969

The Indian Standard Institution (certification of marks) Act, (ISI) 1952 etc.

were passed by the Government for the purpose of protecting the interests of the consumers. But these Acts failed to provide the needed protection to the interests of consumers. To provide for better protection of the interests of the consumers, and to save the consumers from the evils of unfair trade practices, the Government of India enacted the Consumer Protection Act in 1986. Most of the defects in the Act were removed by amendments to the Act in 1991, 1993, 2001, 2002 and 2005

The following points or ground justify the need for consumer protection:

- Consumers do not have adequate product knowledge.
- They are ignorant of their rights and remedies available to them.
- They are in a weak bargaining position.
- Manufacturers and suppliers have the expertise which a consumer does not have.
- Often products are forced on consumers through eye-caching packing materials, sensational media advertisement, etc.
- Fake and spenions products are flooding the market and deceiving the consumers.
- Let the buyer beware' is not realistic in the context of liberalization, privatization and globalization-complex and mass product goods and services. Also it permits seller to disown his/her liability.

Objectives of the Act

The Consumer Protection Act, 1986 seeks to provide for better protection of the interests of consumers. This Act seeks, *inter alia*, to *promote and protect the basic rights of consumers*.

RIGHTS OF CONSUMERS

For the first time in the history of consumer-legislation in India, the Consumer Protection Act, 1986 extended a statutory recognition to the rights of consumers. Section 6 of the Act recognizes to following six rights of consumers.

Right of Protection to Life and Property : The right to be protected against marketing of goods which are hazardous to life and property.

Right to be informed : The right to be informed about the quality, quantity, potency, purity, standard and price of goods to protect the consumers against unfair trade practices.

Right to choose : The right to be assured, wherever possible, access to a variety of goods at competitive prices.

Right to be Heard : The right to be heard and to be assured that consumer's interests will receive due consideration at appropriate forums.

Right to Redress : The right to seek redressal against unfair trade practices or unscrupulous exploitation of consumers, and

Right to Education : It means the right to acquire the knowledge and skill to be an informed consumer.

This is based on the basic rights of consumers as defined by the International Organisation of Consumers (IOCU) viz. Right to safety, to information, of choice, to be heard, to redressal, to consumer education, to healthy environment and to basic needs.

These objects are being promoted and protected by the *consumer protection councils* established at the central, state and district level. The Act seeks to provide *speedy and simple redressal* to consumer disputes. For this purpose a *quasi-judicial machinery* is being set up at the district, state and central level. These quasi-judicial bodies will observe the principles of natural justice. These have been empowered to give reliefs of a specific nature and to award compensation to consumers. Penalties for non-compliance of the orders given by the quasi-judicial bodies have also been provided. The remedies under this Act are additional and supplemental remedies.

Section 3 of the Consumers Protection Act states that the *provision of this Act shall be in addition and not in derogation of the provisions of any other law or Act for the time being in force.*

Advantages of Seeking Relief under the Consumer Protection Act, 1986

Following are the most important advantages of seeking relief before a Consumer Forum instead of approaching of Civil Court. While evaluating the comparative benefits we may also consider the remedy available to consumers under the MRTP Act, 1969 and now under the Competition Act 2002 against restrictive trade practices and unfair trade practices:

Firstly administration of justice under the Consumer Protection Act is ***comparatively cheaper*** than the regular and conventional judiciary.

Secondly consumer courts are expected to deliver ***speedy justice***. Despite criticism on this aspect some of which is justified, one agrees that consumer courts certainly score over the civil courts.

You can be your own lawyer before consumer courts. Though appearance of lawyers is not prohibited *Consumer Courts do not encourage appearance of lawyers* and extensive long winded arguments.

Procedural simplicity and amiable atmosphere prevailing in consumer courts is more encouraging to an ordinary litigant as compared to lengthy and procedure oriented civil court proceedings.

It *applies to all goods and services* unless specifically exempted by the Central Government

The provisions of this Act are in addition to and not in derogation of the provisions of any other Act.

It covers all sectors whether private, public or co-operative While the provisions of Restrictive Trade Practices and Unfair trade practices cannot be invoked against Central Govt., State Govt., and public sector organisations, the provisions C.P. Act, 1986 can be invoked against Govt. run organisations such as railways, post office, air line, telephone boards, electricity boards, insurance companies, banks. Further Consumer Forum is *vested with quasi criminal powers/penal provisions* under section 27 of the Act.

DEFINITIONS

Consumer [Sec 2(i) (d)]

'*Consumer*' means any person who:

(i) "*buys any goods for a consideration* which has been paid or promised, or partly paid and partly promised, or under a system of deferred payment"; or

(ii) *hires any services for a consideration* which has been paid or promised, or partly paid and partly promised, or under a system of deferred payment, *i.e.* in respect of hire-purchase transactions.

(iii) "*uses the goods*" with the approval of the person who has bought the goods for consideration;

(iv) "*beneficiary of services*" with the approval of the person who has hired the service for consideration.

Thus consumer is a person who (i) buys any goods for a consideration, or (ii) hires or avails any services for a consideration. In addition to buyer(s) of goods or hirer(s) or user(s) of services, *any beneficiary of such services, using the goods/services with the approval of the purchaser or hirer or user would also be deemed a 'Consumer' under the Act.*

Nominee of a person insured under LIC is a consumer **[Life Insurance Corporation of India v. Shri Chatur Behari Lal-Appeal No 29/89 (Raj)]**

The widow of the deceased Policy holder was held as a consumer under the Act by the State Commission of A.P. in the case of ***A Vs. LIC of India***. The consideration may be either paid or promised, or partly paid and partly promised or under any system of deferred payment. The Act thus covers transactions for the supply of goods and rendering of services.

Buyer of Goods for consideration : The buyer of goods for a consideration is a consumer. The Act, unlike the Sale of Goods Act, does not insist on money consideration only. Transactions of transfer of services, or barter, or exchange will come within the purview of the Act. The user of such goods, with the approval of the buyer of goods, is also a consumer as per the Act. But according to Section 2 (d) of the Act, *the term consumer does not include a person who obtains such goods for resale or for any commercial purpose.* Thus a purchaser of goods for reselling them, or a purchaser of taxi for plying the same on hire, a purchaser of a V.C.R. for running a video library, or purchaser of machinery for his commercial establishment is not a consumer. However, according to the Consumer Protection (Amended) Act, 1993, *a person who purchases tools or machinery under self-employment scheme is also a consumer.*

Hirer of Services for consideration : Any person who hires services for a consideration is a consumer. Consumer, not only means merely one who hires services for consideration, but also includes a person who is a beneficiary of such services. For example, the user of a telephone, even though he is not himself the subscriber is a consumer under the Act. Services include all kinds of professinal services, be it the ***routine services*** of a barber or the technical services of a highly qualified person. For example, ***supply of electricity*** has been held to be a service and not sale of goods. The services must be of commercial nature in the sense that they must be on payment. The payments may be in cash or kind. It may be made either at once, or partly at once, or partly on credit. The services may be rendered wholly or partly on credit. However, *free services or personal service under a contract have been excluded from the protective spell of the Consumer Protection Act, 1986.*

Union of India. Vs. Mrs. S. Prakash : It was held that the ***subscriber of telephone*** is a consumer as the rental charges paid to the Central Government is the consideration for the services rendered by the *Tele-Communication Department, District Manager, Telephones Patna Vs Lalit Kumar Bajla (1989).*

Mumbai Grahak Panchayat. Vs. Andhra Pradesh Scooters, Ltd : The complainant made an ***advance deposit*** of ₹ 500 with the A.P. Scooters Ltd., ***booking a scooter***. The complinant was not given the refund of the deposit when he demanded the same as per his contract with the opposite party. It was held that the complainant was a consumer, and was entitled to relief asked by him.

Ganapathi. Vs. Post Master, Karnataka State : In this case, ***the remitter of T.M.O.*** was held to be a consumer and was awarded compensation.

Cosmopolitan Hospitals. Vs. Smt. V.P. Nair's : The National Commission held, that a ***patient is a consumer and the medical assistance was a service***. The medical officer's service was not a personal service so as the constitute an exception to the application of the Consumer Protection Act, 1986.

Resale and Commercial Purpose

Commercial purpose does not include use by a person of goods bought and used by him and services availed by him exclusively for the purpose of earning his livelihood, by means of self employment.

A consumer who does not buy the goods for his own consumption or use, but for resale, is excluded from the perview of the definition. When the goods are re-sold in original condition as bought, it is a resale. When the manufacturer sells the goods to the wholesaler who in turn sells the goods to a retailer, the wholesaler will be excluded from the definition of the word consumer as he has bought the goods for 'resale' or for 'commercial purpose.' When the goods are not purchased for immediate final consumption, but for transfer, it is re-sale.

A mere transfer of goods without immediate final consumption could mean purchase of goods for resale or commercial purpose. Similarly, there has to be a direct nexus between the kind of goods purchased and sold. If the goods sold are converted for producing other goods or services, it is buying the goods for commercial purpose or for resale. A person buying the goods for resale or commercial purpose, even if for consideration, is not a consumer.

Commercial purpose should be established. Not buying for one's own use, is not necessarily buying for commercial purpose. A ***purchaser of a cooler*** is a consumer, even if the cooler is installed at a bus- stand for the use of public free of charge ***[T.N. Sethuraman v. Goa, Daman & Diu Industrial Development Corporation - 1992 CPT - 71 (NC)]***.

Goods bought and used by a consumer exclusively for the purpose of earning his livelihood by means of self-employment is not a commercial purpose. In the ***Secretary, Consumer Guidance & Research Society of India v. M/s. B.P.L. India Ltd. - 1992 (1) CPJ 140 MC***, where a lady **purchased a photocopier** for the purpose of earning her livelihood, it was held that the purchase was not for commercial purpose and she was a consumer. The Court should therefore be satisfied that there is no large-scale commercial activity.

Plying of a taxi is purchase of a taxi for commercial purpose. Commercial purpose is commerce, mercantile, having profit as the main aim. There should be profit or loss from further disposal. Commercial purpose includes all business activities. In ***Synco Textiles Pvt. Ltd. v. Greaves Cotton & Co. Ltd. [1991(1) CPR 615 (NC)]***, where Appellant company ***purchased generating sets for generating electricity in the factory*** to be used for operating machinery in the factory for the purpose of commercial production of edible oils and oil cakes, it was held that the purchase was for a commercial purpose and therefore the Appellant company cannot be regarded as consumer. It was observed that Parliament wanted to exclude from the scope of the definition not merely persons who obtain goods for resale but also those who purchase goods with a view to using such goods for carrying on any activity on a large-scale for the purpose of earning profit. Similarly, ***purchase of a computer by a business house*** has been held to be for commercial purpose as the complainant was a large commercial organisation ***[M/s. HCL Ltd. v. Krishna Nanu Naik & Sons & Anr. - 1993 CPJ 11174 (NC)]***.

Where a person enters into a ***contest booking Premier Padmini car*** and is successful in contest, but the Company refuses to give the person reward of the contest as announced, on the complaint filed, it was held that such a person was not a consumer so far as the benefit of the contest was concerned ***[Byford v. S.S. Srivastava — 1993 (II) CPR 83 NC]***.

A ***purchase of a car by a company for use by its business***, by directors and employees is purchase for commercial purpose ***[V.M. Aggarwal v. Byford Leasing Ltd. - 1992 CPJ 29 (Del.)***. Thus, even if a person buys goods for consideration and obtains such goods for any commercial purpose, then he is not a consumer ***[Pushpa Meena v. Shah Enterprises - 1992-CPJ 271 (Raj)]***. It must be noted that during the warranty period, the manufacturer or dealer has to render free service to the consumer, even though he has purchased the goods for the commercial purpose. Thus the defence of purchase of goods for commercial purpose is not available during the warranty or guaranteee period ***(Maruti Udyog Ltd. v. M. S. Hameed Panaji - 1992 (I) CPR 272). Purchase of tractor for agricultural purpose*** is not for commercial purpose ***(Surinder Kumar v. Escorts Ltd - 1993 I CPJ 444 NC)***.

Some instances of Persons who are held as Consumers.

(i) Bank customers;

(ii) Subscribers of telephones;

(iii) consumer of electricity;

(iv) A passenger travelling by train;

(v) A patient receiving medical treatment;

(vi) A depositor of money;

(vii) A beneficiary of services, like a nominee of the insured;

(viii) Persons allotted plots/houses by State Housing Boards;

(ix) Nominee of a person insured under LIC.

(x) an employee-member of Employees' Provident Fund Scheme is a consumer and duties performed by Regional Provident Fund Commissioner under the Scheme is service. Statutory authority not invested with sovereign function while discharging its statutory functions provides service and would be liable in case of any deficiency ***(Regional Provident Fund Commissioner v. Shiv Kumar Joshi - (2000) 1 SCC 98).***

Who are not Consumers?

The following persons are not consumers as per the Consumer Protect Act, 1986

(a) a person who purchased goods for resale or for commercial purpose

(b) a person who buys goods or obtains services without consideration

(c) hires or avails of any services without consideration; or

(d) uses the goods without the approval of the person who has bought the goods for consideration;

(e) is beneficiary of services without the consent of the person who has hired the service for consideration ***[Sec.2(1)(d)]*** or

(f) a person who obtains services under a contract of personal service.

The National Commission, in various cases, had decided that the following are not consumers :

* A client hiring services of an Advocate;
* A student hiring services of a private tutor;
* Purchaser of a taxi;
* Tenant is not a consumer;
* Person presenting documents for registration ***(S.P. God v. Collector of Stamps — AIR 1996 SC 839);***
* Government servant ***(State of Orissa v. Divisional Manager, MC—AIR 1996 SC 2519);***
* Charitable Trust running a diagnostic centre where patients ordinarily are required to pay for CT Scan, purchases of machines made by such Trust is for commercial purpose and such a charitable trust is not a consumer ***(Kalpavarulcsha Charitable Trust v. Toshniwal Brothers (Bombay) Pvt. Ltd. & Anr. -(2000) 1 SCC 512).***
* Tenant of a landlord, where terms of the lease did not contain any provision for cleaning, repairing and maintenance of the building by the landlord ***[Laxmiben Laxmichand Shah v. Sakerben Kanji Chandan & Ors. - (2001) 9 SCC 604).***
* tax-payers to municipality
* contractors
* applicants for jobs
* persons who filed suits in courts, etc.

Consumer Dispute : According to Section 2(1)(e) of the Consumer Protection Act, 1986 '***Consumer Dispute***' means "a dispute where the person against whom a complaint has been made denies or disputes the allegations contained in the complaint". Separate allegation may form separate disputes requiring separate findings on each dispute.

Defect : "Defect" means 'any fault, imperfection or shortcoming in the quality, quantity, potency, purity or standard which is required to be maintained by or under any law for the time being in force or has been undertaken to be performed by a person in pursuance of a contract or otherwise in relation to any service".

From the above definition, it is clear that non-fulfilment of any of the standards or requirements laid down by or under any law for the time being in force or as claimed by the trader in relation to any goods would fall under the ambit of '*defect*'.

Three types of defects are envisaged (i) manufacturing defect, (ii) design defect, (iii) instruction defect.

Manufacturing Defect : A product is said to have manufacturing defect when it is not built according to specification and is consequently unsafe. For instance, there may be negligence on the part of an employee in assembling a part or tightening a nut or a latent defect (hidden flaw) in the raw material out of which the product is made.

Design Defect *:* It appears there is no clear standard with reference to standards prescribed by Government or industry, if any, but courts may liberally interpret the provision to test the complaint from the angle of reasonable care in designing a product. Several High Courts have held that a product is defectively designed if the product is more dangerous than the benefits that accrue on account of product design in the eyes of an ordinary consumer. For instance under Indian conditions if a moped manufacturer does not provide a 'Saree guard' to protect against the possibility of an average woman meeting an accident when loose end of her saree gets in contact with running wheels of moped may be considered as design defect. It is not unreasonable to argue that reasonable and prudent manufacturer should have anticipated or foreseen such a possibility in the Indian Context as large number of even working women wear sarees in India.

Instruction Defect : When a manufacturer fails to provide adequate warning of possible dangers associated with the product in Product Manual, Instruction booklet or on package/label regarding safe use of the product. A drug manufacturer is expected to warn against side effects. It is not a valid defence to argue that manufacturer was not aware of the danger.

Following types of evidence is generally relied upon by complainants to establish defect in product :

(a) Expert Opinion

(b) Manufacturer's records

(c) Government and Industry Standards

(d) Post accident changes

(e) Report of Governmental and other agencies

(f) Past record

(a) **Expert Opinion :** Complainant hires a technical expert to testify about the defective characteristics of a product. A manufacturer has to retain highly qualified experts to rebut the findings of complainant's expert and also educate defence lawyer so well that he can call the bluff of complainan'ts expert.

(b) **Manufacturer's records :** If manufacturer's own exployees expressed concern about product safety it can be extremely persuasive that product defect existed.

(c) **Government and Industry Standard :** Evidence that manufacturer has failed to meet government or industry standards can be compelling proof of existence of defect and when such standards are mandatory it also amounts to automatic findings of negligence.

(d) **Post accident changes :** Post accident changes may be considered as evidence that original designs were deficient. Though this is a contentious factor as to whether such an evidence is admissible a jury may be influenced by the same.

(e) **Report of Govt. and the other agencies :** Generally factual findings of an official investigation forms admissible evidence.

(f) **Past record :** Complainant may show that past record of the product proves his claim. Manufacturer has the obligation of proving that other accidents were not similar.

Who is liable to Pay Compensation?

Who is liable to pay compensation is indeed an important question. The liability extends from manufacturer to retailer or in other words to everyone in the chain of distribution. Even an occasional seller may be held liable for his own negligence to the extent he should have known or discovered that the product was dangerous to users. In most States in USA strict liability applies only to manufacturers.

Therefore, contravention of any of the provisions of enactments such as the Drugs & Cosmetics Act, 1950, Standards of Weights & Measures Act, 1976, the Prevention of Food Adulteration Act, 1955, the Indian Standards Institution (Certification Marks) Act, 1952 etc. or any rules framed under any such enactment or contravention of the conditions or implied warranties under the Sale of Goods Act, 1930 in relation to any goods would also be termed as a '***defect***' under the Act. Fault, imperfection or shortcoming in quality, quantity, potency, purity or standard as claimed by the trader in any manner whatsoever in relation to goods is to be determined with reference to the warrrants or guarantees expressely given by a trader.

Deficiency : Deficiency means any fault, imperfection, shortcoming or inadequacy in the quality, nature and manner of performance which is required to be maintained by or under any law for the time being in force or has been undertaken to be performed by a person in pursuance of a contract or otherwise in relation to any service *[Section 2(1)(g)]*.

Lack of facilities promised by Housing Board is deficiency. *Non-allotment of shares* is not deficiency in service *[L. C. Chandgotiya v. Northern Leasing & Industries Ltd - 1991 (2) CPJ 19 (Raj)]*.

In *Commissioner Officer, Telecom* v. *Bihar State Warehousing, reported in 1991 CPJ - 42*, it has been held that *illegal shifting of the telephone* amounts to deficiency. Likewise, *illegal disconnection of the telephone* would amount to deficiency. Where a *car dealer fails to deliver the car within the stipulated period*, he will be responsible for deficiency in service. Similarly, negligence and deficiency of service on account of the *flight not taking off within a reasonable time of the scheduled departure* can be held as negligence and deficiency of service.

Failure of insurance company to settle claim without sufficient cause is deficiency *(Premlata v. National Insurance Co.q - 1991 CPJ 423 Raj)*.

Failure of Railways to provide cushioned seats in 1st class is deficiency of service *(Gen. Manager, Southern Railway, Madras v. N Prabhakaram —19921 CPJ 323 NC). Delay in installation of telephone, inflated telephone bills* without proper examination and disconnecting the telephone are deficiencies in service *(Union of India v. Aman Dahiya — 1993 I CPJ 13 NC; Union of India v. Dr. (Mrs.) Satya Bhama Thakur — 19911 CPJ 31 NC)*. Where *ornaments in a locker are missing* due to negligence of a Bank, it is deficiency in service. Similarly, *failure of the Bank to credit the amount* in the account is deficiency in service *(Dr. K.T. Shivaiah v. Canara Bank — 1992 1 CPJ 253 NC; Punjab National Bank, Bombay v. K. B. Shetty — 1991 II CPJ 639 NC). Failure of the bank to follow stop payment instructions* is deficiency in service *(Bank of India v. Dr. Mukesh Kumar Shukla — 1993 I CPJ 41)*.

The Supreme court in *Punjab Water Supply & Sewage Board v. Udaipur Cement Works (AIR 1996 SC 557)*, observed, “we do not appreciate the blanket observation of the National Commission to the effect that where the transaction is one of sale and purchase simpliciter no question of deficiency in service can arise so as to entitle the complainant to invoke the jurisdiction of the Consumer Forum.” The order of National Commission was set aside.

When there is a *delay by the banker in making payment under a bank guarantee* on account of delay in grant of permission by Reserve Bank of India, it did not amount to deficiency in service by the Bank *(Union Bank of India v. Seppo Rally Oy - 1999 (8) SCC 357)*.

Excessive Price

It is for complainant to establish that the trader has charged for the goods mentioned in the complaint a price in excess of the price -

(a) fixed by or under any law for the time being in force; or

(b) displayed on goods; or

(c) displayed on any package containing such goods.

A trader can, therefore, be charged for having collected price in excess of what is displayed or published.

Hazardous Goods

In respect of goods which are hazardous to life and safety, traders shall display information regarding the contents, manner and effect of use of such goods. Such goods offered for sale without such display or caution can be a case of complaint.

The definition of '***deficiency***' also has two parts to it like the definition of '***defect***' pertaining to services for which standards are prescribed by the law and services for which express warranties or guarantees are given by the persons concerned, say, traders, etc.

Goods : Goods means goods as defined in the *Sale of Goods Act, 1930 [Section 2(1)(i)]*. As per Section 2(7) of the Sale of Goods Act, 1930 '*Goods*' means every kind of movable property other than actionable claims and money; and includes stock & shares, growing crops, grass and things attached to or forming part of the land which are agreed to be severed before sale or under the contract or sale. Therefore, most consumer products would come under the purview of this definition.

Manufacturer : *Manufacturer* means a person (i) makes or manufactures any goods or (ii) parts thereof, or ii. does not make or manufacture any goods but assembles parts their of made of manufactured by himself, or iii. puts or cause to be put his own mark on any goods made or manufactured by any other manufacturer and claims such goods to be goods made or manufactured by himself. *[Sec. 2(j)]*.

Service [Section 2(O)]

"*Service*" means Service of any description which is made available to potential users and includes the provisions of facilities in connection with banking, financing, insurance, transport, processing, supply of electrical or other energy, boarding or lodging or both, house construction, entertainment, amusement or other information.

The expression "*Service*" includes in its scope provision of facility in connection with telephone provided by Telecommunication Department and houses and plots by Housing & Development Board.

Free services and personal services under a control have been excluded from the protective spell of the Act. Thus services must be of commercial nature in the sense that they must be on payment. The payment may be in cash or kind. It may be made either at once or partly at once or partly later i.e., on credit. For services rendered without consideration, the complaint cannot be maintained in forum. For example, a medical service rendered by Government hospitals will not come within the scope of Consumer Protection Act, 1986.

In *Consumer Unity and Trust Society Vs. State of Rajasthan (1989),* the National Commission, while hearing an appeal from the State of Rajasthan, held that complaints against government hospitals cannot be entertained under the Act on the ground that a person receiving treatment in such hospital is not a 'consumer' as the patient does not 'hire' the services of the hospital; moreover, the treatment provided is free of charge, and therefore, it does not amount to "service".

In the case of *Cosmopolitan Hospitals* Vs. *Smt. Vasantha P. Nair*, (1991) and *Cosmopolitan Hospitals Vs. Smt. V.P. Santha (1992),* the National Commission considered at length whether *service rendered by doctors in private hospitals for consideration* would come under the purview of 'service', whether the medical profession was outside the scope of the Consumer Protection Act, and whether legal representatives of a deceased patient could file a complaint against the hospital alleging negligence. The facts of both cases were similar - the widows of the deceased patients alleged the hospital authorities with negligence - in the diagnosis and treatment in the first case and in the performance of an operation in the second case.

The contentions of the hospital authorities denying the allegation of negligence were that

(i) the complainants were not 'consuners' under the Act, and therefore, were not entitled to initiate the proceedings; and

(ii) the treatment rendered in the hospital did not consitute 'service' under the Act. Their contention was that the Act ensured protection to consumers against unscrupulous traders selling defective goods or indulging in unfair trade practice and against deficiency in service relating to commercial transactions only - and that services rendered to a patient by a medical practitioner, which is a professional service, is of a personal nature and contracts of personal service being outside the purview of the Act, the services rendered in hospitals whether by government or private agencies were not 'services' under the Act.

The National Commission upholding the decision of the State Commission held that

(i) the complainants who were legal representatives of the deceased were clothed by operation of law with the rights which the deceased had to initiate action against the hospital on the ground of alleged deficiency in service and that those rights had not become extinguished by his death but remained enforceable by his legal representatives. Unless such a broad and pragmatic view is taken, the intention of the legislature in enacting the Consumer Protection Act 1986 would be defeated. Therefore, the complainants were "consumers" and had full *locus standi* to maintain the complaint petitions before the Forums.

(ii) the activity carried on by the hospital constituted 'service' under the Act and did not fall within the exempted category of service rendered under a "contract of personal service". The definition of "service" as given in Section 2(1)(0) of the Act mentions "service of any description" made available to potential users and only exempts "service rendered free of charge" or "under a contract of personal service" from its ambit. Restricting the scope of the definition to only "service relating to commercial transactions" would not be warranted, given the intention of the legilsature. Thus, there is no substance in the contention that service rendered by hospitals and members of the medical profession for consideration will not constitute "service" as defined in the Act because it does not relate to a "commercial transaction".

Quoting its own observations in the case of ***A.C. Modagi Vs. Cross Well Tailor (1991)*** the National Commission reiterated that there was a *distinction between contract for service and contract of service. 'Personal service'* stemmed from a master and servant relationship where the master can order what is to be done and how it shall be done and under which, an employee could be turned out of service by the master at will, and therefore, no occasion would arise for the master to complain about the deficiency in the rendering of service by the employee. Where the hirer of the service is not in a position to exercise any sort of control or supervision over the work of the person rendering the service, there would not be any 'personal service'. In the case of hospitals which provide treatment to patients for payment, there could be no reason to hold that there was any element of personal service in such arrangement. ***The provisions of the Consumer Protection Act relating to adjudication of consumer disputes and award of reliefs under Section 14 fully apply to disputes concerning deficiency in the service rendered by hospitals and members of the medical profession also.***

Spurious goods and services means such goods and services which are claimed to be genuine but they are actually not so *[Sec.2(oo)]*.

Contract of Personal Service

A service under a contract of personal service does not come within the perview of service under the Act. A service offered by an *Advocate* to his client is under a contract of personal service and therefore is not included in the definition. A client hiring the services of an Advocate is not a consumer within the meaning of the word 'consumer' under the Act. Service rendered by a *private tutor* is also as an example of personal service.

CONTRACT OF SERVICE AND CONTRACT FOR SERVICE DISTINGUISHED

There is a distinction between a contract for service and a contract of service. The contract of service implies some relationship of a master and a servant. A servant is obliged to obey the order of his master. This is contract of service. Where the person engages the service of another person and where he can only order what is to be done, it is a contract for service.

For the service rendered, the person has to pay a charge or a fee or a price demanded for the service. Where a person contracts for installation of a telephone, he is required to pay installation charges, call charges etc. It is clearly a case of hiring or contract for service. The transport facilities like traveling by railway or airlines by paying for the service. etc. is covered by the term service. Settlement of insurance claims will be covered by the definition of service, contracting with Housing and Development Board is hiring service of the board as the board is engaged in offering services for allotment of plots and houses to the public *[Sushil Dcvi v. Raj Sudha — 1991CPJ 620 (Del)]*. The Banking service is expressly included in the word service. However, if failure to render service is beyond the control of the Bank, no claim for compensation can be sustained *[Federal Bank v. Bion Mishra - 1991 cm 16 (NC))*. The student who pays tuition fees and hires the services of an institution acquires the rights of a consumer.

What are held to be Services?

(i) Services rendered by Housing and Development Board;

(ii) Services rendered by an agency for publication of news;

(iii) Services rendered by Post and Telegraphs Department;

(iv) Services rendered by Insurance Company, including services for settlement of claims;

(v) Services rendered by banking and financial institutions;

(vi) Services rendered by transport agencies like bus, rail, air, sea etc.;

(vii) Processing services;

(viii) Supply of electricity;

(ix) Hotel, lodging and boarding services;

(x) Services rendered by agencies providing entertainment or amusement like cinema houses, theatres, etc;

(xi) Services rendered by a hospital or nursing home on payment of fees;

(xii) Supply of food on board of Aircraft;

(xiii) To provide cushioned seats in first class compartment of Railways;

(xiv) Housing construction or building activity.

A government or semi-government body or a local authority is as much amenable to the Act as any other private body rendering similar service. Truly speaking it would be a service to the society if such bodies instead of claiming exclusion, subject themselves to the Act and let their acts and omissions be scrutinised, as possible accountability is necessary for healthy growth of society. The test is not if a person against whom complaint is made is a stamtory body but whether the nature of the duty and function performed by it is service or even facility.

(xv) Services rendered by medical practitioners I*ndian Medical Association v. V.P. Shantha - AIR 1996 SC 5501*. In the case of *Jacob Mathew v. State of Punjab & Anr. [(2005)65CC l}*, Supreme Court has cautioned on the random prosecutions against Doctors. It is held that it must be shown that accused doctor did something or failed to do something which in the given facts and circumstances, no medical professional in his ordinary senses and prudence would have done or failed to do. It must be shown that hazard taken by accused doctor should be of such a nature that injury which resulted was most likely imminent.

(xvi) Hospital is responsible for the acts of its permanent staff as well as visiting staff whose services are temporarily requisitioned *[Savita Garg v. Director, National Heart Institute (2004) 8 SCC 56]*.

(xvii) Common carrier for loss or damage to the goods entrusted to it for transportation *[Patel Roadways Ltd. v. Birla Yamaha Ltd. - 2000(4) SCC 91]*.

(xviii) Services rendered by statutory and public authorities; misfeasance in public office; personal liability of officials/officers concerned *[Ghaziabad Development Authority v. Balbir Singh (2004) 5 SCC 65]*.

What are held not to be Services?

(i) Faulty or medical treatment offered in the Government hospital;

(ii) Services rendered by Municipal Corporation, as payment of direct or indirect taxes by public is not consideration paid for hiring the services;

(iii) Services rendered by a private tutor, as it is a contract of personal service;

(iv) Services rendered by an Advocate, as it is a contract of personal service;

(v) Any service which is rendered gratuitously, *i.e.,* for which no consideration is paid;

(vi) Non-allotment of shares, in a company;

(vii) Claim for compensation arising out of motor accident as such a claim cannot be said to be in relation to any service hired or availed by consumer *(Thiruvalluvar Transport Corporation v. Consumer Protection Council — AIR 1995 SC 1384)*;

(viii) Service rendered by employee to his employer *(Indian Medical Association v. V P. Shantha - AIR 1996 SC 550)*;

(ix) rendering of service by medical practitioner free of charge to all patients *(Indian Medical Association v. V. P. Shanta — AIR 1996 SC 550)*.

Complaint

"*Complaint*" means any *allegation in writing* made by a complainant with a view to obtaining any relief under the Consumer Protection Act, that :

- as a result of any unfair trade practice or restrictive trade practice, adopted by a trader, the complainant has suffered loss or damage;
- the goods mentioned in the compliant suffer from one or more defects;
- the services mentioned in the complainant suffer from deficiency in any respect;
- a trader has charged for the goods mentioned in the complainant a price in excess of the price fixed by or under any law for the time being in force.
- goods which will be hazardous to life and safety when used are being offered for sale to the public.
- services which are hazardous or likely to be hazardous to life and safety of the public when used, are being offered by the service provider which such person could have known with due diligence to be injurious to life and safety.

The complaint is to made with a view to obtaining any relief provided by or under this Act.

Who can make a Compliant?

A complaint in relation to any goods sold or delivered, or any service provided may be filed with quasi-judicial organs constituted under the Consumer Protection Act, 1986 by any of the following :

(i) the *consumer* to whom such goods are sold or delivered or such service provided;

(ii) any *recognised consumer's association* registered under law, or

(iii) the *Central* or any *State Government*, and

(iv) *one or more consumers* on behalf of many consumers having same interest or

(v) in case of death of a customer, his *legal heir* or *representative [Sec 2 (1) b]*

The Amendment Act 2002 has amended sec. 12. It provides as follows:

1. Every complaint shall be accompanied with such *amount of fee as prescribed.*

2. On receipt of a complaint, the District Forum may, by order, allow the complaint to be proceeded with or rejected.

However a complaint shall not be rejected unless an opportunity of being heard has been given to the complainant.

Further, the admissibility of the complaint shall ordinarily be decided within 21 days from the date on which the complaint was received.

3. Where a complaint is allowed to be proceeded with, the District Forum may proceed with the complaint in the manner as provided under the Act.

Further where a complaint has been admitted by the District Forum, it shall not be transferred to any other court or Tribunal or any authority set up by or under any other law for the time being in force.

Class Complaints : *The Consumer Protection (Amendment) Act 1993* permitted representative complaints. Such a complaint may be filed with a district forum by one or more consumers, on behalf of, or for the benefit of numerous consumers having a common interest. *For the initiation of such a class action complaint, it is necessary to obtain prior permission of the District Forum concerned.* Thus, one or more members of a class or a group may seek relief on behalf of the entire class or group where the complaints, claims or questions of law are common. Thus, the Act can be used on behalf of a group of consumers with a common cause in cases like overcharging in parking lots; or as in the famous *Lohia Machines (LML) case* (two wheeler manufacturers), where the company did not refund the advance deposit of Rs 500 to lakhs of depositors despite cancellation of the booking for scooters.

What Complaints may be Lodged?

[section 2 (1) (c)]. A complaint under may relate to one or more of the following:

(i) that an unfair trade practice or a restrictive trade practice has been adopted by any trader, or service provider;

(ii) that the goods bought by him or agreed to be bought by him suffer from one or more defects;

(iii) that the services hired or availed of or agreed to be hired or availed of by him suffer from deficiency in any respect;

(iv) that a trader has charged for the goods mentioned in the complaint a price in excess of the price fixed by or under any law for the time being in force or displayed on the goods or on any package containing such goods;

(v) that goods which will be hazardous to life and safety when used, are being offered for sale to the public in contravention of the provisions of any law for the time being in force requiring traders to display information in regard to the contents, manner and effect of use of such goods.

Note : 'Recognised Consumer Association' means any *voluntary consumer association* registered under the Companies Act, 1956 or any other law for the time being in force.

To Whom the Complaint is to be made

According to the Consumer Protection (Amendment) Act, 1993, a complaint can be made to the following quasi-judicial agencies in the following manner :

(a) Where the value of goods or services and compensation, if any, claimed *does not exceed ₹20 lakhs*, complaint is to be filed with the *District Forum*;

(b) Where the value of goods or services and compensation, if any, claimed *exceeds ₹ 20 lakhs, but does not exceed ₹1 crore*, complaint is to be filed with the *State Commission.*

Where a joint petition is filed on behalf of a large number of victims, it is the total amount of compensation claimed in the petition (and not the individual claims) that will determine the question of jurisdiction. In case the total compensation claimed exceeds, presently, Rs 20 lakhs but does not exceed Rs one crore, the mailer can be heard by the State Commission [Public Health Engineering Department v Uphokta Sanrakshan Samiti (1992)].

(c) Where the value of goods or services and compensation, if any, claimed *exceeds ₹1 crore*, the complaint to be filed with the *National Commission.*

Where to File a Complaint

A complaint should be filed in a District Forum (subject to pecuniary jurisdiction) within the limits of whose jurisdiction all the opposite parties reside or carry on business, or

Any one of the opposite parties resides or carry on business (with the permission of District Forum or acquiescence of the opposite party not residing there) or where the cause of action wholly or in part arises.

How to File a Complaint

Procedure for filing a complaint are simple and speedy.

(a) Comparatively smaller amount of fee has been prescribed.

(b) Complainant or his authorised agent can present the complaint in person.

(c) The complaint can be sent by post to the appropriate Forum/Commission.

How to Draft a Complaint

A complaint should contain the following information:

(a) Name, description and address of the complainant.

(b) Name, description and address of the opposite party or parties.

(c) The facts relating to complaint and when and where it arose.

(d) Documents, if any, in support of the allegation contained in the complaint.

(e) The relief which the complainant is seeking.

The complaint should be signed by the complainant or his authorised agent.

UNFAIR TRADE PRACTICES

The Consumer Protection Act has adopted the definition of 'Unfare Trade Practices' as given in the MRTP Act.

Section 36-A of the Monopolies and Restrictive Trade Practices Act, 1969, amended in 1993 explains what 'unfair trade practice' means. Unfair trade practice methods are listed in Section 36-A. Where the methods listed in Section 36-A are adopted for the purpose of promoting the sale, use or supply of any goods, or for the provison of any services and thereby some loss or injury is caused to the consumers of such goods or services, it is an unfair trade practice. The practices mentioned in Section 36-A are grouped into the following five categories.

1. **Misleading Advertisement and False Representation :** These include :

(a) *falsely representing* that the goods are of a particular standard, quality, quantity, grade, composition, style or model.

(b) *falsely representing* that the services are of a particular standard, quality or grade.

(c) *falsely representing* that the re-built, second-hand, renovated, reconditioned or old goods as new goods.

(d) *reprsenting* that the goods or services have sponsorship, approval, performance, characteristics, accessories, uses or benefits which such goods or services do not have.

(e) *representing* that the seller or the supplier has a sponsorhip or approval or affiliation which he does not have.

(f) *making a false or misleading representation* concerning the need, for, or the usefulness of any goods or services.

(g) *giving to the public any warranty or guarantee of the performance* or length of life of a product which is not based on adequate test.

(h) *making a materially misleading representation to the public concerning the price* at which a product or like products of goods have been or are ordinarily sold.

(i) *giving false or misleading facts disparaging the goods, services* or trade of another person.

The mode of representation or statement to the public may be by any method. It will be enough if the statement comes to the knowledge of the buyer of those goods etc. The representation may appear on the article or on its wrapper or container or on anything on which the article is mounted.

2. **Sale offer of bargain price :** This includes advertising for supply, at a bargain price, goods or services that are not intended to be offered for supply at the price for a reasonable period or reasonable quantities.

3. **Schemes offering Gifts or Prizes :** This category includes : (a) offering gifts or prizes or other items with the intention of not providing them and conducting promotional contests; (b) the conduct of any contest, lottery or game of chances, etc.

4. **Non-Compliance of Prescribed Standards :** This category includes cases where goods are sold for use by consumers knowing or having reason to believe that they do not comply with the standards prescribed by some competent authority. The prescribed standard may relate to performance, composition, contents, design, construction, finishing or packing as are necessary to prevent or reduce the risk of injury to the person using the goods.

5. **Hoarding, Destruction or Refusal :** The fifth and last category of unfiar trade practices includes cases of hoarding, destruction of goods or refusal to sell goods or services so as to raise the cost of those or similar goods.

Ingredients of Unfair Trade Practices

(a) The trade practices must consist of any of the practices listed as above.

(b) The purpose of such trade practice must be to promote the sale, use or supply of any goods or provision of any services.

(c) The trade practices must have caused loss or injury to the consumer whether by eliminating or restricting competition.

Restrictive Trade Practice

Sec. 2(nn) of the Consumer Protection Act defines "Restrictive Trade Practice" as any trade practice which requires a consumer to buy, hire or avail of any goods or, as the case may be, services as a codition precedent for buying, hiring or availing of other goods or services. While the "Restrictive Trade Practice" covered under C.P. Act relates to tie up sales of slow moving goods with fast moving goods, Sec. 2(o) of MRTP Act has a wider ambit which covers all practices which prevent distort or restrict competition and obstructs free flow of goods and services or obstruct free flow of capital and resources in to production.

Restrictive Trade Practicies under MRTP Act 1969

Restrictive Trade Practices are those trade practices which have the effect of preventing, distorting or restricting competition in any manner and in particular acts intended to result in:

1. Obstruction of capital and resources in to stream of production.
2. Manipulation of price or to abstract production, distribution/supply of goods or provision of services.
3. Agreement falling within the scope of Sec. 33 (of the MRTP Act) which are deemed as Registrable Agreements relating to restrictive trade practices.

REDRESSAL OF CONSUMER DISPUTES

For the purpose of speedy and simple settlement of 'consumer's disputes' Section 9 of the Act, 1986 provides for the establishment of the following three Consumer Disputes Redressal Agencies.

A "*Consumer Disputes Redressal Forum*" to be known as the *District Forum* established by the State Government in each district of the State by notification.

A "*Consumer Disputes Redressal Commission*" to be known as *State Commission* established by the State Government, with the prior approval of the Central Government, in the State by notification, and

A "*National Consumer Disputes Redressal Commission*" to be known as *National Commission* established by the Central Government by notification.

Thus, the Act envisages a hierarchy of three Redressal Agencies: (a) District Forums, (b) State Commissions and (c) National Commission. These are quasi-judicial bodies.

DISTRICT FORUM

District Forum means a *Consumer Disputes Redressal Forum*, established under Section 9 (2) of the Consumer Protection Act, 1986. This is established by the State Government in each district of the State by means of a notification. If reasonable and necessary, the State Government can establish more than one district forum in a district. As per the amended Act, 1993, permission of the Central Government is not necessary for establishing a district forum.

Composition of the District Forum : According to Section 10 of the Act, each district forum shall consist of : (i) a person who is, or has been or is qualified to be a District Judge shall be nominated by the State Government and shall be the *president* of the Forum, (ii) *a person of eminence* in the field of education, trade or commerce, law etc. and (iii) *a lady social worker*.

Appointments to the State Commission shall be made by the State Government on the recommendation of a *Selection Committee* consisting of the President of the State Committee, the Secretary of Law Department of the State and the Secretary in charge of Consumer Affairs in the State.

Every member of the District Forum shall hold office of a *term office 5 years or upto the age of 65 years*, which ever is earlier. Of course, a member may resign by giving a notice in writing to the State Government where upon the vacancy will be filled up by the State Government. The salary or honorarium and other allowances payable to members, and their conditions of service may be prescribed by the State Government. A member shall not be eligible for re-appointment.

Pecuniary and Territorial Jurisdiction of the District Forum

Section 11 provides for the jurisdiciton of the District Forum under two criteria: *Pecuniary* and *Territorial*. The district forum enjoys jurisdiciton to entertain complaints where the value of goods or the services and the compensation, if any, claimed, does not ₹ ceed *₹20 lakhs*. A complaint can be filed either at the *place where the opposite party resides* or carry on business or at the place where the cause of action arises. In case of action arises also at the place where the product is sold.

In the case, *Consumer Education and Research Society Vs. Canara Bank*, it was held that a banking company to be proceeded against the district forum where its branch was located.

Manner of making a Complaint and Complaint by Whom

A complaint, in relation to any goods sold or delivered, or any service period, may be filed with a District Forum by any of the following : The consumer to whom such goods are sold or delivered, or such services provided, any recognised consumer association, whether the consumer is a member of such association or not, the Central or the State Governments, any consumer or consumers on behalf of a number of consumers having same interests.

Every compaint shall be accompanied by a prescribed fee (by notification G.O.No.10(2) 2003 CPU, GSR 175E dated 15.03.2004) as given below:

Fees prescribed for every complaint filed under Section 12 (1) and 21 (1) of the Act

	District Forum	*Fees (₹)*
(i)	Upto ₹ 1 lakh under below poverty line holding Andyodaya Anna Yojana	Nil
(ii)	Upto ₹ 1 lakh other than cited above in (i)	100
(iii)	Above ₹ 1 lakh upto 5 lakh	200
(iv)	Above ₹ 5 lakh to 10 lakh	400
(v)	Above ₹ 10 lakh to 20 lakh	500
	State Commission	
(vi)	Above ₹ 20 lakh to 50 lakh	2,000
(vii)	Above ₹ 50 lakh to 1 crore	4,000
	National Commission	
(viii)	Above ₹ 1 crore	5,000

PROCEDURE ON RECEIPT OF COMPLAINTS

The District Forum has to observe the following procedure as detailed in Section 13 of the Act.

Complaint Relating to the Defects of Goods

The term 'defect' means any fault, imperfection or shortcoming in the quality, quantity, purity or standard which is required to be maintained by any law in force or which the trader claimed that his goods possessed.

(i) If the alleged defect in the goods is such that it cannot be determined without proper analysis or test of the goods, the Forum should *obtain a sample of the goods from the complainant*. The sample of goods should be *protected by a seal*. The sample of goods received *must be sent to 'appropriate laboratory' along with a direction that the goods should be tested or analysed for the alleged defect. The time allowed to the laboratory is 45 days.*

(ii) The District Forum/State Commission may *require the complainant to deposit with it such amount as may be specified towards payment of fees to the 'appropriate laboratory'* for the purpose of carrying out the necessary analysis or tests. [Section 13(1)(d)]. The amount so deposited shall be remitted by them to the appropriate laboratory to enable it to carry out the analysis and send the report.

(iii) On receipt of the report from the laboratory, the *Forum should send a copy of it to the opposite party along with such remarks*, as the District Forum may feel necessary.

(iv) If any party disputes the correctness of the report or the correctness of the methods of analysis, the Forum shall *require him to submit his objections in writing.*

(v) Before issuing any final order in the matter, the Forum will *provide an opportunity to both parties to present their views about the report.* The Forum shall proceed to settle the dispute on the basis of allegations, counter allegations and the evidence produced by the parties in support of their case. *Where the opposition party does nothing (ie., fails to represent his case or fails to appear on the date of heaning before the District forum) in response to the complaint, the matter may be decided on the basis of the evidence produced by the complainant.* The proceedings of the Forum in compliance with the procedure laid down by the Act are to be regarded as valid. The validity cannot be questioned on the ground that the principles of natural justice have not been complied with.

Complaint Relating to Services

Where the above procedure relating to the complaint in respect of goods cannot be followed, or if a complaint relates to any services the District Forum shall -

(a) refer a copy of the complaint to the opposite party directing him to give his version within a period of thirty days or such extended period not exceeding fifteen days as may be granted by the District Forum;

(b) where the opposite party on receipt of a complaint denies or disputes the allegations or fails to take any action to represent his case within the time given by the District Forum, the District Forum shall proceed to settle the consumer dispute as under:

(i) on the basis of evidence brought to its notice by the parties to the dispute; or

(ii) where the opposite party fails to represent his case, then exparte on the basis of evidence brought to its notice by the complainant.

(c) where the complainant fails to appear on the date of hearing before the District Forum, the District Forum may either dismiss the complaint for default or decide it on merits.

Limitation Period for Filing of Complaint

Section 24A provides that the District Forum, the State Commission, or the National Commission shall not admit a complaint unless it is filed *within two years from the date on which the cause of action has arisen.* However, where the complainant satisfies the Forum/Commission as the case may be, that he had sufficient cause for not filling the complaint within one year, such *complaint may be entertained by it after recording the reasons for condoning the delay.*

Administrative Control

Section 24-B provides that the National Commission shal have administrative control over all the State Commission in the matter of calling for periodical returns regarding the institution, pendency and disposal of cases, issuance of instructions regarding adopting of uniform procedure in hearing of matters, serving copies of documents, translation of judgements etc. and generally overseeing the functioning of the State Commission/District fora to ensure that the objects and purposes of the Act are served in the best possible manner.

The State Commission shall have administrative control over all the District fora within its jurisdiction in all the above-referred matters.

Findings of the Forum

If the Forum is convinced that the goods are really defective, or that the complaint about the service is proved, the Forum shall have to order the opposite party to do one or more of the following things :

- *to remove the defect pointed out* by the laboratory from the goods in question.
- *to replace the goods with new goods* of a similar description, which should be free from any defect.
- *to return to the complainant the price of the goods*, or the charges of services paid by the complainant.
- *to pay such amount as may be awarded compensation* to the consumer for any loss or injury suffered by the consumer due to the negligence of the opposite party. The District Forum shall have power to grant punitive damages, if such circumstances as it deems fit.
- *to remove the defects or deficiencies* in the services in question.
- *to discontinue the unfair trade practice or the restrictive trade practice* or not to repeat them.
- *not to offer the hazardous goods* for sale.
- *to withdraw the hazardous goods* from being offered for sale.
- to cease manufacture of hazardous goods, and to desist from offering services which are hazardous in nature;
- to pay such sum as may be determined by it, if it is of the opinion that loss or injury has been suffered by a large number of consumers who are not identifiable conveniently. The minimum amount of sum so payable shall not be less than 5% of the value of such defective goods, sold or service provided, as the case may be, to such consumers. The amount so obtained shall be credited in favour of such person and utilised in such manner as may be prescribed;
- to issue corrective advertisement to neutralise the effect of misleading advertisement at the cost of the opposite party responsible for issuing such misleading advertisement;
- *to provide for adequate costs to parties.*

Every complaint shall be heard as expeditiously as possible. Where the complaint does not require analysis or testing of commodities, endeavour shall be made to decide the complaint within a period of three months from the date of receipt of notice by opposite party and within five months if it requires analysis or testing of commodities.

Every proceeding shall be conducted by the President and at least one member sitting together. Where the member or members for any reason are unable to conduct the proceeding till it is completed, the President and the other member shall conduct such proceeding de-novo.

No adjournment shall be ordinarily granted by the District Forum unless sufficient cause is shown and the reasons for grant of adjournments have been recorded in writing by the Forum. The District Forum shall make such orders as to the costs occasioned by the adjournment as may be provided in the regulations. In the event of a complaint being disposed of after the specified period, the District Forum shall record in writing, the reasons for the same at the time of disposing of the said complaint [Sec.13 (3-A).

The order for the District Forum shall be signed by it's president and the member or members who conducted the proceedings. In case of difference of opinion, the order of the majority of the members shall be the order of the Forum.[Sec 14 (2) (2A)]

The Forums has powers not only to direct the opposite party, to rectify the defect or to replace the goods with the new goods with renewal of guarantee or warranty period but it has powers also to direct payment of compensation to the complainant if the consumer has suffered loss, injury or damage on account of defect or deficiency as a result of negligence of supplier [A.P. State Electricity Board v. A.P. Electricity Consumer Association — 1992 CPJ 148 (NC)].

Replacement of goods will be ordered where removal of defects without sacrificing the quality of goods is not possible (Ravinder Singh v. Premnath Motors — 1991 CPJ 211 HP). Compensation can be awarded only when negligence of the opposite party is established and the loss is suffered by the complainant as a consequence of such negligence [Bharat Tractors v. Sri Ram Chandra — 1991-CPJ-152 (NC)]. Negligence is the failure to exercise care expected of a man of ordinary prudence. Extent of care required differs From case to case. There should be a duty cast on the opposite party to take care. Failure would lead to negligence as a consequence in law. Compensation can be also for mental loss and expenses incurred. When blood purchased from blood bank is contaminated, compensation can be claimed [Harish Kumar v. Sunil Blood Bank - 1991 CPJ 645 (Del.)]

Compensation can also be awarded for late delivery of the telegram if loss or injury is established. Similarly, unnecessary delay by Housing Board in delivering possession of a flat to an allottee can entitle the allottee to compensation.

The amount of compensation is to be quantified to the best of judgement. The loss may be reasonably estimated as having been suffered by the complainant. The Consumer Forums are not debarred from granting reliefs not prayed for by the complainant provided the same are justified on merit (Dist. Manager

Telephones, Patna v. Dr. Tarun Bharthuar — 1992 I CPJ 47 NC]. Merely because complainant due to ignorance has failed to make a specific prayer for reliefs, will be no bar to the Consumer Forums taking cognizance of the same suo motu (United India Ins. Co. Ltd. v. Mohanlal & Sons — 19921 CPR 364 NC). In Air India v. Suganda Ravi Mashelkar (1993 I CPJ 63 NC), it has been held that Consumer Forums are not entitled to grant any compensation under the Consumer Protection Act without proof of negligence on the part of the carrier resulting in loss or injury to the complainant (Also see Indian Airlines v. Rajeshkumar Upadhyay — 1991I CPJ 206).

When the Commission is satisfied that a complainant is entitled to compensation for harassment or mental agony or oppression, which finding of course should be recorded carefully on material and convincing circumstances and not lightly, then it should further direct the department concerned to pay the amount to the complainant from the public fund immediately but to recover the same from those who are found responsible for such unpardonable behaviour by dividing it proportionately where there are more than one functionaries (Lucknow Development Authority v. M.K. Gupta — AIR 1994 SC 787.

The opposite party cannot seek any relief. Orders or directions can be issued against the opposite party. Opposite party cannot have a counterclaim, save and except, if the opposite party itself is a consumer in relation to the complainant.

Interim orders: Where during the pendency of any proceeding before the District Forum, it appear to it necessary, it may pass such interim order as is just and proper in the facts and circumstances of the case [Sec.13(3-8)].

Enforcement of Orders

The orders of District Forum are enforceable in the manner of an order or decree made by a civil court, in a civil suit. If the forum is not able to execute its order, it may forward the same to the court for execution. The court to which the order is sent, shall then execute the orders as if it were a decree or order sent to it for execution.

Appeal

Any person aggrieved by an order made by the District Forum may prefer an appeal against such order to the State Commission *within a period of 30 days from the date of the order*. The period of 30 days would be computed from the date of receipt of the order by the appellant. The appeal to the State Commission is to be made in such form and manner as may be prescribed.

Where no appeal has been preferred, the orders of a District Forum shall be final. In *Kohinor Carpets. Vs. Rajendra Arora, Haryana*, it was held that a penalty become final in the absence of any appeal against it.

Penalties : Every trade or a person against whom complaint is made is bound to comply with the order of the District Forum. If a trader fails to comply with the order, he shall be punishable.

- with *imprisonment for a minimum duration of one month* and *maximum of 3 years*,or
- with *minimum fine of ₹ 2,000* and *maximum of ₹ 10,000* or
- both, with *imprisonment and fine* as mentioned above.

Powers of the District Forum

For the purposes of settling the disputes under section 13, the District Forums have been vested with the same powers as are vested in a civil court under the Code of Civil Procedure, 1908. Such powers are enjoyed by the Forum in respect of the following matters.

1. the *summoning and enforcing the attendance* of any defendant or witness and examining the witness on oath.
2. the *discovery and production of any document* or other material object producible as evidence.
3. the *reception of evidence* on affidavits.
4. the *requisitioning* of the report of the concerned analysis or test from the appropriate laboratory or other relevant source.
5. *issuing of any commission* for the examination of any witness.
6. *dismiss a complaint* which appears to have been filed frivolously or with a view to cause vexation, *order the complainant to make payment of cost, not exceeding ₹ 10,000 to the (under the Sec. 26 of the Act) opposite party.*
7. The authorised officer may *seize such books, papers*, documents or commodities as are required for the purpose of this Act.
8. The Officer has a *right to exercise power of entry and search of any premises of the opposite party.*

Additional Powers

The District Forum shall have power to require any person -

(i) to produce or allow to be examined books, accounts, document or documents or commodities in the custody of the person;

(ii) to furnish such information as may be required;

(iii) to authorise any officer to search any premise and seize books, papers, documents or commodities as required and which are likely to be destroyed, mutilated, altered, falsified or secreted.

After examination of such seized document or commodities, the District Forum may order the retention thereof or may order the return of the same to the party concerned (Rule 10).

It is for the consumer to establish with evidence that the defects alleged in the goods exist. Similarly, onus is on the consumer where he alleges deficiency in service. After being satisfied that the defect or deficiency, as the case may be, exists, the District Forum may pass such orders as it deems fit in accordance with the above provisions.

Forum has power to recall its judgement or orders if it is obtained by fraud. Supreme Court in Indian Bank v. Satyam Fibres (India) RA Ltd. - AIR 1996 SC 2592 has observed: "The authorities, be they Constitutional, Statutory or Administrative (and particularly those who have to decide a us) possess the power to recall their judgments or orders if they are obtained by fraud as fraud and justice never dwell tether."

Isaac Mathew Vs. Maruti Udyog Ltd. : A car which was damaged and was subsequently repaired and supplied as new car was ordered to be replaced and some compensation for inconvenience was also allowed.

Kailash Kumari Vs. Narandra Electronics : A defective television was ordered to be replaced along with compensation.

Vinod Seth Vs. Rathan Road Lines : The carrier was held liable for loss of goods and for mental agony.

Bnany. Vs. Shenoy, Karnataka S.R.T.C. Karnataka : The passenger who could not be conveyed to his destinatin owing to road obstruction was allowed to recover from the bus operators his ticket money to and from.

STATE COMMISSION

State Commission is a "Consumer Disputes Redressal Commission" established by the State Government with the prior approval of the Central Government, in the State notification under Section 9(b) of the Consumer Protection Act.

Composition of the State Commission : According to section 16(1) of the Act, each State Commission shall consist of the following :

- ✶ a person who is or has been a judge of High Court shall be appointed, on the recommendation of a Selection Committee,by the State Government and shall be its *president*.
- ✶ *two other members*, who shall be (i) not lessthen 35 years of age, (ii) possesses a bachelor degree from a recognised univercity, and (iii) persons of ability, integrity and standing. They shall have adequate knowledge or experience of or have shown capacity in dealing with, problems relating to economics, law, commerce, accountancy, industry, public affairs or administration. One of such members shall be a woman.

Note : Not more than 50% of the members shall be from amongst persons having a judicial background. Person having judicial background shall mean persons having knowledge and experience for atleast a period of 10 years as a presiding officer at the district level court or any tribunal at equivalent level.

The provision to this clause states that every appointment made under this clause shall be made by the State Government on the recommendation of a Selection Committee consisting of the President of the State Commission, Secretary-Law Department of the State and Secretary in charge of Consumer Affairs in the State.

Under Section 16(2), the State Government has the power to decide on the salary or honorarium and other allowances payable to the members of the State Commission and the other terms and conditions of service.

Every member of the State Commission shall hold office for a term of *5 years or upto the age of 67 years*, whichever is earlier and shall not be eligible for reappointment.

Jurisdiction of State Commission

According to Section 17 of the Act, subject to the other provision of this Act, the State Commission shall have jurisdiction in the following matters.

1. *Monetary and Origianl :* To entertain complaints where the value of the goods or services and compensation, if any, claimed exceeds ₹ 20 lakhs, but does not exceed ₹ 1crore.
2. *Appellate :* To entertain appeal against the orders of any District Forum within the State, and
3. *Supervisorying and Revisional :* To call for the records and pass appropriate orders in any consumer dispute which is pending before and has been decided by any District Forum within the state.

Therefore, the *State Commission's jurisdiction may be original, appellate or revisional.* In respect of (3) above, the State Commission may reverse the orders passed by the District Forum on any question of fact or law or correct or error of fact of law made by the Forum.

In respect of the original jurisdiction of the State Commission, Section 17 only prescribes pecuniary limits. No territorial limits have been fixed for the exercise of original jurisdiction under the Act though the provision contained in Section 11(2) of the Act apply *matis mutandis* in the matter of entertaining original complaints by the State Commission as was held by the National Commission in *Indian Airlines Vs. Consumer Education and Research Society (1992).* The territorial jurisdiction of the State Commission, therefore, extends to the territorial limit of the State.

In the exercise of its appellate jurisdiction, the State Commission may entertain appeals only against the orders of any District Forum within the State. Similar condition also applies in respect of the State Commission's power to revise orders of the District Forums-only orders of the District Forum within the State may be subject to revision by the State Commission.

Procedure applicable to State Commission : The procedure prescribed for the working of District Forums by sections 12, and 14 and the rules framed under these sections, with suitable modifications, is also applicable to State Commissions.

Findings of the State Commission

According to section 13 of the Act, if the State Commission is convinced that the goods are really defective or that the complaint about the service is proved the State Commission shall issue an order to the opposite party to take one or more of the following things :

1. *To remove the defect pointed out by the appropriate laboratory* from the goods in question.
2. *To replace the goods with new goods* of similar description which shall be free from any defect.
3. *To return to the complainant the price of the goods or the service charges* paid by the complainant.
4. *To pay such amount as may be awarded by it as compensation to the consumer for any loss or injury suffered by the consumer due* to the negligence of the opposite party.
5. To remove the defects or deficiencies in the service in question
6. To discontinue the unfair trade practice or the restricitive trade practice or not repeat them
7. Not to offer the hazardous goods for sale.

8. To withdraw the hazardous goods from being offered for sale.
9. to cease manufacture of hazardous goods, and to desist from offering services which are hazardous in nature;
10. to pay such sum as may be determined by it, if it is of the opinion that loss or injury has been suffered by a large number of consumers who are not identifiable conveniently. The minimum amount of sum so payable shall not be less than 5% of the value of such defective goods, sold or service provided, as the case may be, to such consumers. The amount so obtained shall be credited in favour of such person and utilised in such manner as may be prescribed;
11. to issue corrective advertisement to neutralise the effect of misleading advertisement at the cost of the opposite party responsible for issuing such misleading advertisement;
12. To provide for adequate costs parties.

Appeal : Any person aggrieved by an order made by the State Commission may prefer an *appeal against such order to the National Commission within a period of 30 days* from the date of the order. The appeal must be made in such form and manner as maybe prescribed. National Commission may, however, entertain an appeal after the expiry of the said period of 30 days if it is satisfied that there was sufficient cause for not filing it within that period. Where no appeal has been preferred, the order of the State Commission shall be final. However, *the order of the State Commission on appeal made against the order of a District Forum shall not be entertained by the National Commission.*

Enforcement of Orders : The orders of a State Commission are enforceable in the manner of an order or decree made by a Civil Court in a civil suit. If the State Commission is not able to execute its order, it may forward the same to the civil court for execution.

Penalties : Every trader or a person against whom complaint is made is bound to comply with the order of the State Commission. If a trader fails comply with the order, he shall be punishable as under :

- with *imprisonment for a minimum period of one month and maximum of 3 years*; or
- with *minimum fine of ₹ 2,000* and *maximum of ₹ 10,000*, or
- *both with imprisonment and fine* as stated above.

NATIONAL COMMISSION

In exercise of the powers conferred under sec 9(c) of The Consumers Protection Act, the Central Government established a *"National Consumer Disputes Redressal Commission"* to be known as the '*National Commission*' by notification.

Composition of the National Commission

According to section 20(1) of the Act, the National Commission shall consist of the following :

(a) A person who is or has been a judge of the Supreme Court shall be appointed by the Central Government in consultation with the Chief Justice of India. He shall be its *president.*

(b) *Four other members* shall be persons of ability, integrity and standing. They shall have adequate experience of or have shown capacity in dealing with problems relating to economics, law, commerce, accountancy, industry, public affairs or administration. One of them shall be a woman. The Selection Committee shall consist of a Judge of the Surpreme Court to be nominated by the Chief Justice of India, the secretary in the Department of Legal Affairs and the secretary incharge of consumers Affairs in the Govt. of India. A sitting judge of the Supreme Course can be appointed only after consulting the Chief Justice of the Supreme Court. Every member of the National Commission shall hold office for a term of 5 years of upto 70 years of age whichever is earlier and shall not be eligible for reappointment.

Every appointment made under this clause by the Central Government shall be made on the recommendation of a Selection Committee consisting of a Judge of a Supreme Court to be nominated by the Chief Justice of India, the Secretary in the Department of Legal Affairs and the Secretary in charge of Consumer Affairs in the Government of India.

Section 20(2) gives power to Central Government to fix the salary/honorarium and other allowances payable to the members as well as the other terms and conditions of their service. Every member of the National Commission shall *hold office for term of five years or upto seventy years of age*, whichever is earlier and *shall not be eligible for reappointment*.

Disqualifications for Appointment [Section 20(1)]

A person shall be disqualified for appointment if the -

(a) has been convicted and sentenced to imprisonment for an offence which, in the opinion of the Central Government, involves moral turpitude; or

(b) is an undischarged insolvent; or

(c) is of unsound mind and stands so declared by a competent court; or

(d) has been removed or dismissed from the service of the Government or a Body Corporate owned or controlled by the Government; or

(e) has, in the opinion of the Central Government, such financial or other interest as is likely to affect prejudicially the discharge by him of his functions as a member; or

(f) has such other disqualifications as may be prescribed by the Central Government.

Terms and Conditions of Service of the President and Members of the National Commission:

Period: The President and every member of the National Commission shall give an undertaking, that he does not have, and will not have any such financial or other interest as is likely to affect prejudically his functions as such member. [Rule 12(1)].

The terms and conditions of service of the President and members shall not be varied to their disadvantage during the tenure of office.

Resignation and Vacancy: [Sec. 22D & Rule 12] The President or a member may resign his office at any time. When the office of a President of a District Forum, State Commission, or of the National Commission, as the case may be, is vacant or a person occupying such office is, by reason of absence or otherwise, unable to perform the duties of his office, these shall be performed by the senior most member of the District Forum, the State Commission or of the National Commission, as the case may be. Where a retired Judge of a High Court is a member of the National Commission, such member or where the number of such members is more than one, the senior most person among such members, shall preside over the National Commission in the absence of President of that Commission.

A casual vacancy caused by resignation or removal of the President or any member of the National Commission shall be filled by fresh appointment. When the office of the President of National Commission is vacant or a person occupying such office is by reason of absence or otherwise, unable to perform the duties of his office, the same shall be performed by the senior most member of the National Commission [Rule 12 (6)].

The President or any member ceasing to hold office as such, shall not hold any appointment in, or be connected with the management or administration of any organisation which have been the subject of any proceeding under the Act during his tenure, for a period of five years from the date on which he ceases to hold such office.

Removal of President or Members from Office

The Central Government may remove from office, the President or any member who -

(i) has been adjudged an insolvent; or

(ii) has been convicted of an offence which in the opinion of the Central Government, involves moral turpitude; or

(iii) has become physically or mentally incapable of acting as the President or the member; or

(iv) has acquired such financial or other interest as is likely to affect prejudicially his functions as the President or a member; or

(v) has so abused his position as to render his continuance in office prejudicial to the public interest; or

(vi) remains absent in three consecutive sittings except for reasons beyond his control.

The President or any member shall not be removed from office on any of the above grounds, except on an inquiry held by a sitting Judge of the Supreme Court nominated by the Chief Justice of India in which the President or member has been informed of the charges against him and given a reasonable opportunity of being heard in respect of those charges and found guilty (Rule 13).

National Consumer Disputes Redressal Commission has framed The Consumer Protection Regulations, 2005 for regulating the affairs of the Commission.

Jurisdiction of the National Commission

The jurisdiction of the National Commission shall be as under :

1. *Monetary :* It can entertain complaints where the value of goods or service and compensation, if any, *claimed exceeds Rs. 1 crore.*
2. *Appellate :* It can entertain *appeals against the orders of any State Commission*, and
3. *Supervisory and Revisisional :* It can call for the records and pass appropriate orders in any consumer dispute pending before or has been decided by any State Commission. It can do so where the State Commission has exercised jurisdiction not vested in it by law or has acted in the exercise of its jurisdiction illegally or with material irregularity. Therefore, the *jurisdiction of the National Commission could also he categorised as original, appellate and revisional as that of the State Commission.*

The jurisdiction, powers and authority of the National Commission may be exercised by benches thereof. A Bench may be constituted by the President with one or more members as the President may deem fit.

Difference of Opinion: If the members of the Bench differ in opinion on any point, the points shall be decided according to the opinion of the majority, if there is a majority, but if the members are equally divided, they shall state the point or points on which they differ, and make a reference to the President who shall either hear the point or points himself or refer the case for hearing on such point or points by one or more or the other members and such point or points shall be decided according to the opinion of the majority of the members who have heard the case, including those who first heard it.

PROCEDURE APPLICABLE TO THE NATIONAL COMMISSION

Disposal of Complaint and Relief

The National Commission shall, in the disposal of any complaints or of any proceedings before it, have the powers of a Civl Court. It shall follow such procedure as may be prescribed by the Central Government. The procedure to be followed by the National Commission has been prescribed by the Consumer Protection Rules, 1987 made by the Central Government. The procedure to be followed is as under:

Content of a Complaint

A complaint containing the following particulars shall be presented by the complainant *in person or by his agent to the National Commission or be sent by registered post to the National Commission :*

(a) the name, description and the address of the *complainant.*

(b) the name, description and address of the *opposite party or parties.*

(c) the facts, relating to complaint, and *when* and *where it arose.*

(d) *documents* in support of the allegations contained in the complaint.

(e) the *relief* which complainant claims.

Every complaint shall be accompanied by the relevant fee as is prescribed. Every complaint shall be filed in quadruplicate or with such number of copies as may be required by the National Commission.

Procedure on Receipt of Compliant

The National Commission on receipt of a complaint, has to observe the following procedures as outlined in section 13 of the Act:

A. *Refer a copy of the complaint to the opposite party* directing him to give his version of the case within a period of 30 days or such extended period not exceeding 15 days.

B. Where the opposite party, on receipt of a complaint copy, denies or disputes the allegation contained in the complaint, the omits or fails to take any action to represent his case within the time given by the National Commission, the National Commission shall *proceed to settle the consumer dispute in the manner provided by the Act.*

C. If the complaint relates to some defects in the goods, which cannot be determined without proper analysis or test of the goods, the National Commission shall *obtain a sample of the goods from the complainant and refer the sample to the appropriate laboratory for analysis or test.*

D. The appropriate laboratory has to analyse or test the sample received to find out whether such goods suffer from any defect alleged in the complaint, *within 45 days of the receipt* of the reference or with such extended period as may be granted by the Commission the laboratory shall submit its report the National Commission.

E. On receipt of the report from the appropriate laboratory, the National Commission shall *forward a copy of the report along with such remarks* as the National Commission may feel appropriate to the opposite party.

F. If any of the parties dispute the correctness of the findings of the laboratory, or disputes the correctness of the methods of analysis or test adopted by the laboratory, the National Commission shall *require the opposite party or the complaint to state in writing his objections in regard to the report made by the laboratory.*

G The National Commission, before issuing any final order in the matter, will *provide an opportunity to both parties to present their views about the report of the laboratory.*

Appearance of Parties : On the date ofhearing, it shall be obligatory on the parties or their agents to appear before the National Commission. Where the complainant or his agent fails to appear before the National Commission on the date of hearing, the National Commission may in its discretion, either dismiss the complaint for default or decide its in merits. Where the opposite party or its agent fails to appear on the date ofhearing, the National Commission may decide the complaint *ex parte.*

Time Limit for deciding the complaint: Where the complaint does not require analysis or testing of commodity, the National Commission shall decide the complaint within a period of three months from the date of notice received by Opposite Party. If analysis or testing of commodities is required, the National Commission shall decide the complaint within five months. Every proceedings of the National Commission shall be conducted by the President and at least two members thereof sitting together. Where the member or members for any reason are unable to conduct the proceeding till it is completed, the President shall conduct such proceeding de-novo.

Findings of the National Commission

If the National Commission is convinced that the goods were really defective or that the complain about the service is proved, it shall order the opposite party to do one or more of the following things :

* *to remove the defect pointed out* by the appropriate laboratory from the goods.
* *to replace the goods with new goods* of a similar description, which shall be free from any defect.
* *to return to the complainant the price of the goods or the charges for services paid* by the complainant.
* *to pay to the complainant a sum of money by way of compensation* for any loss or injury suffered by the consumer due to the negligence of the opposite party.
* *to remove the defects or deficiencies in the services in question.*
* *to discontinue the unfair trade practice or the restrictive trade practice* or not to repeat them.
* *not to offer the hazardous goods for sale.*
* *to withdraw the hazardous goods from being offered for sale.*
* to cease manufacture of hazardous goods, and to desist from offering services which are hazardous in nature;
* to pay such sum as may be determined by it, if it is of the opinion that loss or injury has been suffered by a large number of consumers who are not identifiable conveniently. The minimum amount of sum so payable shall not be less than 5% of the value of such defective goods, sold or service provided, as the case may be, to such consumers. The amount so obtained shall be credited in favour of such person and utilised in such manner as may be prescribed;
* to issue corrective advertisement to neutralise the effect of misleading advertisement at the cost of the opposite party responsible for issuing such misleading advertisement;
* *to provide for adequate costs to parties.*

Orders

After the proceedings are conducted, the National Commission, if satisfied with the allegations contained in the complaint shall issue orders to the opposite party. Every order made by the National Commission shall be signed by the President or the senior most member and at least two members who conducted the proceeding. The National Commission shall have the power to direct that any order passed by it, where no appeal has been filed in Supreme Court, or where the Supreme Court has affirmed the order of the National Commission, to publish the order in the Official Gazette or through any other media. No legal proceedings shall lie against the National Commission or any media for such publication.

Appeal : An appeal against the orders of the National Commission can lie to the Supreme Court. *An appeal to the Supreme Court can be made within a period of 30 days* from the date of the order of National Commission. The Supreme Court may permit an appeal even after the expiry of the prescribed period if there was a sufficient cause for not being able to fiel an appeal in time.

Finality of the Orders : Where no appeal has been filed against the order of the National Commission, the same shall be final.

Enforcement of Orders : Every order made by the National Commission may be enforced in the same manner as a decree or order made by a Civil Court.

Penalties : Every trader or a person against whom complaint is made is bound to comply with the order of the National Commission. If a trader or a person fails to comply with the order, he shall be punishable.

- with *imprisonment for a minimum period of one month* and *maximum of 3 years*, or
- with *minimum fine of ₹ 2,000* and *maximum of ₹ 10,000*, or
- *both*, (with imprisonment and fine as stated above)

Appeal to National Commission : According to Section 19 of the Consumers Protection Act, a person aggrieved by an order of the State Commission can prefer an appeal against such order to the National Commission within 30 days from the date of the order in such form and manner as may be prescribed. The procedure for hearing the appeal is laid down by the Consumer Protection Rules, 1987.

No appeal shall be entertained by the National Commission unless the Appellant who is required to pay any amount in terms of an order of the State Commission, has deposited 50% of the amount or ₹ 35,000 whichever is less, in the form of a crossed Demand Draft on a Nationalised Bank in favour of the Registrar, National Commission, payable at Delhi.

Procedure for Hearing an Appeal

1. Memorandum shall be presented by the appellant or his agent to the National Commission in *person or be sent by registered post* to the Commission.
2. The memorandum shall be in *legible hand writing, preferably typed*. The memorandum shall include grounds of appeal without any argument or narattive. The grounds must be numbered consecutively.
3. The memorandum shall be *accompanied by a certified coy of the order* the State Commission appealed against. It shall also be *accompanied by any of the documents* as may be required to support grounds of objection stated in the memorandum.
4. The appellant shall submit *six copies of the memorandum* to the Commission for office use.

5. On the date of hearing, all the *parties or agents must appear* before the National Commission.

6. The appellant shall not, except by leave of the National Commission, urge or be heard in support of any ground of objection not set forth in the memorandum but the National Commission, in deciding the appeal, may not confine to the grounds of objection set forth in the memorandum.

   Provided that the Commission shall not rest its decision on any other ground than those specified in the memorandum unless the party who may be affected thereby, has been given an opportunity of being heard by the National Commission.

7. The National Commission may, on such terms as it deems fit and at any stage of the proceedings, *adjourn the hearing* of the appeal, but *not more than one adjournment shall ordinarily be given* and the appeal should be decided, as far as possible, *within 90 days from the first date of hearing.*

Sitting of National Commission: (Rule 15 A)

Every proceeding of the National Commission shall be conducted by the President or the senior most member and at least two members thereof sitting together, except when a bench is constituted by the President with one or more members as he may deem fit.

Where bench differs on any point, such point shall be referred to the other member for hearing and such point shall be decided according to the opinion of the majority of the National Commission.

8. The order of the National Commission shall be communicated to the parties concerned free of cost.

APPEAL TO SUPREME COURT

An appeal to the Supreme Court, against the order of the National Commission in case of an appeal to it, cannot be made as per law.

An appeal lies to the Supreme Court from an order passed by the National Commission. Order XX(F) of the Supreme Court Rues, 1966 provides the following procedure for filing of appeals to the Supreme Court :

1. Subject to the provisions of Section 4, 5 and 12 of the Limitation Act, 1963, the petition of appeal from the order of the National Commission shall be presented by an aggrieved person within 30 days from the date of the order sought to be appealed against. However, in computing the said period of 30 days, the time required for obtaining a copy of such order shall be excluded.

2. Petition of appeal shall recite succinctly and clearly all the relevant facts leading up to the order from which appeal is sought. The appeal petition shall also set forth in brief, objections to the order appealed from and other grounds relied upon in support of the appeal. The petition shall further state the date of the order appealed from as well as the date on which it was received by the appellant.

3. The petition of appeal shall be accompanied by the following :

   (i) an authenticated copy of the order in appeal.

   (ii) atleast 7 separate sets of petition and the papers filed with it.

4. If the appeal is registered, it is put up for hearing ex-parte before the Court. The Court may dismiss it either summarily or direct issue of notice to all concerned parties or make such order as the cirucmstances of the case may require.

5. A fixed court fee of ₹ 350 shall be paid on the petition of appeal.

Appeal against Order of Penalty [Section 27A]

An appeal against order of penalty, both on facts and on law, shall lie from:

(a) the order made by the District Forum to the State Commission;

(b) the order made by the State Commission to the National Commission; and

(c) the order made by the National Commission to the Supreme Court.

Except as aforesaid, no appeal shall lie to any Court from any order of a District Forum or a State Commission or the National Commission.

Every Appeal shall be preferred within a period of 30 days from the date of an order of a District Forum or a State Commission or, as the case may be, the National Commission. The State Commission or the National Commission or the Supreme Court may entertain an appeal after the expiry of the said period of thirty days, if it is satisfied that the appellant had sufficient cause for not preferring the appeal within the period of thirty days.

Dismissal of Frivolous or Vexatious Complaints [Section 26]

Where a complaint instituted is found to be frivolous or vexatious, the District Forum, the State Commission or the National Commission, as the case may be, shall, for reasons to be recorded in writing, dismiss the complaint and make an order that the complainant shall pay to the opposite party such cost, not exceeding ten thousand rupees as may be specified in the order (Sec. 26).

There are instances where a person takes advantage of his rights under the Act. He does not act bonafide, has no evidence to substantiate his complaint. His complaint is motivated to harass the opposite party, is malicious without thy cause or to settle personal scores. Such a complaint is called "frivolous or vexatious" complaint. Where a complaint was found to be not maintainable under the Act and the complainant had abused the provisions of Consumer Protection Act merely because no Court fee was payable, the National Commission imposed costs of Rs 10,000 on the complainant, payable to the opposite party for filing vexatious complaint (Nava Bharat Land Development & Finance Ltd v. Punjab National Bank — Original Petition No. 71 of 1992 decided on 9.12.1992 (NC)).

POWERS FOR ENFORCEMENT OF ORDER

Enforcement of Orders of the District Forum, the State Commission or the National Commission [Section 25]

Where an interim order made under this Act, is not complied with, the District Forum or the State Commission or the National Commission, as the case may be, may order the property of the person, not complying with such order to be attached.

No such attachment shall remain in force for more than three months at the end of which, if the noncompliance continues, the property attached may be sold and out of the proceeds thereof, the District Forum or the State Commission or the National Commission may award such damages as it thinks fit to the complainant and shall pay the balance, if any, to the party entitled thereto.

Where any amount is due from any person under an order made by a District Forum, State Commission, or the National Commission, as the case may be, the person entitled to the amount may make an application to the District Forum, the State Commission or the National Commission, as the case may be, and such District Forum or the State Commission or the National Commission may issue a certificate for the said amount to the Collector or the district and the Collector shall proceed to recover the amount in the same manner as arrears of land revenue.

For the purpose of settling the disputes, under section, 13 of the Consumer Protection Act, State Commission or National Commission shall have the same powers as are vested in the Civil Court under the Civil Procedures Code in the following matters:

1. the summoning and enforcing the attendance of any defendant and witness and examining the witness on oath.
2. the discovery and production of any document or other material object producible as evidence.
3. the reception of evidence of affidavits.
4. the requisition of the report of the concerned analysis or test from the appropriate laboratory or other relevant source.
5. issuing of any commission for the examination of any witness, and
6. dismissal of frivolous or vexatious complaints.

Consumer Protection Rules, 1987 framed by the Central Government have given additional powers to the National Commission and State Commission : They are :

1. The National Commission or the State Commission shall have power to require any person :
   (a) to produce before and allow to be examined and kept by an officer of the National Commission or the State Commission such books, accounts documents or commodities in the custody or under the control of the person so required described in the requisition.
   (b) to furnish to an office so specified such information as may be required for the purpose of this Act.
2. Where during any proceedings under this Act, the National Commissino or the State Commission has any ground to believe that any book, paper, commodity or document which may be required to be produced in such proceedings are being or may be destroyed, mutilated, altered, falsified or secreted, it may be written order authorise any officer to exercise the power of entry and search of any premises. Such authorised officer may also seize such books, papers, documents or commodities as are required for the purpose of this Act.

CONSUMER PROTECTION COUNCILS

The objects of the Consumer Protection Act are sought to be promoted and protected by the consumer protection councils established at the Central and State levels. The consumer protecton council established at Central level is knwon as *Central Council*. The consumer protection council established at State level is known as *State Council*.

CENTRAL COUNCIL

The Central Government has constituted a Central Protection Council by notification with effect from 1-6-1987. As per the Consumer Protection Rules the *Central Council consist of 150 members*. They are :

1. the Minister-in-charge of Department of Civil Supplies in the Central Government. He shall be the Chairman of the Central Council.
2. the Minister of State or Deputy Minister in the Department of Civil Supplies in the Central Government. He shall be the Vice-Chairman of the council.
3. the Minister of Food and Supplies in States.

4. eight Members of Parliament-Five from the Lok Sabha and three from Rajya Sabha.
5. the Commissioner of scheduled castes and scheduled tribes.
6. 10 representatives of women.
7. 20 representatives of farmers, trade and industries.
8. 15 persons capable of representative consumer interests.
9. 35 representatives of the consumer organisation or consumers.
10. the Secretary in the Department of Civil Supplies. He shall be the members secretary of the Central Council.

Procedure of the Central Council

The Central Council shall meet as and when necessary. Atleast one meeting of the council shall be held every year. The Central Council shall meet as at such time and place as the Chairman may think fit. It shall observe such procedure in regard to the transaction of its business as may be prescribed.

The procedure which the Central Council shall observe in regard to the transaction of its business is as under:

(i) The meeting of the Central Council shall be presided over by the Chairman. In the absence of the Chairman, the Vice-Chairman shall preside over the meeting of the Central Council. In the absence of the Chairman and the Vice Chairman, the Central Council shall elect a member to preside over that meeting of the Council.

(ii) Each meeting of the Central Council shall specify the place and the day and hour of the meeting and shall contain statement of business to be transacted thereat.

(iii) Every notice of a meeting of the Central Council shall specify the place and the day and hour of the meeting and shall contain statement of business to be transacted thereat.

(iv) No proceedings of the Central Council shall be invalid merely by reason of existence of any vacancy in or any defect in the constitution of the Council.

For the purpose of performing its functions under the Act, the Central Council may constitute from amongst its members necessary working groups. Every working group shall perform such functions as are assigned to it by the Central Council. The findings of such working groups shall be placed before the Central Council for its consideration. The resolutions passed by the Central Council shall be recommendatory in nature.

The non-official members, non-official members from Island territories, non-official members who senior citizens and Members of Parliament attending the meetings of the Council or its working group shall be entitled to avail of travel facilities, incidental charges as prescribed in Rule 3(6) of Consumer Protection Rules, 1987 as amended by Consumer Protection (Amendment) Rules, 2004.

Objects of the Central Council : Section 6 of the Consumers Protection Act, 1986 lays down the objects of the Central Council. The objects of the Central Council shall be to promote and protect the right of the consumers.

1. *The right to be protected against the marketing of goods which are hazardous to life and property :* For example, adulterated goods are dangerous to life as well as to property. The consumer is assured by this Act that if he has been victimised into purchasing goods which have injured his person or property, he will have simple, speedy and effective remedy under the hierarchy constituted under the

Act. The subjec tmatter of dangerous goods is generally taken care of under law of Torts. All such matters can now be taken before the authorities constituted under the Act. It has become an established principle that a producer sending goods into the market would be liable to the ultimate user if his person or property is injured in the normal use of goods.

2. *The right to informed about the quality, quantity, potency, purity, standard and price of goods so as to protect consumer against unfair trade practices :* This is intended to save the consumer from unfair trade practices like false and misleading descriptions about the nature and quality of the goods, and exaggerated statements about their power and potency. In all cases of unfair trade practices or restrictive trade practices, the consumer would have the option of either apply to the Monopolies Commission under the Monopolies and Restrictive Trade Practices Act, 1969 or the Redressal Agencies constituted under the Consumer Protection Act. Viz., (a) District Forum, (b) State Commission, (c) National Commission.

3. *The right to be assured, wherever, possible, access to variety of goods at competitive price :* The Central Council constituted under this Act has been charged with the responsibility or bringing about the organisation of markets and market practices in such a way that all dealers are supplied with a variety of goods for the benefit of consumer and that the goods with a variety are being offered at competitive prices. It is only then that the consumer will have success to variety and will be able to enjoy the benefit of competitive prices.

4. *The right to be heard and to be assured that consumer's interest will receive due consideration at appropriate Forums :* The Central Council is charged with the responsibility of assuring the consumers that they would be heard of right by the appropriate Forums and the consumers will receive due attention and consideration from such Forums.

5. *The right to seek redressal against unfair trade practices, or unscrupulous exploitation of consumers:* Three redressal agencies have been established to provide simple and speedy redressal to consumer disputes. These agencies have been empowered to give relief of specific nature and to award compensation to consumers. They will observe the principles of natural justice. Their orders are final unless appealed.

6. *The right to consumer education :* The consumer has been given the right to education by section 6 of the Consumer Protection Act, 1986. The Central Council has been charged with the responsibility to provide to the people proper education in terms of their remedies under Act. People's awareness is likely to prove a better for putting the trade on some level of discipline that of Governments Controls.

STATE COUNCIL

The objects of every State Council shall be the same as those of the Central Council. The objects of every State Council shall be to promote and protect within the State the rights of consumers as laid down in section 6 of the Consumer Protection Act.

Section 7 provides for the establishment of State Consumer Protection Councils by any State Government (by notification) to be known as Consumer Protection Council for (name of the State). The State Council shall consist of a Minister incharge of consumer affairs in the State Government who shall be its Chairman and such number of other official or non-official members representing such interests as may be prescribed by the State Government. The State Council shall meet as and when necessary but not less than two meetings shall be held every year. The procedure to be observed in regard to the transaction of its business at such meetings shall be prescribed by the State Government.

Consumer Protection Council. Vs. National Dairy Development Board : The complainant wanted to known in what way the Dairy Board and using the imported palm oil. The Board was refusing to give the information on the ground that the disclosure was against the public interest. Without that information the complainant was to able to make out his case. It was held that the consumer had the right to the requisite information.

DISTRICT COUNCIL [Section 8(A)]

The State Government shall establish for every district, a District Consumer Protection Council.

The District Consumer Protection Council shall consist of the following members, namely:

(a) the Collector of the district, who shall be its Chairman; and

(b) such number of other official and non-official members representing such interests as may be prescribed by the State Government.

The District Council shall meet as and when necessary but not less than two meetings shall be held every year. The District Council shall meet at such time and place within the district as the Chairman may think fit and shall observe such procedure in regard to the transaction of its business as may be prescribed by the State Government.

Objects of the District Council: [Section 8B]

The objects of every District Council shall be the same as the objects of the Central Council to promote and protect within the district the rights of the consumers. (The objects of the Central Council have been detailed above).

REVIEW QUESTIONS

1. What are the objectives of Consumer Protection Act, 1986?
2. Who is a 'Consumer'? Who is not a consumer under the Consumer Protection Act, 1986?
3. What do you mean by 'Service'? What services will come under the purview of the Consumer Protection Act, 1986?
4. What do you mean by 'Complaint'? Who can make a complaint and to whom a complaint can be made?
5. What do you mean by 'Unfair Trade Practices'? State its ingredients and instances. Support your answer with few decided cases.
6. What is meant by (a) defect in goods and (b) deficiency in service?
7. What are the rights of consumers and how the Consumer Protection Act, 1986 seeks to protect such rights of consumers?
8. Write short notes on (a) Defect in goods, (b) Deficiency in service, (c) Public interest complaints, (d) Consumer Rights, (e) Consumer Welfare legislations, (f) Unfair trade Practices, (g) Restrictive trade practices.
9. What are the consumer disputes redressal agencies provided under the Consumer Protection Act, 1986?
10. What is the nature and scope of remedies under the Consumer Protection Act?
11. In what way Consumer Protection Act can help the consumers in the redressal of their grievances?
12. What is the jurisdiction of the various forums/commissions for the purpose of Consumer Protection Act, 1986?
13. What is a 'District Forum'? Explain the procedure to be adopted by the forum on receipt of a complaint.
14. State the jurisdiction, powers and procedure and settlement of disputes by the National Commission.
15. State the jurisdiction, powers and procedure and settlement of disputes by the State Commission.

16. State the objects and compositioin of the Central Consumer Protection Council and State Consumer Protection Council.
17. What are the enactments promoting and protecting consumer interest?
18. State the grounds justifying the need for separate consumer protective legislation.
19. Who can make a complaint under the Consumer Protection Act, 1986?
20. What are the advantages of seeking remedy or redressal under the Consumer Protection Act. 1986?
21. How to file a complaint for redressal of grievances under the Consumer Protection Act 1986?
22. In What way Consumer Protection Act can help the consumers in the redressal of their grievances?
23. What are power s vested with consumer disputes redressal commission to enforce its order against the opposite party?
24. Explain the procedure of appeal to supreme court against order of National Commission.
25. What is the time limit to decide the case under the Consumer Protection Act, 1986?
26. Explain the procedure to be followed in deciding consumer dispute, by a District Forum under the Consumer Protection Act, 1986
27. What are the powers of the National Consumer Disputes Redressal commission?
28. What type of remedies for consumer grievances or disputes measures are ordered by the consumer disputes redressal machineries provides under the Consumer Protection Act, 1986?
29. What are the penalties imposed on a trader failing to comply with the order of the Forum or commission under the Consumer Protection Act, 1986?
30. Write short notes on:

    (a) Jurisdiction of the National Consumer Disputes Redressal Commission

    (b) The District Consumer Protection Council

❒ ❒ ❒

Chapter 16

THE INDUSTRIES (DEVELOPMENT & REGULATION) ACT, 1951

The Industries (Development & Regulation) Act, 1951 came into force on 8th May, 1952. It has been amended from time to time, the latest being in 1991. The Act has three important oh/relives, viz. (i) to implement the Industrial Policy, (ii) regulation and development of important industries, (iii) planning future development of new undertakings. The Act applies to the whole of India including the State of Jammu & Kashmir.

Objectives of the Act

The objectives the Industries (Development and Regulation) Act 1951, sought to accomplish were as follows:

1. The regulation of industrial investment and production according to plan priorities and targets.
2. Protection of small entrepreneurs against competition from large industries.
3. Prevention of monopoly and concentration of ownership of industries.
4. Balanced regional development with a view to reducing disparities in the levels of development of different regions of the economy.

It was hoped that through the instrument of industrial licensing, the State would be able to (i) direct investment into the most important branches, (ii) correlate supply and demand in the domestic market, (iii) eliminate competition, and (iv) ensure the optimum utilisation of social capital.

Main Provisions of the Act

The following are the main provisions of the Act:

1. All scheduled undertakings should be registered with the Government.
2. All undertakings which wish to have substantial expansion should get licences from the Government. Similarly, all new undertakings should also obtain licences from the Government.
3. The Government was empowered to enquire into the affairs of any scheduled undertaking.
4. If any undertaking failed to abide by the instructions of the Government, the Government was empowered to takeover defaulting industry.
5. Licenses are to be obtained and categories on the basis of new industries having substantial expansion, industries engaged in the production of new articles, industries seeking change of location and industries carrying on business.
6. An advisory licensing body was set up with the representation of Planning Commission and the Ministries to advise the government in the matters dealing with issue and grant of licences.

Scope and Coverage (Scheme) of the Act

The Act confers very wide powers on the Government in relation to industries. The *main provisions of the Act* are given below:

1. It provides for the registration *of the existing industrial enterprises.*

2. The Act empowers the Government to start an *investigation into the a/fain of any industrial undertaking* in the case of unsatisfactory working of the undertaking and can even take it under its own management if it fails to carry out its instructions.

3. It provides for the licensing of new industrial undertakings. Licensing is a permission from the Government which may include conditions such as the location, minimum size etc. Licence is required for (a) the establishment of new industrial undertakings pertaining to a scheduled industry; (h) substantial expansion to produce the same item or diversification to produce a new licence but which has not been licensed previously; and (d) change of location of licensed/registered undertaking.

4.The Act also provides for the establishment of (a) a Central, Advisory Council to advise the Government on the regulation and development of scheduled industries, (b) a Development council to each major industry, and (c) a Licensing Committee.

The provisions of the Act may be grouped into three board categories:

(i) Preventive (Regulatory) Measures	(ii) Curative (Control) Measures	(iii) Developmental (Creative) Measures
(a) Registration & Licensing of industrial undertakings.	(a) Direct management or control by Government.	(a) The Central Advisory Council
(b) Investigation of scheduled industries.	(b) Control of supply, distribution, price etc.	(b) The Reviewing Committee.
(c) Revocation of Registration or Licence		(c) Standing Committee
		(d) Licensing Committee
		(e) Development Councils.
		(f) Industrial Panels
		(g) Imposition of Cess

CENTRAL ADVISORY COUNCIL (Section 5)

Constitution and Functions : The Central Government may by a notified order, establish a council to be called the Central Advisory Council. for the purpose of advising it on matters concerning (i) the development and regulation of scheduled industries, (ii) the administration of the Act when called for, and (iii) also in the making of rules under the Act. It shall consist of a chairman and such other members not exceeding thirty in number, all of whom shall be appointed by the Central Government from among person who arc in its opinion capable of representing the interest of : (a) owners of industrial undertaking in scheduled industries (b) persons employed in industrial undertakings in scheduled industries (c) consumers of goods manufactured by scheduled industries; (d) such other class of persons including primary products, as in the opinion of the Central Government ought to be represented on the Advisory Council. The term of office or the procedure to be followed in the discharge of their functions and the manner of filling casual vacancies among members of the Advisory Council, shall be such as may be prescribed.

The Central Government shall consult the Advisory Council in regard to (a) the making of. any rules, (b) in regard to any other matter connected with the administration of the Act in respect of which the Central Government may consider it necessary to obtain the advise of the Advisory Council.

The Reviewing Sub-Committee of the Central Advisory Council reviews the industrial licenses issued, varied, amended or revoked from time to time. The Standing Committee of the Central Advisory Council, Minister of Industry as its chairman, reviews the position of industries wherever required.

Development Council (Section 6)

Constitution and Functions : The Central Government may, by a notified order, establish for any scheduled industry or group of scheduled industries a body of persons to be called a Development Council which shall consist of members who in the opinion of the Central Government are:

(a) Persons capable of representing the interests of owners of industrial undertakings in the scheduled industry or group of scheduled indusries;

(b) Person having special knowledge of matters relating to the technical or other aspects of the scheduled industry or group of scheduled industries;

(c) Person capable of representing the interest of persons employed in industrial undertakings in the scheduled industry or group of scheduled industries;

(d) Persons not belonging to any of the aforesaid categories who are capable of representing the interests of consumers of goods manufactured by the scheduled industry to group of scheduled industries.

The number and term of office of, and the procedure to be followed in the discharge of their functions and the manner of filling casual vacancies among members of a Development Council shall be such as may be prescribed.

The Central Government may assign to the Development Council the following functions in order to increase the efficiency or productivity in the scheduled industry or group of scheduled industries for which the Development Council is established, improve or develop the service that such industry or group of industries renders, or enable such industry or group of industries to render such services more economically

(i) Recommending targets for production, coordinating production programmes and reviewing progress from time to time.

(ii) Suggesting norms of efficiency with a view to eliminating waste, obtaining maximum production, improving quality and reducing costs.

(iii) Recommending measures for securing the fuller utilisation of installed capacity and for improving the working of the industry, particularly of the less efficient units.

(iv) Promoting arrangements for better marketing and helping in devising of a system of distribution and sale of the produce of the industry which would be satisfactory to the consumer.

(v) Promoting standardisation of products

(vi) Assisting in the distribution of controlled materials and promoting arrangements obtaining materials for the industry.

(vii) Promoting or undertaking inquiry as to materials and equipment and as to methods of production, management and labour utilisation, including the discovery and development of new materials, equipment and methods and of improvement in those already in use, the assessment of the advantages of different alternatives and the conduct of experimental operation and of tests on a commercial scale.

(viii) Promoting the training of persons engaged or proposing engagement in the industry and their education in technical or artistic subjects relevant thereto.

(ix) Promoting the re-training in alternative occupations of personnel engaged in or retrenched from the industry.

(x) Promoting or undertaking scientific anti industrial researci4 research into matters affecting industrial psychology and research into matters relating to production and to the consumption or use of goods and services supplied by the industry.

(xi) Promoting improvements and standardisation of accounting and costing methods and practices.

(xii) Promoting or undertaking the collection and formulation of statistics.

(xiii) Investigating possibilities of decentralising the stages and processes of production with a view to encouraging the growth of allied small scale and cottage industries.

(xiv) Promoting the adoption of measures for increasing tile productivity of labour, including measures for securing safer and better working conditions and provision and improvement of amenities and incentives for workers.

(xv) Advising on any, natters relating to the industry (other than remuneration and conditions of employment) as to which the Central Government may request the Development Council to advise and undertaking inquiries for the purpose of enabling the Development Council so to advise.

(xvi) Undertaking arrangements for making available to the industry information obtained and for advising on matters with which the Development Councils are concerned in the exercise of any of their functions.

(xvii) Such other functions as it may be required to perform.

Annual Report : 'A Development Council shall prepare and transmit to the Central Government and the Advisory Council annually a report (including a statement on the audited accounts together with a copy of audit report) on its functions during the financial year last completed. A copy of each such report shall be laid before the Parliament by the Central Government.

Dissolution o council : A Development Council established under Sec. 6 may be dissolved by the Central Government if the Central Government is satisfied that the existence of such a Development Council is not necessary. On such dissolution, the assets of such a council shall vest in the Central Government after meeting liabilities the Development Council, if any. The assets vested in the council shall be used by the Central Government for the purpose of this Act.

Levy and Collection of Cess (Section 9)

The Central Government may levy and collect cess on all goods manufactured and produced in any specified scheduled industry and hand over the pioceeds to the Development Council of that industry to be utilised:

(a) to promote scientific and industrial research with reference to the scheduled industry or group of scheduled industries in respect of which the Development Council is established

(b) to promote improvements in design and quality with reference to the products of such industry or group of industries;

(c) to provide for the training of technicians and labour in such industry or group of industries;

(d) to meet such expenses in the exercise of its functions and its administrative expenses as may be prescribed.

REGULATION OF SCHEDULED INDUSTRIES

The development of industries listed in Schedule I of the Act is regulated through (i) Registration of existing industrial undertakings: (ii) Licensing of new industrial undertakings: (iii) Licence for producing or manufacturing New Articles; (iv) Certain powers vested in the Central Government under the Act to cause investigation into the affairs of such scheduled industries or industrial undertakings: and (v) to take-over its management. These are discussed in the following pages.

Registration of Existing Industrial Undertakings (Section 10)

The owner of every industrial undertaking (except the Central Government) shall register the undertaking in the prescribed manner within such times as the Central Government may specify by notification in the Official Gazette. The Central Government shall also get registered those existing industrial undertakings which are owned by the Central Government. After registration of industrial undertakings, the owner shall he issued a Certificate of Registration containing production capacity of the industrial undertaking and other particulars as prescribed by the Central Government. While mentioning the production capacity in the Certificate of Registration, the Central Government shall also take into consideration the production or installed capacity of the industrial undertakings, along with the level of production before the date of application for registration, the level of highest annual production during last three years, immediately before the Industrial (D&R) Amendment Act, 1973, the limit to which production during this period was utilised for export and such other factor as the Central Government may think relevant.

The application for registration of an existing industrial undertaking shall be made in triplicate to the Secretariat of Department of Industrial Development, Government of India, New Delhi. This application must be made at least three months before the expiry period fixed by Central Government for making application by that industrial undertaking.

However, if the application is not made in time, the same may be entertained by the Ministry if the application satisfied that there was sufficient cause for delay in making the application must be accompanied by a fee of ₹ 1,000 by a demand draft. The demand draft should be made payable to the Pay and Accounts Officer, Ministry of Industry, New Delhi. The Ministry or authority entertaining the application may require the application to furnish such other additional information as may be considered necessary for the purpose of registration of the industrial undertaking. In case the application is found in order, a Certificate of Registration shall be issued by the Ministry to the applicant.

Power to revoke registration : However, the registration of the existing industrial undertakings can be revoked or cancelled under Section IOA if the Central Government is satisfied that (i) the registration of any industrial undertaking has been obtained by misrepresentation as to essential facts, (ii) the undertaking ceased to be registrable by reason of any exemption granted tinder the Act, or (iii) For any other reason, the registration has become useless or ineffective and therefore, requires to be revoked. The Central Government may i-evoke the registration granted under Section 10 after giving an opportunity to the owner of the industrial undertaking to explain.

Licensing of New Undertakings, New Articles, etc.,

(i) Licence for establishing any new industrial undertaking (Sec. 11) : No person or authority other than the Central Government after the commencement of the Act, viz., May 8, 1952, shall establish any new industrial undertaking without a licence from the Central Government. A State Government may, however establish a new industrial undertaking with permission of the Central Government. The licence may contain such conditions including in particular the location-and size of the undertaking as the Central Government may deem fit.

(ii) Licence for producing manufacturing new articles : The owner of an industrial undertaking (other than Central Government) registered under section 10 or licenced under Section 11, shall not produce or manufacture any new articles unless (a) in the case of an industrial undertaking registered under Section 10, he has obtained a licence for producing or manufacturing such new articles, and (b) in the case of an undertaking licensed under Section II - lie has had the existing licence amended in the prescribed manner.

Power to revoke licenses : Under Section 12, the Central Government may revoke the licence grant under Sections 10 and 11 if effective steps to establish the new industrial undertaking or produce or manufacture new articles are not taken within the prescribed time. The Central Government may also vary or amend any licence but only before any effective steps had been taken.

(iii) Licence for carrying on business without registration [Sec. 13(1)(a)] : Where an industrial undertaking is required under Section 10 of the Act but which has not got itself registered within the prescribed time, a licence or permission as the case may he, is required to be, obtained from the Central Government by the owner of such undertaking for the purpose of carrying on its business after the expiry of the period within which ii ought to have got registered.

(iv) Licence for carrying on business afer the revocation of certificate of registration: Under Section 10A of the Act, the certificate of registration granted by the Central Government can be revoked under certain circumstances, aftere such revocation, the owner shall not carry on the business unless a license or permission for this purpose has been obtained from the Government.

(v) Licence for carrying on business by an industrial undertaking to which the Act become applicable: There may be cases where the Act did not originally apply to an industrial undertaking but became applicable after the commencement of the Act for any reason. In such case, the owner of the undertaking concerned shall not carry on the business after the expiry of three months from the date on which the provisions became so applicable unless a licence or permission as the case may he has been obtained from the Central Government.

(vi) Licence for effecting substantial expansion : Owner of an industrial undertaking (other than Central Government) cannot effect any substantial expansions of an industrial undertaking, registered or licenced, without a licence from the Central Government. The Central Government may, however, impose conditions as to location and size of the undertaking or vary or amend the licence.

(vii) Licence for change hi location : Owner of an industrial undertaking (other than Central Government) cannot change the location of the whole or any part of industrial undertaking which has been registered. The Central Government may, however, impose conditions as to location and size of the undertaking or vary or amend the licence at any time. If any question arises as to whether there has been a substantial expansion of an industrial undertaking or an industrial undertaking is producing or manufacturing any new articles, the decision of the Central Government thereon shall be final

POWERS OF THE CENTRAL GOVERNMENT

To take-over management and control of undertakings [Section 18(A)]

The Central Government may, by giving a notification in the Official Gazette, authorise any person or body of persons to take-over, either in part in full, the management or control of the undertaking. This may be done if the Central Government is of the opinion that any industrial undertaking to which directions have been issued under Section 16 has failed to comply with such directions. This may also be done in the case of any industrial undertaking about which an investigation has been conducted under Section 15 of the Act and in both the cases, it is proved that the affairs of such industrial undertaking are managed in such a manner which is quite detrimental to public interest or against the interest of the schedriled industry.

Such an order for the take-over shall remain in force for a period not exceeding 5 years, but if the Central Government is of the opinion that is necessary that such notification should continue even after a period of 5 years. The Central Government may issue directions for continuing of such an order for such period not exceeding 2 years at a time but a copy of such order shall be laid before both the House of Parliament as soon as possible. However, such order shall not exceed more than 17 years in any case.

Take-over of management and control of industrial undertaking without any investigation (Section 18AA)

The Central Government may authorise any person or body of persons to take-over the management of the whole or any part of the industrial undertaking or to exercise such functions of control as may be specified by the Central Government in its order.

The management and control may be taken-over in case the Central Government is satisfied on the basis of any documentary or other evidence relating to any industrial undertaking engaged in any reckless investment or creating of charge on the assets of the industrial undertaking or by way of diversion of funds and has created such a situation which is likely to adversely affect the production of industrial undertaking and that immediate action is necessary to present the situatin. If the Central Government is of the opinion that any industrial undertaking has been closed for 3 months by way of voluntary winding tip or otherwise and such closure is detrimental to the scheduled industry and looking to the financial position of the undertaking together with the condition of plant and machinery, it is possible to restart the undertaking in the public interest, a notification to take-over shall be issued for a period not more than 5 years. However, it can he extended for a further period of 2 yeas at a time subject to the condition that the total period of notification shall not exceed 17 years.

Section 18AA does not require any enquiry before taking over the management and control of any industrial undertaking. Any person or body of persons so appointed to take over shall undertake the control and management with immediate effect. It further provides that any person or body of persons who is in charge of the management or control of the industrial undertaking whether by or under the orders of any court or tinder any contract or otherwise at the time of passing on order by the Central Government, shall hand over charge to any person or authority whom the Central Government nominates. However, the Central Government should comply with the princples of natural justice before passing any order tinder this Section.

Effect of taking-over on matters concerning management : 1. Those persons who are in charge of the management, including those working as managers, directors of-the industrial undertaking immediately before the issue of the notification to take-over (by the Central Government), shall be deemed to have vacated their respective offices. 2. All contracts of management between the undertaking and the managing director/holding office before the issue of notification shall be treated as terminated. 3. The managing director, if any, appointed under Section 18A shall be deemed to have been duly relieved.

Any person or body of persons who is authorised to take-over the management and control of an industrial undertaking has been given powers under to cancel or change certain contracts which have been entered into between the industrial undertaking and any other person in had faith. Any person or body of persons who is empowered to exercise its authority as laid down tinder Section 18(c) shall make an application to the appropriate High Court which has jurisdiction Such an application to the High Court shall he made after taking prior permission of the Central Government. The application shall he made for the purpose of cancelling or changing any such contract. If the High Court is satisfied, after an enquiry, that such contract including any agreement had been entered into in bad faith and which is detrimental to the interest of the industrial undertaking, it shall give an order thereby cancelling or changing that contract. Thereafter, such contract or agreement he treated as cancelled or amended.

Effects of takeover by Central Government on employment and compensation (Sec. 18D): Any person who ceases to hold any office whose contract of management has been terminated for the reason mentioned above, shall not be entitled to any compensation on account of loss of office or for premature termination of the contract of management, but the right of any such person for recovering moneys other than compensation from the industrial undertaking shall not be affected,

Effects of take-over by Central Government of Winding up of companies (Sec. 18E): In case where the management of any industrial undertaking which is a company has been taken over by the Central Government then inspite of any other things mentioned in the Companies Act, 1956, or in the Memorandum and Articles of Association of the Company, it shall be unlawful for shareholders of such undertakings or any other person to nominate any other person to be a director of the industrial undertaking. Further, any resolution passed at any meeting of the shareholders of such an industrial undertaking shall not be given effect to unless the same is approved by the Central Government. This section further provides that no proceedings for winding up of such undertaking or for appointment of receiver shall be maintainable in any court unless the Central Government's consent is received. Even if the proceedings are pending, it would not be maintainable.

Powers of the Central Government to authorise to take-over management/Control of industrial undertaking owned by companies in liquidation: The powers entrusted to the Central Government go to authorise it to appoint any person or body of persons to take over the management and control of the industrial undertakings owned by companies which are in liquidation. But this can only be done with the permission of the High Court.

In case the Central Government is of the opinion that possibilities are visualised to run or restart the industrial undertakings in respect of which investigations have been made which show that such undertakings should be restarted for increasing production supply and distribution of articles relating the scheduled industry which would be in the interest of public, then the Central Government may present an application to the High Court concerned asking for permission to appoint any person to take-over the management of the undertaking. The High Court on such application by the Central Government may pass an order giving powers to the Central Government to authorise any person to take-over the management of the whole or part of industrial undertaking for a period not exceeding 5 years. 11w High Court may extend the period further for two years on such application by the Central Government subject to the maximum period of 12 years after the expiry of 5 years thereby making a total period of 17 years.

The official liquidator before taking over the management and control of the industrial undertaking to the person appointed by Central Government shall make full inventory of all the assets and liabilities of the industrial undertaking and deliver a copy of the inventory to the person appointed by the Central Government who shall acknowledge it by giving a receipt. The appointed persons shall take immediate steps to run the industrial undertaking for maintaining production. He may also be competent to raise our loan on such terms and conditions as may be prescribed, together with creating a charge on the current assets of the industrial undertaking.

In case the person specified by the Central Government is of the view that the repairs or replacement of any machinery of the undertaking is necessary for efficient and smooth running, he shall replace or repair the machinery on such terms as may be prescribed. It further provides that he may also employ such number of former employees of the undertaking whose services were terminated due to winding up of the company owning the industrial undertaking. Every such person employed shall be treated as having entered into a fresh contract of service with the establishment.

Powers of the Central Government to provide relief to industrial undertaking in certain eases (Sec. 18FB)

The Act empowers the Central Government to take certain with the aim of maintaining proper production in any scheduled industry. If the Central Government is satisfied that it is necessary to do so hi the public interest to prevent a fall in the, production of such industrial undertaking of which management and control has been taken over by the Central Government. The Central Government may issue a notification to the effect that the provisions of Industrial Disputes Act. 1947. Minimum Wages Act, 1948 and Industrial Employment Standing Orders Act, 1946 shall not apply or if applied, with certain modifications, Notification may also suspend any of the contracts, settlements awards etc., which were in force before the date of notification. Such order if issued, shall remain in force for one year which may be extended from time to time for one year at a time, subject to the total time, including the original order shall not exceed 8 years or the orders for taking over management, whichever is earlier.

Powers of Central Government to order liquidation or reconstruction of companies: During the period of assumption of management and control of an industrial undertaking, the Central Government may call for a report from the authorised person/persons relating to the functioning of the industrial undertaking and the person so authorised shall submit his report containing a list of members and creditors of the undertaking if it is a company.

After receipt of such a report, if the Central Government is satisfied that the financial conditions and surrounding circumstances of the company are such that the company is not in a position to meet its current liabilities out of existing assets, then the Central Government may decide that the industrial undertaking should be sold as a running concern in the interest of the general public and side by side the winding up proceedings be started by the High Court. In the case of a company owning an industrial undertaking which has been wound up by the High Court, the Central Government, on the basis of assets and liabilities of the company, may decide to sell it as a running concern.

In place of sale of the undertaking as a running concern, the Central Government may also decide to frame a scheme of reconstruction of the company if the Central Government is satisfied that the reconstruction of the company is in general public interest or in the interest of its shareholders. However, a scheme of reconstruction shall not be prepared by the Central Government in regard to a company which is being would up by under supervision of the High Court. However, this can be done by taking prior approval of the High Court.

Powers of the Central Government to control supply and price of articles (Sec.18G)

In pursuance of any order made with reference to clause 2(d) requiring any producer, manufacturer or any person to sell any article, the price of which shall be paid to him thereof shall be as under

1. In case the price is fixed by agreement which price is in accordance with the control price, the price so agreed upon shall be paid.

2. In case no such agreement is arrived at, the price calculated in reference to the control price shall be fixed and paid.

3. In case clauses 1 and 2 do not apply, the price calculated at the market rate shall be fixed which is prevailing in the locality on the date of sale of the artcile.

4. If any order or orders have been made in accordance with the provisions of the section, such orders shall not be challenged in any court.

5. In case an order which has been made and signed by an authority in accordance with the powers given under this section, it shall be presumed by the court, if required, that such orders have been given by the authority under the meaning of the Indian Evidence Act. 1872. Any articles relating to any scheduled industry shall also include any articles or class of articles which have been imported into India which is of the same nature or description as articles producer or manufactured in India in any scheduled industry.

The object of such orders under this section is to secure an equitable distribution and availability of certain ariticles (like cement, sugar etc.) at a fair price as decided in the case of Shiv Prakas Vs. Union of India / 968 by Mysore High Court.

Powers of Inspector (Sec. 19)

Any person authorised by the Central Government shall have the following powers under the Act or Rules I. To cute; any premises and inspect it. 2. To order production of documents, registers. records, or books in possession of any pet-son having the control of any industrial undertaking. 3. To examine any person who is in control of the records and who has been employed in the industrial undertaking. Any person so authorised by the Central Government as above shall be deemed to be a public servant within the meaning of Section 21 of the Indian Penal Code.

General Prohibitions of taking over the management or control of industrial undertaking

After the commencement of this Act, it shall not be competent for any State Government or a local authority to take-over the management or control of any industrial undertaking under any law which is in force for the time being which authorises any government or local body to take-over the management. If any action is required to he taken under this Act, it is only the Central Government to take action but the State Government is debarred from taking action under this Act.

ANNEXURE

SCHEDULES TO INDUSTRIAL POLICY RESOLUTION, 1956

Schedule A (Industries reserved for the public sector)

1. Arms and ammunition and allied items of defence equipment.
2. Atomic energy.
3. Iron and steel.
4. Heavy castings and forgings of iron and steel.
5. Heavy plant and machinery required for iron and steel production, for mining, for machine tool manufacture and for such other basic industries as may be specified by the Central Government.
6. Heavy electrical plant including large hydraulic and steam turbines.
7. Coal and lignite.
8. Mineral oils.
9. Mining of iron ore, manganese ore, chrome ore, gypsum, sulphur, gold and diamond.
10. Mining and processing copper, lead, zinc, tin, molybdenum and wolfram.
11. Minerals specified in the Schedule to the Atomic Energy (Control of Production and Use) Order, 1953.

12. Aircraft.
13. Air transport.
14. Railway transport.
15. Shipbuilding.
16. Telephones and telephone cables, telegraph and wireless apparatus (excluding radio receiving sets).
17. Generation and distribution of electricity.

Schedule B (Industries where public sector had priority in establishing new unit)

1. All other minerals except "minor minerals" as defined in Section 3 of the Minerals Concession Rules, 1949.
2. Aluminium and other non-ferrous metals not included in Schedule 'A'.
3. Machine tools.
4. Ferro-alloys and tool steels.
5. Basic and intermediate products required by chemical industries such as the manufacture of drugs, dye-stuffs and plastics.
6. Antibiotics and other essential drugs.
7. Fertilisers,
8. Synthetic rubber.
9. Carbonisation of coal.
10. Chemical pulp.
11. Road transport.
12. Sea transport.

REVIEW QUESTIONS

1. Briefly explain the objective and scope of the IDR Act, 1951.
2. What is meant by a Scheduled Industry? How are such industries regulated by the Act?
3. Enumerate the Central Governments power to order investigation into scheduled industries.
4. Under what circumstances the Central Government can assume management or control of an industrial undertaking.
5. What are the different licences specified by the Act? Are there any exemptions from licensing provisions?
6. Can any industrial undertaking be takenover by the Central Government without any investigation?
7. Write short notes on: (a) The Central Advisory Council (b) Development Councils
8. Explain the main provisions of Industries Development and Regulation Act?
9. What considerations are generally applied while examining investment proposal for the purpose of licensing?

10. State the proposals which do not require an industrial licence under the Industries Development and Regulation Act, 1951.
11. Briefly explain the procedure of the IDR Act 1951 for regulating scheduled industries.
12. What are the powers of Central Government to revoke Registration Licence?
13. Explain the previsions of registration of existing industrial undertaking. When can it be revoked?
14. Explain the constitution and functions of Central Advisory Council for industries.
15. Explain the constitution, functions of Development Councils for industries.
16. Explain the power of Central Government to control, supply distribution, price etc., of certain articles.
17. Under what circumstances may the Central Government takeover the management of a licensed undertaking.
18. Under what circumstances may the Central Government investigate the affairs of licensed undertakings?

❑ ❑ ❑

THE FOREIGN EXCHANGE MANAGEMENT ACT, 1999

Industrialisation of the country depends on the extent of investments made in the economy for starting many projects. Resources in the form of money and material are very essential for development. Capital for investment may be forthcoming within the country or it may also from foreign countries. Non-Resident Indians would be interested in investing in the Indian ventures. Further, industrialists and big businessmen would have earned lot of foreign exchange for further investments. It has become an imperative need for the Government to regulate the flow of foreign capital and also stimulate investment for purposes of industrialisation and economic development of the country.

During the Second World War period, the then Government passed several ordinances regulating the foreign exchanges transactions. In 1947, a full-fledged Foreign Exchange Regulation Act was passed by the Government of India. In the year 1973, the Act was modified and the Foreign Exchange Regulation Act, 1973 was passed. The term foreign Exchange includes foreign deposits and balances payable in foreign currency and also foreign securities.

As a stated earlier, the Foreign Exchange Management (FEMA) Act was passed by the Government of India in Parliament in 1999. The Act aims "to consolidate and amend the law relating to foreign exchange with objective of faciliating external trade and payments and for promoting the orderly development and maintenance of foreign exchange market in India.

★ The stated objective of the new Act is to facilitate external trade and payment.

★ It seeks to promote the orderly development and maintenance of the foreign exchange market.

★ On the capital account, the forex outflow is allowed only for transactions that are permitted.

★ Current account transactions can be restricted by the Centre in consultation with the RBI.

This Act extends to the whole of India and shall also apply to all branches, offices and agencies outside India owned or controlled by a person resident in India.

DEFINITIONS

An Act to consolidate and amend the law relating to foreign exchange with the objective of facilitating external trade and payments and for promoting the orderly development and maintenance of foreign exchange market in India.

In this Act, unless the context otherwise requires-

(a) "*Adjudicating Authority*" means an officer authorised under sub-section (1) of Sec. 16.

(b) "*Appellate Tribunal*" means the Appellate Tribunal for Foreign Exchange established under Sec. 18.

(c) "*authored person*" means an authorised dealer, money changer, off-shore banking unit or any other person for the time being authorised under sub-section (1) of Sec. 10 to deal in foreign exchange securities;

(d) "*Bench*" means a Bench of the Appellate Tribunal;

(e) "*Capital accountant transaction*" means a transaction which alters the assets or liabilities, including contingent liabilities, outside India of persons resident in India or assets or liabilities in India of persons resident outside India, and include transactions to in sub-section (3) of Sec. 6.

(f) "*Chairperson*" means the Chairpersons of the Appellate Tribunal;

(g) "*Chartered Accountant*" shall have the meaning assigned to it in CI. (b) of sub-section (1) of Sec. 2 of the Chartered Accountants Act, 1949 (38 of 1949);

(h) "*currency*" includes all currency notes, postal notes, postal orders, money orders, cheques, drafts, travellers cheques, letters of credit, bills of exchange and promissory notes, credit cards or such other similar instruments, as may be notified by the Reserve Bank.

(i) "*currency notes*" means and includes cash in the form of coins and bank notes;

(j) "*current account transaction*" means a transaction other than a capital account transaction and without prejudice to the generally of the foregoing such transaction includes,-

(i) payments due in connection with foreign trade, other current business, services, and short-term banking and credit facilities in the ordinary course of business,

(ii) payments due as interest as loans and as net income from investments,

(iii) remittances for living expenses of parents, spouse and children residing abroad, and

(iv) expenses in connection with foreign travel, education and medical care of parents, spouse and children;

(k) "*Director of Enforcement*" means the Director of Enforcement appointed under sub-section (1) of Sec. 36;

(j) "*export*", with its grammatical variations and cognate expressions means-

(i) the taking out of India to a place outside India any goods,

(ii) provision of services from India to any person outside India;

(m) "*foreign currency*" means any currency other than Indian currency;

(n) "*foreign exchange*" means foreign currency and includes-

(i) deposits, credits and balances payable in any foreign currency,

(ii) drafts, travellers cheques, letters of credit or bills of exchange, expressed or drawn in Indian currency but payable in any foreign currency,

(iii) drafts, travellers cheques, letters of credit or bills of exchange, expressed or drawn by banks, institutions or persons outside India, but payable in Indian currency;

(o) "*foreign security*" means any security, in the form of shares, stocks, bonds, debentures or any other instrument denominated or expressed in foreign currency and includes securities expressed in foreign currency, but where redemption or any form of return such as interest or dividends is payable in Indian currency;

(p) "*import*" with its grammatical variations and cognate expressions, means bringing into India any goods or services;

(q) "*Indian currency*" means currency which is expressed or drawn in Indian rupee but does not include special bank notes and special one rupee notes issued under Sec. 28A of the Reserve Bank of India Act, 1934 (2 of 1934);

(r) "*legal practitioner*" shall have the meaning assigned to it in CI. (i) of sub-section (1) of Sec. 2 of the Advocates Act, 1961 (25 of 1961);

(s) "*Member*" means a Member of the Appellate Tribunal and includes the Chairperson thereof;

(t) "*notify*" means to notify in the Official Gazette and the expression "notification" shall be construed accordingly;

(u) "*person*" includes-

- (i) an individual
- (ii) a Hindu undivided family
- (iii) a company
- (iv) a firm
- (v) an association of persons or a body of individuals, whether incorporated or not,
- (vi) every artificial juridical person, not falling within any of the preceding sub-clauses, and
- (vii) any agency, office or branch owned or controlled by such person;

(v) "person resident in India" means -

- (i) a person residing in India for more than one hundred and eighty-two days during the course of the preceding financial year but does not include-
  - (A) a person who has gone out of India or who stays outside India, in either case-
    - (a) for or on taking up employment outside India, or
    - (b) for carrying on outside India a business or vocation outside India, or
    - (c) for any other purpose, in such circumstances as would indicate his intention to stay outside India for an uncertain period;
  - (B) a person who has come to or stays in India, in either case, otherwise than-
    - (a) for or on taking up employment in India, or
    - (b) for carrying on in India a business or vocation in India, or
    - (c) for any other purpose, in such circumstances as would indicate his intention to stay in India for an uncertain period;
- (ii) any person or body corporate registered or incorporated in India;
- (iii) an office, branch or agency in India owned or controlled by a person resident outside India;
- (iv) an office, branch or agency outside India owned or controlled by a person resident in India;

(w) "*person resident outside India*" means a person who is not resident in India.

(x) "*prescribed*" means prescribed by rules made under this Act.

(y) "*repatriate to India*" means bringing into India the realised foreign exchange and-

(i) the selling of such foreign exchange to an authorised person in India in exchange for rupees, or

(ii) the holding of realised amount in an account with an authorised person in India to the extend notified by the Reserve Bank, and includes use of the realised amount for discharge of a debt or liability denominated in foreign exchange and the expression "repatriation" shall be construed accordingly;

(z) "*Reserve Bank*" means the Reserve Bank of India constituted under sub-section (1) of Sec. 3 of the Reserve Bank of India Act, 1934 (2 of 1934);

(za) "*Security*" means shares, stocks, bonds and debentures, Government securities as defined in the Public Debt Act, 1944 (18 of 1944), savings certificates to which the Government Savings Certificates Act, 1959 (46 of 1959); applies, deposit receipts in respect of deposits of securities and units of the Unit Trust of India established under sub-section (1) of Sec. 3 of the Unit Trust of India Act, 1963 (52 of 1963), or of any mutual fund and includes certificates of title to securities, but does not include bills of exchange or promissory notes other than Government promissory notes or any other instruments which may be notified by the Reserve Bank as security for the purposes of this Act;

(zb) "service" means service of any description which is made available to potential users and includes the provision of facilities in connection with banking, financing, insurance, medical assistance, legal assistance, chit fund, real estate, transport, processing, supply of electrical or other energy, boarding or lodging or both, entertainment, amusement or the purveying of news or other information, but does not include the rendering of any service free of charge or under a contract of personal service;

(zc) "Special Director (Appeals)" means an officer appointed under Sec. 18;

(zd) "specify" means to specify by regulations made under this Act and the expression "specified" shall be construed accordingly;

(ze) "transfers" includes sale, purchase, exchange, mortgage, pledge, gift, loan or any other form of transfer of right, title, possession or lien.

'Resident' Section 2 (sub-section v) *defines 'person resident in India'* as (i) a person residing in India for more than 182 days during the course of the preceding financial year; (ii) any person or body corporate registered or incorporated in India; (iv) an office, branch or agency outside India owned or controlled by a person resident in India

'*Person resident outside India*' means a person who is not resident in India

REGULATION AND MANAGEMENT OF FOREIGN EXCHANGE

Chapter II of the Act deals with the regulation and management of foreign exchange. *Section 3* states that except as otherwise provided in this Act, no person shall in any manner deal in or transfer any foreign exchange of foreign security to any person not being an authorised person. *Section 4* states that except as otherwise provided in this Act, no person resident in India shall acquire, hold, own possess or transfer any foreign exchange, foreign security or any immovable property situated outside India.

Current Account

Sections 5 and 6 deal with current account and capital account transactions. According to Section 5, any person may sell or draw foreign exchange to or from an authorised person if such sale or drawal is a current account transaction. However, the Central Government may, in public interest and in consulation with the Reserve Bank, impose such reasonable restrictions for current account transactions as may be prescribed.

Capital Account Transactions

According to Sub-section 1 of Section 6, any person may sell or draw foreign exchange to or from a authorised person for a capital account transaction subject to provisions of Sub-section 2. Sub-section 2 states that Reserve Bank may, in consultation with the Central Government, specify: (a) any class or classes of capital account transactions which are permissible; (b) the limit up to which foreign exchange shall be admissible for such transactions. However, the Reserve Bank shall not impose any restriction on the drawal of foreign exchange for payments due on account of amortisation of loans or for depreciation of direct investments in the ordinary course of business.

Sub-section 3 of Section 6, nevertheless, lays down that without prejudice to the generality of the provisions of Sub-section 2, the Reserve Bank may, by regulation prohibit, restrict or regulate the following

(a) transfer or issue of any foreign security by a person resident in India;

(b) transfer or issue of any security by a person resident outside of India;

(c) transfer or issue of any security or foreign security by a branch, office or agency in India of a person resident outside India;

(d) any borrowing or lending of foreign exchange in whatever form or by whatever name called;

(e) any borrowing or lending in rupees in whatever form or by whatever name called between a person resident in India and a person resident outside India;

(f) deposits between persons resident in India and persons resident outside India;

(g) export, import or holding of currency or currency notes;

(h) transfer of immovable property outside India, other than a lease not exceeding five years, by a person resident in India;

(i) acquisition or transfer of immovable property in India, other than a lease not exceeding five years, by a person resident outside India;

(j) giving of a guarantee or surely in respect of any debt, obligation or other liability incurred;

(i) by a person resident in India and owed to a person resident outside India; or (ii) by a person resident outside India.

Sub-section 4 of Section 6 states that a person resident in India may hold, own, transfer or invest in foreign currency, foreign security or any immovable property situated outside India if such currency, security or property was acquired, held or owned by such person when he was resident outside India or inherited from a person who was resident outside India. Sub-section 5 states that a person resident outside India may hold, own, transfer or invest in Indian currency, security or any immovable property situated in India if such currency, security or property was acquired, held or owned by such person when he was resident in India or inherited from a person who was resident in India.

According to Sub-section 6 of Section 6, without prejudice to the provisions of this Section, the Reserve Bank may by regulation prohibit, restrict, or regulate establishment in India of a branch, office or other place of business by a person resident outside India, for carrying on any activity relating to such branch, office or other place of business.

Export of Goods and Services

Sub-section 1 of Section 7 of the Act lays down that every exporter of goods shall-

(a) furnish to the Reserve Bank to such other exchange to or from an authorised person for a capital account transactions which are permissible;

(b) the limit up to which foreign exchange shall be admissible for such transactions. However, the Reserve Bank shall not impose any restriction on the drawal of foreign exchange for payments due on account of amortization of loans or for depreciation of direct investments in the ordinary course of business.

Sub-section 2 of Section 7 lays down that the Reserve Bank may direct any exporter to comply with such requirements as it deems fit for the purpose of ensuring that the export value of goods is received without any delay. Sub-section. 3 lays down that every exporter of services shall furnish to the Reserve Bank, in a specified manner, the details regarding the true and correct material particulars in relation to payment for such services.

Realisation and Repatriation of Foreign Exchange

Section 8 lays down that save as otherwise provided in the Act, where any where any amount of foreign exchange is due or has accrued to any person resident in India such person shall take all reasonable steps to realise and repatriate to India such foreign exchange within such period and in such manner as may be specified by the Reserve Bank.

Section 9 Provides the following exemptions from realisation and repatriation of foreign exchange:

(a) possession of foreign currency or foreign coins by any person upto such limit as the Reserve Bank may specify; (b) foreign currency account held or operated by such person or class of persons and the limit up to which the Reserve Bank may specify; (c) foreign exchange acquired or received before the 8th day of July, 1947 or any income arising or accruing thereon which is held outside India by any person in pursuance of permission granted by the Reserve Bank; (d) foreign exchange held by a person resident in India upto such limit as the Reserve Bank may specify, if such foreign exchange was acquired by way of gift or inheritance from a person referred to in clause (c) including any income arising therefrom; (e) foreign exchange acquired from employment, business, trade, vocation, services, honorarium, gifts, inheritance or any other legitimate means upto such limit as the Reserve Bank may specify; and (f) such other receipts in foreign exchange as the Reserve Bank may specify.

AUTHORISED PERSON - AUTHORISED DEALERS - MONEY CHANGER

Authorised Dealers

A major portion of actual dealing in foreign exchange from the customers (importers, exporters and others receiving or making personal remittances) is dealt with by such of the banks in India which have been authorised by the Reserve bank to deal in foreign exchange Section 19 of FEMA states that the Reserve Bank may, on an application made to it in this behalf, authorise any person to deal in foreign exchange. However, authorisation in the form of licence to deal in foreign exchange is ordinarily granted only to scheduled banks in India. Authorisations have also been granted to certain finance institutions to undertake specific types of foreign exchange transactions incidental to their main business.

Chapter III of the Act relates to the authorisation of a person by the Reserve Bank to deal in foreign exchange, Reserve Bank's powers to issue directions to authorised person and the power of Reserve Bank to inspect authorised person. Section 10 of the Act says that the Reserve Bank may authorise any person to deal in foreign exchange or in foreign securities, as an authorised dealer, money changer or off-shore banking unit or in any other manner as it deems fit. The authorisation shall be in writing and shall be subject to the condition laid down therein.

The Reserve Bank may refuse to grant authorisation if in its opinion the applicant is not properly equipped or otherwise unfit to undertake foreign exchange business.

An authorised dealer should comply with the directions and instructions of the Reserve Bank given from time to time. The Exchange Control Manual (latest 1993 edition) embodies such directions of standing nature issued by the Reserve Bank to authorised dealers. All amendments to the Exchange Control Manual are intimated to authorised dealers by the Reserve Bank in the form of its AD (MA Series) circulars. Further, general and procedural directions are given in the form of its AD (OP Series) circulars. Thus in carrying out its dealings, an authorised dealer should be guided by the latest edition of the Exchange Control Manual, as amended upto date by AD (MA Series) circulars.

The FERA states that an authorised dealer shall, before undertaking any transaction in foreign exchange on behalf of any person, require that person to make such declarations and give such information as will reasonably satisfy that the transaction will not be in contravention or evasion of foreign exchange regulations. The authorised dealer should refuse to undertake the transaction if the condition is not complied with. If the authorised dealer believes that the other person contemplates any contravention or evasion of foreign exchange regulations, the matter should be reported to the Reserve Bank.

With regard to charging of commission, quotation of rates, etc., the authorised dealer should also comply with the rules of Foreign Exchange Dealers Association of India (FEDAI).

However, the Reserve Bank may revoke the authorisation (a) if it is in public interest to do so, or (b) if the authorised person has failed to comply with the condition subject to which the authorisation was granted or has contravened any of the provisions of the Act or any rule, regulation, notification, direction or order made thereunder.

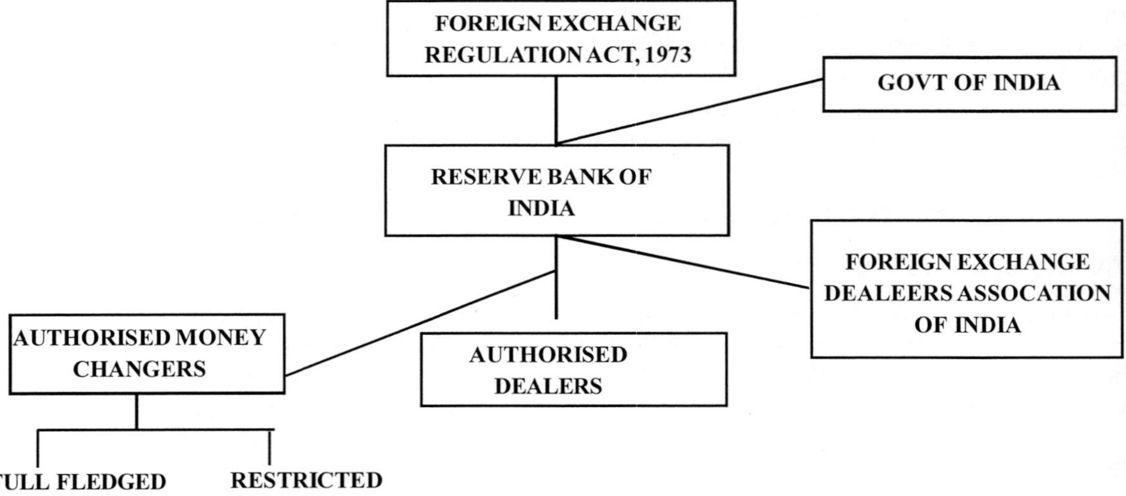

Figure – 1: ***Administration of Foreign Exchange in India***

However, no such authorization shall be revoked on any ground referred to in clause (b) unless the authorised person has been given a reasonable opportunity of making a representation in that matter.

Duties of Authorised Person

The duties of an authorised person as provided in the Act are summarised hereunder.

1. **To comply with RBI directions [Sec.10 (4)]**- An authorised person shall, in all his dealings in foreign exchange or foreign security, comply with such general or special direction or order as the Reserve Bank may, from time to time, think fit to give.

2. **Not to engage in unauthorized transactions [Sec.10 (4)]**. Except with the previous permission of the Reserve Bank, an authorised person shall not engage in any transaction involving any foreign exchange or foreign security which is not in conformity with the terms of authorization under this section.

3. **To ensure compliance of FEMA provisions [Sec.10(5)].** An authorised person shall, before undertaking any transaction in foreign exchange on behalf of any person, require that person to make such declaration and to give such information, as will reasonably satisfy him that the transaction will not involve and is not designed for the purpose of any contravention or evasion of the provisions of this Act or of any rule, regulation, notification, direction or order made thereunder. Where the said person refuses to comply with any such requirement or makes only unsatisfactory compliance therewith, the authorised person shall refuse in writing to undertake the transactions and shall, if he has reason to believe that any such contravention or evasion as aforesaid is contemplated by the person, report the matter to the Reserve Bank.

   Any person, other than an authorised person, who has acquired or purchased foreign exchange for any purpose mentioned in the declaration made by him to authorised person under sub-section (5): (a) does not use it for such purpose; or (b) does not surrender it to authorised person within the specified period; or (c) uses the foreign exchange so acquired or purchased for any other purpose for which purchase or acquisition of foreign exchange is not permissible under the provisions of the Act or the rules or regulations or direction or order made thereunder shall be deemed to have committed contravention of the provisions of the Act for the purpose of this section.

4. **Duty to produce books, accounts, etc. [Sec.12(2)].** It shall be the duty of every authorised person, and where such person is a company or a firm, every director, partner or other officer of such company or firm, as the case may be, to produce to any officer making an inspection under s.12(1) such books, accounts and other documents in his custody or power and to furnish any statement or information relating to the affairs of such person, company or firm as the said officer may require within such time and in such manner as the said officer may direct.

   Section 12(1) empowers the Reserve Bank to cause an inspection to be made, by an officer of the Reserve Bank specially authorised in writing by the Reserve Bank in this behalf, of the business of any authorised person as may appear to it to be necessary or expedient for the purpose of-(a)verifying the correctness of any statement, information or particulars furnished to the Reserve Bank; (b) obtaining any information or particulars which such authorised person has failed to furnish on being called upon to do so; (c) securing compliance with the provisions of this Act or of any rules, regulations, directions or orders made thereunder.

Powers of the Authorised Person

1. To deal in or transfer any foreign exchange or foreign security to any person [Sec.3(a)]
2. Receive any payment by order or on behalf of any person resident outside India in any name. [Sec.3(c)1

   However, an authorised person is not allowed to credit the account of any person without any corresponding remittance from any place outside India.
3. To open NRO, NRE, NRNR, NRSR and FCNR accounts.
4. To sell or purchase foreign exchange for current account transactions. [Sec.5]
5. To sell or purchase foreign exchange for permissible capital account transactions. [Sec.6]

Section 11 empowers the Reserve Bank to give directions to the authorised person in regard to making of payment or the doing or desisting from doing any act relating to foreign exchange or foreign security to ensure compliance with the provisions of the any act relating to foreign exchange or foreign security to ensure compliance with the provisions of the Act.

Section 12 empowers the Reserve Bank to inspect the business of any authorised person for the purpose of-

(a) verifying the correctness of any statement, information or particulars furnished to the Reserve Bank;

(b) obtaining any information or particulars which such authorised person has failed to furnish on being called upon to do so;

(c) securing compliance with the provisions of the Act or of any rules, regulations, directions or orders made thereunder.

It shall be the duty of every authorised person, and where such person is a company or a firm, every director, partner or other officer of such company or firm, as the case may be, to produce to any officer making an inspection under sub-section (1), such books, accounts and other documents in his custody or power and to furnish any statement or information relating to the affairs of such person, company or firm as the said officer may require within such time and in such manner as the said officer may direct.

Authorised Money Changers

To provide facilities for encashment of foreign currency for tourists, etc., Reserve Bank has granted limited licences to certain established firms, hotels and other organisations permitting them to deal in foreign currency notes, coins and travellers' cheques subject to directions issued to them from time to time. These firms and organisations are called 'authorised money changers'. An authorised money changer may be a 'full-fledged money changer' or a 'restricted money changer'. A full-fledged money changer is authorised to undertake both purchase and ale transactions with the public. A restricted money changer is authorised only to purchase foreign currency notes, coins and travellers' cheques subject to the condition that all such collections are surrendered by him in turn to an authorised dealer in foreign exchange.

CONTRAVENTION AND PENALTIES

Chapter IV deals with the issue of contravention and penalties. Section 13 says that if any person contravenes any provisions of this Act, he shall, upon adjudication, be liable to penalty upto thrice the sum involved in such contravention where such amount is quantifiable, or upto two lakh rupees where the amount is not quantifiable, and where such contravention is a continuing one, further penalty which may extend to

five thousand rupees for every day after the first day during which the contravention continues. Section 14 says that if the person concerned fails to make full payment of the penalty imposed on him within a period of ninety days, he shall be liable to *civil imprisonment*. According to Sub-section 1 of Section15 any contravention under Section 13 may, on an application made by the person committing such contravention, be compounded by the Director of Enforcement or such other officers as may be prescribed by the Central Government. Sub-section 2 of Section 15 says that were a contravention has been compounded under Sub-section 2 of Section 15 says that where a contravention has been compounded under Sub-section I, no proceeding or further proceeding, as the case may be, shall be initiated or continued as the case may be, against the person committing such contravention under that section, in respect of the contravention so compounded.

ADJUDICATION AND APPEAL

Chapter V deals with the issue of adjudication and appeal. Section 16 states that the Central Government may appoint *Adjudicating Authorities* for holding an inquiry in the manner prescribed after giving the accused person a reasonable opportunity of being heard for the purpose of imposing any penalty. The Adjudicating Authority shall have the same *powers of a civil court* which are conferred on the Appellate Tribunal under Sub-section (2) of Section 28 (discussed later). Section 17 provides for the appointment of one or more Special Directors (Appeals) under this Act. *The Appellate Tribunal* shall consist of a chairperson and such number of Members as the Central Government may deem fit. Section 21 states that a person shall not be qualified for appointment as the *chairperson* or a *Member* unless he (a) is or has been or is qualified to e a Judge a District Court. A person shall not be qualified for appointment as a *Special Director* (Appeals) unless he - (a) has been a member of the Indian Legal Service and has held a post in grade I of that service; or (b) has been a member of the Indian Legal Service and has held a post equivalent to a Joint Secretary to the Government of India.

Sub- section 2 of Section 28 which deals with the powers of the Appellate Tribunal and the Special Director (Appeals) states that they shall have, for the purposes of discharging their functions under this Act, the *same powers as are vested in a civil court under the Code of Civil Procedure*, 1908 while trying a suit, in respect of the following matters, namely.

(a) summoning and enforcing the attendance of any person and examining him on oath:

(b) requiring the discovery and production of documents:

(c) receiving evidence on affidavits:

(d) subject to the provision of Sections 123 and 124 of the Indian Evidence Act, 1872, requisitioning any public record or document from any office:

(e) issuing commissions for the examination of witnesses or documents;

(f) reviewing its decisions:

(g) dismissing a representation of default or deciding it *ex parte*:

(h) setting aside any order of dismissal of any representation for default or any order passed by it ex parte; and

(i) any other matter which may be prescribed by the Central Government.

Section 34 or the Acts states that no civil court shall have jurisdiction to entertain any suit or proceedings in respect of any matter which an Adjudicating Authority or the Appellate Tribunal or the Special Director (Appeals) is empowered by or under this Act to determine and no injunction shall be granted by any court or other authority in respect of any action taken or to be taken in pursuance of any power conferred by or under this Act. Section 35 lays down that any person aggrieved by any power conferred by or under this Act. Section 35 lays down that any person aggrieved by any decision or order of the Appellate Tribunal may file an appeal to the High Court within sixty days from the date of communication of the decision or order of the Appellate Tribunal to him on any question of law arising out of such order.

DIRECTORATE OF ENFORCEMENT

Chapter VI deals with the establishment of the *Directorate of Enforcement* and its powers, etc. Sub-section I of Section 36 states that the Central Government shall establish a Directorate of Enforcement with a Director and such other officers or class of officers as it thinks fit, who shall be called *Officers of Enforcement*, for the purpose of this Act. Sub-section I of Section 37 lays down that the Director, shall take up for investigation the contravention referred to in Section -section 2 lays down that, without prejudice to the provisions of Sun-section I, the Central Government may also, by notification, authorise any officer or class of officers in the Central Government, State Government or the Reserve Bank, not below the rank of an Under Secretary to the Government of India to investigate any contravention referred to in Section 13. According to Sub-section 3 of this section, the Director of Enforcement and other officers of Enforcement shall exercise the like powers which are conferred on Income-tax authorities under the Income- tax Act, 1961 (43 of 1961) and shall exercise such powers, subject to such limitations laid down under that Act. Section 38 empowers the *Central Government to authorise any officer of customs or any central excise officer or any police officer or any other officer of the Central Government or a State Government to exercise such of the powers and discharge such of the duties of the Director of Enforcement or any other officer of Enforcement under this Act as may be stated in the order.*

MISCELLANEOUS PROVISIONS

The last chapter, chapter VII consisting of Sections 39 to 49 deals with miscellaneous issues. Sub-section I of Section 40 empowers the Central Government in the public interest and by notification to suspend or relax the provisions of the Act in certain circumstances. Sub-section 3 provides that notification issued thereunder shall be laid before each House of Parliament. Section 41 empowers the Central Government to give general or special directions to the Reserve Bank. Section 42 provides that where contravention of any of the provisions of this Act is committed by a company, the person responsible for the conduct of its business shall be deemed to be guilty of the contravention. Section 44 bars the prosecution of legal of its business shall be deemed to be guilty of the contravention. Section 44 bars the prosecution of legal proceeding against the officers of the Central Government or the Reserve Bank or any other person exercising any powers or discharging any functions or performing any duties under the provisions of this Act for anything done is good faith. Section 45 empowers Central Government to remove the difficulties in giving effect to the provisions of the Act. Section 46 empowers the Central Government to frame the rules and Section 47 empowers the Reserve Bank of make regulations to carry out the provisions of this Act and the rules made thereunder. Section 48 provides for laying before Parliament the rules and regulations made under this Act. Section 49 provides for repal of the Foreign Exchange Regulation Act, 1973 and for dissolution of the Appellate Board constituted under Section 52 of the said Act. Sub-section 3 of this Section says that notwithstanding anything contained contained in any other law for the time being in force, no court shall take cognizance of an offender under the repealed Act and adjudicating officer shall take notice of any contravention under Section 51 of the repealed Act after the expiry of a period of two years from the date of the commencement of this Act. According to Sub-section 4, subject to the provisions of Sub-section 3 all offences committed under the repealed Act shall continue to be governed by the provisions of the repealed Act as if that Act had not been repealed. Sub-section 5 states that-

(a) anything done or any action taken or purported to have been done or taken including or declaration made or any licence, permission, authorization or exemption granted or any document or instrument executed or any direction given under the Act hereby repealed shall, in so far as it is not inconsistent with executed or any direction given under the corresponding provisions of this Act:

(b) any appeal preferred to the Appellate Board under Sub-section 2 of Section 52 of the repealed Act but not disposed of before the commencement of this Act shall stand transferred to and shall be dispose of by the Appellate Tribunal constituted under this Act;

(c) every appeal from any decision or order of the Appellate Board under Sub-section 3 or Sub-section 4 of Section 52 of the repealed Act shall, if not field before the commencement of this Act, be filed before the High Court within a period of sixty days of such commencement. Provided that the High Court may entertain such appeal after the expiry of the said period of sixty days if it is satisfied that the appellant was prevented by sufficient cause from filing the appeal within the said period.

ACQUISITION AND TRANSFER OF IMMOVABLE PROPERTY OUTSIDE INDIA

The Reserve Bank of India in exercise of the powers conferred under Section 6(3)(h) and Section 47(2) of the Foreign Exchange Management Act, 1999 prescribed regulations in respect of acquisition arid transfer of immovable property outside India.

Holding of Immovable Property

A person resident in India is prohibited from acquiring or transferring any immovable property situated outside India without general or special permission of the Reserve Bank. However, this prohibition is not applicable to the property held by a person resident in India who is a national of a foreign state; and acquired by a person resident In India on or before 8th July, 1947 and continued to be held by him with the permission of the Reserve Bank.

Acquisition of Immovable Property

A person resident in India may acquire immovable property outside India by way of gift or Inheritance from a person who was resident outside India, in terms of Section 6(4) of FEMA or who is a national of a foreign state or such property was acquired by a person resident in India on or before July 8, 1947 and continued to be held by him with the permission of RBI.

A person resident in India may acquire immovable property outside India by way of purchase out of foreign exchange held iii Resident Foreign Currency (RFC) account maintained in accordanct4 with the Foreign Exchange Management (Foreign Currency Accounts by a person resident in India) Regulations, 2000.

A person resident in India who has acquired immovable property outside India as above may transfer it by way of gift to his relative who is a person resident in India. For this purpose, relative in relation to an individual means husband, wife, brother or sister or any lineal ascendant or descendant of that individual.

ACQUISITION AND TRANSFER OF IMMOVABLE PROPERTY IN INDIA

The Foreign Exchange Management (Acquisition and Transfer of Immovable Property in India) Regulations, 2000, issued by the RBI defines the term 'A person of Indian origin' as to mean an individual (not being a citizen of Pakistan or Bangladesh or Sri Lanka or Afghanistan or China or Iran or Nepal or Bhutan), who—

(i) at any time, held Indian passport; or

(ii) who or either of whose father or whose grandfather was a citizen of India by virtue of the Constitution of India or the Citizenship Act, 1955.

The term 'Repatriation outside India' has been defined as to mean the buying or drawing of foreign exchange from an authorised dealer in India and remitting it outside India through normal banking channels or crediting it to an account denominated in foreign currency or to an account In Indian currency maintained with an authorised dealer from which it can be converted In foreign currency.

Acquisition and Transfer of Property in India by an Indian Citizen Resident Outside India

An Indian citizen resident outside India is permitted to—

(i) acquire any immovable property in India other than agricultural/plantation/farm house,

(ii) transfer any property in India to a person resident in India, and

(iii) transfer any property other than agricultural or plantation property or farm house to an Indian citizen or to a person of Indian origin, resident outside India.

Acquisition and Transfer of Properly in India by a Person of Indian Origin

A person of Indian origin resident outside India may acquire any immovable property other than agricultural land/farm house/ plantation property in India by purchase, from out of funds received In India by way of inward remittance from any place outside India or funds held in any non-resident account maintained in accordance with the provisions of the Act and the regulations made by the Reserve Bank under the Act. He may also acquire any immovable property in India other than agricultural land/farm house/plantation property by way of gift from a person resident in India or from a person resident outside India who is a citizen of India or from a person of Indian origin resident outside India.

A person of Indian origin resident outside may also acquire any immovable property in India by way of inheritance from a person resident outside India who had acquired such property in accordance with the provisions of the foreign exchange law in force at the time of acquisition by him or the provisions of these Regulations or from a person resident in India. He has been permitted to transfer any immovable property in India other than agricultural land/farm house/plantation property, by way of sale to a person resident in India; transfer agricultural land/farm house/ plantation property in India, by way of gift or sale to a person resident in India who is a citizen of India; and transfer residential or commercial property in India by way of gift to a person resident in India or to a person resident outside India who is a citizen of India or to a person of Indian origin resident outside India.

Acquisition of Immovable Properly for Carrying on a Permitted Activity

A person resident outside India who has established in India in accordance with the Foreign Exchange Management (Establishment in India of Branch or Office or other Place of Business) Regulations, 2000, a branch, office or other place of business for carrying on in India any activity, excluding a liaison office, may acquire any immovable property in India, which is necessary for or incidental to carrying on such activity, provided, however that all applicable laws, rules, regulations or directions for the time being in force are duly complied with; and the person files with the Reserve Bank a declaration in the Form IPI not later than ninety days from the date of such acquisition. Such a person is also allowed to transfer by way of mortgage to an authorised dealer as a security for any borrowing, the acquired immovable property.

Repatriation of Sale Proceeds

A person resident outside India, or his successor shall not, except with the prior permission of the Reserve Sank, repatriate outside India the sale proceeds of any immovable property. In the event of sale of immovable property other than agricultural land/farm house/plantation property in India by a person resident outside India who is a citizen of India or a person of Indian origin, the authorised dealer may allow repatriation of the sale proceeds outside India, provided the following conditions are satisfied —

(a) the immovable property was acquired by the seller in accordance with the provisions of the foreign exchange law in force at the time of acquisition by him or the provisions of Foreign Exchange Management (Acquisition and Transfer of Immovable Property in India) Regulations, 2000;

(b) the sale takes place after three years from the date of acquisition of such immovable property or from the date of payment of final instalment of consideration for its acquisition, whichever is later; and

(c) the amount to be repatriated does not exceed the amount paid for acquisition of the immovable property in foreign exchange received through normal banking channels or out of funds held in Foreign Currency Non-Resident Account or the foreign currency equivalent, as on the date of payment, of the amount paid where such payment was made from the funds held in Non-Resident External account for acquisition of the property.

In the case of residential property, the repatriation of sale proceeds is restricted to not more than two such properties.

FEMA *VERSUS* FERA

The salient features of Foreign Exchange Management Act, (FEMA), 1999, which replaced the Foreign Exchange Regulation Act, (FERA), 1973, with effect from June 1, 2000, are as follows:

1. FEMA is civil law unlike FERA being a criminal one. There are only 12 operational Sections of FEMA unlike FERA's 32.
2. FEMA clearly defines forex transactions viz. "Current" and "Capital" for which RBI) Government has issued notifications. Now, authorized dealers (AD)/persons viz. Banks etc. are authorized to allow foreign exchange towards such permitted transactions. Documentation part is left to the ADs. Banks should therefore use discretion for document requirement and users of foreign exchange should also cooperate with banks. RBI now issues directives circulars to banks where necessary. However, RBI has no discretionary powers as in the FERA. But ADs have now responsibility to satisfy about the genuineness of the transactions. If banks decline to release exchange they will have to refuse in writing giving reasons for rejection of the case.
3. RBI may authorise any person to be known as authorised person to deal in foreign exchange or in foreign securities as an authorised dealer money changer or off-shore banking unit.
4. New structure of Exchange Control under FEMA is: (a) Rules by GOI Via Notifications (b) Directions by RBI via Circulars (c) Regulations by RBI Via Notifications.
5. FEMA defines for the first time a "resident" as a person resident in India for more than 182 days during the course of preceding financial year. This definition is now based on physical stay, comparable to the definition under the Income Tax Act. The word "person" has also been comprehensively defined.
6. FEMA seeks to check compensatory payments (hawala transactions) by prohibiting any financial transaction within the country, which results in acquisition or transfer of assets abroad
7. FEMA also seeks to prohibit foreign exchange dealings undertaken other than through an "authorized person", also makes it clear that if any person residing in India receives any forex

payment without there being a corresponding inward remittance from abroad, then the concerned person shall be deemed to have received the payment from a non- authorized person.

8. Compounding of contravention is provided in FEMA. On payment of penalty, contravention stand fully condoned. Imprisonment is prescribed upto 3 years only in case of nonpayment. The penalty for such contravention will be under subject to a maximum of three times the sum of money involved. Rarely, does a statue provide compounding of penalty like FEMA. Both Enforcement Directorate and RBI can do compounding.
9. Thus, FEMA removes the rigorous of FERA particularly, doctrine of Means-rea, and stringent penalities (i.e. fine equal to five times the value of the offences, 7 years imprisonment and publication of convicted company's name). Now, the onus of proving contravention's rests with the enforcement agency and not on person who is charged with such contravention.
10. PEMA contains "Sun Set clause" {Section 49 (3)} according to which no court shall take cognizance of an offence under the repealed Act and no adjudicating officer shall take notice of any contravention under section 51 of the repealed Act after the expiry of two years from the date of commencement of this Act.
11. FEMA provides a suitable mechanism for appeals and Appellant Authority viz. Special Director (Appeals), Appellate Tribunal etc. have been appointed for the purpose.

FOREIGN EXCHANGE MANAGEMENT (CURRENT ACCOUNT TRANSACTIONS) RULES, 2000.

1. Remittance out of lottery winnings.
2. Remittance of income from racing/riding, etc., or any other hobby.
3. Remittance for purchase of lottery tickets, banned/prescribed magazines, football pools, sweepstakes, etc.
4. Payment of commission on exports made towards equity investment in joint ventures/wholly Owned Subsidiaries abroad of Indian companies.
5. Remittance of dividend by any company to which the requirement of dividend balancing is applicable.
6. Payment of commission on exports under Rupee State Credit Route.
7. Payment related to "Call Back Services" of telephones.
8. Remittance of interest income on funds held in Non-resident Special Rupee Scheme account.
9. Drawal of foreign exchange is prohibited for a travel to Nepal and Bhutan; or a transaction with a person resident in Nepal or Bhutan.

Under Rule No. 4, no person shall draw foreign exchange for a transaction mentioned below, without prior approval of the Government of India with the concerned Ministry.

(a) Cultural Tours

(b) Advertisement abroad by any PSU/State and Central Government Department

(c) Remittance of Freight of Vessel charted by a PSU.

(d) Payment of import by a Govt. Department or a PSU on c.i.f. basis (i.e., other than f.o.b. and f.a.s. basis)

(e) Multimodal transport operators making remittance to their agents abroad

(f) Remittance of container detention charges exceeding the rate prescribed by Direct-General of Shipping

(g) Remittance under technical collaboration agreements where payment of royalty exceeds 5% on local sales and 8% on exports and lump-sum payment exceeds USdollar 2 million

(h) Remittance of prize money/sponsorship of sports activity abroad by a person other than International/National/State level Sports bodies, if the amount involved exceeds US dollar 1,00,000.

(i) Payment for securing insurance for health from a company abroad.

The above rule shall not apply where the payment is made out of funds held in Resident Foreign Currency (RFC) Account or Exchange Earner's Foreign Currency (EEFC) Account of the remitter.

Under Rule No. 5, no person shall draw foreign exchange for the following transactions without prior approval of the Reserve Bank of India.

(i) Remittance by artiste, e.g., wrestler, dancer, entertainer, etc. (This restriction is not applicable to artists engaged by tourism related organisations in India like ITDC, State Tourism Development Corporations, etc., during special festivals or those artistes engaged by hotels in five-star category, provided the expenditure is met out of EEFC (account)

(ii) Release of exchange exceeding US dollar 5000 or its equivalent in one calendar year, for one or more private visits to any country (except Nepal and Bhutan)

(iii) Gift remittance exceeding US dollar 5,000 per beneficiary per annum.

(iv) Donation exceeding US dollar 5,000 per annum per beneficiary

(v) Exchange facilities exceeding US dollar 5,000 for person going abroad for employment.

(vi) Exchange facility for emigration exceeding US dollar 5,000 or amount prescribed by country of emigration.

(vii) Remittance for maintenance of close relatives abroad exceeding US dollar 5,000 per year per recipient.

(viii) Release of foreign exchange, exceeding US dollar 25,000 to a person irrespective of period of stay, for business travel, or attending a conference or specialised training or for maintenance expenses of a patient going abroad for medical treatment or check-up.

(ix) Release of exchange for meeting expenses for medical treatment abroad exceeding the estimate from the doctor in India or hospital/doctor abroad.

(x) Release of exchange for studies abroad exceeding the estimates from the institution abroad or US dollar 30,000 whichever is higher.

(xi) Commission to agents abroad for sale of residential flats/commercial plots in India, exceeding 5% of the inward remittance.

(xii) Short-term credit to overseas offices of Indian Companies.

(xiii) Remittance for advertisement on foreign television by a person whose export earnings are less than ₹ 10 lakhs during each of the preceding two years.

(xiv) Remittance of royalty and payment of lump-sup fee under the technical collaboration agreement which has not been registered with Reserve Bank.

(xv) Remittance exceeding US dollar 1,00,000 for architectural/consultancy services procured from abroad.

(xvi) Remittances for use and/or purchase of trade mark/franchise in India.

The above state rule shall not apply where the payment is made out of funds held in Resident Foreign Currency (RFC) Account or Exchange Earner's Foreign Currency (EEFC) Account of the remitter.

FOREIGN EXCHANGE MANAGEMENT
(PERMISSIBLE CAPITAL ACCOUNT TRANSACTIONS) REGULATIONS, 2000

Permissible Capital Account Transactions

Regulation No. 3(1) : Capital account transactions of a person may be classified under the following heads, namely :

(A) transactions, specified in Schedule I, of a person resident in India;

(B) transactions specified in Schedule II, of a person resident outside India.

(2) Subject to the provisions of the Act or the rules or regulations or direction or orders made or issued thereunder, any person may sell or draw foreign exchange to or from an authorised person for a capital account transaction specified in the Schedules : Provided that the transaction is within the limit specified in the regulations.

Schedule : I [Regulation 3(1)(A)]

Classes of Capital account transactions of persons resident in India:

(a) Investment by a person resident in India in foreign securities.

(b) Foreign Currency loans raised in India and abroad by a person resident in India.

(c) Transfer of immovable property outside India by a person resident in India.

(d) Guarantees issued by a person resident in India in favour of a person resident outside India.

(e) Export, import and holding of currency/currency notes

(f) Loans and overdrafts (borrowings) by a person resident in India from a person resident outside India.

(g) Maintenance of foreign currency accounts in India and outside India by a person resident in India.

(h) Taking out of insurance policy by a person resident in India from an insurance company outside India.

(i) Loans and overdrafts by a person resident in India to a person resident outside India.

(j) Remittance outside India of capital assets of a person resident in India.

(k) Sale and purchase of foreign exchange derivatives in India and abroad and commodity derivatives abroad by a person resident in India.

Schedule II : [Regulation 3(1)(B)]

Classes of capital account transactions of persons resident outside India:

(a) Investment in India by a person resident outside India, that is to say,

(i) issue of security by a body corporate or an entity in India and investment therein by a person resident outside, India; and

(ii) investment by way of contribution by a person resident outside India to the capital of a firm or a proprietorship concern or an association of persons in India.

(b) Acquisition and transfer of immovable property in India by a person resident outside India.

(c) Guarantee by a persons resident outside India in favour of or on behalf of, a person resident in India.

(d) Import and export of currency/currency notes into/from India by a person resident outside India.

(e) Deposits between a person resident in India and a person resident outside India.

(f) Foreign currency accounts in India of a person resident outside India.

(g) Remittance outside India of capital assets in India of a person resident outside India.

Regulation No. 4 : Prohibition

Save otherwise provided in the Act, rules or regulations made thereunder :

(a) no person shall undertake or sell or draw foreign exchange to or from an authorised person for any capital account transaction,

(b) no person resident outside India shall make investment in India, in any form, in any company or partnership firm or proprietary concern or any entity, whether incorporated or not, which is engaged or proposes to engage-

(i) in the business of Chit Fund, or

(ii) as Nidhi Company, or

(iii) in agricultural or plantation activities, or

(iv) in real estate, business, or construction of farm houses, or

(v) in trading in Transferable Development Rights (TDRs)

Explanation : For the purpose of this regulation "real estate business" shall not include development of townships, construction of residential/commercial premises, roads or bridges.

"*Transferable Development Rights*" means certificates issued in respect of category of land acquired for public purpose either by Central or State Government in consideration of surrender of land by the owner without monetary compensation, which are transferable in part or whole.

Method of Payment for Investment

Regulation No. 5 : The payment for investment shall be made by remittance from abroad through normal banking channels or by debit to an account of the investor maintained with an authorised person in India in accordance with the regulations made by the Reserve Bank under the Act.

Declaration to be Furnished

Regulation No. 6 : Every person selling or drawing foreign exchange to or from an authorised person for a capital account transaction shall furnish to the Reserve Bank, a declaration in the form and within the time specified in the regulations relevant to the transaction.

FOREIGN EXCHANGE MANAGEMENT (EXPORT AND IMPORT OF CURRENCY) REGULATIONS, 2000

Export and Import of Indian Currency Notes

Regulation : 3(1) : Save as otherwise provided in these regulations, any person resident in India,

(a) may take outside India (other than to Nepal and Bhutan) currency notes of Government of India and Reserve Bank of India notes upto an amount not exceeding ₹ 5,000/- per person;

(b) may take or send outside India (other than to Nepal and Bhutan) commemorative coins not exceeding two coins each.

Explanation : 'Commemorative Coin' includes coin issued by Government of India Mint to Commemorate any specific occasion or event and expressed in Indian currency;

(c) who had gone out of India on a temporary visit, may bring into India at the time of his return from any place outside India (other than from Nepal and Bhutan), currency notes of Government of India and Reserve Bank of India notes upto an amount not exceeding ₹ 5,000/- per person.

According to *Regulation No. 4*, no person shall take or send out of India the Indian coins which are covered by the Antique and Art Treasure Act, 1972.

According to *Regulation No. 5,* except as otherwise provided in these regulations, no person shall, without the general or special permission of the Reserve Bank, export or send out of India, or import or bring into India, any foreign currency.

Import of Foreign Exchange into India

Regulation 6 : A person may (a) send into India without limit foreign exchange in any form other than currency notes, bank notes and travellers cheques; (b) bring into India from any place outside India without limit, foreign exchange (other than unissued notes); provided that bringing of foreign exchange into India under clause (b) shall be subject to the condition that such person makes, on arrival in India, a declaration to the customs authorities in Currency Declaration Form (CDF). This declaration shall not be necessary if the aggregate value of the foreign exchange at any one time does not exceed 10,000 US Dollars.

Export of Foreign Exchange and Currency Notes

Regulation : 7

(1) An authorised person may send out of India foreign currency acquired in normal course of business;

(2) any person may take or sent out of India

(i) cheques drawn on foreign currency account maintained in accordance with Foreign Exchange Management (Foreign Currency Accounts by a person resident in India) Regulations, 2000;

(ii) foreign exchange obtained by him by drawal from an authorised person in accordance with the provisions of the Act or the rules or regulations or directions made or issued thereunder;

(iii) currency in the safes of vessels or aircrafts which has been brought into India or which has been taken on board a vessel or aircraft with the permission of the Reserve Bank;

(3) any person may take out of India;

(i) foreign exchange possessed by him in accordance with the Foreign Exchange Management (Possession and Retention of Foreign Currency) Regulation, 2000;

(ii) unspent foreign exchange brought back by him to India while returning from travel abroad and retained in accordance with the Foreign Exchange Management (Possession and Retention of Foreign Currency) Regulations, 2000;

(4) any person resident outside India may take out of India unspent foreign exchange not exceeding the amount brought in by him and declared in accordance with the proviso to clause (b) of Regulation 6, on his arrival in India.

Export and Import of Currency to or from Nepal and Bhutan

Regulation No. 8 : Notwithstanding anything contained in these regulations a person may-

(i) take or send out of India to Nepal or Bhutan, currency notes of Government of India and Reserve Bank of India notes (other than notes of denominations of above ₹ 100 in either case)

(ii) bring into India from Nepal or Bhutan, currency notes of Government of India and Reserve Bank of India notes (other than notes of denominations of above ₹ 100 in either case);

(iii) take out of India to Nepal or Bhutan, or bring into India from Nepal or Bhutan, currency notes being the currency of Nepal or Bhutan

Note : As required under Regulation 6, the format of Currency Declaration Form (CDF) has been furnished by the Regulations. This form contains 'Instructions for Passengers' and also the necessary format for mentioning the 'Name of the Currency' and other particulars connected therewith, including details to be filled in by the Customs Officer.

FOREIGN EXCHANGE MANAGEMENT REGULATION, 2000
(ACQUISITION AND TRANSFER OF IMMOVABLE PROPERTY OUTSIDE INDIA)

Regulation No. 3: Restriction on acquisition or transfer of immovable property outside India : Save as otherwise provided in the Act or in these regulations, no person resident in India shall acquire or transfer any immovable property situated outside India without general or special permission of the Reserve Bank.

Regulation No. 4 : Exemptions : Nothing contained in these regulations shall apply to the property;

(a) held by a person resident in India who is a national of Foreign State;

(b) acquired by a person resident in India on or before 8th July 1947 and continued to be held by him with the permission of the Reserve Bank.

Acquisition and Transfer of Immovable Property Outside India

Regulation No. 5(1) : A person resident in India may acquire immovable property outside India :

(a) by way of gift or inheritance from a person referred to in sub-section (4) of Section 6 of the Act, or referred to in clause (b) of regulation 4;

(b) by way of purchase out of foreign exchange held in Resident Foreign Currency (RFC) account maintained in accordance with the Foreign Exchange Management (Foreign Currency accounts by a person resident in India) Regulation, 2000.

(2) A person resident in India, who has acquired immovable property outside India under sub-regulation (1) of this regulation, may transfer it by way of gift to his relative who is a person resident in India.

Explanation : For the purpose of this regulation 'relative' in relation to an individual means husband, wife, brother or sister or any lineal ascendant or descendant of that individual.

FOREIGN EXCHANGE MANAGEMENT REGULATIONS, 2000
(FOREIGN CURRENCY ACCOUNTS BY A PERSON RESIDENT IN INDIA)

According to *Regulation No. 2*, under this, Foreign Currency Account means an account held or maintained in currency other than the currency of India or Nepal or Bhutan.

According to *Regulation No. 4*, a person resident in India may open, hold and maintain with an authorised dealer in India, a *Foreign Currency Account* to be known as *Exchange Earner's Foreign Currency (EEFC)*

Account, subject to the terms and conditions of Exchange Earner's Foreign Currency Account Scheme specified in the schedule.

Opening, Holding and Maintaining a Resident Foreign Currency Account

Regulation No. 5 (1) : A person resident in India may open, hold and maintain with an authorised dealer in India a Foreign Currency Account to be known as a Resident Foreign Currency (RFC) Account out of foreign exchange-

(a) received as pension or any other superannuation or other monetary benefits from his employer outside India; or

(b) realised on conversion of the assets referred to in sub-section (4) of the Section 6 of the Act, and repatriated to India; or

(c) received or acquired as gift or inheritance from a person referred to in sub-section (4) of Section 6 of the Act; or

(d) referred to in clause (c) of Section 9 of the Act, or required as gift or inheritance therefrom

(2) the funds in a Resident Foreign Currency Account opened or held or maintained in terms of sub-regulation (1) shall be free from all restrictions regarding utilisation of foreign currency balances including any restrictions on investment in any form, by whatever name called, outside India;

Regulation No. 6

A shipping or airline company incorporated outside India or its agents in India may open, hold and maintain a Foreign Currency Account with an authorised dealer in India for meeting the local expenses in India of such airlines of shipping company : provided that the credits to such accounts are only by way of freight or passage fare collection in India or by inward remittances through normal banking channels from its office outside India and, in the case of agent, from his principal outside India.

Opening, Holding and Maintaining a Foreign Currency Account Outside India

Regulation No. 7(1) : An authorised dealer in India may open, hold and maintain with his branch or head office or correspondent outside India, a Foreign Currency Account for the purpose of transacting foreign exchange business and other matters incidental thereto, in accordance with the provisions of the Act or the rules or regulations made or the directions issued thereunder.

(2) A branch outside India of a bank incorporated or constituted in India may open, hold and maintain with a bank outside India, a Foreign Currency Account for the purpose of carrying on normal banking business outside India, subject to compliance with the directions or guidelines issued from time to time by the Reserve Bank, and the regulatory authority in the country where the branch is located.

(3) A shipping or airline company incorporated in India may open, hold and maintain with a bank outside India, a Foreign Currency Account for the purpose of undertaking transactions in the ordinary course of its business.

(4) Life Insurance Corporation of India or General Insurance Corporation of India and its subsidiaries may open, hold and maintain with a bank outside India, a Foreign Currency Account for the purpose of meeting the expenditure incidental to the insurance business carried on by them and for that purpose, credit to such account the insurance premia received by them outside India.

(5) A person resident in India, being an exporter who has undertaken a construction contract or a turnkey project outside India or who is exporting services or engineering goods from India on deferred payment terms may open, hold and maintain a Foreign Currency Account with a bank outside India, provided that-

(a) approval as required under the Foreign Exchange Management (Export of Goods and Services) Regulations, 2000 has been obtained for undertaking the contract/project/export of goods or services, and

(b) the terms and conditions stipulated in the letter of approval have been duly complied with.

(6) A person resident in India who has gone abroad for studies or who is on a visit to a foreign country may open, hold and maintain a Foreign Currency Account with a bank outside India during his stay outside India, provided that on his return to India, the balance in the account is repatriated to India.

Provided that short visits to India by a person who has gone abroad for studies, before completion of his studies, shall not be treated as his return to India.

(7) A person resident in India who has gone out of India to participate in an exhibition/trade fair outside India may open, hold and maintain a Foreign Currency Account with a bank outside India for crediting the sale proceeds of goods on display in the exhibition/trade fair. Provided that the balance in the account is repatriated to India through normal banking channels within a period of one month from the date of closure of the exhibition/trade fair.

Limit on Holding in a Foreign Currency Account

Regulation No. 8 : Unless otherwise stipulated by the Reserve Bank, a person resident in India who has opened and is maintaining a Foreign Currency Account in accordance with the provisions of Regulations 6 and 7, may hold therein foreign exchange without any limit.

Types of Accounts

Regulation No. 9 : A Foreign Currency Account with an authorised dealer in India under these Regulations may be opened, held and maintained-

(1) in the form of current or savings or term deposits account in cases where the account holder is an individual and in the form of current account or term deposit account in all other cases;

(2) singly or jointly in the name of person eligible to open, hold and maintain such account

Remittances out of the Accounts after the Account Holder's Death

Regulation No. 10 : On the death of a foreign currency account holder :

(1) the authorised dealer with whom the account is held or maintained may remit to a nominee being a person resident outside India, funds to the extend of his share or entitlement from the account of the deceased account holders.

(2) a nominee being a person resident in India, who is desirous of remitting funds outside India out of his share for meeting the liabilities abroad of the deceased, may apply to the Reserver Bank of such remittance.

Responsibility of Authorised Maintaining Foreign Currency Accounts

Regulation No. 11 : An authorised dealer maintaining foreign currency accounts shall-

(1) comply with the directions issued by the Reserve Bank from time to time; and

(2) submit periodic returns of Statements; if any, as may be stipulated by the Reserve Bank.

In the Schedule under these 'Regulations', 'Exchange Earner's Foreign Currency (EEFC) Account Scheme' has been furnished in detail.

REVIEW QUESTIONS

1. Briefly summaries the essential features of FEMA
2. What is Money Changer?
3. What is Overseas Corporate body?
4. What is Person of Indian origin?
5. What is Non-resident Indian?
6. Summarise the dealings in Foreign Exchange under this Act, in Current Account Transactions and Capital Account Transactions.
7. What are the definitions of the following expressions and terms according to Foreign Exchange Management Act, 1999?

   (a) Authorised person (b) Capital Account Transaction (c) Current Account Transaction

   (d) Director of Enforcement (e) Foreign Currency (f) Foreign Security

   (g) Foreign Exchange (h) Person Resident in India (i) Adjudicating Authority
8. Who is an 'Authorised person' according to FEMA? When can the authority of an 'authorised person be revoked?
9. What are the duties and powers of an 'authorised person' under FEMA, 1999?
10. State the powers of the Reserve Bank with respect to:

    (i) Issue of directions to auhorised persons, (ii) Inspection of an authorised person.
11. What are the obligations of an exporter of goods and services out of India? Explain.
12. State the provision of FEMA with respect to regulation of export of goods and services out of India.
13. State the duties of an exporter with respect to realisation and repatriation of foreign exchange regarding goods and services exported out of India. Give exemptions, if any.
14. Can an appeal be filed against the order of the Adjudicating Authority? If yes, then with whom shall the appeal be filed and within what period?
15. State the powers of Special Director (Appeals) and of the Appellate Tribunal in disposing off the appeals.
16. Explain the consequences of contraventions of the provisions of FEMA. State the procedure to be adopted by the aggrieved for redressal of his grievances against the order of adjudication authority.
17. Write short note on :

    (a) Overseas Corporate body, (b) Person of Indian origin, (c) Non-Resident Indian
18. Explain the regulations relating to acquisition and transfer of immovable property outside India?
19. Explain the regulations in respect of acquisition and transfer of immovable property inside India?

❑ ❑ ❑

MODULE - III

COMPANY LAW

---

18. The Nature of a Company
19. Formation of a Company
20. Prospectus
21. Directors
22. Meetings and Resolutions
23. Winding Up

18 Chapter

THE NATURE OF A COMPANY

The Company Legislation in India has developed on the lines almost parallel to the English Company Law. The Companies Act, passed from time to tome in India have been following the English Companies Act with certain modifications to suit Indian conditions. The English Companies Act of 1844 is trated to be the first enactment on modern system of joint stock enterprises. On that very line, the first Indian Companies Act providing for the registration of joint stock companies was passed in the year 1850.

THE COMPANIES ACT, 1956

The Indian Companies Act, 1913 was repealed by the present Companies Act of 1956 which came into force on 1st April, 1956. The present Companies Act is based largely on the recommendations of the Company Law Committee (Bhabha Committee) which submitted its report in March, 1952. This Act is the largest statute ever passed by our Parliament. It consists of 658 sections and 12 schedules. The Act was amended several times since 1956. The latest amendments were effected in 2000 and 2001.

Definition of Company

According to *Section 3(1)(i) of the Companies Act, 1956* a company means, "*A company formed and registered under this Act or an existing company*". An existing company means a company formed and registered under any of the previous Companies Law.

According to ***Lord Justice Lindley*** a company is,

> *"An association of many persons who contribute money or money's worth to a common stock and employed for a common purpose. The common stock so contributed is denoted in money and is capital of the company. The persons who contribute it or to whom it belongs are members. The proportion of capital to which each member is entitled is his share. Shares are always transferable although the right to transfer them is often more or less restricted*".

A company, thus may be defined as an incorporated assocation, which is an artificial person, having an independent legal entity, with a perpetual succession, a common seal, a common stock capital comprised of transferable shares and carrying limited liability in relation to its members.

Corporation or Body Corporate

A *corporation sole* is a corporation and constituted in a single person who, in right of some office or function, has corporate status. Examples of corporate sole are to be found in perpetual offices such as the President, Governors, Crown, Ministers, a public trustee. A corporation sole is not a "body corporate" for the purposes of the Companies Act 1956. It is still a legal person and as such can be member of a compnay. A *corporation aggregate* consists of a group of persons contemporaneously associated so that they form a single person, e.g., a limited compnay, a municipality, or a municipal corporation.

CHARACTERISTICS OF A COMPANY

1. ***Separate Legal Entity :*** A company formed and registered under the Companies Act is a distinct legal entity. It is a creation of law and is sometimes called *artificial person* being invisible and intangible. It is a fiction of law with legal, but no natural or physical existence. The principle that a company is a legal entity separate from the individuals who compose it is very clearly illustrated in the leading case of ***Saloman Vs. Saloman & Co. Ltd. (1897).*** Saloman had a boot business. He sold the business to a company named Saloman & Company Ltd., which he formed. There were seven members-his wife, daughter and four sons who took one share each and Saloman himself who took 20,000 shares. The price paid by the company to Saloman was £30,000; but instead of paying him cash, the company gave him £20,000 fully paid shares of each one £ and £10,000 in debentures. Owing to strike in the boot trade, the company was wound up. The assets of the company amounted to £ 6,000 only. Debts amounted to £ 10,000 due to Saloman and secured by debentures and a further £ 7,000 due to unsecured creditors. The unsecured creditors claimed that as Saloman & Company Ltd. was really the same person as Saloman, he could not owe money to himself and that they should be paid their £ 7,000 first. It was held by the House of Lords that Saloman was entitled to £ 6,000 as the compnay was an entirely separate person from Salomia. the unsecured creditors got nothing.

   Thus, Saloman's case established beyond doubt that in law, a registered compnay is an entity distinct from its members, even if one person holds all the shares in the company. There is no difference in principle between a company consisting of only two shareholders and a company consisting of two hundred members. In each case the company is a separate legal entity.

   Lee Vs. Lee's Air Farming Co. Ltd. (1960) Of the 3,000 shares in a company, L held 2,999. He voted himself as the governing director and chief pilot at a salary. L was killed in an air crash while working for the company. His widow claimed compensation for the death to her husband while in the course of his employement. It was argued that no compensation was due because L and Lee's Air Farming Ltd. were the same person. The Privy Council applied Saloman's case and said that L was a separate person from the company he formed and compensation was payable.

2. ***Perpetual succession :*** Unlike a natural person a company never dies. It is an entity with a perpetual succession. Its existence is not affected by the death, lunacy and insolvency of its members.

3. ***Limited liability :*** Limited liability of members is another most important characteristic of a company. Their liability is limited to the face value of shares subscribed by them. If the shares are fully paid up, their liability is nil. Where the assets of the company are insufficient to meet the claims of the creditors of the company, the members cannot be asked to pay anything more than what is due on the shares of the company held by them.

4. ***Common seal :*** As a company is an artificial person it cannot sign its name on a contract. Common seal is used as a substitute for its signature. Every company must have a seal with its name engraved on it. Anything done under an agreement between the company and the third party requries recognition of the company in the form of an official seal.

   Every company must have a *common seal* and the name of the company must be engraved in legible characters on its seal; the penalty for contravention is `500 (Section 147 of the Companies Act). The seal is used for execution of all important documents. "A company may be bound by a deed even when it has not affixed its seal if it acted on the deed and taken the benefits of the covenants therein". *(Mcdonold Vs.Johan Twiname Ltd. 1953. (A.E.I.R. 589)}.*

   Though the Companies Act or the model regulations in *Table A* of *Schedule I* do not provide for the form and manner in which the common seal of a company should be kept, i.e., whether a metallic one or a rubber stamp, the Department of Company Affairs, vide its Circular No.8/70 (147) 64-P.R, dt.8.12.64 observed that the working of Section 147 (1)(b) suggests that the view that only a metallic seal should be used is correct. Thus, in view of the above, *common seal of the company should be a metallic seal and not a rubber stamp.*

5. ***Transferability of shares*** : The shares of a company are freely transferable and can be sold or purchased in the share market. Section 82 of the Companies Act recognises the right of transferability of shares and provides that, "*the shares or other interest of any member shall be movable property transferable in the manner provided for in the articles of the company*".

6. ***Capacity to sue and be sued*** : On incorporation, a company acquires a separate and independent legal personality. As a legal person, it can sue and be sued in its own name.

7. ***Not a citizen*** : Although a company is a legal person having both nationality and domicile, it is not a citizen. As such, a company cannot, therefore, claim the protection of those fundamental rights which are explicitly guaranteed to citizens only, namely, the right of franchise.

8. ***Company's actions limited*** : A company cannot go beyond the powers of its charter-the memorandum of association. But once the powers have been laid down, it cannot go beyond unless the memorandum of association is itself altered prior to doing so.

9. ***Separate property*** : As a legal person, a company can own, enjoy and dispose of any property in its own name. No member can claim himself to be the owner of the company's property. The property of the company is not the property of the shareholders; it is the property of the company.

Consequences of the Principle of Separate Corporate Personality

★ The shareholders shall have no insurable interest in the property of the company, (*Macaure Vs. Northern Assurance Co. Ltd.*)

★ The persons who own its capital may also be its creditors or employees.

★ When a shareholder dies, the company continues to exist. His shares, and not the assets of the company, vest in his personal representatives or legal heir.

★ The nationality of the company does not depend on the nationality of the shareholder. (*Janson Vs. Driefontein Mines Ltd.*)

★ The property of the company is not the joint property of its shareholders.

★ A company can also be prosecuted for wrongs done in its name. Being an artificial person, it can, however, be only fined, it cannot be imprisoned.

LIFTING THE CORPORATE VEIL

The general rule is that a *company is a legal person and is distinct from its members*. The principle is regarded as a curtain, a veil, or shield between the company and its members, thus protecting the latter from the liability of the former. But when the notion of legal entity is used to defeat public convenience, justify wrong, protect fraud or defend crime, the law will regard the company as an association of persons. These cases are *exceptions to the principle in Saloman Vs Saloman &Co. Ltd.* In these exceptional cases, the law either goes behind the corporate personality to the individual members or ignores the separate personality of each company in favour of the economic reality constituted by a group of associated concerns. When this protection is taken away, the veil is said to have been lifted or pierced. The corporate veil is lifted in the followig cases :

1. ***Determination of the Character*** : In times of war the court will lift the veil to see whether a company is controlled by enemy/aliens. Consequently, a company registered in England may be '*alien enemy*' if its agents or the persons who infact control its affairs, are alien enemies. [*Daimler Company Ltd. Vs. Continental Tyre & Rubber Ltd. (1960)*].

2. ***Where company is a mere cloak or sham*** : The court will lift the veil where the company is a mere cloak or sham i.e. where the device of incorporation is used for some illegal or improper purpose. [(*Jones Vs. Lipman (1962)*].

3. ***Where the comany is acting as an agent of the shareholders:*** Where a company is acting as an agent for its shareholders, they will be liable for its acts. Whether it is acting as an agent is a question of fact in each case.

4. ***Protection of revenue*** : The courts may disregard the corporate entity of a company where it is used for tax evasion or to circumvent tax obligation. Further, where it is desired to establish the residential status/character of a company for tax purposes the court will lift the veil and find out where is central management its, and the place determines its residence.

Statutory Exceptions

1. ***Number of members below statutory minimum*** : If at any time the number of members of a compnay is reduced below two in the case of a private company or below seven in the case of a public company and it carries on business for more than six months while the number is so reduced, every member, who knows of this fact, will become liable to an unlimited extent for the payment of the whole debts of the company contracted during the time (Section 45).

2. ***Company name not mentioned on a bill of exchange etc.***: Where an officer of the company or any person signs on behalf of the company, a bill of exchange, promissory note, cheque or order for money or goods, wherein the name of the company is not mentioned, he is personally liable unless the amount is paid by the company. (Section 147).

3. ***Group accounts*** : The principle of separate legal entity may be disregarded where a compnay has subsidiaries and group accounts must be laid before the company in general meeting when the company's own Profit and Loss Account and Balance Sheet is so laid. (Section 212).

4. ***Fraudulent trading*** : If in the course of the winding up of a company it appears that any business of the company has been carried on with intent to defraud creditors, the court may declare that any person(s) who were knowingly parties to the carrying on of such business are to be personally liable for the debts and other liabilities of the company. (Section 542).

5. ***Investigation into related companies*** : An inspector appointed under Section 239 by the Central Government may lift the veil of incorporation if he thinks it necessary for the purpose of investigation into the affairs of its subsidiary or holding company.

KINDS OF COMPANIES

1. Chartered Companies

The Crown, in the exercise of the royal prerogative, has power to create a corporation by the grant of a charter to persons assenting to be incorporated. Such companies or corporations are known as *Chartered Companies*. Examples of this type of companies are Bank of England, East India Company, Peninsular and Oriental Steam Navigation Company (1840) etc. The powers and the nature of business of a chartered company are defined by the charter which incorporates it.

2. Statutory Companies

A company may be incorporated by means of a special Act of the Parliament or any State legislature. Such companies are called *Statutory Companies*. They are generally formed to carry out some special public undertaking. For example railway, waterworks, gas, electricity generation etc. Instances of statutory companies, (which are also known as *Public Corporations*) in India are Reserve Bank of India (RBI), The Life Insurance Corporation of India (LIC), The Food Corporation of India (FCI), Unit Trust of India (UTI), State Trading Corporation (STC) etc.

Statutory companies are governed by the Acts creating them. They are not required to have any memorandum or articles of association. Changes in their structure are possible only by amendment in the Acts creating them. The annual report on the working of each statutory company is required to be placed before the Parliament or the State Legislature as the case may be. A statutory company though owned by the Government has a separate legal entity. It cannot be regarded as a department of the Government. The provisions of the Companies Act, 1956 apply to the statutory companies except where the said provisions are inconsistent with the provisions of the Act creating them.

3. Registered Companies

Companies registered under the Companies Act, 1956, or the earlier Companies Act are called *registered companies*. Such companies come into existence when they are registered under the Companies Act and a certificate of incorporation is granted to them by the Registrar. Section 12(2) provides that a company registered under the Act may be (a) a company limited by shares, (b) a company limited by guarantee, and (c) an unlimited company.

CHART SHOWING KINDS OF COMPANIES

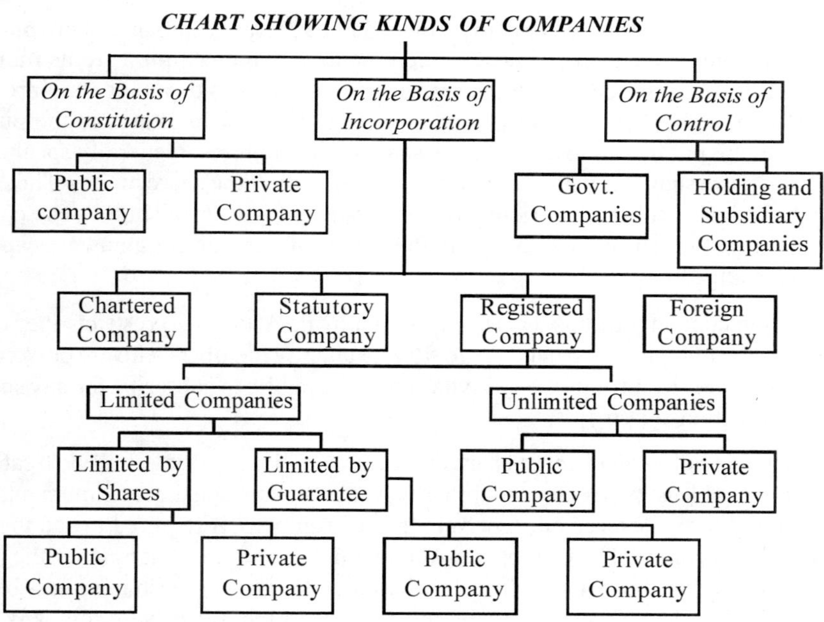

(i) ***Companies limited by Shares :*** Companies limited by shares are the most common type of companies. This is a company where the liability of its members is limited to the amount fixed by the memorandum of the company, if any, unpaid on the shares respectively held by them. The liability can be enforced during the existence of the company as well as during the winding up. Where the shares are fully paid up, no further liability rests on them.

(ii) ***Companies limited by Guarantee :*** This is a company where the liability of its members is limited to such amounts as they may respectively undertake as fixed by the memorandum to contribute to the assets of the compnay in the event of its being wound up. In the case of such companies, as in the case of companies limited by shares, the liability of its members is limited, but it is limited to the amount of guarantee undertaken by them. For example, the Madras Stock Exchange is a company limited by guarantee. A company limited by guarantee may or may not have a share capital. If it has a share capital, the liability of the members is twofold; (i) liability to pay the share amount and (ii) the amount guaranteed. A guarantee company may not be suitable for ordinary business purposes. Clubs, trade associations, research associations and societies for promoting various objects are the examples of guarantee companies. Many such companies obtain permission of the Central Government to dispense with the word 'limited'.

(iii) ***Unlimited Companies :*** It is a company where the liability of its members is not limited at all. In such a company, the liability of each member extends to the whole amount of the company's debts and liabilities, but he will be entitled to claim rateable contribution from other members. The Articles shall state the number of members with which the company is to be registered and if the company has a share capital, the amount of share capital with which the company is to be registered. An unlimited company may be converted into a limited company either limited by shares or limited by guarantee.

PUBLIC AND PRIVATE COMPANIES

Public Company : A public company means a company which is not a private company. There must be at least seven persons to form a public company. However, there is no maximum limit as to its number of shareholders or members. It is the essence of a public company that its articles do not contain provisions restricting the number of its members or excluding generally the transfer of its shares to the public or prohibiting any invitation to the public to subscribe for its shares or debentures. Generally speaking any member of the public may acquire shares in a public company on payment of the share money. The Articles of a public company may, however, contain restrictions on the issue or transfer of shares. The company remains a public company despite such restrictions. Only the shares of a public compnay are capable of being dealt in on a stock exchange.

Private Company : A private company means a company which by its Articles (i) restricts the rights to transfer its shares, (ii) limits the number of its members to fifty (excluding members who are or were in the employment of the company), and (iii) prohibits any invitation to the public to subscribe for any shares or debentures of the company. [Section 3(1)(iii)].

Where two or more persons hold one or more shares in a company jointly, they shall be treated as a single member. There should be at least two persons to form a private company and the maximum number of members in a private company cannot exceed 50. A private limited company is required to add the words "*Private Limited*" at the end of its name. The Companies Act does not specify in what manner the right to transfer shares must be restricted in the Articles. The restriction as to transfer of shares must be made applicable in respect of all shareholders. There cannot be any discrimination. If a private company fails to comply with any of the restrictions contained in the articles, it ceases to be entitled to some of the privileges of a private company.

Section 3(1) (iii) of the Amendment Act, 2000 further provided (prohibited) that a *private company* should include following restrictions in its Articles i.e.,

(i) *Prohibit an invitation or acceptance of deposits* from persons other than its members, directors or their relatives.

Note : Question may arise as to whether the Articles of existing companies need be amended to include this condition. Even if the articles are not amended, the provisions of Section 9 will apply wherein it is stated that the provisions of the Act will supercede the provisions of the Articles. However, it is desirable advisable as a good secretarial practice to alter the Articles. It these restrictions are not there, the company will be treated as public company. Therefore, the Articles of Association should be amended immediately by passing *Special Resolution* under Section 31 to provide for restriction, in particular item (d) above.

(ii) It may be noted that after the above amendment no private limited company can take any loan/ deposit or retain any loan/deposit taken from any outsider (other than its members, director's or their relatives.) Therefore, all private limited companies will have to regularise this matter immediately.

(iii) Every private company should have paid up capital of ₹ One lac. Existing companies will have to issue new shares to ensure paid up capital of ₹ 1 lac within 2 years of commencement of Amendment Act. Such capital may be Equity or Preference

(iv) If paid up capital is not increased to ₹ 1 lac within 2 years the company will be deemed to be a defunct company under Section 560, name of such a company will be struck off by Register of Companies.

Privileges of a Private Company : The provisions of the Companies Act apply to public and private companies alike. But certain provisions of the Companies Act do not apply to a private company but are applicable to public companies. These may be regarded as the *privileges or advantages of a private company* which are as under :

1. A private company may consist of *two members only.*
2. A private company is *entitled to commence business immediately on incorporation.*
3. A private company may allot shares *without issuing a prospectus or delivering to the Registrar a* statement in lieu of prospectus.
4. A private company is not required to hold a *statutory meeting* or file a statutory report with the Registrar.
5. A private company can have a *minimum of two directors.*
6. The provisions of Section 81 as regards *further issue of capital* do not apply to a private company.
7. A private company may issue not only equity and preference shares but also deferred shares or any other kind of *shares with disproportionate voting rights* as it may think fit.
8. A private company can give *financial assistance for purchase of its shares* or its holding company's shares.
9. Copies of Balance Sheet and Profit and Loss Account filed with the Registrar cannot be *inspected by* the public.
10. A director of a private company need not hold *the share qualification.*
11. Restrictions in regard to *overall managerial remuneration* imposed by Section 309 do not apply to a private company.
12. An *interested director* can participate in the Board proceedings and exercise his vote.

The privileges mentioned above are not available to a private company which is a subsidiary of a public company. It also applies to a private company which becomes a deemed public company by virtue of Section 43-A. Further, a private company ceases to be entitled to privileges mentioned above if, having made provisions required of a private company in its Articles, the company makes a default in complying with any one of those provisions.

DISTINCTION BETWEEN PUBLIC COMPANY AND PRIVATE COMPANY

1. ***Minimum number of members*** : The minimum number of persons required to form a public company is *seven*, whereas in private company it is only *two*.
2. ***Maximum number of members*** : There is *no limit* as to the maximum number of members of a public company, but a private company cannot have more than *fifty* members excluding past and present employees.
3. ***Commencement of Business*** : A private company can commence its business as soon as it is incorporated. But a public company shall not commence its business immediately unless it has been granted the *certificate of commencement of business*.
4. ***Invitation to public*** : A public company by *issuing a prospectus* may invite public to subscribe to its shares/debentures whereas a private company cannot extend such invitation to the public.
5. ***Transferability of shares*** : There is no restriction on the transfer of shares in the case of a public company whereas a private company by its Articles must restrict the right of members to transfer the shares.
6. ***Number of directors*** : A public company must have at least *three* directors whereas a private company may have *two* directors.
7. ***Statutory Meeting*** : A public company must hold as statutory meeting and file with the Registrar a statutory report. But in a private company there are no such obligations.
8. ***Restrictions on appointment of directors*** : A director of a public company shall file with the Registrar a consent to act as such. He shall sign the Memorandum and enter into a contract for *qualification of shares*. He cannot vote or take part in the discussion on a contract in which he is intersted. Two-thirds of the directors of a public company must *retire by rotation*. These restrictins do not apply to a private company.
9. ***Managerial remuneration*** : Total managerial remuneration in the case of a public company cannot exceed 11% of the net profits, but in the case of inadequacy of profits, a minimum of ₹ 50,000 can be paid. These restrictions do not apply to a private company.
10. ***Further issue of capital*** : A public company proposing further issue of shares must offer them to the existing members. A private company is free to allot new issues to outsiders.

CONVERSION OF PRIVATE COMPANY INTO PUBLIC COMPANY

Conversion by Choice

A private company may deliberately choose to become a public company. If a private company deletes from its Articles the requirements of Section 3(i)(iii) by *passing a special resolution*, the company will cease to be a private company from date of the alteration of the Articles. When a private company chooses to become a public company, it will have to comply with all the provisions of the Companies Act, applicable to a public company. Within 30 days of its becoming a public company, it shall *file with the Registrar a prospectus* or *a statement in lieu of prospectus.*

Converion by Default

A private company is entitled to certain privileges and exemptions. It can enjoy those privileges as long as it complies with the requirements of its definition as given in Section 3(i)(iii). Where any default is made in complying with these provisions (viz, restriction on transfer of shares,limitation of the number of members to 50 and prohibition of invitation to public to buy shares and debentures), the company loses the privileges and the exemptions and the provisions of the Act apply to the company as if it was not a private company. However, the company may be relieved of the consequences on an application made to the court, and the court is satisfied that the failure to comply with the conditions is not wilful or that it is just and equitable to grant relief. (Sec. 43).

Conversion by the Operation of Law

Private companies are exempted from the operation of several provisions of the Act and enjoy certain privileges principally on the ground that they are family concerns in which the public is not directly interested. As public money is invested in such companies, there is no reason for treating such companies as private companies. The law tries to tackle the problem by creating another type of company viz., *Deemed Public Company*. Actually it is a private company which, under certain circumstances, can be treated by the laws as the public company. Firstly where a private company is a subsidiary of a public company, it is dealt with as a public company for all purposes of the Act.

A private company shall also be deemed as a public company in the following cases :

(a) Where it *invites public deposits* through an advertisement;

(b) it *holds 25% or more of the paid up share capital of a public company*;

(c) it has public company(ies) or deemed public company(ies) as its shareholders *holding in aggregate 25% or more of its paid up share capital*;

(d) its average annual turnover for the last three consecutive financial ₹ars is ***₹25 crores or more.*** A private company which has become a public company by virtue of these provisions shall continue to be so until it has, with the approval of the Central Government and in accordance with the provisions of the Act, again become a private company. *Provisions regarding 'deemed public companies' are deleted by the Companies Amendment Act, 2000.*

Conversion of Public Company into Private Company

A public company may be converted into a private company by altering the Articles incorporating the three restrictions mentioned in Section 3(i)(iii). Such alteration of Articles will be made by a *special resolution* and the *approval of the Central Government* is necessary for such alteration. A copy of the special resolution has to *be filed with the Registrar within 30 days* and when the approval of the Central Government for conversion of a public company into private company is obtained, a copy of such approval shall also be filed within one month. A printed copy of the Articles as altered shall be filed by the company with the Registrar within one month of the date of receipt of the order of approval.

Holding Company and Subsidiary Company

A company which controls another company is known as the '*holding company*' and the company so controlled is termed as 'subsidiary company'.

A holding company is one of it :

(i) controls the composition of board of directors of another company; or

(ii) holds *more than half of the nominal value of equity* share capital of another company; or

(iii) controls *more than 1/2 of the total voting* power of the other company. .

(iv) is a subsidiary of any company which is in turn a subsidiary of another company.

Illustration : Company B is a subsidiary of company A, and company C is a subsidiary of company B. Company C will be a subsidiary of company A.

GOVERNMENT COMPANY

Section 617 of the Companies Act defines a government company as a company in which not less than fifty one per cent of the paid up share capital is held by the Central Government, or by any State Government, or Governments, or partly by the Central Government and partly by one or more State Governments. It also includes a company which is a subsidiary of a Government company.

Certain special provisions have been laid down in the Act regarding a government company. They are discussed below :

1. The *auditor* of a Government company shall be appointed or re-appointed by the Central Government on the advice of the Comptroller and Auditor General (GAG) of India.
2. The auditor will *submit a copy of the audit report* to the CAG of India who may comment upon or supplement the audit report in such manner as he may think fit. Such a comment or supplementary report shall be placed before the annual general meeting along with the audit report. (Section 619).
3. Where the Central Government is a member of the Government company it shall cause an *annual report on the working and affairs of the company to be prepared and laid before both Houses of Parliament* alongwith the audit report and the comments, if any, of the Comptroller and Auditor General of India. The report shall be prepared within 3 months of the Annual General Meeting. Where the State Government is also a member, the report shall also be laid before the *State legislature.*

Distinction between Government Company and NonGovernment Company

Basis of Difference	*Government Company*	*Non-Government Companies*
1. Ownership or Capital	Not less than 51% of the share capital is held by the Central Government and/ or one or more State Governments.	The share capital is held by the promoters and/or the investing public.
2. Auditing of Accounts	The accounts of Government companies are audited by the auditors appointed by the Government and their reports are commented by the Comptroller and Auditor General of India.	The accounts of Non- Government Companies are audited by a private practising auditor at the discretion of the Board of Directors.
3. Annual Report	The annual report of Government companies are submitted to Parliament or to the special committee formed by parliament for the purpose.	The annual reports are not required to be submitted to the parliament.
4. Modification	The Central Government with the approval of parliament may declare that the provisions of the Companies Act other than Sections 618 and 619 shall not be applicable to the Government Companies or shall be applicable with certain exceptions, modifications and adaptations. (Sec.620)	In case of Non-Government Companies the Central Government cannot issue any such orders.

FOREIGN COMPANIES

It means a company *incoporated outside India and having a place of business in India.* The Companies Amendment Act, 1974 provides that where *not less than 50% of the share capital is held by Indian citizens* and/or companies incorporated in India it shall have to comply with such of the provisions of the Act as may be prescribed as if it were a company incorporated in India.

1. **Documents :** Every foreign company shall, within 30 days of the establishment of the business in India, furnish with the Registrar for registration the following documents :
   (i) *A certified copy* of the Charter, Statute, Memorandum and Articles of the company, containing the constitution of the company and if the instrument is not in English language a certified translation thereof.
   (ii) The full *address of the registered or principal office* of the company.
   (iii) *A list of the directors* and secretary of the company with particulars as to name, nationality etc.
   (iv) The names and addresses of *any person* or persons resident, in India, *authorised to accept service of legal processes* and notices on behalf of the company.
   (v) *The full address of the principal place* of business in India. (Section 592) Where any change occurs in the above particulars, the company shall file with the Registrar a return of such alterations within the prescribed time. (Section 593).
2. **Accounts :** Every foreign company, unless exempted by the Central Government, shall *file with the Registrar every year three copies of its Balance Sheet and Profit and Loss Account* and other documents required under the Act. Such documents must be in English language. Apart from these documents, it shall also send to the Registrar, three copies of a list in the prescribed form of all places of business established by the company in India. (Section 594).
3. **Names :** Every foreign company shall *exhibit on the outside of every office or place of business its name and the country of incorporation* in English and in one of the local languages. It shall also have the name of the company and the country of incorporation stated in English on *business letters, bill heads, and letter papers and on all notices and other official publications of the company.*
4. **Winding up :** All foriegn companies carrying on business in India may be wound up by an order of the Court as unregistered companies. It can also be wound up even if it has been dissolved or cease to exit according to its own law of incorporation (Section 584).

One-man Company and Family Company

These are companies in which one man holds virtually the whole of the share capital with a few extra members holding the remainder, who may be his relations or nominees. Being the largest holder, such a person is generally the sole or the managing director and enjoys complete control over the company. This is done with a view to fulfil the statutory requirement of at least seven members in the case of a public company and at least two members in the case of a private company. He is, thus, in a position to enjoy the profits of the business with limited liability. Such types of companies are perfectly valid and not illegal. As already established in *Saloman Vs. Saloman & Co. Ltd.,* such companies are legal entities distinct from the members.

Licensed Companies (or Companies not for Profit)

Section 25 of the Companies Act relates to licensed company. These licensed companies are *formed for a non-trading object or for a noble cause*, like the promotion of art, science, education, commerce, etc. Charitable associations, sports clubs, trade associations, chambers of commerce, etc, are examples of companies not for profit. Such companies can be formed only on obtaining the license from the Central Government or State Government i.e. they can be registered only after such licence. The Government has power to revoke the licence granted to such companies if it thinks fit on giving the company notice and after an opportunity to object.

Illegal Associations

Section 11 of the Act provides that *no company, association or partnership consisting of more than 10 pesons in case of banking business and of more than 20 persons in the case of any other business* which has for its objects the acquisition of gain, can be legally formed unless it is registered under the Companies Act or is formed in pursuance of some other Indian law. If they are not so registered, they would be considered as illegal associations. The law does not recognise them being illegal.

Effect of an Illegal Association : An association or partnership which is not registered under Section 11 can have *no legal recognition as a separate legal entity*. The result of this is (a) Such an association cannot enter into any binding contract. (b) It cannot sue or be sued. But such an association may get itself registered and enforce its claims. (c) Such an association cannot be dissolved under the Act either at the instance of a creditor, a member, or the association itself. Every member of such an association shall be *personally liable for all liabilities incurred* in such business and shall also be liable to a fine which may extend upto ₹ 1,000.

DISTINCTION BETWEEN PARTNERSHIP AND COMPANY

1. ***Registration :*** Registration of a firm is not compulsory even under the Partnership Act, 1932 whereas incorporation/registration of a company is compulsory under the Companies Act, 1956.
2. ***No. of Members :*** Minimum two persons may constitute a partnershpi. Maximum membership in case of partnership doing banking business is ten persons and for other business is twenty persons, while minimum two and maximum fifty constitute private limited company and minimum seven and no maximum (unlimited) constitute a public limited company.
3. ***Legal Status :*** A firm has no individual legal status while a company has a separate legal existence of its own, and is considered a separate person from its members.
4. ***Property :*** Property of the firm is the property of the partners. On the contrary, in case of a company property always belongs to the company.
5. ***Contracts :*** A partner cannot contract with the firm whereas a shareholder can contract with the company.
6. ***Management :*** Management in case of partnership vests in the hands of the active partners whereas in case of a compnay, management vests in the Board of Directors elected by the shareholders.
7. ***Life Duration :*** Partnership unlike company has no perpetual existence.
8. ***Liability :*** Partners of the firm are liable to an unlimited extent, i.e., in partnership there is an unlimited liability whereas the liability of shareholders is usually limited.

9. ***Creditors :*** Creditors of the firm are also creditors of the partners individually, whereas in the case of company, creditors are only the creditors of company and not of the individual shareholders.

10. ***Dissolution on Death :*** Death of a partner may mean dissolution of partnership while the death of a shareholder or even of a director does not affect the existence of a company.

11. ***Agency Relationship :*** Every partner is an agent of the other partner, whereas the shareholder of a company is not an agent of the company.

12. ***Transfer of interest :*** A partner cannot transfer his interest in the firm without the consent of the other partners. A transferee becomes a partner of the firm only with the consent of the other partners whereas in case of a company shares are easily transferable and the transferee of a share becomes a members of the company without any difficulty.

13. ***Statutory obligations :*** Partnership has less statutory obligations under the Partnership Act, 1932 whereas a company is regulated strictly under the Companies Act, 1956.

REVIEW QUESTIONS

1. Define the term company.
2. What are the characteristics of a company?
3. "The company is a legal entity distinct from its members". In what cases do the courts disregard this principle?
4. Define a Private company.
5. Distinguish from a Public Company.
6. Discuss the privileges enjoyed by a private company over a public company.
7. How can a private company be converted into a public company and vice versa?
8. Define a Government company. How far it is governed by the Companies Act 1956.
9. What is a Foreign Company? Discuss the various provisions of Companies Act, 1956 relating to foreign companies.
10. Write notes on : (a) Holding company, (b) One man company; (c) Statutory companies (d) Licensed Companies; (e) Illegal Association; (f) Deemed Public Company.
11. State the differences between a partneship firm and a company.
12. What is an illegal association? What are its legal effects?

❒ ❒ ❒

19 Chapter

FORMATION OF A COMPANY

Documents to be Filed for Registration of a Company

The application for registration of a company should be presented to the Registrar of Companies of the State in which the business office of the company is to be situated. The application shall be accompanied with the following documents.

1. The Memorandum of Association
2. The Articles of Association, if any, duly signed by the subscribers of the Memorandum.
3. A statement of the nominal or authorised capital.
4. A notice of address of the registered office of the company. This may also be done within 30 days of registration if it cannot be filed at the time of registration.
5. A list of directors and their consent to act as such, signed by each.
6. An undertaking in writing signed by each such diretors to take and pay for their qualification shares.
7. A declaration that all the requirements (provisions) of the Companies Act have been complied with. Such a declaration may be signed by an *advocate* of the Supreme Court or High Court, an *attorney* or *pleader* entitled to appear before a High Court, or a *Chartered Accountant* practising in India, who is engaged in the formation of the company, or by a person named in the Articles as *director, manager or secretary of the company*.

Note : Items number 5 and 6 listed above are not required to be filed in the case of a private company.

If the Registrar is satisfied that all the requisite documents delivered to him are in order, he shall register the Memorandum and the Articles, if any, provided he is satisfied on the following points :

(a) the relevant provisions of the Act have been complied with,

(b) the objects of the company are lawful.

(c) the requisite number of persons required under the Act have subscribed and duly signed,

(d) the Memorandum and the Articles comply in all respects with the provisions of the Act,

(e) the name selected by the company is acceptable; and

(f) the statutory declaration has been properly made. If the Registrar of Companies is satisfied that all the aforesaid requirements have been complied with, he will register the company and place its name on the register of companies. It is clear that once the statutory requirements have been complied with, the Registrar has no option but no register it. On refusal to register a company on improper grounds, he may be compelled by a *Writ of Mandamus*.

Certificate of Incorporation

On registration, the Registrar will issue a certificate of incorporation whereby he certifies that the company is incorporated. From the date of incorporation mentioned in the certificate, the company becomes a legal person separate from its shareholders and secures a perpectual succession. Hence it is the *birth certificate* of the company. The certificate of incorporation prevents the reopening of matter prior to the registration and places the existence of the company as a legal person beyond doubt. Consequently, even if the seven signatures to a memorandum were written by one peson or were all forged, the certificate would be conclusive that the company was duly registered. Similarly, if the signatories were all infants, the certificate would still be conclusive.

Certificate of Commencement of Business

A private company may commence its business immediately on incorporation but a public company cannot commence business immediately after incorporation, unless it has obtained a certificate of commencement of business (also known as *Trading Certificate*) from the Registrar. If the company has a share capital and has issued a prospectus inviting the public to subscribe for its shares or debentures it cannot commence business until

(a) shares payable in cash have been allotted to the extent of the minimum subscription :

(b) every director has paid in cash the application and allotment money on the shares taken by him;

(c) no money is liable to be repaid to the applications for failure to apply or obtain permission for the shares or debentures to be dealt in on any recognised stock exchange;

(d) a statutory declaration duly verified by one of the directors or the secretary in the prescribed form that the above conditions have been complied with has been filed with the Registrar [Section 149(1)].

On the above requirements being duly fulfilled, the Registrar shall certify that the company is entitled to commence business. *This certificate is a conclusive evidence that the company is so entitled. [Section 149(3)]. Contracts made by the company before it has obtained the certificate of commencement are provisonal* only and do not become binding on the company until it has become entitled to commence business. [Section 149(4)]. Where a company is wound up before it becomes entitled to commence business, anybody who has supplied goods cannot have any claim against the company. *A company is bound to commence business within a year of its incorporation or else it is liable to be would up by the Court.* [Section 433(c)].

PROMOTER

A promoter is one "*who undertakes to form a company with reference to a given object and to set it going and who takes the necesary steps to accomplish that purpose*" The promoters of a company decide the scope of its business activities. They negotiate, if necessary, for the purchase of an existing business. They instruct the solicitors to prepare the necessary documents and secure the services of directors. They provide the registration fees and carry out other duties involved in the formation of a company. They also make arrangements for advertising and circulating the prospectus, and placing the capital.

A promoter is not an agent for the company which he is forming because a company cannot have an agent before it comes into existence. For the same reason, he cannot be the trustee of the company. However, from the moment he acts with the company in mind, a *promoter stands in fiduciary position towards the company.*

Liabilities of Promoters

A promoter can be compelled by the company to hand over any *secret profit* which he has made without full disclosures to the company. The company can also sue for the rescision of the contract of sale by the promoter where the promoter has not disclosed his interest therein.

A promoter is liable for any *untrue statement in the prospectus* to a person who has subscribed for any shares or debentures on the faith of the prospectus. Such a person may sue the promoter for compensation for any loss or damage sustained by him.

Remuneration of Promoters

The nature of the promoters work in the formation of a company calls for considerable skill for which he should be adequately remunerated. A promoter has no right against the company for his remuneration unless there is a contract to that effect. In the absence of such a contract, he cannot even recover from the company payments he has made in connection with the formation of the company.

Preliminary or Pre-Incorporation Contracts

Preliminary contracts are purported to be made on behalf of a company before its incorporation. Prior to this, a company has no capacity to contract. A contract entered into by promoters on behalf of a proposed company is void so far as the company is concerned. The promoters cannot be the agents for a principal of a which has not yet come into company existence. In such a case the company cannot sue or sue on it. The company has no legal existence until it is incorporated. The preliminary contracts made by promoters generally provide that if the company adopts the agreement, the promoters' liability shall cease and if the company does not adopt the agreement within a certain time either party may rescind the contract. In such a case the promoters, liability would cease after the lapse of the fixed time.

Provisional Contracts

Pre-incorporation contracts must be distinguished from contracts entered into by a company after incorporation, but before it becomes entitled to commence business. Contracts entered into by a company after its incorporation and before it is entitled to commence business are provisional only and are not binding on the company until the trading certificate is issued. Consequently, should the company go into liquidation, without commencing business, such contracts cannot be enforced at all.

Before 1963 (i.e. before passing of Specific Relief Act): A pre-incorporation contract never binds company, since a person (legal or artificial) cannot contract before his or its existence, and the company before incorporation has no legal existence. Even where Articles purport to enforce such a contract, the company cannot be bound because ratification is not possible as the ostensible principal did not exist at the time the contract was made (*Kelner Vs. Baxter year?*).

After 1963 (i.e After passing of the Specific Relief Act, 1963) : Until the passing of the Specific Relief Act, 1963 the promoters found it very difficult to carry out the incorporation. Since contracts prior to incorporation were void and also could not be ratified, people hesitated to either supply any goods or work for the cause of incorporation. Promoters also felt shy of accepting personal responsibility. *The Specific Relief Act, 1963* came as a sigh of relief to the promoters. Secs 15 (h) and 19 (e) of the Act provide that when the promoters of a company have before its incorporation entered into a contract for the purposes of the company and such a contract can be enforced by or against the company. Thus, contracts like a contract for the preparation and printing of the Memorandum or Articles of association is the contract envisaged under this Act.

Distinction between Pre-Incorporation and Provisional Contracts

Pre-incorporation Contracts	Provisional Contracts
1. Contracts which are entered into before the company comes into existence	Provisional Contracts are entered by a company after its incorporation but before commencement of its business.
2. No effect so far as the company is concerned.	Not binding until the company is entitled to commence business.
3. Can be enforced against the company only if warranted by terms of incorporation.	Cannot be enforced the company goes into without commencing business.

MEMORANDUM OF ASSOCIATION

Meaning : Memorandum of Association is one of the core documents which has to be filed with the Registrar of Companies at the time of incorporation of a company. It is a document which sets out the *constitution* of the company and is really the foundation on which the structure of the company is based.

It contains the fundamental conditions upon which alone the company is allowed to be incorporated. A company may pursue only such objects and exercise only such powers as are conferred expressly in the memorandum or by implication therefrom i.e. such powers as are incidental to the attainment of the objects. A company cannot depart from the provisions contained in its memorandum, however, great the necessity may be. If it does, it would be *ultra vires* the company, and therefore wholly void. It defines its relation with the outside world and the scope of its activities. The purpose of the memorandum is to enable shareholders, creditors and those who deal with the company to know what is the permitted range of the activities of the enterprise.

Contents of Memorandum

According to Section 13, the Memorandum of Association of every company must contain the following clauses :

1. The *Name* of the company with 'Limited' as the last word of the name in the case of a public limited company and with 'Private Limited' as the last word in the case of a private limited company.
2. The State in which the *registered office* of the company is to be situated.
3. The *objects* of the company to be classified as (i) the main objects of the company to be pursued by the company on its incorporation and objects incidental to the attainment of the main objects, and (ii) other objects not included above.
4. The *Liability* of members is limited if the company is limited by shares or by guarantee.
5. In the case of a company having a share capital, the amount of *share capital* with which the company proposes to be registered and its division into shares of a fixed amount. An unlimited company need not include items 4 and 5 in its Memorandum. A brief discussion of the various clauses is as follows :

Name Clause : A company may be registered with any name it likes. But no company shall be registered by a name which in the opinion of the Central Government is undesirable and in particular which is identical or which too nearly resembles the name of an existing company. Every public company must write the word 'limited' after its name and every private *limited* company must write the '*private limited*' after its name. A company cannot adopt a name which violates the provisions of the *Emblems and Names (Prevention of Improper Use) Act 1950*. Every company is required to publish its name outside its registered office, and outside every place where it carries on business, to have its name engraved on a seal and to have its name on all business letters, bill heads, notices and other official publications of the company (Section 147).

Registered Office Clause : This clause states the name of the State where the registered office of the company is situated. The registered office clause is important for two reasons. Firstly, it ascertains the domicile and nationality of a company. This domicile clings to it throughout its existence. Secondly, it is the place where various registers relating to the company must be kept and to which all communications and notice must be spent.

Objects Clause : The objects clause is the most important clause in the Memorandum of association of a company. It is not merely a record of what is contemplated by the subscribers, but it serves a two-fold purpose - (a) It gives an idea to the prospective shareholders the purposes for which their money will be utilised. (b) It enables the persons dealing with the company to ascertain its powers. In case of companies which were in existence immediately before the commencement of the Companies (Amendment) Act 1965, the objects clause has simply to state the objects of the company. But in the case of a company to be registered after the amendment, the objects clause must state separately.

(i) ***Main Objects :*** This sub-clause has to state the main objects to be pursued by the company on its incorporation and objects incidental or ancillary to the attainment of the main objects.

(ii) ***Other objects :*** This sub-clause shall state other objects which are not included in the above clause.

Liability Clause : This clause states that the liability of the members of the company is limited. In the case of a company limited by shares, a member is liable only to the amount unpaid on the shares taken by him. In the case of a company limited by guarantee, the members are liable to the amount undertaken to be contributed by them to the assets of the company in the event of its being wound up. However, this clause is omitted from the Memorandum of association of the unlimited companies.

Capital Clause : The Memorandum of a company limited by shares must state the authorised or nominal share capital, the different kinds of shares, the nominal value of each share. The chief point to consider in regard to this class is what funds are necessary to set the business going or, if it is proposed to by an existing concern, what sum is needed to pay its price and what, in addition, is wanted to keep the business going. It is generally advisable to have a reasonable amount of more capital and have some shares in reserve as unissued so that further capital may be raised as and when requried.

Association or Subscription Clause : This clause provides that those who have agreed to subscribe to the memorandum, must signify their willingness to associate and form a company. According to Section 12 of the Act, atleast *seven persons are required to sign the Memorandum in the case of pubic company, and at least two persons in the case of private company*. The Memorandum has to be signed by each subscriber in the presence of at least one witness who must attest the signatures. Each subscriber must write opposite his name the number of shares he shall take. No subscriber of the memorandum shall take less than one share. This clause need not be numbered.

ALTERATION OF MEMORANDUM

The Memorandum of association of a company being its charter, the right of the company to alter its contents is rigidly limited by the provisions of the Act. Section 16 of the Act provides that a company shall not alter the conditions contained in its memorandum except in the cases, in the manner and to the extent provided in the Act.

Change of Name

A company can change its name. For this purpose it must first pass a *special resolution* and then obtain *approval of the Central Government* in writing. However, no such approval is necessary for merely including or deleting the word 'Private' consequent on the conversion of the public company into private company and vice versa. (Section 21).

The Registrar shall enter the new name the register in place of former name and shall issue a fresh certificate or incorporation. Necessary alteration shall also be made in the Memorandum by the Registrar. The change of name shall be complete and effective only on the issue of such a certificate. The rights and obligations of a company will not be affected on the change of its name (Section 23).

Change of Registered Office

A company can shift its registered office from one place to another within the same city, town or village, provided a *notice of change is given to the Registrar within 30 days of such change*. But, where the registered office is to be changed outside the local limits of any city, town or village in the same State, *special resolution* to that effect must be passed. However, the alteration of the change of the place of the registered office of a company from one State to another shall take effect only on the *confirmation by the Company Law Board* on petition. A notice of such change shall also be given to the Registrar within 30 days of the change. These two changes in the registered office do not involve alteration of Memorandum.

Procedure for shifting Registered Office from one State to another

A company can change its registered office from one State to another only for purpose specified in Section 17 (1) of the Companies Act, 1956 and for no other purpose.

1. *Resolution of the Board of Directors:* The first step in changing registered office is that the board of directors must adopt a resolution to that effect.
2. *Special resolution*: A special resolution must be passed by the company in the general body meeting of share holders/members (Sec.17(1).
3. *Confirmation by the CLB:* the change shall not take effect unless and until it is confirmed by the CLB on a petition by the company .(Sec17(2). Consequent to the Companies (Amendment) Act, 1996, the change of registered office requires no confirmation by CLB.
4. *Notice to affected parties*: Before confirming the change the CLB shall ensure that sufficient notice has been given to every person whose interest will be affected by the change and that the consent of the creditors of the company has been obtained or their debts or claims have been discharged or secured. (Sec.17(3)
5. *Notice to Registrar:* The CLB shall cause notice of the petition for confirmation of the change to be served on the Registrar. The Registrar shall also be given a reasonable opportunity to appear before the CLB and state his objections and suggestions, if any, with respect to the confirmation of the alteration. (Sec.17(4).
6. The CLB as it may think fit impose such terms and conditions.
7. *Copy of the order to be filed with ROC's*: A certified copy of the order confirming the alternation, together with a printed copy of altered Memorandum shall be filed by the company with the registrar of each of the States who shall registrar the same. All the records of the company shall be transferred.

The aforesaid copy of the order must be filed within three months from the date or the order. The CLB before confirming a resolution will satisfy itself that sufficient notice has been given to every creditor and all other persons whose interest are likely to be affected by the alternation to every creditor and all other persons whose interest are likely to be affected by the alternation including the Registrar of Companies and the Government of the State in which registered office is situated. In *Orient Paper Mills Ltd. Vs. State of AIR (1957) Ori.232*, it was observed that a State whose interests are affected by the change of the registered office to a different States High Court declined to confirm of the shifting of the registered office from Orissa to West Bengal on the ground that the State has the right to protect its revenue and therefore the interest of the State must be taken into account.

But in *Minerva Mills Ltd. Vs. Govt. of Maharashtra,* the Bombay High Court held that the CLB cannot refuse confirmation of the shifting of the registered office on the ground of loss of revenue to a state or would adversely affect on the general economy of the State. Similar view was expressed in *Rank Film Distributors of India Ltd Vs. Registrar of Companies, West Bengal.*

Change of Registered Office within a State

1. No company shall change the place of its registered office from one place to another within a State unless such change is confirmed by the Regional Director.
2. The company shall make an application in the prescribed form to the Regional Director for confirmation under sub-section .
3. The confirmation referred to in sub-section (1), shall be communicated to the company within four weeks from the date of receipt of application for such change.

   Explanation - For the purposes of this section, it is hereby declared that the provisions of this section shall apply only to the companies which change the registered office from the jurisdiction of one Registrar of Companies to the jurisdiction of another Registrar of Companies within the same state.
4. The company shall file, with the Registrar a certified copy of the confirmation by the Regional Director for change of its registered office under this section, within two months from the date of confirmation, together with a printed copy of the memorandum as altered and the Registrar shall register the same and certify the registration under his hand within one month from the date of filing of such document.
5. The certificate shall be conclusive evidence that all the requirements of this Act with respect to the alteration and confirmation have been complied with and hence forth the Memorandum as altered shall be the Memorandum of the company".

Change of the Objects Clause

Section 17 of the Act only gives a limited right to the company to alter its objects clause. This sectin provides specific purposes that the objects clause can be altered only if the change enables the company :

(a) to carry on its business more economically or more efficiently;

(b) to attain its main object by new or improved means;

(c) to enlarge or change the local area of its operation;

(d) to carry on some business, which under existing circumstances may be conveniently or advantageously combined with the business of the company;

(e) to restrict or to abandon any of the objects specified in the memorandum;

(f) to sell or dispose of the whole or any part of the undertaking of the company;

(g) to amalgamate with any other company or body of persons.

The company can alter its objects clause only to the above named purposes. The Company Law Board has no jurisdiction to confirm any alteration which is not covered by Section 17(i). The alteratin must leave the business of the company substantially the same what it was before with only such changes in the mode of conducting it as will enable it to be carried on more economically or more efficiently. The additions or alterations should be a step in aid to improve efficiency and generate more resources.

Procedure : Before the company can alter object clause, it shall pass a *special resolution*, sanctioning the alteration. A copy of the special resolution shall be filed with the Registrar within 30 days of its passing. But the alteration shall not take effect unless it is *confirmed by the Company law Board on petition*. Before confirming, the Company Law Board (CLB) shall see that sufficient notice of the petition has been given to all persons whose interests are likely to be affected by the proposed alteration. It may confirm the alteration either wholly or in part and on such terms and conditions as it may think fit. *A certified copy of the order of the Company Law Board together with a printed copy of the altered memorandum must be filed with the Registrar within three months of the order,* who shall register the same and issue a certificate of registration within one month. (Section 18). If the copy of the order is not registered within the prescribed period, the proceedings connected with the order will become void and inoperative. However, the Board may revive the order on an application made within one month of its lapse. (Section 19).

Change of Liability Clause

Ordinarily the liability clause cannot be altered so as to make the liability of members unlimited. Any alteration in the Memorandum will be void if the effect of the alteration is the enhancement of the liability of members. This privision, however, will not apply to a case where the members agree in writing to be bound by the alteration. (Section 38). A limited company, if authorised by its articles by a special resolution, may alter its Memorandum to make the liability of its directors or manager unlimited. This rule applies to future appointees only. Such alteration will however not affect the existing directors and managers unless they have accorded their consent. (Section 323).

Change of the Capital Clause

A limited company, having a share capital may alter its capital clause subject to the provisions of its Articles by a resolution in the general meeting. The confirmation of the court is not required if alteration is made for any of the following purposes : (i) to increase its share capital. (ii) to consolidate and divide its capital into shares of larger amount. (iii) to convert its fully paid shares into stock and reconvert the stock into fully paid up shares. (iv) to sub-divide its shares into shares of smaller amount, and (v) to cancel its shares. *But for reduction of share capital, special resolution and confirmation by the court are necessary.* For detailed discussion on the above, see chapter, "*Shares and Debentures*".

DOCTRINE OF ULTRA-VIRES

A company has power to carry out the objects set out in the Memorandum and also everything which is reasonably necessary to enable it to carry out those objects. Any activities not expressly or impliedly authorised by the Memorandum are ultra-vires to the company. An act is said to be *ultra-vires* (beyond the powers) when it is performed which, though legal in itself, is not authorised by the objects clause in the Memorandum of association or the statute.Such an act is *void and cannot be ratified* even by an unaniminous resolution of all the shareholders.

The doctrine of ultra vires was put in its modern form in the famous case of ***Ashbury Railway Carriage and Iron Co. Ltd. Vs. Riche***. year? There may be certain acts which are ultra-vires the directors or ultra-vires the Articles but which are intra-vires the company. If an act is *ultra-vires the directors* only and the shareholders have ratified it, the company would be bound by it. Where an act is *ultra-vires the articles*, it can be ratified by altering the Articles through a *special resolution*. Further, it an act is within the powers of the company, any irregularities seen can be cured by the consent of all the shareholders.

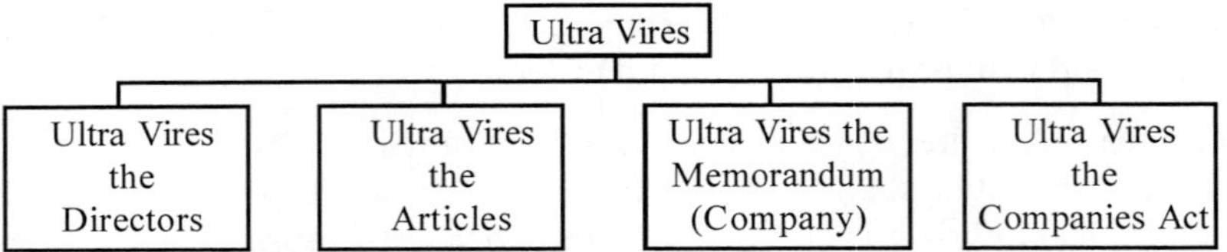

Effects of Ultra-vires Acts

An act which is ultra-vires the company is *absolutely void*. A company is not bound by and cannot enforce an ultra-vires contract. The effects of an ultra-vires are as follows.

1. **Injunction :** As such a company may be *restrained by an injunction* to do an act if it is ultra-vires of its objects.
2. **Subrogation :** If the money borrowed has been used to pay-off debts which could have been enforced against the company, the lender may *sue the company being subrogated* to the rights of the creditors who were paid-off.
3. **Tracing Order :** If the lender can identify his money, or other property purchased with it, he is entitled to what is known as a *tracing order* and can *recover*.
4. **Personal Liability of Directors :** The lender may *hold the directors personally liable* for contracting an ultra-vires loan of the company. The directors are *liable for damages to the lender* for the breach of the implied warranty of authority.
5. If any money is unlawfully disbursed, the directors shall be personally liable to make good the amount.
6. **Breach of Warranty of Authority :** Where the officers of a company persuade a third party to enter into a transaction which is ultra-vires the company, an action may lie against them in *breach of warranty of authority.*
7. An ultra-vires contract *cannot become intra-vires by reason of estoppel, lapse of time, ratification or delay.*
8. A company can *protect its property* acquired by an ultra-vires expenditure.
9. A company will be *liable for torts or crimes committed* in the pursuit of its stated objects.

ARTICLES OF ASSOCIATION

Meaning : The word '*Articles*' means the Articles of association of a company as originally framed or as altered from time to time in pursuance of any previous companies law or of this Act. The Articles of association are the rules and regulations of a company framed for the purpose of internal management of its affairs. It deals with the rights of the members of the company *inter-se*. The Articles are framed for carrying out the aims and objects of the Memorandum of Association. The Articles of association of a company are subordinate to and are controlled by the Memorandum of Association.

It is not obligatory to register Articles in the case of a public company limited by shares. In such a case, *model Articles contained in 'Table A' of Schedule I of the Act* will apply. However, a private company, a compnay limited by guarantee and an unlimited company must register their Articles alongwith the Memorandum.(Section 26). In the case of an unlimited company, the Articles shall state the number of the numbers, with which the company is to be registered, and if it has a share capital, the amount of share capital with which it is to be registered. [Section 27(1)]. In the case of a company limited by guarantee, the Articles shall state the number of members with which the company is to be registered. [Section 27(2)].

In the case of a private company, the Articles must contain provisions which (a) restrict the right to transfer its shares; (b) limit the number of its members to fifty excluding past and the present employees of the company; (c) prohibit any invitation to the public to subscribe for any shares in or debentures of the company. [Section 27(3)].

The Articles must be printed and divided into paragraphs, numbered consecutively. The Articles must be signed by each subscriber of the Memorandum in the presence of at least one witness who will atleast the signature and likewise add his address, description and occupation, if any. [Section 30].

Contents of Articles

1. Exclusion wholly or in part of *Table A*.
2. Adoption of preliminary contracts.
3. Number and value of shares.
4. Allotment of shares.
5. Calls on shares.
6. Lien on shares.
7. Transfer and transmission of shares.
8. Forfeiture of shraes.
9. Alteration of share capital.
10. Share certificates.
11. Conversion of shares into stock.
12. Voting rights and proxies.
13. Rules of conducting Meetings.
14. Directors, their appointment etc.
15. Borrowing powers.
16. Accounts and audit.
17. Dividens and reserves.
18. Winding up.

ALTERATION OF ARTICLES

Companies have wide powers to alter their Articles. Any restriction on the exercise of their powers will be invalid. Articles of Association may be altered by a company by passing a *special resolution* to that effect. The altered Articles will bind the members in the same way as did the original Articles. The company must *file with the Registrar a copy of the special resolution within one month from the date of its passing.*

Section 31 of the Companies Act, 1956 vests companies with powers to alter or add to its Articles. A company cannot divest itself of these powers (*Andrews Vs. Gas Meter Co.(1897) I Ch.361*}. Matters as to which the Memorandum is silent can be dealt with by the alteration of Articles (Section 31(1)}. The alteration must be effected subject to the following limitations:

(i) the alteration must not exceed the powers given by Memorandum or conflict with the provisions thereof.

(ii) It must not be inconsistent with any provisions of the Companies Act or any other statute.

(iii) It must not be illegal.

(iv) It should not be in fraud of a minority or inflict a hardship on a minority subject to an important provision that whatever is done in the interest of the company can never be regarded as oppressive to the minority, however, hurtful it may be to the minority. *(Brown British Abrasive Wheel Co. (1919) I Ch.290: Side bottom Vs. Kershaw Least and Co.Ltd. I Ch.154.)*

(v) The alteration must not be inconsistent with an order of the Court. Where a company is compelled by a Court's order to change its Articles in cases of oppression or mismanagement any subsequent alteration thereof which is inconsistent with such an order can be made by the company only with the leave of the Court.

(vi) It may be regarded as having a retrospective effect so long as it does not affect the things already done by the company (*Allen Vs.Gulf Line (1909) S. C.732.)*

(vii) If a public company is converted into a private company then the approval of the Central Government is necessary {Section 31 (1) Provision}. Printed copy of altered Articles shall be filed with the Registrar within one month of date of the Central Government's approval [Section 31(2)].

It may further be noted than an injunction cannot be granted to prevent the adoption of new Articles which constituted a breach of contract. But if the company acts on them it may be liable to damages/*[Shirtlaw Vs.Southern Foundries Ltd.1940 A.C. 701(760)]*

(viii) An alteration that has the effect of increasing the liability of a member to contribute to the company is not binding on a present member unless he has agreed there to in writing (Section 38.)

(ix) A reserve liability once created cannot be undone but may be cancelled on a reduction of capital (*Midland Railway Carriage Wagon Co.(1907) W.N.175*; (Section 99).

(x) Any irregular alternations which have been made and acted upon for many years are binding.

DISTINCTION BETWEEN MEMORANDUM AND ARTICLES

1. **Contents and scope :** Memorandum of Association is the charter of the company and defines the scope of its activities. Articles of Association of the company is a document which regulates the internal management of the company. These are rules made by the company for carrying out the objects of the company as set out in the Memorandum.

2. **Relationship between company, members and outsiders:** Memorandum of Association defines the relation of the company with the outside world, whereas Articles of Association deals with the rights of the members of the company *inter-se* and also establishes the relationship of the company with the members.

3. **Alteration :** Memorandum of Association cannot be altered except in the manner and to the extent provided by the Act, whereas the Articles being only the byelaws of the company, can be altered by a special resolution.

4. **Supremacy :** Memorandum is a supreme document of the company, whereas Articles are subordinate to the Memorandum. They cannot alter or control the Memorandum.
5. **Adoption :** Every company must have its own Memorandum. But a company limited by shares need not register its Articles. In such a case *Table 'A'* applies.
6. **Ratification of Ultra-vires Acts :** A company cannot depart from the provision contained in its Memorandum, and if it does, it would be ultra-vires the company. Anything done against the provisions of Articles, but which is intra-vires the Memorandum, can be ratified.

LEGAL EFFECT OF MEMORANDUM AND ARTICLES

The Memorandum and the Articles shall, when registered, bind the company and the members thereof to the same extent as if they respectively had been signed by the company and by each member and contained covenants by the company and each member to observe all the provisions of the Memorandum and the Articles [Section 36(1)].

The effect of these provisions is to constitute through the Memorandum and the Articles of Association of a company a contract between each member and the company. The effect and the implications of this section may be appreciated by considering, how far the memorandum and the articles bind. (i) The members to the company, (ii) the company to the members. (iii) the members inter-se and (iv) the company to the outsiders.

Members to the Company : As between the members and the company, each member of the company is bound to observe the various provisions of the Memorandum and Articles of association as if he had actually signed the same.

Company to the Members : The company is bound to the members by the various provisions contained in the Memorandum and the Articles of association in the same way as the members are bound to the company. The company can, therefore, exercise its rights as against any members only in pursuance of and in accordance with the Articles and the Memorandum. Any member is entitled to sue the company to prevent any breach of the Articles which would affect his right as a member of the company. Thus, where a right is conferred by the Articles on a shareholder to record his vote at a company meeting, the chairman of the meeting cannot deprive him on this right.

Members Inter-se : The Articles and the Memorandum do not constitute express agreement between the members of the company. Yet each member of the company is bound by the Memorandum and Articles on the basis of an implied contract to the other members. The articles regulate the rights of the members inter-se but such rights can be enforced only through the company.

Company to the Outsiders : Articles do not constitute any contract between the company and an outsider. This is because the outsider is not a party to the contract, and therefore, cannot sue on it. An outsider is not entitled to enforce the Articles against the company for any breach of right that is conferred on him by the Articles. Thus, a provision in the Articles to pay remuneration to the promoters constitutes no contract between them and the company on which they can sue the company for damages, if the remuneration is not paid to them. The term 'outsider' means a person who is not a member of the company. Even a member will be regarded as an outsider and he will not be in a position to enforce a right against the company if he enjoys the right in the capacity of a solicitor or a director and not in the capacity of a member.

CONSTRUCTIVE NOTICE OF MEMORANDUM AND ARTICLES OF ASSOCIATION

The Memorandum and Articles of association of every company are required to be registeed with the Registrar of Companies. *On registration they become public documents, and are open for public inspection on payment. Everyone dealing with the company, whether a shareholder or an outsider, is presumed to have read the two documents. He will be presumed to know the contents of these documents.* This deemed knowledge of the two documents and their contents is known as the constructive notice of Memorandum and Articles. Accordingly, where a person deals with a company in a manner which is inconsistent with the provisions of the Memorandum or Articles, he must take the consequences in respect of such dealing.

Moreover, *the parties dealing with the company must be taken not only to have read these documents but also to have understood according to their proper meaning.*

Doctrine of Indoor Management (Rule in *Turquand* Case)

The Doctrine of Indoor Management is an exception to the rule of constructive notice. A person dealing with a company is deemed to have knowledge of the Memorandum and the Articles of Association of the company. So, if he enters into a transaction with the company which is ultra-vires of the Memorandum or Articles, he cannot treat the transaction as binding on the company. On the other hand, if the transaction appears to be proper one, when compared with the Memorandum and Articles, it would be grossly unfair if the company could escape liability under it by showing that there was some irregularity in the conduct of the company's affairs leading upto the transaction, when the other party did not know of the irregularity and had no means of discovering it.

The doctrine of indoor management is eminently practical and is based on business convenience, for business could not be carried on smoothly if a person dealing with the company was compelled to call for evidence that all internal regulations have been duly observed. The doctrine is not only convenient, it is also just. The lot of creditors of a company is not a particular happy one; it would be unhappier still if the company could escape liability by denying the authority of the officials to act on its behalf. The Memorandum and the Articles of a company are *public documents* and accessible to all who are to consult them; but the details of the internal procedures are not registered and not accessible to all.

The doctrine is however, subject to the following ***exceptions*** :

1. **Knowledge of irregularity :** A person, who deals with the company and who has knowledge in its internal management in connection with the subject-matter of his dealings, cannot claim the benefit of the rule in Turquand's case.
2. **Negligence :** A person cannot claim the benefit of the rule in Turquand's case in circumstances under which he would have discovered the irregularity if he had made proper inquiries.
3. **Forgery :** The rule in Turquand's case will not apply where a document on which the person seeks to rely is a forgery.
4. **Acts outside the apparent autority :** The rule in Turquand's case does not apply where a person acting on behalf of the company exceeds any actual or ostensible authority given to him.
5. **No Knowledge of the contents of the Articles :** A person who has not actually read the Memorandum and Articles of a company and who was not at the time, he entered into the contract, aware of their contents, cannot seek to rely on statement contained therein. The doctrine of indoor management is based on the principle of estoppel, and therefore, it cannot be invoked in favour of a person who has not consulted the company's Memorandum and Articles of association.

REVIEW QUESTIONS

1. Describe the procedure relating to the incorporation of companies under the Companies Act 1956.
2. Enumerate the various documents to be filed with the Registrar in connection with it.
3. What is the effect of issuing a certificate of incorporation?
4. Can a court annual a certificate of incorporation which has been improperly issued?
5. Explain the term *promoter* and describe his legal status vis-a-vis the company.
6. Discuss the duties and liabilities of a promoter.
7. How can a promoter realise the remuneration for the services which he renders to the company?
8. Discuss the steps that are to be taken before a company can commence its business.
9. 'The Memorandum of Association is the charter of the company'. Comment.
10. Discuss the contents of the Memorandum of Association.
11. By what method and to what extent may a company alter its Memorandum of Association?
12. Explain fully the doctrine of ultra-vires in relation to companies?
13. What are the liabilities of a company and its agents for ultra-vires acts?
14. Define Articles of Association and give its contents.
15. Distinguish between Memorandum and Articles of Association.
16. What do you understand by the doctrine of indoor management? State the exceptions to it.
17. Explain the legal effects of Memorandum and Articles of Association of a company.
18. Write short notes on

    (a) Alteration of Object clause in a Memorandum (b) Constructive Notice (c) Doctrine cf Indoor Management.

❐ ❐ ❐

20 Chapter

PROSPECTUS

A public company may raise its capital by issuing shares or debentures. The public is invited to subscribe for its shares or debentures. The invitation containing the offer states the prospects of the company and the purposes for which the capital is required. The document inviting the public to purchase the shares or debentures of the company is called a *Prospectus*.

Definition of Prospectus : Section 2(36) defines a prospectus as

> "*any document described or issued as a prospectus and includes any notice, circular, advertisement or other document inviting deposits from the public or inviting offer from the public for the subscription or purchase of any shares in, or debentures of, a body corporate*".

A prospectus is usually a circular or newspaper advertisement published by the promoters after the formation of the company to induce the public to take up shares in the company. The invitation must be sent to the public if the document is to be a prospectus.

FORMALITIES IN ISSUING A PROSPECTUS

1. Every prospectus issued by or on behalf of a company must be *dated* and that date shall unless the contrary is proved, be regarded as the date of its publication.
2. A copy of the prospectus *signed by every director* or proposed director or by his agent must be delivered to the Registrar on or before the date of publication. The prospectus issued to the public should mention that a copy of the prospectus along with the specified documents have been filed with the Registrar.
3. SEBI's Consent or authorisation i.e. acknowledgement from *Securities Exchange Board of India.*
4. *Every form of application* for subscribing the shares or debentures of a company shall not be issued, unless *it is accompanied by a copy of the prospectus*.
5. A prospectus must *contain the necessary information* to enable the public to decide whether or not to subscribe for its shares or debentures. Every prospectus shall state the particulars specified in part I and II of Schedule II.

CONTENTS OF A PROSPECTUS

The Government has revised the format of prospectus given in Schedule II of the Companies Act, 1956 w.e.f. 1-11-99. This has been done to provide for greater disclosure of information regarding the company, its management, the project proposed to be undertaken by the company, the *financial performance* of the company for the last five years and *management perception of risk factors* so as to enable the investors to take an informed decision regarding investment in shares or debentures offered through public issue. The company will also be required to furnish particulars in regard to *other listed companies under the same management* within the meaning of Section 370(1B) of the Companies Act, which have made any capital issue during the last three years. The company will inform whether they have obtained *credit rating for* debenture/preference share issue. A declaration will also have to be furnished to the effect that all the relevant provisions of the Companies Act, 1956 and the *guideliines issued by the government have been complied with* and no statement made in prospectus is contrary to the provisions of Companies Act, 1956 and rules made thereafter.

The Government has also prescribed rules on similar lines regarding salient features of the prospectus for the purpose of Sub-section (3) of Section 56 (*abridged prospectus*) of the Companies Act, 1956 and has prescribed new Form 2A in this regard.

Keeping in view the requirement of Schedule II of the Companies Act, 1956 and the SEBI guidelines for disclosure and investor protection, the prospectus to be issued by companies should provide for the following matters:

1. General Information

(a) *Name and address of Registered office* of the company;

(b) *Details of letter of intent/industrial licence* obtained and disclaimer clause of SEBI about non-responsibility for financial soundness or correctness of statements;

(c) *Names of stock exchanges* where listed (if applicable) and where listing applications have been made for the issue;

(d) Provisions of Section 68A(1) of Companies Act, 1956 regarding fictitious applications.

(e) *Declaration regarding minimum subscription* and *refund of application money* in terms of Schedule II of Companies Act, 1956 and SEBI guidelines;

(f) *Dates of opening, closing and earliest closing of the issue*;

(g) *Names and addresses of lead managers, co-managers, trustees* (if applicable), legal advisors to the company, auditors, bankers to the issue, brokers to the issue and the secretary.

(h) Whether or not *credit rating* from any other recognised agency has been obtained for the proposed debenture issue should be mentioned. If rating is obtained, it should be indicated, preferably with implications of the rating symbol. In terms of SEBI guidelines, rating of a credit agency is mandatory for debentures with maturity period of more than 18 months.

(i) *Underwriting arrangements* made for the issue, names of underwriters, amount underwritten and declaration by Board of directors and the lead managers that in their opinion the resources of the underwriters are sufficient to discharge their underwriting obligations.

2. Capital Structure of the Company and Issue Details

(a) Authorised, issued, subscribed and paid-up capital of the company.

(b) Size of the issue with break up of reservation for *preferential allotment* to promoters, shareholders of group/associate companies, financial institutions, mutual funds. NRI, permanent employees, etc. The *lock-in-period* in respect of shares/debentures to be allotted to promoters and shareholders of group and associate companies/employees/financial institutions should be mentioned. The maximum number of shares/debentures that can be allotted to each employee and the number of permanent employees in the company should be mentioned.

(c) Paid-up capital after the present issue and after conversion of debentures, if applicable.

3. Details of the Issue

(a) Authority for the issue and details of resolutions passed for the issue.

(b) Terms of Payment : The amount payable on application, allotment and on calls should be stated.

Further, in case of premium issues, the appropriation of application, allotment and call money towards capital and premium should be indicated. For debenture issues with each debenture having several parts, the appropriation of application, allotment and call money towards each part of the debenture should be stated with further split between capital and premium.

(c) Rights of the instrument holders.

(d) Objects of the issue

(e) Tax benefits available to the company and its shareholders.

(f) Justificaiton for the premium on the issue, if any, disclosure of net asset value on the basis of the last audited results.

4. Details about the Company Management

(a) History, main objects and present business of the company.

(b) Subsidiaries of the company

(c) Promoters and their background.

(d) Names, addresses and occupation of manager, managing director and other directors including nominee directors, whole-time directors and their directorships in other companies.

5. Details about the Project

(a) Cost of the project and means of financing

(b) Location of the project

(c) Plant and machinery for the project, technology adopted and process of manufacture.

(d) Collaboration, performance guarantee or assistance in marketing by the collaborators.

(e) Infrastructure facilities for raw materials.

(f) Utilities like water, power etc.

(g) Schedule of implementation of the project, with separate details of land acquisition, civil work, installation of plant and machinery and the progress till the date of the prospectus.

(h) Expected date of trial production and commercial production.

(i) Nature of the products, consumer/industrial and end users and approach to marketing and proposed marketing set up.

(j) Export prospectus and export obligation

(k) Expected capacity utilisation during the first 3 years from the date of commencement of production for each of the major product groups.

(l) Expected year when the company would be able to earn cash profits and net profits and the expected cash profits and net profits for the next 3 years.

(m) High/Low equity prices of the shares/debentures of the company for each of the last 3 years and monthly high/low prives for the last 6 months (applicable to existing listed companies).

6. Other Information

(a) In respect of *any issue made by the company* and other listed companies under the same management, the following details:

(i) Name of the company;

(ii) Year of issue;

(iii) Type of issue;

(iv) Amount of issue;

(v) Date of completion of delivery of share/debenture certificates/letters of allotment;

(vi) Date of completion of the project, where the object of the issue was for financing a project;

(vii) Rate of dividend paid during the previous year(s).

(b) *Declaration about the issue of allotment letter, refunds* within a period of 10 weeks and liability to pay interest in case of delay in refund under Section 73 of Companies Act, 1956.

(c) *Outstanding litigation pertaining to* :

(i) matters likely to affect operation and finances of the company, including disputed tax liabilites;

(ii) criminal prosecution launched against the company and directors for alleged offences under the following statutes:

The Indian Stamp Act, 1899.

The Central Excises and Salt Act, 1944

The Imports and Exports (Control) Act, 1951

The Industries Development and Regulation Act, 1951

The Prevention of Food Adulteration Act, 1954

The Essential Commodities Act, 1955

The Companies Act, 1956

The Wealth-tax Act, 1957

The Income-tax Act,1 961

The Customs Act, 1962

The Monopolies and Restrictive Trade Practices Act, 1969

The Foreign Exchange Management Act, 1999.

(d) *Particulars of default in meeting statutory dues*, institutional dues, due to holders of instruments like debentures, fixed deposits and arrears of cumulative preference shares, pertaining to the company and/or other companies promoted by the same promoters, which are listed on stock exchanges.

(e) *Any material development after the date of the last Balance Sheet* and its impact on the performance and prospectus of the company.

(f) *Management's perception of risk factors* relating to the project like exchange rate fluctuations, difficulty in availability of raw materials, or on marketing of products, cost and time over-run etc.

(g) *Consent of directors*, auditors, solicitors, managers to issue, registrar to issue, bankers, brokers to the issue to the company, bankers to the issue and experts.

(h) *Changes in directors* and auditors in the last three years, if any, and reasons there of.

(i) *Procedure for making application* and availability of forms, prospectus and mode of payment.

(j) Procedure and time schedule for *allotment and issue of certificates.*

7. Financial Information

A report from the auditors on:

(a) *Profits and losses of the company* (where there is no subsidiary company) and the combined profits and losses of the subsidiaries or individual profits and losses of each subsidiary for each of the five financial years preceding the issue of prospectus (where there are subsidiaries);

(b) *Assets and liabilities of the company* (where there is no subsidiary company) at the last date to which the accounts are made up and the combined assets and liabilities of the subsidiaries or individually with the assets and liabilities of each subsidiary (where there are subsidiaries);

(c) *Rates of the dividends paid by the company* in respect of each class of shares for each of the five financial years preceding the issue of prospectus.

If no accounts have been made up in respect of any part of the period of five years ending three months before the date of issue of prospectus, the report should contain a statement of the fact. Further, a statement of accounts of the company should be made in respect of a part of the said period upto a date not earlier than six months of the date of issue of prospectus and the assets and liabilities position as at the end of that period. There should be a *certificate from the auditors that such accounts have been examined and found correct by them.*

The report should distinguish items of a non-recurring nature and indicate the nature of provisions or adjustments made or are yet to be made.

8. Statutory and Other Information

(a) Minimum subscription, as laid down in the SEBI guidelines.

(b) Expenses of the issue giving separately fees payable to advisers, registrars to the issue, managers to the issue and trustees for debenture holders.

(c) Underwriting commission and brokerage.

(d) Previous issue for cash or consideration otherwise than for cash.

(e) Details of public or right issue during the last five years.

   (i) Date of allotment and refund;

   (ii) Date of listing on the stock exchange;

   (iii) Amount of premium or discount, if applicable.

(f) Details of premium received in respect of any issue of shares made in the two years preceding the date of issue of prospectus or to be made stating the proposed date of the issue, the reasons for differentiation of premium for different categories, if applicable and the disposal of premia received or to be received.

(g) Commission or brokerage paid on previous issue.

(h) Debentures and redeemable preference shares and other instruments outstanding on the date of propsectus and the terms of their issue.

(i) Option to subscribe;

(j) Particulars of property purchased or proposed to be purchased from vendors to be paid for wholly or partly out of the proceeds of the issue and the interest of the promoters or directors in any transaction relating to the property within the last two years.

(k) Details of directors, proposed directors, whole-time directors, their remuneration, appoiment and remuneration of the managing director(s).

(l) Interests of directors, their borrowing powers and qualification shares.

(m) Any amount or benefit paid or given within the two preceding years or intended to be paid or given to any promoter or officers and consideration for the payment or giving of the benefit.

(n) The dates of, parties to, and general nature of

(i) every contract of appointment or remuneration of a managing director or manager;

(ii) every other material contract, not being a contract entered into in the ordinary course of business of the company or entered into more than two years prior to the date of prospectus; Reasonable time and place for inspection of the contract should be provided for.

(o) Full particulars of the nature and extent of interest of every director or promoter.

(i) in the promotion of the company; or

(ii) in any property acquired by the company within two years of the date of the prospectus or proposed to be acquired by it.

(p) Rights of members regarding voting, dividend, lien on shares, modification of rights and forfeiture of shares/debentures.

(q) Restriction on transfer and transmission of shares/debentures and on consolidation/splitting.

(r) Revaluation of assets, if any, during the last 5 years.

ADDITIONAL DISCLOSURES TO BE MADE IN PROSPECTUS

SEBI has directed that *lead managers* should ensure proper disclosures to the investors, keeping in mind their increased responsibilities consequent upon the notification of the Merchant Bankers Rules and regulations. The lead managers should, therefore, not only furnish adequate disclosures but also ensure due compliance with the *Guidelines for Disclosure and Investor Protection* issued by SEBI, both in letter and in spirit.

Lead Manager should ensure inclusion of the following information in the offer documents :

(i) *Disclaimer clause :* (To be printed in both in the offere document in Part I after Issue Details under the head "*General Inforamation*"). "It is to be distinctly understood that the vetting of the draft prospectus/letter of offer by SEBI should not in any way be deemed/construed as approval from SEBI for the proposed Issue. SEBI does not take any responsibility for the financial soundness of any scheme or project of for the statements made or opinions expressed in the offer document. SEBI merely ensures, on the basis of information furnished to it, that adeauate disclosures have been made in the offer document to enable the investors to take informed investemnt decisions".

(ii) *Reservation for Non-Resident (NRIs) Overseas Corporate Bodies (OCBs) in Public Issues :*

(a) "Name and addres of at least one source in India from where individual NRI applicants can obtain the application forms" - at the appropriate place.

(b) "NRI applicants may please note that only such applicants as are accompanied by payment in free foreign exchange will be considered for allotment under the reserved category. Such

NRIs who wish to make payment through Non-Resident Ordinary (NRO) accounts shall not use the forms meant for reserved category but must use the form meant for Resident Indians"- at the appropriate place.

(iii) *Stockinvest :* Manner of obtaining Stockinvest and disposal of applicants accompanied by Stockinvest as also a paragraph, on the following lines, at the appropriate place. "Registrars to the issue have been authorised by the Company (through Resolution of the Board passed on ...) to sign on behalf of the Company to realise the proceeds of the Stockinvest from the issuing bank or to affix non-allotment advice on the instrument or cancel the stockinvest of the non-allotees or partially successful allottees who have enclosed more than one stockinvest. Such cancelled stockinvest shall be sent back by the Registrars directly to the investors".

(iv) *Buy-back arrangement for purchase of non-convertible portion (khokha) of partly convetible debentures:*

(a) Full information relating to the terms of offer or purchase including the name(s) of the party offering to purchase the Khokhas, the discount at which such offer is made and the ultimate price that would work out to the investor including the discount portion.

(b) Where no such arrangement has been disclosed in the offer document, the Lead Manager may not allow such offer being made during the period he is associated with the issue.

(v) *Performance vis-a-vis promises relating to previous issues :* In case of issuer has come out with a public or rights issue within the previous 3 years of the proposed issue, details relating to the objects of the previous issues, schedule of implementation thereof and the status against the same should be disclosed under the head.

(vi) *Deployment of proceeds of the issue :* The offer document shall give details of avenues of investment in which the management proposes to deploy issue proceeds pending utilisation in the proposed project.

(vii) *Stock market data :* Along with high/low and average prices of shares of the Company, during preceding 3 years details relating to volumes of business transacted should also be stated for respective periods.

(viii) *Statement relating to allotment and refund :* Lead manager shall ensure that the offer document does not contain statements to the effect that "... or in the event of unforeseen circumstances within such further time as may be allowed by the Stock Exchange Extension, if any, granted by the Stock Exchange would be without prejudice to the Company's liablity to pay interest under Section 73 of the Companies Act, 1956".

The SEBI has also in its recent guidelines for disclosure and investor protection stated that every prospectus submitted to it shall, in addition to the requirements of Scheduled II of the Companies Act, contain/specify the followings information. Some of them to mention are:

An index of the contents of the prospectus, details of actual project expenditure, and its financing, details of bridge-loan, bifurcated details of turnover (separately) into products manufactured traded, not normally traded in, statement of assets and liabilities after providing for revaluation, a statement by directors regarding last financial statements affecting materially the profitability of the company if any, details of shareholding by the promoter group, stock market data, management perception of internal and external risk factors, discussion of the financial condition and results of the operations, details regarding major shareholders etc.

Legal significance : It was stated in earlier pages of this book that a company cannot normally vary at any time the terms of a contract in the prospectus and that it can do so only with the approval and authority obtained from its general meeting [Section 61]. Suppose, there is a condition in the prospectus, which requires or binds an applicant for shares or debentures to waive compliance with any of the requirements relating to statutory matters and reports. In such a case it will be void. Similarly, if there is a condition which has the effect of affecting him with the notice of any contract, document or a matter not specifically referred to in the prospectus, then such a condition shall be void [Section 56(2)].

Suppose, the requirement of Section 56 have not been complied with but the application for shares has been accepted by the company. Can the applicant ask for the rescission of the contract or rectification of the register? The answer is "no". But he can sue the person responsible for the issue of the prospectus for any damages he may have suffered *[South of England Natural Gas and Petroleum Co. (1911)].*

STATEMENT IN LIEU OF PROSPECTUS (Section 70)

In some cases, companies are able to raise the original capital without inviting the public to subscribe. In such cases, the company need not issue a prospectus. Where a public company, which has a share capital does not issue a prospectus on its formation, it cannot allot any shares without first filing with the Registrar a document called '*Statement in lieu of Prospectus*'. This document must be in the form set out in Schedule III and must contain practically the same information as is required in the prospectus.

The document shall be delivered to the Registrar at least *three days before the first allotment of shares.* The statement must be *signed by every director* or proposed director or his agent. If a company fails to deliver a statement in lieu of prospectus, it cannot allot any shares or debentures. An allotment, if made, is *voidable if the allottee notifies the company within 2 months after the statutory meeting* or in case where there is no such meeting within two months after allotment.

If a company fails to fulfill the above conditions, the company and every director who has been knowingly a party to this contravention shall be *liable for fine upto ₹ 1,000.* If a statement in lieu of prospectus delivered to the Registrar contains an untrue i.e., a misleading statement, every person who authorised the delivery of the statement shall be *liable to imprisonment for two years and fine of ₹ 5,000.*

OFFER FOR SALE AND DEEMED PROSPECTUS (Section 64)

The provisions relating to a prospectus (as regards registration, contents and full disclosure) are very stringent and the duty of preparing and filing a prospectus in accordance with the law is extremely onerous. These requirements used to be evaded by companies in the past by allotting the whole of an issue of shares or debentures to an *Issuing House* at a certain price. The Issuing House then published an advertisement in the nature of an offer for sale inviting public to buy the shares or debentures from it at a higher price. *Sec. 64 now specifically provides that a document by which an 'offer for sale' is made to the public is within the definition of the prospectus.*

When applications are received by the Issuing House, it renounces its interest in the shares or debentures to the extent of the number of shares or debentures allotted in favour of the applicant. When this is done, the applicant becomes an allottee of the company. By this method of allotment, stamp duty is saved.

SHELF PROSPECTUS

Any public financial institution, public sector bank or scheduled bank whose main object is financing shall file as *shelf prospectus.* A company filing a shelf prospectus with the Registrar shall not be required to file prospectus afresh at every stage of offer of securities by it within a period of validity of such shelf prospectus. A company filing a shelf prospectus shall be required to file an *information memorandum* on all material facts relating to new charges created, changes in the financial position as have occurred between the first offer of securities, within such time as may be prescribed by the Central Government, prior to making of a second or subsequent offer of securities under the shelf prospectus. An information memorandum shall be issued to the public along with shelf prospectus field at the stage of the first offer of securities and such prospectus shall be valid for a period of one year from the date of opening of the first issue of securities under that prospectus: Provided that where an update of information memorandum is filed every time an offer of securities is made, such memorandum together with the shelf prospectus shall constitute the prospectus.

Explanation - For the purpose of this section-- "*financing*" means making loans to or subscribing in the capital of, a private industrial enterprise engaged in infrastructure financing or, such other company as the Central government may notify in this behalf; "*Shelf prospectus*" means a prospectus issued by any financial institution or bank for one or more issues of the securities or class of securities specified in that prospectus.

INFORMATION MEMORANDUM (Section 60B)

A public company making an issue of securities may circulate information memorandum to the public prior to filing of a prospectus. A company inviting subscription by an information memorandum shall be bound to file a prospectus prior to the opening of the subscription lists and the offer as a *red-herring prospectus*, at least three days before the opening of the offer. The information memorandum and red-herring prospectus shall carry same obligations as are applicable in the case of a prospectus. Any variation between the information memorandum and the red-herring prospectus shall be highlighted as variations by the issuing company.

Explanation - For the purposes of sub-sections (2), (3) and (4) "*red -herring prospectus*" means a prospectus which does into have complete particulars on the price of the securities offered and the quantum of securities offered.

Every variation as made and highlighted in accordance with sub-section above shall be individually intimated to the persons invited to subscribe to the issue of securities. In the event of the issuing company or the underwriters to the issue have invited or received advance subscription by way of cash or post-dated cheques or stock-invest, the company or such underwriters or bankers to the issue shall not encash such subscription moneys or post-dated cheques or stock invest before the date of opening of the issue, without having individually intimated the prospective subscribers of the variation and without having offered an opportunity to such prospective subscribers to withdraw their application and cancel their post-dated cheques or stock -invest or return of subscription paid. The applicant or proposed subscriber shall exercise his right to withdraw from the application on any intimation of variation within seven days from the date of such intimation and shall indicate such withdrawal in writing to the company and the underwriters. Any application for subscription which is acted upon by the company or underwriters or bankers to the issue without having given enough information of any variations. or the particulars of withdrawing of offer or opportunity for cancelling the post-dated cheques or stock invest or stop payments for such payments shall be void and the applicants shall be entitled to receive a refund or return of its post-dated cheques or stock invest or stop payments for such payments shall be void and the application had never been made and the applicants are entitled to receive back their original application and *interest at the rate of fifteen percent* for the date of encashment till payment of realisation. Upon the closing of the offer of securities, a final prospectus stating there in the total capital raised, where by way of debt or share capital and the closing price of the securities and any other details as were not complete in the red-herring prospectus shall be filed in a case of a listed public company with the Securities and Exchange Board and Registrar, and in any other cases with Registrar only.

Abridged Form of Prospectus

Section 56(3), as amended by the Amendment Act of 1988, states that no application form can be issed for shares or debentures of a company unless it is accompanied by an abridged prospectus which complies with the requirements of the Act. However full prospectus is to be furnished on a request being made by any person before the closing of the subscription list.

The Central Government has prescribed on 13-10-91 the salient features of 'abridged prospectus. For the purpose. Rule 4cc has been inserted in the *Companies (Central Government's) General Rules and Forms, 1956*. As per the rule the 4cc, the the sailent features required to be included in the 'abridged prospectus' shall be in "From 2A",. The abridged prospectus contains information very much similar to a 'Prospectus' in a concise and compact manner so that cost of public issue of capital my be reduced.

The abridged prospectus (in Form 2A) and the share application form should bear the same printed number. The investor may detach the share application form along the perforated line after he has had an opportunity to study the contents of the abridged prospectus, before submitting the same to the company or its designated bankers. The same procedure may be also followed while making available copies of the prospectus under Section 56 of the Act.

LIABILITY FOR MIS-STATEMENTS OR OMISSION IN A PROSPECTUS

Where an untrue or fraudulent statement occurs in a prospectus there may be-(a) civil liability, and (b) criminal liability. The liability for fradulent or misstatement in a Statement in lieu of Prospectus is the same as in the case of prospectus.

Civil Liability

A person who has been induced to subscribe for shares in a company on the strength of misstatement or omission in the prospectus may have a remedy either against the company or against the promoters or directors or experts.

Remedies against the Company

A person who has been induced to subscribe for shares may (a) *rescind the contract to take the shares*; (b) *claim damages*.

(a) ***Rescission of contract :*** Where a person has purchased the shares of a company on the faith of a prospectus which contained an untrue or misleading, but not necessarily fraudulent statement, he can seek rescission of the contract i.e., *return the shares allotted to him get back his purchase money with interest and get his name removed from the register of members*. This remedy is available only to those persons who subscribed for any shares on the faith of the prospectus.

(b) ***Damages :*** Any person induced by fraud to take up shares is entitled to sue the company for damages provided he has rescinded his contract in time. He cannot both retain the shares and get damages against the company. The company is liable in damages where the misrepresentation is an innocent one, unless it proves that it had reasonable grounds to believe.

Remedies against the Directors, Promoters and Experts

Any person who has purchased shares or debentures on the faith of the prospectus containing the untrue statement may sue (a) every director; (b) every person whose name appeared in the prospectus as a proposed director; (c) every promoter; and (d) every person who authorised the issue of the prospectus; The aggrieved person may claim (1) compensation under Section 62; (2) damages for non-compliance with the requirements of Section 56; (3) damages under the general law.

Defences available to a Director

A director may escape liability if he proves:

(i) that the prospectus was *issued without his knowledge or consent* and that on becoming aware of its issue, he gave reasonable public notice to that effect;

(ii) that after the issue of prospectus and before allotment, he on becoming aware of the untrue statement in it, *withdrew his consent and gave reasonable public notice of the withdrawal* and the reasons for it;

(iii) that he had *reasonable grounds to believe* and did believe upto the time of allotment of shares or debentures *that the statement was true*;

(iv) that *he made the statement upon the authority of an expert whom he had reasonable ground* to believe;

(v) that the statement was a correct and true copy of an official document.

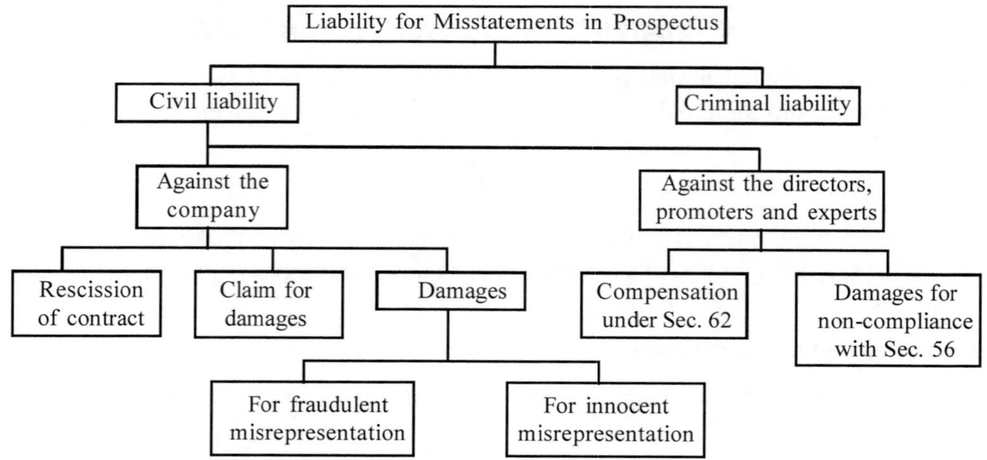

Criminal Liability of Directors

Every person who authorised the issue of a prospectus containing an untrue statement shall be *punishable with imprisonment which may extend to two years or with fine which may extend to ₹5,000 or with both.* The accused person, however, may not be liable if he proves; (a) that the statement was immaterial, or (b) he had reasonable ground to believe and did believe upto the time of the issue of the prospectus that the statement was true. (Section 63). The punishment for issuing an application for shares or debentures which is not accompanied by a prospectus is a fine upto ₹ 5,000.

MINIMUM SUBSCRIPTION (Section 69)

Where the public company for the first time invites the public to subscribe for its shares, it cannot allot those shares until the minimum amount stated in the prospectus has been subscribed. This amount stated in the prospectus is known as the '*minimum subscription*'.

The minimum subscription is not a sum fixed by the Articles or calculated as a percentage of the shares issued under the prospectus. It is the minimum amount stated in the prospectus which in the opinion of the directors must be raised in order to provide for :

(a) the purchase price of any property purchased or to be purchased;

(b) the preliminary expenses and any underwriting commission payable by the company;

(c) repayment of money borrowed by the company in respect of any of the foregoing matters;

(d) working capital; and

(e) any other expenditure stating the nature and purpose thereof and the estimated amount in each case.

The object of the 'minimum subscription' provision is to prevent the company getting underway until it has raised the capital needed to carryout the objects in which it has invited the public to participate. This also affords protection to the creditors by ensuring that a limited company is not able to incur commitments if it is grossly under-capitalised.

All moneys received from applicant shall be deposited and keep deposited in a scheduled bank until minimum subscription has been received by the company. An allotment made in contravention of the restriction of the minimum subscription is not void but only voidable and the applicant may avoid the allotment within the time specified in Section 71(1).

Where such minimum subscription is not received by the company *within 120 days from the first issue of the prospectus*, all moneys received from applicants shall be returned within 130 days of the issue of the prospectus. On failure to pay, the directors shall be jointly and severally liable to *repay that money with interest at the rate of 12 per cent per annum*. [Sec. 69(5)].

As per the guideline the promoters should make their subscription in advance before the public issue opens and give a certificate to this effect to the regional stock exchange concerned. *The SEBI's guidelines* provides in this regard that companies will undertake in the prospectus, letters of offer, advertisement or publicity literature etc., to refund the amount at the end of 90 days from the date from the closure of the issue, if not subscribed up to 90% and to pay interest @ 15% p.a. if refunds are delayed by more than 10 days after this period.

The minimum subscription stated in the prospectus must be reckoned exclusively of any amount payable otherwise than in cash. *The amount payable on application on each share must not be less than five per cent of the nominal amount of the shares. All moneys received from applicants for shares are required to be deposited in a scheduled bank until the certificate to commence business is obtained.*

Underwriting Commission [Section 76]

The Board of Directors enters into underwriting contracts with underwriters. When a company offers its shares to the public, it often wants that the whole issue should be taken up. Consequently a company is usually willing to pay a small commission on all the shares offered to the public to any one who undertakes to take up all the shares, which the public do not take. This is known as '*underwriting*'. It consists of an undertaking by some person or persons that if the public fails to take up the issue, he or they will do so. In return for this undertaking, the company agrees to pay the underwriters a commission on all shares, whether taken by the public or by the underwriters. It is, thus, *in the nature of an insurance against the possibility of inadequate subscription.*

Sec. 76 prescribes certain conditions subject to which underwriting may be paid. A company may pay a commission (called an *underwriting commission*) to any person in consideration of his subscribing or agreeing to subscribe for shares, or procuring or agreeing to procure subscription for any shares in the company. Underwriting commission may be paid only if the following conditions are satisfied.

1. The payment of the commission must be *authorised by the Articles of association* The authority in Memorandum is not sufficient. [*Republic of Bolivia Exploration Syndicate Ltd. (1914)*].
2. The Commission can be paid only on shares issued to the public.
3. The payment of commission must be strictly by way of 'Commission' and not merely a device to issue shares at a discount.
4. The rate of commission must *not exceed 5% of the price of the shares and 2½% of the price of the debentures* at which they are issued or the rate authorised by the Articles whichever is less.
5. The amount paid or agreed to be paid must be-(a) disclosed in the prospectus if shares are offered to the public, or (b) in other cases, disclosed in the statement in lieu of prospectus delivered to the Registrar.
6. The number of shares or debentures which persons have agreed for a commission to subscribe for absolutely or conditionally is disclosed in the prospectus or statement in lieu of prospectus.
7. A copy of the contract for the payment of the commission must be delivered to the Registrar along with the prospectus or statement in lieu of the prospectus.

REVIEW QUESTIONS

1. Explain the meaning and importance of prospectus.
2. What constitutes the public issue of the prospectus?
3. Explain the legal provisions relating to the issue and registration of a prospectus?
4. Discuss the civil and criminal liabilities of directors for misstatement in a prospectus.
5. What are the remedies open to an allottee of shares who had applied for them on the faith of a false and misleading prospectus and what are the defences available to the directors of the company who have issued such a prospectus?
6. What do you understand by minimum subscription?
7. Who is an underwriter? What are his functions?
8. Write short notes on : (a) Deemed Prospectus; (b) Shelf Prospectus; (c) Information Memorandum; (d) Abridged Prospectus.

❐ ❐ ❐

21 Chapter

DIRECTORS

According to Section 2(13) of the Companies Act 1956, "*director*" includes any person occupying the position of director by whatever name called. Only an individual can be appointed a director [Section 253].

Number of Directors : Every public company must have atleast 3 directors and every private company must have atleast 2 directors. Subject to the minimum number of directors a company should have, the Articles of a company may prescribe the maximum and the minimum number of directors for its Board of directors. A company in a general meeting may by ordinary resolution increase or reduce the number of its directors within the limits fixed in that behalf by its Articles (Section 258). A public company or a private company which is a subsidiary of a public company cannot increase the number of directors beyond the permissible maximum under its Articles without the approval of the Central Government. However, no approval of the Central Government is required if such permissible maximum is twelve or less than twelve, and the increase in the number of its directors does not exceed twelve. (Section 259).

APPOINTMENT OF DIRECTORS

Directors may be appointed in the following ways:

1. By the Articles as regards first directors (Section 254).
2. By the company in general meeting (Sections 255 to 263, 264).
3. By the directors (Sections 260, 262, 313).
4. By third parties eg., lending institutions for nominee directors. (Section 255).
5. By the principle of proportional representation (Section 265).
6. By the Central Government (Section 408).

LEGAL POSITION OF DIRECTORS

The directors are not servants of the company or members of its staff. They cannot be treated as the employees of the company. For certain matters under the Companies Act, the *directors are treated as Officers of the Company*. As such, they are liable to certain penalties if the provisions of the Act are not strictly complied with.

Directors are Trustees of (a) the company's money and property; and (b) the powers entrusted to them. They are trustees of a the company's money and property in the sense that they must to them. They are trustees of a the company's money and property in the sense that they must account for all the company's money over which they exercise control and must refund to the company any of its money which they have improperly paid away. Directors are trustees of their powers and they must exercise their powers honestly and in good faith and in the interest of the company.

Company being an artificial person, is governed by the human agency. *Directors control the affairs of the company as its Agents*. Acts of the directors for and on behalf of the company exclude directors from personal liability, provided they are within the scope of their authority.

The liabilities of directors follow mostly from their duties, they are also accountable to the company for damage suffered as a result of negligence in performance of their duties. They are also liable to the company when they commit a breach of trust reposed in them by the shareholders, and misuse or avail of misappropriate profits or assets of the company. If the directors fail in the performance of their statutory functions of accounts, etc., they render themselves liable to prosecution and penalties prescribed by the Statue.

The directors of a company are usually protected by an Indemnity Clause contained in the Articles of Association in order to provide recompensation and protection for bonafide acts of the directors in discharge of their functions as directors. Such indemnity, however, is not available where director has not acted in good faith and where he is charged with gross negligence, bad faith and disregard of his duties in the conduct of his office as a director.

Penalties imposable on directors for the contravention or defaults are of two types : (a) those imposable on them directly as "*directors*" and (b) those imposable on them directly as "*officers who are in default*". Under each category, there is a long list of offences dealt with in different sections of the Companies Act with specific penalties prescribed thereunder.

Share Qualification : The Act does not make it obligatory on any director to hold shares in the company. The articles of association generally requires that the qualification of a director shall be the holding of a specified number of shares known as *qualification shares*. The nominal value of these shares must not exceed ₹ 5,000 or one share where it exceeds ₹ 5,000.

DISQUALIFICATION OF DIRECTORS

A Person who can not be appointed as a Director

The circumstances in which a person can not be appointed as a director of a company are enumerated in Section 274. According to this section, a person cannot be appointed as a director of a company, if

(i) he has been found to be of *unsound mind* by a competent court and the finding is in force;

(ii) he is an *undischarged insolvent*;

(iii) he has *applied to be adjudicated as an insolvent* and his application is pending

(iv) he has been *convicted of an offence involving moral turpitude* and sentenced to imprisonment for not less than 6 months and a period of 5 years had not elapsed since the expiry of his sentence;

(v) he has *not paid any call in respect of shares of the company held by him* for a period of six months from the last day fixed for the payment.

(vi) he has been *disqualified by an order of the Court under* Section 203, of an offence in relation to promotion, formation or management of the company or offence in relation to promotion, formation or management of the company or fraud or misfeasance in relation to the company.

(vii) It may be noted that section 274 (1) (g) now provides that a person who is a director of a public company which has *defaulted in filing its annual accounts and returns* for a continuous period of 3 years from 1.4.1999 or has failed to *repay its deposits or interest on due date or redeem its debentures on due date* or pay dividend and such failure continues for one year or more, is disqualified from appointment as director of any company. Such disqualification will continue for a period of 5 years from such default.

Restriction or Ceiling on Number of Directorships

No person can be a director in *more than twenty companies*. The following companies shall be excluded in calculating the number of companies of which a person may be a director;

(a) a *private company* which is neither a subsidiary nor a holding company of a public company;

(b) an *unlimited company*;

(c) an *association not carrying on business for profit* or which profits the payment of a dividend;

(d) a company in which such person is only an *alternate director*.

Position after 2000: At present a person can be a director of 20 companies. This number has *now been reduced to 15 companies*. If a person is director of more than 15 companies, he has to regularise the position within 2 months of commencement of the Amendment Act of 2000 (i.e. within 2 months from 14.12.2000)

In calculating the above number, directorship in a private company, which is not a subsidiary or holding company of a public company, should be excluded. If a person in an alternate director of a company, the same should not be counted for this purpose. (Refer Section 287 which has not been amended.)

Vacation of Office by Directors (Section 283)

The office of a director shall become vancant if

(a) he fails to obtain or *ceases to hold the share qualification* required of him by the articles of the company;

(b) he is found to be of *unsound mind* by a competent court;

(c) he *applies to be adjudicated an insolvent*;

(d) he is *adjudged an insolvent*;

(e) he is *convicted by a Court of an offence involving moral turpitude* and sentenced to imprisonment for not less than 6 months;

(f) he *fails to pay any calls on the shares* held by him within six months from the date fixed for payment; unless the Central Government has by notification in the Official Gazette removed his disqualification.

(g) he *absents himself from three consecutive meetings of the Board* of directors or from all the meetings of Board for a continuous period of 3 months whichever is longer without obtaining leave of absence from the Board.

Minimum Number of Directors in the Board of Directors of a Company

Under this Act every public company should have *atleast 3 directors*. It is now provided that a public company with (a) paid-up capital of ₹ 5 crores or more and (b) 1000 or more small share holders shall have atleast shall have atleast *one director elected by small shareholders* to be elected in the prescribed manner. For this purpose small shareholders means a shareholder holding shares of the nominal value of ₹ 20,000 or less in the company.

Removal of Directors : A director of a company can be removed by (a) Shareholders, (b) Central Government; or (c) the court.

Remuneration of Directors : The remuneration payable to directors is usually determined by the Articles of Association or a resolution passed by the company in its general meeting. However, this will be subject to the provisions of Sections 198 and 309 of the Act. According to Section 198, total managerial remuneration payable to directors, managing director(s), or manager and whole-time director, in respect of any financial year should not exceed 11% of the net profits of the company for the financial year. In years of inadequate profits, a sum not exceeding ₹ 50,000 per annum may be paid to all managerial personnel with the prior approval of the Central Government.

REMUNERATION OF MANAGERIAL PERSONNEL

Section 198 provides that the total managerial remuneration payable by a public company or a private company which to its directors or manager in respect of any financial year must not exceed. 11 percent of the net profit of that company for that financial year, in computing the above ceiling of 11 percent computed in the manner laid down in sections 349 and 359. The fees payable to directors for attending Board meetings is not included.

What is included in Managerial Remuneration?

Explanation to s.198 describes the term *remuneration*. According to it, for the purposes of Sections 309, 310, 311, 381 and 387, 'remuneration' includes the following: (a) any expenditure incurred by the company in providing *rent-free accommodation*, or any other benefit or amenity in respect of accomodation free of charge, to any of its directors or manager; (b) any expenditure incurred by the company in providing any other benefit or *amenity free of charge or at a concessional rate* to any of the persons aforesaid; (c) any *expenditure incurred by the company in respect of any obligation or service*, which, but for such expenditure by the company, would have been incurred by any of the persons aforesaid; and (d) any expenditure incurred by the company to effect *any insurance on the life of, or to provide any pension, annuity or gratuity* for, any of the persons aforesaid or his spouse or child.

Section 309 contemplates three kinds of directors, i.e., (i) Managing Director; (ii) Whole-time director; (iii) Director pure and simple. Further, Section 309 provides that subject to the general provisions of section 198, dealing with the total managerial remuneration, the remuneration be determined by the Articles, or by a resolution or, if the articles or require, by a special resolution, passed by the company in general meeting. Any remuneration paid for services in any other capacity shall not be included if: (a) the services rendered are of a professional nature; and (b) in the opinion of the Central Government, the director possesses the requisite qualifications for the practice of the profession.

A director who is neither in the whole-time employment of the company nor a managing director may be paid remuneration. (a) by way of a monthly, quarterly or annual payment with the approval of the Central Government; or (b) by way of commission, if the company by special resolution authorises such payment; or (c) by both.

However, in either of the above cases, the remuneration paid to such director, or where there is more than one such director, shall not exceed: (i) one per cent of the net profit of the company, if the company has managing or wholetime director or manager; (ii) three per cent of the net profits of the company in any other case. The company in general meeting may, however, with the approval of the Central Government, authorise the payment of a commission at a rate higher than one per cent, or as the case many be, three per cent of its net profits.

Each director is entitled to receive a *sitting fee* for each meeting of the Board or a committee thereof, provided the same is authorised by the Articles.

A whole-time director or a managing director may be paid remuneration either by way of a monthly payment or at a specified percentage of the net profits of the company or partly by one way and partly by the other; provided that except with the approval of the Central Government such remuneration shall not exceed 5 per cent of the net profits for one such director and if there is more than one such director, 10 per cent for all of them together. Furthermore, a managing or whole-time director who is in receipt of any commission from the company cannot receive any remuneration from any subsidiary of the company.

If any director draws or receives, directly or indirectly, by way of remuneration any sum in excess of the limits stated above, without the sanction of the Central Government, where it is required, he shall have to refund such sums to the company and until the refund is made the money will be held by him in trust for the company. The company cannot waive the recovery of any sum refundable to it, unless permitted by the Central Government.

The provisions of Section 309 will not apply to a private company unless it is a subsidiary of a public company.

Increase in Remuneration

Section 310 provides that every increase in the remuneration of any director including a managing or whole-time director granted or provided by any amendment in his term of appointment which has the effect of increasing, whether directly or indirectly, the amount payable to him would not be operative unless the same has been approved by the Central Government. *But no approval oj the Central Government would be required if the increase in remuneration made is a accordance with the conditions specified in Schedule XIII.* Also no approval of the Central Government is necessary, if the increase in the remuneration is only by way of fee for each meeting of the Board or a committee of the Board attended by any such director and the amount of the fee after such increase does not exceed such sum as may be prescribed. *The Central Government has laid down differential scale of sitting fee according to the paid-up capital of the companies.*

As regards remuneration payable to a Manager, section 387 provides that he may receive remuneration either by way of a monthly payment or by way of a specified percentage of the 'net profits' of the company, or partly by one way and partly by the other. Such remuneration, however, must not exceed in the aggregate 5 per cent of the net profits except with the approval of the Central Government.

Managerial Remuneration vis-a-vis Schedule XIII

A public company, is entitled to appoint its managerial personnel and fix their remuneration so long as the same is in accordance with the conditions laid down in Schedule XIII without seeking the prior approval of the Central Government. Schedule XIII, provides as follows:

Remuneration Payable by Companies having Profits

Subject to the provisions of Section 198 and Section 309, a company having profits in a financial year may pay any remuneration, by way of salary, dearness allowance, perquisites, commission and other allowances, which shall not exceed 5 per cent of its net profits for one such managerial person and if there are more than one such managerial persons, 10 per cent for all of them together.

Remuneration Payable by Companies having No Profits or Inadequate Profits

Where in any financial year during the currency of tenure of the managerial person, a company has no profits or its profits are inadequate, it may pay remuneration to a managerial person, by way of salary, dearness allowance, perquisites and other allowance, not exceeding ceiling limit of Rs 24,00,000 per annum or Rs 2,00,000 per month calculated. on the following scale:

Where the effective capital of the company is	*Monthly remuneration payable shall not exceed*
(i) Less than ₹ 1 crore	₹75,000
(ii) ₹ 1 crore or more but less than ₹ 5 crores	₹ 1,00,000
(iii) ₹ 5 crores or more but less than ₹ 25 crores	₹ 1,25,000
(iv) ₹ 25 crores or more but less than ₹ 50 crores	₹ 1,50,000
(v) ₹ 50 crores or more but less than ₹ 100 crores	₹ 1,75,000
(vi) ₹ 100 crores or more	₹2,00,000

In addition to the above, certain perquisites like contribution to provident fund, gratuity, leave encashment may be paid. Non-resident Indians may also be paid children education allowance, holiday passage for children studying outside India or family staying abroad, leave travel concession. These additional benefits shall be subject to the limits laid down in Schedule XIII.

*The expression '**effective capital**' shall mean* the aggregate of the paid-up share capital (excluding share application money or advances against shares); amount, if any, for the time being standing to the credit of share premium account, reserves and surplus (excluding revaluation reserve); long term loans and deposits repayable after one year (excluding working capital loans,overdrafts, interest due onloans unless funded, bank guarantee, etc. and other short term arrangements) as reduced by the aggregate of any investments (except in case of investments by an investment company whose principal business is acquisition of shares, stock, debentures or other securities), accumulated losses and preliminary expenses not written off.

Sitting Fee (Section 310). The sitting fee payable to a director for each meeting of the Board of Directors or a committee thereof shall not exceed ceiling prescribed by the Central Government (presently, ₹ 5,000). Any increase in the sitting fee payable to a director shall not require the prior approval of the Central Government if it falls within the prescribed limits.

Managerial Remuneration again Raised

The Department of Corporate Affairs (DCA) has issued a notification enhancing the managerial remuneration in the corporate sector from the existing ₹ 75,000 to ₹ 1.50 lakhs per month for companies with effective capital of less than ₹ 1 crore and a maximum of ₹ 4 lakhs for companies with effective capital of ₹ 100 crores or more from the existing ₹ 2 lakhs per month.

According to an official release, the managerial remuneration, which has been doubled, will be ₹ 2 lakhs for companies, whose effective capital is over ₹ 1 crore but less than ₹ 5 crores; between ₹ 5 crores and ₹ 25 crores, the maximum remuneration per month will be ₹ 3 lakhs and between ₹ 25 crores and ₹ 50 crores, it will be ₹ 3.50 lakhs per month. The last revision was made in March 2000.

The enhanced managerial remuneration willbe subject to approval by a resolution of the Remuneration Committee of a company provided the company has not defaulted to repayment of any of its debts including public deposits or debentures or interest payable thereon for a continuous period of 30 days in the preceding financial year before the date of appointement of such managerial person. Besides, the company should mention disclosures regarding managerial remuneration in the board of directors' report under the heading "*Corporate Governance*" attached to the annual report.

DIRECTORS RESPONSIBILITY STATEMENT

A new sub-section (2AA) has now been inserted to provide that the Report of Board of Directors shall also include a Directors' Responsibility Statement as under:

(i) That the applicable accounting standards have been followed in preparing the annual acccunts. If there is material departure, explanation for the same should be given

(ii) That the directors have selected such accounting policies and applied the consistently and made judgements and estimates that are reasonable and prudent so as to give to true and fair view of the state of affairs of the company while preparing the annual accounts.

(iii) That the Directors have taken proper and sufficient care (a) for maintenance of adequate accounting records as required by the Act. (b) for safeguarding the assets of the company and (c) for preventing and detecting fraud and other irregulations.

(iv) That the Directors have prepared the annual accounts on a going concern basis.

MEETINGS OF BOARD

The directors of a company exercise most of their powers in a joint meeting called the *Meetings of the Board*. In the case of every company, a meeting of the Board of directors must be held at least *once in every three months and atleast four such meetings shall be held in every year*. However, the Central Government is empowered to relax the rule with regard to any class of companies (Section 285).

Notice of every meeting of the Board of directors must be given in writing to every director for the time being in India and at the usual address in India to every other director. The *quorum for a meeting* of the Boad shall be one-third of its total strength (any fraction contained in that one-third being rounded off as one) or *two directors* whichever is higher. When the meeting of the Board could not be held for want of quorum, then unless otherwise provided by the Articles, the meeting shall automatically stand adjourned till the same day in the next week. (Section 288).

POWERS OF BOARD

As the company is an artificial person, it acts through its directors. The directors enjoy such powers as are given to them by the Act, Memorandum or Articles, Sections 291 to 293-A contain the powers of the Board and the restrictions thereon. The powers of directors are discussed under the following heads :

General Powers : Section 291 empowers the Board to exercise all such powers and do all such acts and things, as the company is authorised to exercise and do. But the Board cannot do any act which is to be done by the company in general meeting. In exercising any power, the Board will be subject to the provisions of this or any other Act, the Memorandum or the Articles.

Powers to be exercised by Board only at Meeting : Under Section 292, the following powers can be exercised by the Board, only by resolutions passed at the Board meeting : (i) the power to make calls; (ii) the power to issue debentures; (iii) the power to borrow money otherwise than on debentures; (iv) the power to invest the funds of the company; (v) the power to make loans. Powers specified in points (iii), (iv) and (v) the above can be delegated by the Board, at a meeting by means of a resolution to a committee of directors, to the managing director, to the manager or to other principal officer of the company.

Duties of Directors

1. In discharging the duties of his position, a director must *exercise some degree of skill and diligence*.
2. A director must *act honestly* in the performance of his duties.
3. A director is not bound to give continuous *attention to the affairs of his company*.

4. Though all books of account and other *books and papers of the company are open to inspection by the director*, he is not bound to examine individual entries in the books.

5. The directors must *perform their duties personally*. The maxim"delegatus non-potest delegate" (a delegate cannot delegate further) applies to them like all agents. Hence, unless permitted by the Articles specifically, *the directors must not delegate any of their powers to some other person.*

6. A director or his relative or any firm in which he or his relative has any interest or any private company of which he is a member or a director shall not *enter into any contract with the company for the sale, purchase or supply of goods, materials or services* or for underwriting the subscription of any shares or debentures.

LIABILITIES OF DIRECTORS

The liabilities of directors may be discussed under three heads; (a) Liability to outsiders, (b) Liability to company and (c) Criminal liability.

A. **Liability to outsiders :** The directors are not personally liable to outsiders if they act within the scope of powers vested in them. *The directors are personally liable to third parties of contract in the following cases :*

(a) They contract with outsiders in their *personal capacity.*

(b) They contract as agents of an *undisclosed principal.*

(c) They enter into a contract on *behalf of a prospective company.*

(d) When the contract is *ultra-vires the company.*

In *default of statutory duties*, the directors shall be personally liable to third parties in the following cases : (i) misstatement in prospectus. (ii) irregular allotment. (iii) failure to repay application money if allotment of shares and debentures is not dealt in on the stock exchange as provided in the prospectus.

B. **Liability to company :** The directors shall be liable to the company for the following:

(i) Where they have *acted ultra vires the company.*

(ii) When they have *acted negligently*.3

(iii) Where there is a *breach of trust.*

(iv) Directors are liable to the company for *misfeasance.*

C. **Criminal liabilities of directors :** For acts of fraud, default in discharging their duties and misdemeanour, the Act penalties by way of fine or imprisonment. Sections 75,93,113,115,143,162,168,303, etc. impose penalty upon the directors for omitting to comply with or contravening certain provisions of the Act.

MANAGING DIRECTOR [Section 2(26)]

Managing Director means a director who is entrusted with substantial powers of management which would not otherwise be exercisable by him. It includes a director occupying the position of a managing director by whatever name called. The *'substantial powers of management'* may be conferred upon him by virtue of an agreement with the *powers of management'* may be conferred upon him by virtue of an agreement with the company, or of a resolution passed by the company in its general meeting or by its Board of Directors, or by virtue of its Memorandum or Articles of association.

The appointment of a managing director can be made by any one of the following modes :

1. By an agreement with the company; or
2. By a resolution passed by the company in its general meeting; or

3. By a resolution of the Board of Directors; or

4. By a clause in the Memorandum of Association or Articles of Association of the company.

Remember that, the managing director of a company shall exercise his powers subject to superintendence, control and direction of its Board of Directors. Since the managing director must be a director, he has also the duties, responsibilities and liabilities of an ordinary director.

Articles of a company generally authorise the directors to appoint one of them as managing director. A public company or a private company being subsidiary of a public company must get the approval of the Central Government before appointing the managing director for the first time or within 3 months of doing so.

It is to be noted that the Government shall not grant approval unless it is satisfied that:

(i) it is in the interest of the company to have a managing director or whole-time director;

(ii) the proposed person is a fit and proper person and the appointment is not against public interest; and

(iii) the terms and conditions of appointment are fair and reasonable.

The Central Government is empowered to reduce the period of appointment proposed by the company. Further, Section 269(5) provides that in case the appointment is not approved, then the proposed name (person) would vacate office from the date on which the decision of the Government is communicated to the company.

Disqualifications of Managing Director (Section 267)

Following persons cannot be appointed as a managing director.

1. A person who is an *undischarged insolvent* or who has at any time been adjudged an insolvent;
2. A person who suspends or has at any time *suspended to his creditor* or who makes or has at any time *made a composition with them.*
3. A person who is or has at any time been *convicted* by a Court of an offence involving moral turpitude.

Term of Office and Re-appointment of Managing Director (Sections 269 and 317) : The re-appointment of a person as managing director shall also be approved by Central Government. Note that, *a company cannot appoint a managing director for more than 5 years at a stretch* but under the Act, the re-appointment is not forbidden and such re-appointment cannot be sanctioned earlier than 2 years from the date on which it is to come into force. Such provision does not apply to private company unless it is a subsidiary of a public company.

Again, *a person cannot be a managing director of more than 2 companies* where at least one of the two companies is a public company. But the Central Government may allow a person to be managing director of more than two companies provided it is of the view that the companies should have for their proper working functions as a single unit and have a *common managing director* (Sec. 316).

The managing director works in a two fold capacity. As a director he has a seat on the board and can take part in the board meeting proceedings. As a manager, he is responsible for routine management of the company. *He may be given a fixed salary and a certain rate of commission on the net profits of the company*, so that he may have extra incentives to work hard and take more personal interest in securing efficiency and economy in the administrative machinery of the company. A managing director of a public company cannot vote in the matter of his appointment or of fixing his remuneration.

The managing director is also exempted from the normal rule of a retirement by rotation. So he need not retire at the end of every three years as long as he is acting as managing director. Thus *he may be termed as a non-retiring director*. But if he ceases to act as a director on account of any disqualification, eg. non-payment of a call within six months thereof, his managing directorship is automatically terminated.

Whole-Time Director : A '*Whole-time Director*' includes '*a director in the whole-time employment of the company*'. The provisions applicable to the appointment of a Managing Director are also applicable to the appointment of a whole-time director.

MANAGER

According to Section 2(24), '*Manager*' means *an individual who, subject to the superintendence, control and direction of the Board of Directors, has the management of the whole, or substantially the whole, of the affairs of a company*. It includes a director or any other person occupying the position of a manger, by whatever name called, and whether under a contract of service or not. It is to be noted that the provisions applicable to a managing director regarding his appointment, term of office and the number of companies which can be managed are also applicable to a 'manager'.

Disqualifications of a Manager

A firm, body corporate (company) or association cannot be appointed as a 'Manager' of the company. Besides, the following persons cannot be appointed as manager of a company.

1. A person who is an *undischarged insolvent* or who has at any time within the preceding 5 years been adjudged an insolvent.
2. A person who suspends or who has at any time within the preceding 5 years *suspended payment to his creditors* or who has at any time within the preceding 5 years composition with them.
3. A person who is or who has at any time within the preceding 5 years been *convicted by a court in India of an offence involving moral turpitude.*

The Central Government may, by notification in the Official Gazette, remove the above disqualifications, either generally or in relation to any company or companies specified in the notification.

Appointment of Manager (Section 386)

No company can appoint any person as 'manager', if he is either the manager or managing director of any other company. Even then, if the company wants to employ him, then : (a) it must be approved by a resolution passed at the meeting; (b) specific notice of such appointment must be given to every director present in India; (c) it is approved by Central Government who will approve only if a *common manager* is necessary for the proper working of more than two companies.

Remuneration : The manager of a company may, subject to the provisions of Section 198 as applicable to the managing director, receive *remuneration either by way* of a *monthly payment, or by way of a specific percentage of the net profits* of the company or partly by one way partly by the other. Except with the approval of the Central Government, such remuneration shall not exceed in the aggregate 5% of the net profits (Sec. 387).

REVIEW QUESTIONS

1. Briefly state the provisions of the Companies Act regarding the appointment of the directors of a company.
2. "Directors of a company are not only its agents, but they are also in some sense trustees of the company", Discuss.
3. What is the legal position of directors of a company?
4. How can the directors of a company be removed from office before the expiry of their terms?
5. Explain the procedure for filling the vacancy caused by the removal of a director.
6. What are the qualifications of a director?
7. When is a person disqualified for appointment as a director of the company?
8. State the powers of the Board of Directors of a company and the restrictions on them.
9. What are the duties and liabilities of the board of directors of a company?
10. What is the ceiling on number of directorships of a director?
11. What do you know about Director's Responsibility Statement
12. Who is a managing director? How a managing director is appointed?
13. Discuss disqualifications of managing director.
14. Write short notes on (a) whole time director; (b) Manager. (c) Managerial remuneration.

❑ ❑ ❑

Chapter

MEETINGS AND RESOLUTIONS

Need for Meetings

Whenever a decision has to be taken by more thanone person, it is necessary that the people concerned should meet. They should exchange their veiws, discuss the matter, debate on points of dis-agreements, and arrive at a decision which would be binding on all people concerned. In respect of Business Organisations where the process of decision making is involved, and the decision have to be taken collectively by more than one person, the importance of meetings gains added significance. As has been discussed earlier in this chapter the hierarchy of a company form the organisation consists of

1. a body of individuals who own the company, namely of shareholders;
2. a body of directors collectively called the Board of Directors who are the overall in charge of the management of the affairs of the company.
3. In many cases there is also a body of creditors in the form of Debentureholders, who have lent money to the company, though generally have less to do with the affairs of the Company, except when their rights are effected. If all these peoples have to participate in the decision making process, the most convenient medium of making the decision is a meeting.

To facilitate proper conduct of the meettings and to arrive at and record the decisions of these bodies of individuals at the meetings, and to prepare and preserve the records of these meetings, a set of rules, regulations and conditions are absolutely essential. Recognising the importance of the meetings for a company, the Company Law has framed extensive rules governing the meetings. The law relating to the Meetings, and the procedures are proposed to be discussed in this chapter.

It is at the meeting of the directors, members, creditors, etc., of a company express their will be passing resolutions. Such meetings are (i) Board of Directors, (explained in the previous chapter), (ii) Statutory, (iii) Annual, (iv) Extra-ordinary, (v) Class of shareholders and (vi) Creditors.

The meetings of the Shareholders can also be broadly divided into three categories, namely, : (a) Mandatory Meetins (b) Optional Meetings, and (c) Contingent Meetings. Mandatory Meetings are those meetings of the Shareholders, which must be compulsorily held by the Companies according to the Act. Statutory Meeting Required to be held section 165 of the Act, and the Annual General Meeting required to be held under Section 166 of the Act. Optional Meetings are such meetings, the convening of which is not mandatory under the Law. These meetings are convened at the discretion the Board of Directors, should they feel the need for convening the meeting of the Sharehloders. The meetings falling under this category are Extra Ordinary General Meetings, voluntarily convenced by the Board of Directors. Contingent meetings are such meetings of the Shareholders, the need for which arises only if Certain contingencioes and circumstances arises. These meetings become mandatory, as when the cintingencies provided for in the Law take place.

Extra Ordinary General Meetings on Requisition under Section 169 of the Act. Meetings of a Class of Shareholders, called Class Meetings to approve the prolposal for the variations of the rights of that Class of shareholders, Meetings of Shareholders held under the orders of the High Court to applrove2 the Schemes of Arrangements or Compromise under Section 391 of the Act. or the Scheme of Reconstruction of Amalgamation proposed by the Company, or the meetings of Winding up of the Company, ordered by the Court.

STATUTORY MEETING (Section 165)

Every company limited by shares and every company limited by guarantee and having a share capital share within a period of not less than one month and not more than six months from the date at which the company is entitled to commence business, hold a general meeting of the members of the company. Such a meeting shall be called the "*Statutory meeting*". [Section 165(1)].

This meeting is held once during the life time of the company. A private company, an unlimited company or a company limited by guarantee and not having a share capital is not required to hold a statutory meeting.

Notice of the Meeting : The notice for calling the meeting must be given at least 21 days before the meeting. The notice convening the statutory meeting must specifically state that the meeting is the statutory meeting.

Object fo Holding the Statutory Meeting

1. The object of such a meeting is to ensure that at an early date, the members may have an opportunity of ascertaining the precise position progress made by the company since its formation and prospect of the company. According to Palmer, "The object of the statutory meeting is to put the shareholders of the company at as early a date as possible in possession of all the important facts relating to the new company".

2. To provide an opportunity to the members to discuss the various matters connected with the formation of the company and its working without any previous notice.

3. To approve or to effect any modification to contracts mentioned in the prospectus.

Statutory Report : In order to achieve this object, the directors, are required to send a report called the 'statutory report' to every member of the company at least 21 days before the date of the meeting. Even if the report is sent later than is required, it shall be deemed to have been duly forwarded if it is so agreed to by all the members entitled to attend and vote at the meeting.

Contents of the Statutory Report (Section 165(3)) : The statutory report shall contain the following particulars : (a) The total number of *shares allotted* distinguishing those allotted as fully or partly paid up otherwise than in cash, and stating in the case of shares partly paid up the extent to which they are so paid up and in either case the consideration for which they have been allotted. (b) The total amount of *cash received* by the company in respect of all the shares allotted. (c) An abstract of *receipts and payments made* there at upto a date within seven days of the date of the report (d) An account or estimate of the *preliminary expenses.* (e) *Names, addresses and occupations of its directors and auditors* and also if its manager and secretary, if any, and the changes which have occurred since the date of the incorporation. (f) The particulars of any *contract and the modification* or the proposed modification of any contract which is to be submitted for the approval of the members at the meeting. (g) The extent to which the *underwriting contracts* have not been carried out and the reasons therefor. (h) The arrears, if any, due on *calls from any director and the manager.* (i) The particulars of any *commission or brokerage paid or to be paid* to any director or to the manager in connection with the issue or sale of shares or debentures of the company.

Certification of the Report : The statutory report must be certified as correct by not less than two directors, one of whom shall be the managing director if any. The auditors of the company then shall certify it as correct regarding the shares allotted, cash received in respect of such shares and the receipts and payments of the company.

Filing of the Report : A certified copy of the statutory report shall be delivered to the Registrar for registration immediately after the same have been sent to the members of the company.

Procedure at the Meeting : At the commencement of the meeting, the Board shall place a list showing the names, addresses and occupation of the members of the company and the number of the shares held by them. The list shall remain open for inspection by members during the continuance of the meeting. The members present at the meeting may discuss any matter relating to the formation of the company or arising out of statutory report, whether previous notice has been given or not. But the meeting cannot pass a resolution on any item or on a subject of which notice has not been given as required by the Act. The meeting, however, may adjourn from time to time and a resolution may be passed at any such adjourned meeting if due notice thereof has been given in the meantime. The adjourned meeting is treated as if it is an original meeting for the purpose of transacting business.

Consequences of default or Effect of non-compliance : If any default is made either in delivering the statutory report to the Registrar or in holding the statutory meeting, every director and officer of the company who is in default will be liable to a fine which may extend to ₹ 500. Failure to comply with the provisions of Section 165 of the Act will be a ground for winding up of the company by the Court under Section 433 of the Act, the Court may, however, give directions for the statutory report to be filed or a meeting to be held, as the case may be and refuse to order the winding up of the company. [Section 433].

ANNUAL GENERAL MEETING

Every company must in each year hold in addition to any other meeting, an annual general meeting. The notice convening the meeting must specify that it is a notice of the annual general meeting.

Time gap between two meetings : The first annual general meeting must be held within 18 months from the date of incorporation of the company. The year of incorporation or in the following year. Year means calendar year [Park V. Lawton (1911) K.B. 588] The registrar has no power to extend the time limit to hold the first Annual General Meeting. [Dalmia Cement (Bharat) Co Ltd. V. Registrar of companies.]

Example: A company incorporated on October 1, 2003 may hold its first annual general meeting by April 1, 2000 and then no other meeting will be necessary either for 2004 or 2005. Similarly, a company incorporated on January 1, 2004 may hold its first annual general meeting within 18 months, i.e. up to July 1, 2005. If the meeting is held, say in June 2005, the company need not hold any other meeting in the years 2004 and 2005.

Thereafter, (i) it must be held in each and every calendar year; (ii) there shall not be a gap of more than fifteen months between two annual general meetings. However, the Registrar has the power to extend the time for holding the annual general meeting (except the first annual general meeting) by a period not exceeding three months. (iii) The Annual General Meeting must be held within six months of the close of the Accounting Year.

In the case of Sree Meenakshi Mills Co. Ltd. V. Assistant Registrar of Companies, A.I.R. (1938) Mad. 640, the annual general meeting of a company called in December 1934 was adjourned and held in March 1935. The next meeting was held in January 1936, no other meeting being held in1935. The company was prosecuted for failure to call the annual general meeting in1935. The company contended that it did hold a meeting in the year 1935, but the Court held that the meeting of March 1935 was the adjourned meeting of 1934.

It should be noted that the all the above time limits should be adhered to for holding Annual General Meeting. This means that the earlier of the above dates will become the last date for holding the annual general meeting.

The following *example* will explain the provision clearly.

Let us assume that for company X Ltd.

The closure of the accounting year is	31st March
The date of the 4th Annual General Meeting was	28th August, 2004

The deadlines for holding the 5th Annual General Meetings as per the above points would be:

1.	To be every Calendar Year	31st December, 2005
2.	Maximum Gap of 15th months fromt the previous AGM	28th November, 2005
3.	6 Months from the expiry of the Financial Year	30th September, 2005

The 5th Annual General Meeting must be held before the earliest of the above three dates, namely, 30th September, 2005.

In the above illustration, had the 4th Annual General Meeting been held on the 29th May, 2004, the deadline as per Criterion 2 would have been 29th August 2005.

In that case, the 5th Annual General Meeting will have to be held before the 29th August, 2005, though the deadline as per Criterion 3 is 30th September 2005.

First Annual General Meeting – An Exception

Provisio to Sub section (1) provides the exception to the above rule relating to the time limit for the Annual General Meeting. According to this, the first Annual General Meeting of the company should be held within 18 months of the date of its incorporation. This proviso states that if first AGM is so held, there need not be an Annual General Meeting either in the year of incorporation, or the following year.

Correspondingly, sub section (3) fo Section 210 also states that the closure of the first financial year should not precede the date of the first annual general meeting by a period of nine months (instead of six months as in case of subsequent AGMs).

The following illustration will clarify the point

Let us assume that

The date of Incorporation of the Company is	10th November 2007
The closure of the Accounting Year is	30th September

As per the criterial 1 in Previous illustration, the Company has hold the Annual General Meeting in the years 2006, as well as 2007.

However the deadline for the First Annual General Meetings would be:

As per the Proviso to Section 166(1)	
(18 months from date of incorporation)	10th May, 2008
As per Section 210 (3) (Nine months from the closure of the first	
Accouting year, i.e., 30th September 2007	30th June 2008

In this case, the first Annual General Meeting must be held before the earlier of the above two deadlines, namely 10th May, 2008.

Day, time and place of the Meeting : Every annual general meeting must be held on a working day and during business hours. It should be either held at the registered office of the company or at some other place within the city, town or the village in which the registered office of the company is situated. However, the Central Government may exempt any class of companies from these provisions subject to such conditions as it may impose. Public companies and private companies which are subordinates of public companies may fix the time of their annual general meeting. A private company may also in a like manner and by a resolution agreed to by all the members fix the time as well as the place for its annual general meeting.

With regard to the holding of the annual general meeting, no distinction is made between a public company and a private company. It was decided in the case of **Registrar of Companies *V.* Cabral & Co. Pvt. Ltd**

Notice of the Meeting: According to Sec. 171(1) of the Act, a 21 clear days notice is necessary to hold an Annual General Meeting. However, a shorter notice is sufficient if all the members give their consent. The notice should specifically state that it is the notice of the Annual General Meeting.

Contents of the Notice : The notice of the meeting should contain the following:

1. The Place where it is to be held.
2. The Date and Hour of the meeting.
3. A Statement of the business to be transacted.
4. Any Special Business to be transacted.

Annual Accounts : The Balance Sheet and the Profit and Loss Account and the Report of the Directors must accompany the notice of the Annual General Meeting. The annual accounts should be made for a period up to a date not more than six months before the date of the meeting and they should be laid before the meeting.

From the wordings of the Secs. 173 and 200, it is implied that the annual accounts must be laid only before the Annual General Meeting and not at any other meeting. In case the annual accounts are not ready, it is open to the company concerned to adjourn the said Annual General Meeting to a specific date when the annual accounts are expected to be ready for placing before it.

An adjourned meeting is the continuation of the original meeting. The statutory requirement as to laying of the accounts before the annual general meeting would be satisfied if the accounts are laid before the adjourned meeting. It was decided in the case of **Sudhir Kumar Seal *V.* Assistant Registrar of Companies.**

To whom the Notice Should be Sent: Notice of the Annual General Meeting must be sent to: (a) Every member of the company. (b) Every person entitled to shares due to transmission. (c) Auditor or Auditors of the company.

Business Transacted at the Annual General Meeting: Sec. 173 of the Act has classified the business to be transacted at an Annual General Meeting into two kinds namely,

(a) Ordinary Business, and (b) Special Business.

The ordinary business to be transacted at an Annual General Meeting may relate to the following matters:

1. Consideration and adoption of the accounts and the reports of the directors and auditors.
2. Declaration of dividend.

3. Appointment of directors in the place of those retiring.
4. Appointment of auditors and fixing remuneration to them.

All other businesses transacted at this meting are called special business. Also every business transacted at any other general meeting other than the Annual General Meeting is also a special business. Some of the examples of special business are -

1. Removal of a director.
2. Issue of rights/bonus shares.
3. Election of a person (other than a retiring director) as director.

Drafting the Notice of the Annual General Meeting

The following points must be considered while drafting the notice of the annual general meeting of a company.

1. The meeting should be held either at the registered office or at a place within the city, town or village in which the registered office is situated.
2. The meeting should not be convened on a day which is a public holiday within the meaning of the Negotiable Instruments Act.
3. The meeting should be convened during the usual business hours.
4. The first item for consideration at an annual general meeting is adoption of the accounts. It must be ensured that the gap between the period up to which accounts are prepared and the date of the annual general meeting should not be more than six months.
5. If the provision of Sec. .224 A of the Act are applicable to the company, the appointment of auditors will require approval by means of a special resolution.
6. In case any special business is proposed to be transacted at an annual general meeting, then the resolution must be set out for each of the items proposed to be considered.
7. Notice should be under proper authority. Therefore, the words **"By Order of the Board"** should be added before the name of the secretary.
8. The gap between the date of the notice and the date of the meeting should not be less than 25 days so that after excluding 48 hours for effecting the notice as per Sec. 53 (2) (b), the date of service of notice and the date of holding the meeting, there is left a clear period of 21 days.
9. Section 176 provides that it must be indicated in the notice that a member entitled to attend and vote at a meeting is entitled to appoint a proxy to attend and vote instead of himself and such proxy need not be a member of the company. Therefore, it is necessary to include this by means of a note with the notice of the annual general meeting. Similarly, an additional note is to be given in the notice is that proxies to be valid should be lodged 48 hours before the time of the meeting though there is no statutory provision.
10. A note should be added to the notice indicating the period for which the register of members would be closed.
11. A note is to be added to the notice indicating the date by which the dividend warrants will be posted.
12. In case of special business, which is proposed to be transacted, the explanatory statement under section 173 (2) of the Act must be attached to the notice.

Default in holding the Annual General Meeting: If any company fails to hold an annual general meeting within the prescribed period, the Central Government on the application of any member, may either call or direct the calling of a general meeting of the company. It may give such directions as it thinks fit in regard to the calling, holding or conducting of such meetings. The Central Government may direct that one member of the company present in person or by proxy shall be deemed to constitute a meeting. A general meeting held at the directions of the Central Government shall be regarded as an annual general meeting.

It must be noted that the Company Law Board has not been given the powers to all, hold and conduct the annual general meetings of the companies beyond the period specified in Section 166. Section 186(1) excludes these meetings from its purview. Under Section 186(1) the Company Law Board is empowered to call, hold and conduct extraordinary meetings of the companies in certain circumstances.

If default is made in holding the meeting of the company in accordance with Section 166, or in complying with any directions of the Central Government, the company and every other officer of the company who is in default shall be punishable with fine which may extend to ₹ 5,000 and in the case of a continuing default with a further fine which the default continues. [Section 168].

The company is liable for mere default but for the prosecution of a director or an officer of the company, it must be shown that he was knowingly a party to the default. Further, the company would not be liable for the default, if it is due to a cause beyond its control. In re Bank of Deacon Ltd. AIR 1960. Kerala-15, the books of the company had been seized by the police and produced in the criminal court, the Kerala High Court held that the company would not be punished because the default was beyond the control of the company.

EXTRAORDINARY GENERAL MEETING

Every general meeting of the company which is not statutory or the annual general meeting is an 'extraordinary general meeting.' This meeting is generally held for the purpose of dealing with any extraordinary matter which cannot be postponed till the next annual general meeting. eg. issue of right shares, increase in the remuneration of managing director, Persons authorised to convene the Meeting.

Meeting convened by the Board : The extraordinary general meeting can be *convened either by the Board of whole time director, etc. directors whenever they think fit or on the requisition of the members of the company*. Where the directors think fit to convene a meeting, they do so by resolution passed at a duly convened and constituted meeting of the Board. If it any time sufficient number of directors to form a quorum are not present in India, any director or any two members of the company may call an extraordinary general meeting.

On the requisition of the Members : The directors are bound to call an extraordinary general meeting of the company if the requisition is made by members :

(i) holding not less than $1/10^{th}$ or 10% of the paid-up share capital of the company and having a right to vote at the date of the deposit of the requisition; or

(ii) if the company has no share capital, members having not less than $1/10^{th}$ or 10% of the voting powers of all the members having a right to vote at the date of the requisition.

(iii) 100 members can requisition a meeting even if their collective shareholding is less than 10%.

Contents of a Valid Requisition

(a) The requisition should be in writing (b) It should state the business to be transacted at the requisitioned meeting. (c) It should be signed by all the requisitions. (d) It should be deposited in the Registered Office of the Company. While the Act does not specifically require proof of the fact that requisitionists hold sufficient number of shares or voting powers as required above, it is always a good practice for the requisitionsists to spell out of the company rejecting the requisition on technical grounds.

On receipt of the requisition, the Board shall proceed within 21 days to convene a meeting which must be held within 45 days from the date of the deposit. If the Board does not, within 21 days from the date of the deposit of a valid requisition, proceed duly to call a meeting on a day not later than 45 days from the date of the deposit of the requisition, the meeting may be called-

(a) by the requisitionists themselves;

(b) in the case of a company having a share capital, by such of them as represent either a majority in value of the paid-up share capital held by all of them or not less than one-tenth paid-up share capital of the company, whichever is less; or

(c) in the case of a company not having share capital, by such of the requisitionists as represent not less than one-tenth of the voting power of the members of the company.

The extraordinary general meeting requisitioned by the members must be held within three months of the deposit of the requisition. Where a meeting is called by the requisitionists themselves and the registered office is not made available to them, for holding the meeting, they may hold the meeting elsewhere. The company is bound to repay all reasonable expenses incurred by the requisitionists in calling such a meeting and the company can recover the said sum from the directors at default.

Power of the National Company Law Trubunal to Call Meeting (Section 186) : The National Tribuanal has been vested with the power to call a meeting of the company other than the annual general meeting. This power which was earlier vested in the court, has after the passing of the Companies (Amendment) Act, 1974, been transferred to the National Tribunal. Where for some reason it is impracticable to call a meeting of the company, other than the annual general meeting, the National Tribunal Law may either on its own motion or on the application of any director or member of the company order a meeting to be called, held and conducted in such manner as it thinks fit. It can give such directions in regard to the calling, holding and conducting of the meeting. It can also direct that even one member of the company present in person or by proxy shall be deemed to constitute a meeting. The word 'impracticable' means impracticable from a reasonable point of view. The National Tribunal should take a common sense view of the matter and act as a prudent person of business.

Time and Place : Unlike in the case of Annual General Meetings, the Act does not contain any restrictions on the time and place of Extra-Ordinary General Meeting. Hence an Extra-Ordinary General Meeting can be held on a public holiday. It is also not essential that the extra-ordinary general meeting must be held in the town or city where the Registered Office of the Company is situated.

Business Transacted : The Extra-Ordinary General Meeting can transact any business as may be contained in the Notice excepting the items of business specifically reserved for the Annual General Meeting, viz, adoption of annual accounts, election of directors in place of those retiring by rotation. appointment of Auditors etc. All the items of business transacted in Extra-Ordinary General Meeting are treated as Special Business. An Explanatory Statement should accompany the Notice for every item of business proposed in the Extra-Ordinary General Meeting.

Meeting Convened by any Director or any two Members : Regulation 48(2) of Table A provides that if any time the directors capable of acting and forming sufficient quorum, may call for an extra-ordinary general meeting. Such meeting is also deemed as a meeting conducted by the Board of Directors

Drafting of the Notice of Extraordinary General Meeting

There is no statutory restriction that extra-ordinary general meetings should not be called on date which is a public holiday. However, they are usually called on a date, which is not a public holiday during usual business hours either at the registered office or within the city, town or village in which the registered offices is situated. As all business at extra-ordinary general meetings are special, it is not necessary to say so in the notice of the meeting. All business must be given in the form of resolution indicating whether they are ordinary or special. Proper authority must issue notice. A note covering the right of a member to appoint a proxy must be indicated in the notice. In terms of Section 173(2) of the Act, an explanatory statement must always be annexed to the notice covering an extra-ordinary general meeting since all business at such meeting will be special.

CLASS MEETINGS

Class Meetings are generally held for obtaining the consent of a particular class of shareholders for altering their rights and privileges or for the conversion of one class into another. For instance, there may be a meeting of preference share holders for paying their rate of dividend or investing them into equity shares.

Class Meeting for the purpose of Compromise or Arrangements

When there is a proposal for the Compromise ofArrangement, or flor the Amalgamation or Reconstruction of Companies under Section 291 of the Act, the Court normally orders that a Meeting of each case of the shareholders has to be held separately.

These Class Meetings held on the orders of the Court have to follow the procedureas directed by the Board. Usually, the procedure is the same as the procedure for the other general meetings, but the Chairman of the Meeting is Companies (Court) Rules, 1959.

Thus for effecting such changes it is necessary that a separate meeting of the holders of those shares is to held and the matter is to be approved at the meeting by a special resolution. For example, for cancelling the arrears of dividends on cumulative preference shares, it is necessary to call for a meeting of such shareholders and pass a resolution as required by Sec. 106 of the Act. In case of such a class meeting, the holders of other class of shares have no right to attend and vote.

REQUISITES OF A VALID MEETING

1. Proper Authority

A meeting to be valid must be called by a proper authority. It is the Board who can normally convene a meeting. But under certain circumstances meetings can also be convened by the members, National Company Law Tribunal or the Central Government.

2. Notice

The Second requirement of a valid meeting is that all those who are concerned with the business of the meeting and are entitled to attend it, are communicated of the date, time, place and business of the meeting. Such a communication is called '*Notice of the Meeting*, Not less than 21 clear days notice in writing should be given to the members to call a meeting of any kind. 'Not less than 21 clear days' means that both the date of the meeting and the date on which it is served are to be excluded, i.e., 21 clear days notice. Where the notice is sent by post, it shall be deemed to have been received at the expiration of forty-eight hours after the posting.

Length of the Notice : The requirement of 21 days notice' of the meeting overrides any provision in the Articles for a shorter period. But the Articles can validly provide for longer notice than the statutory minimum period.

Shorter Notice : The meeting can, however, be called by giving a shorter notice in the following cases.

(a) In the case of an annual general meeting, by the consent of all the members entitled to attend and vote.

(b) In the case of any other meeting, by the consent of the members holding not less than 95 per cent paid-up share capital of the company, or holding not less than 95 per cent of the total voting power of the company (when a company does not have a share capital).

Place, day and time: Every notice of a meeting of a company must specify the place, day and hour of the meeting and shall contain a statement of the business to be transacted there at.

To whom Notice to be given: Notice of every meeting must be given to the following person: (i) Every members of the company, (ii) Every person entitled to a share in consequence of the death or insolvency of a member, (iii) The auditor or auditors of the company. If notice of a meeting of the company is not given to every person entitle to receive notice, any resolution passed at the meeting will he of no effect.

Where notice of the meeting is given by advertisement in a newspaper circulating in the neighbourhood of the registered office of the company under Section 53(3) of the Act, explanatory statement need not one annexed to the notice under Section 173 of the Act. But it is necessary to mention in the advertisement that the explanation statement has been forwarded to the members of the company. The accidental omission to give notice to or non-receipt of the notice by any members, shall not invalidate the proceedings at the meeting.

Content of Notice/Business to be Transacted : Notice of meeting must contain a statement of nature of the business to be transacted in the meeting. Section 173 classifies the business into ordinary business and special business.

Ordinary Business : The following business which is transacted at every annual general meeting is considered as ordinary business :

(i) The consideration of accounts, balance sheet and the report of the Board of directors and auditors.

(ii) The declaration of a dividend.

(iii) The appointment of directors in place of those retiring.

(iv) The appointment of and fixing the remuneration of auditors.

Special Business : Any business other than ordinary business transacted at an annual general meeting and all business transacted at the statutory meeting and at any extraordinary general meeting is deemed as special business.

Explanatory Statement : In case of any items of special business to be transacted in the general meeting, an explanatory statement shall be annexed to the notice of the meeting. The statement must set out all materials facts concerning each such item of the business including in particular the nature of the concern or the interest if any, therein of any director and the manager. Where any item of such business relates to or affects any other company, the statement must set out the extent of share holding interest in such other company, of every director and the manager if any, of the company, if such interest is not less than 20 per cent of the paid-up share capital of such other company. Where the item of such business relates to the according of approval to any document by the meeting, the statement annexed to the notice must specify the time and the place where the document can be inspected. The purpose of the statement is to enable the members to understand and appreciate the nature of the business or items of business proposed to be considered at the meeting and make up their mind whether to go to attend and vote at the meeting or abstain from voting.

Who Signs the Notice Convencing the Meeting

The Annual General Meeting is convenced by the Board of Directors of the Company. The Notice of the Annual General Meeting, and every other general meeting is usually signed by the Secretary under the Authority of the Board. If a company does not have a Secretary, the Notice is signed either by a Director or any other officer of the Company duly authorised by the Board.

3. Quorum (Section 174)

A quorum may be defined as the minimum number of members who must be present at a meeting in order that the business of the meeting may be validly transacted. Unless the articles of the company provide for a larger number, *five members* personally present in the case of public companies (other than a public company which has become such by virtue of Section 43-A) and *two persons* personally present in the case of private company will be the quorum for a meeting of the company. It may be noted that the articles cannot provide for a smaller quorum. No proxy is counted in forming the quorum.

Consequences of Incomplete Quorum : If within half an hour from the time fixed for the meeting, the quorum is not present, the meeting shall stand dissolved if it was called at the requisition of the members. In any other case, the meeting shall stand adjourned to the same day next week, at the same time and place. If at the adjourned meeting also, the quorum is not present within half an hour, the members present shall be the quorum.

In Re Hartley Baird Ltd. (1954) 3 A.E.R. 695 the court helt that the quorum required is the quorum to be present at the time of beginning to consider the business and it need not be present through out or at the time of taking the vote on any resolution.

One Member forming the Quorum : Where the total number of members of a company becomes reduced below the quorum fixed for a meeting, it would appear that the rule as to quorum would be satisfied, if all the members of the company, though less than the quorum are present. But, where only one person is present, he cannot form a quorum as a single member cannot constitute a meeting. However, the Company Law recognizes certain *exceptions* which are as follows :

(i) If all the shares of a particular class or all the debentures are held by only one person them he will constitute a valid quorum for the meeting.

(ii) One member may constitute a quorum for an annual general meeting when it is called by the Central Government under Section 167 of the Act

(iii) One member of the company present in proxy or by person shall be deemed to constitute a meeting where the Company Law Board orders a meeting of the company to be held. (Section 186).

4. Agenda for the Meeting

The term Agenda means the "**things to be done**" or "**business to be transacted at a meeting**". In order to transact the business of a meeting systematically and without omission of any important item, it is necessary to put down the items of business to be done on a paper called the "**Agenda Paper**" or "**Agenda**".

The Agenda should be circulated amongst the members along with the notice of the meeting. No business should be transacted at a meeting unless it is specified in the Agenda Paper.

The preparation of the agenda is the work of the Company Secretary. He should do this job in consultation with the Chairman of the company. In preparing the agenda, the Secretary should take care to include therein all the business to be transacted. The matters should be presented clearly and in a summary form so that the members can grasp the matter in advance, and form some opinion.

The agenda should be so drafted as to help the quick disposal of the business. The usual practice is to put the routine items first and complicated matters later. So the routine matters can be disposed of first and the latter part of the meeting can be utilised for discussion of more important items. It is also considered advisable that matters of similar or related nature should be placed in continuous order.

There are generally two ways in which the agenda for a meeting can be prepared. They are as follows:

1. By referring to the business very briefly by writing just one line about each item. For example:
   (a) To read the minutes.
   (b) To pass the transfers.
   (c) To produce financial statement.
2. By giving more details about each item and even sometimes including suggested drafts of the resolutions for the consideration of the meeting. For example.
   (a) To read and sign minutes of the meeting held on 25th March 2002.
   (b) To pass transfer of shares numbered 208 to 215.

The second method is found more suitable as it helps the Secretary or his assistant to write the munutes easily.

5. Chairman (Section 175)

A meeting cannot proceed to transact any business without electing a chairman. The chairman is necessary element for the proper conduct by Company meeting. He is the presiding officer of the company. Chairman is elected in every meeting before at it starts its business. He is neither a judicial officer nor an administrative head. The articles of the company may provide who will be the chairman at a general meeting. Where the articles are silent, the members present at the meeting may elect one of themselves to be the chairman thereof. Election may be by show of hands shall immediately take the poll. If some other person is elected as a result of the poll, he shall be the chairman for the rest of the meeting.

The chairman presides over the meetings of the company. His main function is to keep order and see that the business is properly conducted. He must decide questions arising at the meeting and must take care that the sense of the meeting is properly ascertained with regard to any question before it. He must give a reasonable chance to the members present to discuss any proposed resolutions. The chairman cannot arbitrarily adjourn the meeting or dispose it at his own choice without the consent of the shareholders unless the business for which it was convened has been concluded. The power of adjournment vests in the majority and they can appoint another chairman and conduct the business unfinished by the former chairman.

Powers and Duties of a Chairman

Powers

(i) A Chairman has *prima facie* authority or Power to decide all the questions and points of order.

(ii) He can adjourn the meeting when it is not possible, by reason of disorder etc., to conduct the meeting and complete business.

(iii) He has right to decide priority amongst the speakers to demand poll.

(iv) Power to exercise a casting vote.

(v) Power to expel unruly member behaving disorderly and

(vi) He can, with the support of a majority, apply closure to the discussion after it has been reasonably debated.

Duties

He must act all times *bona fide* and in the interest of the company as a whole. A Chairman who presides over a meeting of a company is neither wholly a ministerial officer nor wholly a judicial officer; his duties are of a mixed nature. He is not liable for damages, if acting *bona fide* according to the best of his judgement and without malice.

(i) It is his duty to see that the meeting is duly convened as to notice, quorum. etc.

(ii) It is his duty to preserve order, and to see that the business is properly conducted.

(iii) He must ensure that the sense of the meeting is properly ascertained in regard to any question before it.

(iv) He must ensure that the provisions of the Companies Act and the Articles of Association are observed, and that the business is taken in the order set out in the agenda, and that business is within the scope of the meeting.

(v) He must ensure that proper opportunity is given to the members to express their views that the voting is fair.

(vi) He must exercise his casting vote *bona fide* in the interests of the company.

(vii) He must decide questions arising for decision during the meeting, and must see to it that the majority do not refuse to bear the minority.

(viii) He must ensure that proceedings of the meeting are correctly and properly recorded in the minutes book.

6. Minutes of the Meeting

The term 'minutes' mean the official record of the meetings of a company. Minutes looks contain a summary of the business transacted, decisions and the resolutions arrived at the meeting. It is incumbent on the company to maintain minutes of proceedings of general meetings and of the Board of Directors and other meetings. Every company shall cause entries in the minutes of proceedings of every meeting within 30 days of the conclusion of every such meeting concerned. The minutes book shall be bound and its pages consecutively numbered. Each page of every minutes of proceedings shall be initiated or signed and the last page of the record of proceedings of each meeting in such book shall be dated and signed :

(a) In the case of minutes of the proceedings of a meeting of the Board or of a committee thereof, by the chairman of the said meeting or the chairman of the next succeeding meeting.

(b) In the case of minutes of proceedings of a general meeting, by the chairman of the same meeting or in the event of the death or in ability of the chairman by a director duly authorised by the Board for the purpose.

Minutes of the proceedings of a meeting shall not be attached to any such book by pasting or otherwise. The minutes of each meeting shall contain (a) a fair and correct summary of the proceedings; and (b) all appointments of officers made there at. In the case of a meeting of the Board of directors or of a Committee of the Board, the minutes shall also contain (a) the names of the directors who dissent from or do not concur in the resolution passed at the meeting. The minutes must not contain any matter which, in the opinion of the chairman of the meeting: (a) is or could reasonably be regarded as defamatory of any person; (b) is irrelevant or immaterial to the proceedings; or (c) is detrimental to the interests of the company. The discretion in regard to such inclusion or non-inclusion of any matter in the minutes lies with the chairman. If default is made in complying with the foregoing provisions, the company and every other officer of the company who is in default, shall be punishable with fine which may extend to ₹ 500 *(Section 193).*

Minutes of the meetings kept in accordance of the provisions of Section 193 shall be evidence of the proceedings, recorded therein. *(Section 194)*. Until the contrary is provided, every general meeting of the company or meeting of the director or a committee of directors in respect of the proceeding thereof, minutes have been so made and signed, shall be deemed to have been duly called and held. The proceedings at these meetings shall be deemed to have duly taken place, and in particular, all appointments of directors or liquidators made at the meeting shall be deemed to be valid. *(Section 195)*.

Location and Inspection of Minutes Book : The minutes books of the general meetings of a company must be kept at the registered office of the company and be open during business hours for the inspection of any member without charge for at least two hours a day. A member is entitled to be furnished within 7 days, after he has made a request in that behalf to the company, with a copy of any minutes on payment of thirty seven paise for every one hundred words, or fractional part thereof, required to be copied. If inspection is refused or if any copy is not furnished within the specified time, the company and every other officer of the company who is in default shall be punishable with fine which may extend to ₹ 500 for each offence. Moreover, the court may, by order, compel an immediate inspection of the books or direct that the copy required shall forthwith be sent to the person requiring it. *(Section 196)*.

Publication of Reports : No document purporting to be a report of the proceedings of a general meeting of a company can be circulated or advertised at the expense of the company, unless it includes the matters required by Section 193, to be contained in the minutes of the proceedings of such meeting. Contravention is punishable with fine which may extend to ₹ 5,000 *(Section 197)*.

7. Voting or Poll (Sense of Meeting)

Every person whose name appears on the register of members, has a right to vote. A shareholder's right to vote is a right of property which he may use in any manner he likes. In other words, he can exercise his right to vote for his own interest and even against the interest of the company. In the case of a company which has no share capital, each member is entitled to one vote only. But, where a company has a share capital, if the Articles are silent every shareholder has one vote is respect of each share.

A company is authorised to make provisions in its articles restricting the voting rights of a member on the ground that (i) calls on his shares or any other sum presently payable have not been paid, or (ii) the company has exercised right of lien in respect of those shares. Where the articles of a company do not contain such provisions, a member cannot be prevented from voting even though calls payable by him have not been paid (Section 181). A public company shall not put any restrictions put on the right of voting will be void even though such provisions are contained in the articles. *(Section 182)*. A member entitled to more than one vote is free to split his votes in favour of and against the same resolution. Such use of votes is possible only on a vote by poll, for on a show of hands no member can register more than one *(Section 183)*.

Methods of Voting

In order to ascertain the sense of a meeting, voting may be only (i) show of hands, or (b) by poll.

Voting by a Show of Hands : Questions arising at a general meeting are to be decided in the first instance by a show of hands. But, where a poll is demanded it is not necessary that the resolution should be put to vote by show of hands. On a show of hands each member has one vote and a proxy cannot vote unless the articles otherwise provide. The declaration by the chairman that a resolution on a show of hands has or has not been carried and an entry to that effect in the minutes book shall be conclusive evidence of that fact. *(Section 178)*.

Voting by Poll : A vote by a show of hands is only a rough and ready method of taking the sense of a meeting. It is not an accurate method of ascertaining the wishes of the members of a company because the votes of those voting by proxy are not counted. Again it does not pay due regard to the wishes of a member holding a large number of shares since he has only one vote on a show of hands. A poll is more proper and effective means of arriving at the wishes of all the members. A poll may be demanded before or on the declaration of the result of the voting on any resolution on a show of hands. Such a poll cannot be demanded after the declaration of result and after the chairman has taken up any other item from the agenda for consideration of the meeting. A poll may be ordered either by the chairman of his own motion or on a demand of the members. The chairman is bound to order a poll if demand is made by the following persons :

(a) In the case of a public company at least by five members having the right to vote on the resolution and present in person or by proxy.

(b) By any number of members present and having not less than one-tenth of total voting right of all the members entitled to vote at the meeting.

(c) By any member or members present and holding shares paid upto the extent of not less than 10 per cent of the total sum paid-up on all the shares having a voting right.

In the case of a private company, the number of members demanding for a poll depends on the number of members present at the meeting. Where the number of members present personally at the meeting does not exceed seven, one member can demand a poll if he has a right to vote on the resolution and is present in person or by proxy. But if the number of the members present personally at the meeting exceeds seven, two members can demand poll who have the right to vote on the resolution and are present in person or by proxy.

The demand for poll may be withdrawn at any time by the person or persons who made the demand *(Section 179)*. If a poll is demanded on the election of chairman, it must be taken forthwith. Similarly, a poll demanded on the question of adjournment must be taken forthwith. But a poll demanded on any other question must be taken at such time, not being later than 48 hours from the time when the demand was made. *(Section 180)*.

The chairman of the company shall appoint two scrutineers to scrutinise the votes given on the poll and to report thereon to him. A scrutineer may be removed at any time by the chairman before the result of the poll is declared. The chairman in such case will fill the vacancy in the office of the scrutineer. He is also empowered to fill the vacancy in the office of scrutineer arising from any other cause. One of the scrutineers shall always be a member (not being an officer or employee of the company) present at the meeting provided that such a member is available and willing to be appointed. *(Section 184)*.

The chairman of the meeting shall have the power to regulate the manner in which a poll shall be taken. The result of poll shall be deemed to be a decision of the meeting on the resolution on which the poll was taken. *(Section 185)*.

8. Proxies

Any member of a company entitled to attend and vote may do so either in person or by proxy. A proxy may be defined as a person authorised to attend and vote for another at a meeting. According to Lord Hanworth M.R., Proxy is a personal representative of the shareholder who may be described as his agent to carry out a course which the shareholder himself has decided upon. It also refers to the instrument by which the appointment is made.

Meaning and Definition : A proxy need not be a member of the company. The proxy has no right to speak at a meeting, but he can demand a poll.

Cases where a Proxy cannot be appointed : A member of a private company cannot appoint more than one proxy to attend on the same occasion and a member of a company without a share capital cannot appoint a proxy.

Form of Proxies : Two forms have been provided under Schedule IX of the Act. The instrument of proxy, however, need not necessarily be in either forms. The company can make its own form. The only advantage of these two forms is that the appointment of proxy made in any of such forms cannot be questioned on the ground that it has not complied with any special requirements contained in the Articles of the company.

Procedure for appointing a Proxy : The instrument appointing a proxy must be in writing in the form prescribed and signed by the appointed or by his attorney duly authorised in writing. If the appointer is a corporate body, it must be under its seal or signed by an officer or attorney duly authorised. Every notice calling a meeting of the company having a share capital or the Articles of which provide for voting by proxy at a meeting, must mention with reasonable prominence a statement that a member entitled to attend and vote, is entitled to appoint a proxy and a proxy need not be a member. Every officer of the company who is in default in complying with this provision is punishable with fine which may extend upto ₹ 500.

Lodging of Proxies : The instrument appointing a proxy must be deposited with the company 48 hours before the meeting. Any provision in the Articles which requires the instrument appointing a proxy to be received by the company more than 48 hours before the meeting shall have effect as if a period of 48 hours had been specified in such provision. There is, however, nothing in the Act to prevent the lodging of such instruments less than 48 hours before the meeting. Subject to this the instrument must be deposited within the time specified by the articles.

Revocation of Proxy : A proxy is always revocable unless made irrevocable for valuable consideration. A proxy can be revoked at any time before the proxy has voted. A latter proxy revokes one of earlier date. Death of a member revokes the proxy but if the company has no notice of such death, then the vote given by the proxy will be valid. Where a shareholder who having given a proxy personally attends and votes at the meeting, the proxy is revoked thereby.

Inspection : Every member entitled to vote at the meeting is authorised to inspect the proxies during the 24 hours preceding the meeting till the conclusion of the meeting. For such inspection the member must give at least three days notice in writing to the company. Such inspection cannot be taken by a proxy.

Invitation to appoint a person as Proxy : Where a company issues invitations at its expense to members, giving names of persons to be appointed as proxies for the purpose of any meeting, then every office of the company who knowingly issued the invitation or permitted the same shall be liable to a fine which may extend to ₹ 10,000. *(Section 176).*

Representation of Corporations in Meetings : A body corporate can be a member or creditor of another company. It may authorise a person not necessarily an employee to attend and vote at any meeting of the company. The representative thus appointed is a member personally present for the purposes of quorum and voting by the show of hands and is not merely in the position of a proxy. A representative can appoint a proxy to attend and vote at the meeting instead of himself. *(Section 187).*

Representatives of the President and Governors : Where the President of India or the Governor of a State is a member of a company, he may appoint such person as he thinks fit to act as the representative to attend and vote at any meeting of the company. Such a representative shall be deemed to be a member of such a company and shall be entitled to exercise the same rights and powers (including the right to vote by proxy) as the President or Governor could exercise as a member of the company. *(Section 187-A).*

9. Adjournment of the Meeting

The term adjournment literally means an act of putting off or breaking off for a later resumption. In relation to meetings, it denotes an act of dissolving or suspending a duly convened meeting after it has been duly commenced, to be reconstituted at a later time or date. The date or time of the meeting can be decided in the same meeting at the time of adjournment or to be decided later on if the meeting is adjourned *sine die.* It should also be noted that the discussion on a particular business or motion can also be adjourned without adjourning the meeting itself.

Adjournment and Postponement

The terms adjournment and postponement are different in their scope and meaning. The following are the points of distinction between the two.

1. Adjournment refers to the suspension of a meeting to a future date after it commences its deliberations. In other words, a meeting can be adjourned only after it is convened, whereas a meeting can be postponed only before the meeting is convened.
2. A meeting can be adjourned only by the meeting itself, whereas a meeting can be postponed by the person who convenes the meeting. In other words, postponement is the act of the convening authority, whereas adjournment is the act of the meeting itself.
3. It is generally said that the power to convene a meeting also imply the power to postpone the meeting. But this proposition is not followed in many cases. From the decisions of the Courts, it appears that a meeting properly convened cannot be postponed unless there is some irregularity.

But a meeting can be adjourned to a later date.

Reasons for Adjournment

A meeting can be adjourned due to the following reasons-

1. If no quorum is present.
2. If it is not possible to obtain the required information within the date of the meeting and the same is to be placed before it.
3. If the meeting passes a resolution to this effect.
4. If the Chairman by virtue of the powers conferred upon him does so.

STATUTORY PROVISIONS REGARDING ADJOURNMENT

The statutory provisions relating to adjournment can be summed up as follows:

1. **Right to Adjourn :** The power of adjournment generally vests in the majority of those present at the meeting. If the majority of the members present at a meeting decides so, the Chairman has no other alternative other than to adjourn the meeting. A resolution is to be passed to this effect.
2. **Adjournment by the Chairman :** For the proper conduct of the meeting, the right of adjournment is generally conferred upon the Chairman. Therefore, the Chairman should exercise this power only for the proper conduct of the meeting and not for his own willing and discretion. If the Chairman acts *bona fide*, the meeting stands adjourned and hence the dissenting members have no right to continue the proceedings and the proceedings thereat shall be null and void.
3. **Malafide Adjournment by the Chairman :** If the Chairman adjourns a meeting on his ownaccord ignoring the views of the majority, the following consequences shall follow:
    1. The remaining members can appoint another Chairman and transact the business left unfinished.
    2. The proceedings of the meeting shall be valid and binding on the company.

4. **Adjournment for Want of Quorum :** If a meeting is adjourned due to want of sufficient quorum, the adjourned meeting is to be held on the same day and time in the next week. If the quorum is not present within half an hour even in the adjourned meeting, the members present shall constitute the quorum and the proceedings thereat will be valid.

5. **Notice for the Adjourned Meeting :** An adjourned meeting is merely the continuation of the original meeting and so no fresh notice is necessary for the adjourned meeting. However, it is usual to serve a fresh notice (i) If the time gap between the original and adjourned meeting exceeds 30 days, and (ii) If the original meeting is adjourned *sine die*.

6. **Business at the Adjourned Meeting :** Only those businesses, not completed in the original meeting should be transacted in the adjourned meeting. Therefore, no fresh business can be transacted in the adjourned meeting. However, in case of an adjourned statutory meeting, a new business, after proper notice, can be brought up for discussion in the meeting.

MOTIONS AND RESOLUTIONS

Decisions of the company are made by motions and esolutions of its members, passed at meeting of members. A proposal promotion when passed and accepted by the members become resolution. Three kinds of resolutions are recognised by Companies Act.

1. Ordinary Resolution,
2. Special Resolution,
3. Resolutions requiring a Special Notice.

Ordinary Resolution

An ordinary resolution is one which is passed at a general meeting by a simple majority of members entitled to vote therein. Simple majority means that the votes cash either by show of hands or on a poll in favour of a particular proposal including the casting vote of the chairman exceeds the votes cast against it. The votes may be cast by the members either in person or by proxy, if allowed. An ordinary resolution is sufficient to affect any transaction which is within the powers of the company and is not required either by the articles or the Companies Act to be effected in some other manner. All resolutions which are not special or which do not require special notice are ordinary resolutions.

Business Transacted with Ordinary Resolution : The important items usually transacted with ordinary resolutions are the following:

1. Adoption of the Statutory Report.
2. Adoption of the Balance Sheet and Profit and Loss Account at the Annual General Meeting [Sec. 210].
3. Election of Directors.
4. Appointment of auditors and fixing their remuneration [Sec. 224].
5. Issue of shares at a discount.
6. Declaration of dividends and sanction of the sums to be transferred to the reserves.
7. Authorising the Board to sell or dispose of the undertaking of the company.
8. Rectification of name or adoption of new name by a company where it resembles the name of an existing company with the previous approval of the Central Government [Sec. 22 (1)(a)].

9. Alteration of share capita [Sec. 94 (2)].
10. Re-issue of redeemed debentures who are liable to retire by rotation [Sec. 255 (1)].
11. Appointment of first directors who are liable to retire by rotation [Sec. 255 (1)].
12. Increase or reduction in the number of directors within the limit fixed by the Articles [Sec. 258].
13. Appointment of managing/whole-time director [Sec. 269].
14. Removal of a director and appointment of a director in his place [Sec. 284 (1)].
15. Approval of appointment of sole-selling agents [Sec.294].
16. Appointment and fixation of remuneration of liquidators in a members' voluntary winding up [Sec. 490 (1)].
17. Nomination of a liquidator in a creditors' voluntary winding up [Sec. 502 (1)].

Meaning and Essentials of Special Resolution

A resolution shall be a special resolution when

(a) the intention to propose the resolution as a special resolution has been duly specified in the notice;

(b) the notice required under the Act (21 clear days) has been duly given, and

(c) the votes casted in favour of the resolution by member entitled to vote either in person or by proxy are not less than three times the number of votes, if any, cast against the resolution. The votes may be cast either on a show of hands or by poll. There is no question of a casting vote in case of a special resolution.

(d) An explanatory statement setting out all material facts concerning the subject matter and the interest of the directors and the Manager if any should be set out in the notice calling the meeting.

(e) A copy of each special resolution together with the copy of an explanatory statement should be filed with the Registrar within 30 days from the date of passing the resolution.

A special resolution is a most useful part of the mechanism of a company. It is by and through the instrument of a Special Resolution that the companies carries important executive or administrative acts which are, or may be necessary for the company's benefit. The aim of passing a special resolution is to ensure that every important change shall be made only after due deliberation and with the sanction of the greater body of shareholders of the company.

Circumstances in which a Special Resolution is Necessary

The Articles of association may provide that certain types of business shall be approved by a special resolution. The Act also provides that in certain specified cases, a company must pass a special resolution. A special resolution is required for the following purposes.

1. To alter the provisions of the Memorandum for changing the place of registered office from one State to another or objects of the company. (Section 17).
2. To change the name of the company. (Section 21).
3. To alter the Articles of the company (Section 31)
4. To offer further issue of subscribed capital when shares are offered to outsiders, (Section 81)

5. To create Reserve capital. (Section 99).
6. To reduce the share capital of the company. (Section 100).
7. Commencement of a new line of business (Seciton 149)
8. To authorise payment of interest out of capital. (Section 208)
9. To request the Central Government to appoint inspectors for investigation of the affairs of the company. (Section 237)
10. To authorise payment of remuneration to directors who are not in the whole time employment of the company. (Section 309)
11. To make the liability of directors unlimited. (Section 323)
12. Authorisation of inter-company loans (Section 370)
13. To have the company wound up by the court. (Section 433)
14. To wind up the company voluntarily. (Section 484)
15. Permission to liquidator to accept shares as a consideration for the sale of the property of the company (Section 484)
16. Omission or addition of the word "**Private**" from, or to, the name of a company (Section 21)
17. Change of name of a charitable or other non-profit company by omitting the word or words "**Limited**" or "**Private Limited**" (Section 25 (3))
18. Variation of share holders' rights (Section 106)
19. Keeping registers and returns at a place other than the registered office (Section 163 (1))
20. Applying to the Central Government for appointing an Inspector for investigating a company's affairs in some cases (Section 237 (a))
21. Appointment of sole selling or buying agent in the case of companies having paid-up share capital of ₹ 50 lakhs or more (Section 294-AA (3))
22. Allowing a director to hold an office of profit under a company (Section 314 (1) and (1-B))
23. Applying to the National Company Law Tribunal to wind up a company (Section 433 (a))
24. Authorising the liquidator of a company to accept shares as consideration (Section 494 (1))
25. Disposal of books and papers of a company in voluntary winding up when its affairs have been completely wound up (Section 550 (1) (b))

Resolutions requiring Special Notice (Section 190)

In addition to the above two types of resolutions, there is another class of resolutions provided under the Companies Act which require a special notice to be given in respect of them.

Circumstances in which a Special Notice is required

Special notice is required in the following cases.

1. For the appointment of an auditor other than the retiring auditor. *(Section 225).*
2. For express resolution that the retiring auditor shall not be reappointed. *(Section 225).*

3. For removing a director before before the expiry of his term. *(Section 284).*
4. For appointing another person as director in place of the director removed. *(Section 284).*

In the above cases, the proposer should give a special notice, of his intention to move the resolution to the company not less than 14 days before the meeting. In computing 14 days, the day on which the notice is served and the day of the meeting are excluded.

The company must, immediately after receiving the notice, give its members notice of the proposed resolution in the same manner as it gives notice of any meeting. If that is not practicable, the company must give notice either by advertisement in a local newspaper or in any other mode allowed by the Articles at least 7 days before the meeting. *(Section 190).*

CIRCULATION OF MEMBERS RESOLUTIONS

Section 188 provides a method by which members desirous of moving a resolution at the annual general meeting can give notice and explanation in advance to the other members of what they intend to do.

Notice to the Members of the Company: A company is bound on requisition in writing by a specified number of members (a) to give notice to the members of any resolution which is intended to be moved at the next annual general meeting; (b) to circulate to the members any statement of not more than one thousand words with respect to the proposed resolution or any business to be dealt with at the meeting. The expenses of any such notice and circulation will be borne by the requisitionists.

Requisition to Company : The requisition for circulating resolution shall be deposited with the company at its registered office not less than six weeks and any other requisition not less than two weeks before the next annual general meeting. The requisition must be signed by the required for requisition must either be (i) one hundred or more members having the right to vote on the resolution and holding shares on which a total amount of not less one lakhs of rupees has been paid up, or (ii) members representing not less than l/20th of the total voting power of all the members having the right to vote on the resolution.

On receipt of the requisition the company shall give notice of the proposal resolution to all members of the company entitled to receive notice of the next annual general meeting. The company shall also circulate the statement among its members entitled to notice of the general meeting. The company is not bound to circulate the resolution or statement if the court finds, on application by the company or an aggrieved person, the same to be defamatory or abuse of the provisions of the section. The cost of such application may be recovered from the requisitionists.

Passing of Resolution by Postal Ballot (Section 192 A)

1. Notwithstanding anything contained in the provisions of this Act,a listed public company may, and in this case of resolutions relating to csuch business as the Central Government may, by notification, declare to be conducted only by postal ballot, shall get any resolution passed by means of a postal ballot, instead of transacting the business in general meeting of the company.
2. Where a company decides to pass any resolution by resorting to postal ballot, it shall send a notice to all the shareholders, along with a draft resolution explaining the reasons therefore,and requesting them to send their assent or dissent in writing on a postal ballot within a period of thirty days form the date of posting the letter.
3. The notice shall be sent by registered post acknowledgement due, or by any other method as may be prescribed by the Central government in this behalf, and shall include with the notice, a postage pre-paid envelope for facilitating the communication of the assent or dissent of the shareholder to the resolution within the said period.

4. If a resolution is assented to by a requisite majority of the shareholders by means of postal ballot, it shall be deemed to have been duly passed at a general meeting convened in that behalf.

5. If a shareholder sends under sub-section (2) his assent or dissent in writing on a postal ballot and thereafter any person fraudulently defaces or destroys the ballot paper or declaration of identity of the shareholder, such person shall be punishable with imprisonment for a term which may extend to six months or with fine or with both.

6. If a default is made in complying with sub-sections (1) to (4), the company and every officer of the company, who is in default shall be punishable with fine which may extend to fifty thousand rupees in respect of each such default.

   Expalnation.-For the purposes of this section, "postal ballot" includes voting by electronic mode.".

DIRECTORS RESOLUTIONS

Just like the shareholders, the Directors give effect to their decisions by passing resolutions in the meeting of the Board. Questions that come up for discussion are generally decided by a simple majority of votes. The following points are to be noted in this connection.

1. **No voting by Poll :** No provision is made for voting by poll at the Board Meeting. This is because, each director has only one vote. Hence, voting by show of hands is generally followed.

2. **Proxies are not Allowed :** Proxies are not allowed in the Board Meetings as in the case of General Meetings. However, if alternate director is appointed to act for an absentee director he can cast his vote.

3. **Cases Where Unanimous Consent is Necessary :** It is already noted that a simple majority is sufficient to decide the questions in the Board Meeting. But, as an exception to the above rule, there are three instances in which an unanimous decision is necessary. They are the following:

   1. To appoint or employ a person as its Managing Director under Sec. 316.
   2. To appoint or employ a person as its Manager if he is already a Managing Director or Manager of another company.
   3. To invest the funds of the company in any shares or debentures of any other body corporate under Sec. 372.

REGISTRATION OF RESOLUTIONS AND AGREEMENTS

Section 192 provides that certain resolutions and agreements shall be registered with the Registrar so that he can maintain a complete record of the important transactions of the company. It affords an opportunity to the members of the public to ascertain the position of the company in certain respects.

The following are the resolutions of agreements which are to be registered.

1. Special resolutions

2. Resolutions which have been agreed to by all members on a subject, which otherwise required a special resolution.

3. Any resolution of the Board of directors of a company or agreement executed by a company relating to the appointment or variation of the terms of appointment of a managing director.

4. Resolutions or agreements which have been agreed to by all the members of any class of shareholders on a subject which required to be passed by a resolution of a particular majority in a particular manner.

5. All resolutions and agreements which effectively bind members of any class of shareholders even though not agreed upon by those members.
6. Resolutions authorising the directors of a company to: (i) sell, lease or otherwise dispose of the whole or any part of the company's undertaking; (ii) borrow money beyond the limits of the paid-up-capital and free reserves; (iii) contribute to charitable or other funds exceeding ₹ 50,000 or 5 per cent of the average of the net profits of the last three years, whichever is greater.
7. Resolutions approving the appointment of sole-selling agents.
8. Resolutions requiring a company to be wound up voluntarily.

Resolutions and agreements to be printed or typewritten and certified by an officer of the company shall be filed within 30 days of the passing of the resolution or the making of the agreement. In case of non-compliance the company and every officer of the company who is default shall be fined upto ₹ 20 for every day during which the default continues.

REVIEW QUESTIONS

1. What are the essentials of a company meeting?
2. Define meetings. State the different kinds of meetings.
3. What is the significance of a statutory meeting?
4. What is an ordinary business?
5. What is a requisitioned meeting?
6. Describe briefly a class meeting?
7. List out the objects of holding a statutory meeting?
8. What is company meeting? What are its essentials?
9. What are the different kinds of meeting?
10. What is statutory meeting? State its objects.
11. Describe the procedure far holding statutory meeting.
12. What is extra-ordinary general meeting? Who are authorized to convene it?
13. What is board meeting?
14. Explain the various kinds of company meetings.
15. Indicate clearly the law relating to holding of a statutory meeting.
16 What should be the contents of statutory report?
17. Explain the provisions of the Companies Act, 1956, relating to annual general meeting.
18. Write an essay on extra-ordinary general meeting.
19. Enumerate the legal provisions; regarding the board meeting.

❐ ❐ ❐

Chapter 23

WINDING UP

Winding up of a company is a process of putting an end to the life of a company. It is a proceeding by means of which a company is dissolved and in the course of such a dissolution its assets are collected, its debts are paid off out of the assets of the company or from contribution by its members, if necessary. If any surplus is left, it is distributed among the members in accordance with their rights.

MODES OF WINDING UP

There are three modes of winding up of a company. These are : (a) Compulsory winding up by the court, (b) Voluntary winding up, which is itself of two kinds: (i) Members' voluntary winding up, (ii) Creditors voluntary winding up, (c) Winding up under the supervision of the court

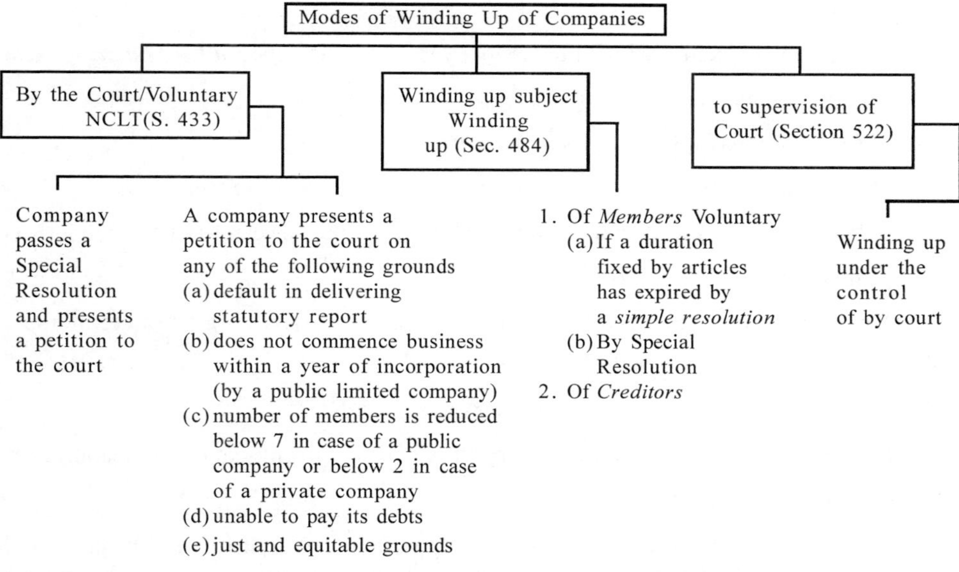

Note : Winding up under the control of court has been abolished by the *Companies (Amendment) Act of 2004*.

COMPULSORY WINDING UP BY NCLT

A company may be wound up by an order of the court. This is called *Compulsory Winding up*. Section 433 lays down the following grounds for the winding up of a company by the NCLT.

1. If the company has by a *special resolution* resolved that it may be wound up by the court.

2. If a company makes a *default in delivering the Statutory Report to the Registrar or in holding the statutory meeting*, the court may order winding up of the company either on the petitition of the Registrar or on the petition of the Contributory.

3. Where a company *does not commence its business within a year* from its incorporation, or suspends its business for a whole year, the court may order for its winding up.

4. Where the *number of members is reduced below 7* in the case of a public company and below 2 in case of a private company, the court may order the winding up of the company.

5. The NCLT may order for the winding up of a company if it is *unable to pay its debts.* The basis of an order for winding up under this clause is that the company has *ceased to be commercially solvent.*

6. The last ground on which the NCLT can order the winding up of a company is when the NCLT is of the opinion that is *just and equitable* that the company should be wound up. The following are the instances where the Courts have exercised their discretion under this clause :
   (i) Where there is a *deadlock in the management*,
   (ii) Where it is impossible to carry on the business of the company *except at a loss,*
   (iii) Where the company has ceased to carry on its authorised business and is engaged in an *illegal business*,
   (iv) Where the object for which the company is formed is *impossible of further pursuit*,
   (v) Where the *minority is being disregarded or oppressed*,
   (vi) Where there is *lack of confidence in directors*,
   (vii) Where a company has been *conceived and brought forth in fraud.*

Persons eligible to file petition for Winding up : The following persons can file a petition :

1. The Company;
2. Any Creditor or creditors including any contingent prospective creditor or creditors;
3. Any Contributory or contributories;
4. All or any of the aforesaid parties, together or separately;
5. The Registrar; 6. Any person authorised by the Central Government under Section 243.

Commencement of Winding up

The winding up of a company by the NCLT is deemed to commence at the time of the presentation of the petition for winding up. But where, before the presentation of the petition, a resolution has been passed by the company, for voluntary winding up, the winding up shall be deemed to have commenced at the time of the passing of the resolution. [Section 441].

OFFICIAL LIQUIDATOR

Under the present Act, the only person who is competent to act as the liquidator in a winding up is the Official Liquidator. For the purpose of winding up, there shall be attached to each High Court an *Official liquidator* appointed by the Central Government, who may be either a whole time or part time officer. In District Courts, the *official receiver* will be the official liquidator. The Central Government may appoint one or more deputy or assistant official liquidators to assist the official liquidator. On a winding up order being made, the official liquidator, by virtue of his office, becomes the liquidator of the company.

Statement of Affairs of the Company

After a winding up order is made or the official liquidator is appointed as provisional liquidator, a statement as to the affairs of the company must be made out and submitted to the official liquidator. It must be in the prescribed form and verified by an affidavit. The statement must contain the following particulars : (a) The assets of the company stating separately the cash balance in hand and at the bank, if any, and the negotiable securities, if any, held by the company. (b) Debts and liabilities of the company. (c) The names, residences and occupations of its creditors, stating separately the amount of secured and unsecured debts. (d) The debts due to the company and the names, residences and occupations of the persons from whom they are due and the amount likely to be realised on account thereof. (e) Such further or other information as may be prescribed, or as the official liquidator may require.

Duties of the Liquidator

The liquidator of a company in compulsory winding up must perform such duties in reference thereto as the court may impose. These are as under :

1. To submit preliminary report,
2. To take over company's assets
3. To convene meetings of creditors and contributories,
4. To keep proper books
5. To submit accounts,
6. To submit information in pending liquidation.

Powers of Official Liquidator

The powers of the liquidator can be divided into two classes : (a) those which can be exercised with the sanction of the NCLT; and (b) those which do not require such sanction.

Powers to be exercised with the sanction of the NCLT : (i) To institute or defend suits, prosecutions or other legal proceedings in the name and on behalf of the company. (ii) To carry on business of the company so far as it may be necessary for the beneficial winding up of the company. (iii) To sell the immovable and movable property and actionable claims of the company by public action or private contract. (iv) To raise money on the security of any asset of the company. (v) To do all other acts as may be necessary to wind up the company and to distribute assets.

Powers to be exercised without the sanction of the NCLT : The following powers do not require sanction of the court for their exercise : (i) To do all acts and execute in the name of the company all deeds, receipts, documents etc. and to use the company's seal for that purpose, where necessary. (ii) To inspect the records and returns of the company on the files of the Registrar without payment of any fees. (iii) to prove, rank and claim in the insolvency of any contributory and to receive dividend out of his estate. (iv) to draw, accept, make and endorse bill of exchange, hundi or promote in the name of and on behalf of the company. (v) To take out in his official name, letters of administration to any deceased contributory and in his official name to do all things necessary for obtaining any money from a contributory or his estate. (vi) To appoint agents where necessary.

CONTRIBUTORY

Section 428 defines the term '*contributory*'. It means every person who is liable to contribute to the assets of the company in the event of its being wound up and includes the holders of fully paid up shares. A debtor to the company is not a contributory nor a person who guarantees such debts. When a company goes into liquidation, every member whether past or present, has to contribute to the assets of the company. The list of contributories is made out in two parts A and B in accordance with Section 426. The *A list* comprises the present members and the *B list* those of past members, who have ceased to be members within one year preceding the winding up. The 'A' contributories, i.e., those in the list of present members are primarily liable for everything and must be first individually exhausted before any 'B' contributory can be called upon.

A past member is not required to contribute in the following cases : (a) Where he had ceased to be a member for a period of one year or upward before the commencement of winding up. (b) Where the debt or liability of the company was incurred after he ceased to be a member. (c) Where the present members are able to satisfy the contributions required to be made by them under the Act.

VOLUNTARY WINDING UP

The object of a voluntary winding up is that the company and its creditors are left to settle their affairs without going to the Court, but they may apply to the Court for any directions or orders if and when necessary. This form of winding up is by far the most common and the most popular form. A company may be wound up voluntarily when-(a) the period fixed by the Articles for the duration of the company has expired or an event upon which the company is to be wound up has happened and the company in general meeting has passed a special resolution; (b) the company has for any cause, whatever passed a *special resolution* to wind up voluntarily (Section 484). The company may be wound up by special resolution even if it is prosperous.

A voluntary winding up commences from the date of the passing of the resolution. (Section 486). From the commencement of the winding up, the company ceases to carry on its business except so far as may be required for the beneficial winding up of such business. But the corporate status and powers continue until it is dissolved.

Types of Voluntary Winding Up : A voluntary winding up may be: (a) A members' voluntary winding up. (b) A creditor's voluntary winding up.

Members's Voluntary Winding Up and Declaration of Solvency : Section 488 provides that where it is proposed to wind up a company voluntarily, the directors or a majority of them, may, at a meeting of the Board, make a declaration of solvency verified by an affidavit that the company has no debts or that it will be able to pay its debts in full within a period not exceeding 3 years from the commencement of winding up as may be specified in the declaration. Such declaration shall be made within five weeks immediately preceding the date of the passing of the resolution for winding up and shall be delivered to the Registrar before that date. Where such a declaration is duly made and delivered, the winding up following shall be called members voluntary winding up.

Creditor's Voluntary Winding Up : Where the declaration of solvency is not made the winding up is referred to as creditors' voluntary winding up. The provisions for creditors' voluntary winding up are similar to those applicable to the members' voluntary winding up except that in the former, it is the creditors who appoint the liquidator, fix his remuneration and generally conduct the winding up. Sections 500 to 509 deal with creditors voluntary winding up.

Distinction between Members' Voluntary Winding up and Creditors' Voluntary Winding up.

Members' Voluntary Winding up	*Creditor's Voluntary Winding up*
1. Such winding up takes place only when the company is in a position to pay is debts.	1. Such winding up takes place only in case when the company is not in a position to pay its debts.
2. Declaration of solvency is made by the Directors	2. No such declaration is made.
3. Only meeting of members is called	3. Meeting of the members and creditors is called.

4. The liquidator is appointed and remuneration is fixed by the company itself	4. The liquidator in fact is appointed by the creditors and remuneration is fixed by the committee of inspection.
5. No committee of inspection is appointed.	5. Committee of inspection is appointed.
6. The liquidator can exercise some powers with the sanction of a special resolution of the company	6. The liquidator exercises powers with the sanction of the court.
7. Meeting of members is called on completion of proceedings of winding up.	7. Meeting of members and creditors is called when the proceeding for winding up has been completed

Winding Up subject to Supervision of Court

(Now this type of winding up is not allowed. It is only for academic interest)

At any time after a company has passed a resolution for voluntary winding up the court may make an order that the voluntary winding up will continue, but subject to the supervision of the court and with such liberty for creditors, contributors and others to apply to the court on such terms and conditions as the court thinks fit. [Section 522]. A petition for the continuance of a voluntary winding up subject to the supervision of the court must be deemed to be a petition for winding up by the court [Section 523]. The court on making a supervision order may appoint an additional liquidator or liquidators. The court may remove any liquidator so appointed. The court may appoint or remove a liquidator on the application of the Registrar [Section 524]. A liquidator appointed by the court will have the same powers and be subject to the same obligations as if he had been duly appointed as a liquidator in a voluntary winding up. [Section 25].

CONSEQUENCES OF WINDING UP

1. **Consequences as to Shareholders :** A shareholder is liable to pay the full amount upto the face value of the shares held by him. Not only the present members but past members are also liable in the event of winding up of the company. The liabilities of present member is the amount remaining unpaid on the shares held by him while a past member can be called upon to pay if the contributions made by the present members are not adequate.

2. **Consequences as to Creditors :** A company, whether solvent or insolvent, can be wound up under the Act. In case of solvent company, all claims of its creditors when proved are fully met. But in case of an insolvent company, the rules under the *Law of Insolvency* shall apply.

As regards the secured creditor, he need not prove his claim against the company. He may realise his security and satisfy the debts. For deficiency (if any), he may put up his claim before the liquidator. The secured creditor has also the option to relinquish his security and to prove the amount as if he were an unsecured creditor.

ORDER OF PAYMENT

As soon as the assets are realised and the list of claimants is finalised the liquidator to commence making payment. From the provisions of Section 511, 520, 529 and 530 it appears that : first comes the claims of the *secured creditors*, second comes costs, charges and *expenses of the winding up* including liquidators, remuneration; third comes *preferential creditors*; fourth comes the *creditors secured* by floating charge; fifth comes *unsecured* or ordinary creditors, and at the end, comes *members or contributories*.

Regarding members, if any of them has paid in excess of the amount of call made on him, that will be returned to him first and then the preference shareholders are given their capital and thereafter, if any, surplus is left-that will be distributed among the equity shareholders if the Articles of the company so provide.

Any surplus still left, will also go to the equity shareholders unless the preference shares are the participating preference shares as per terms of the issue.

Preferential Payments (Section 530)

'Preferential Payments' are the payments made to certain unsecured creditors in priority to all other debts on winding up of the company. The preferential payments are :

(a) *All revenues, taxes, cesses and rates due from the company to the Central or State Government or to a local authority* which have become due and payable within 12 months before : (i) the date of appointment of provisional liquidator, or (ii) the date of winding up order in case of compulsory winding up, and (iii) the date of the passing of the resolution for winding up on the case of voluntary winding up.

(b) *All wages or salary of an employee* in respect of services rendered to the company and due for a period not exceeding 4 months within 12 months before the above relevant date.

(c) Any *compensation payable to any workman* under any of the provisions of Chapter V-A of the *Industrial Disputes Act, 1947*. The total amount must not exceed ₹ 1,000 in the case of any one claimant.

(d) All *accrued holiday remuneration becoming payable to any employee or in the case of his death* to any other person in his right, on the termination of his employment before or by the effect of, the winding up order or resolution.

(e) All amount due in respect of *contributions payable during 12 months* next before the relevant date, by the company as the employer of any persons under the *Employees' State Insurance Act, 1948*, or any other law for the time in force. But this is not payable if the company is being wound up voluntarily for the purpose of reconstruction and amalgamation.

(f) All amount due in respect of death or disablement of any employee under the *Workmen's Compensation Act, 1923*, but this is not payable if the company is being wound up voluntarily for reconstruction or amalgamation.

(g) All sums due to any employee from a *provident fund, a pension fund, a gratuity fund or any other fund for the welfare of the employees* maintained by the company.

(h) The *expenses of any investigation* held in pursuance of Section 235 or 237, in so far as they are payable by the company.

It is to be noted that the above preferential creditors will rank equally amongst themselves. They have to be paid in full, unless the assets are insufficient in which case they shall abate in proportion to their total amount. They shall have preference even over those creditors who are secured by a floating charge on the assets.

DISSOLUTION OF A COMPANY (Section 481)

The Court makes an order for the dissolution of a company on any of the grounds stated below :

(i) when the affairs of a company have been completely wound up, or

(ii) when the court is of the opinion that the liquidator cannot proceed with the winding up of a company for want of funds or assets; or

(iii) when it is just and reasonable in the circumstances of the case that an order of dissolution of the company should be made, or

(iv) for any other reason whatsoever.

The company is dissolved from the date of the order of the Court. Within 30 days of the order of the court, the liquidator must send a copy of the order to the Registrar, failing which he is punishable with fine which may extend to ₹ 50 for every day of default.

Where a company has been dissolved by process of winding up, or by order of court under Section 481 or for facilitating reconstruction and amalgamation or otherwise, the Court may at any time within 2 years of the date of dissolution make an order declaring the dissolution to have been void. A certified copy of such an order shall be filed with the Registrar within 30 days after the making of such an order.

DEFUNCT COMPANY

A '*defunct company*' means a company which has never commenced business or which has ceased to carry to business. Under Section 560, the Registrar of Companies can strike the name of such a company from the Companies' Register and for striking off the name, he is supposed to adhere to the following steps :

1. He has to send to the company by post a *letter* enquiring whether the company is carrying on business or is in operation.
2. If no reply is received within one month, then he must send within the next 14 days a *registered letter* referring to the first letter and stating that no answer thereto has been received and that if an answer is not received to the second letter within one month from the date thereof, a *notice* will be published in the Official Gazette with a view to striking the company's name off the Register.
3. If no satisfactory reply is received within one month from the date thereof, he must send to the company by post and publish in the Official Gazette a notice stating that unless cause is shown to the contrary, the name of the company will be struck off the Register after 3 months and the company will be dissolved.

REVIEW QUESTIONS

1. What do you understand by the winding up of a company?
2. What are the various modes of winding up?
3. Discuss the circumstances in which a company may be wound up by the NCLT.
4. Under what circumstances will the NCLT order a compulsory winding up of a company?
5. What is the effect of the winding up of a company?
6. Explain the grounds on which the NCLT would consider it just and equitable to wind up a company.
7. Who can present a petition for the winding up a company by the NCLT?
8. State the procedure for the members voluntary winding up of a company.
9. Explain the provisions of the Companies Act in respect of the creditors' voluntary winding up. How does it differ from a members' voluntary winding up?
10. Who is a contributory? What is the nature and extent of his liability?
11. Describe the duties and powers of liquidator appointed by the Court.
12. What do you understand by 'winding up subject to the supervision of the court?
13. Write short notes on (a) Defunct company; (b) Official Liquidator; (c) Contributory; (d) Preferential Payments.

❐ ❐ ❐

CASE STUDY

Company Law

1. A husband and wife, who were the only two members of a private limited company, are shot dead by dacoits. Does the company also die with them?
2. A company was promoted to carry on the business of crop-spraying from the air. X, one of its promoters, held bulk of its shares and was its Managing Director. Subsequently, the company entered into a service agreement with him and engaged him as its chief pilot also. While piloting one of the aircrafts of the company, in the course of letter's business, he was killed in an air-crash. His wife has claimed compensation under the provisions of the Workmen's Compensation Act. The claim is being resisted by the solicitor of the company who contends that X and the company were one and the same person and as a person cannot employ himself, no compensation is payable.

   The above case is referred to you for your decision as to whether the compensation is payable. Decide.
3. A was employed as an accountant with P, a sole trader, under an agreement of service for ten years. Before the expiry of the term of agreement, P's business was purchased by a company and all his assets and liabilities were transferred to it. All employees of P reported for duty at the company but A did not. The company charged A with being unlawfully absent from work in contravention of his service agreement. State whether in your opinion there is any default on the part of A.
4. H was appointed as a Managing Director of X Ltd. On the condition that he shall not entice away the customers of the company during his stay in the company or afterwards.

   He left the services of the company and formed a new company, Y, which enticed away X's customers. What remedy is available to X company?
5. 40% of the income of a tea company was taxable as income from manufacture and sale of tea, and the rest 60% of its income was exempt from income tax as it was deemed to be agricultural income.

   X, as a member of the company, was in receipt of dividend from shares held by her in the company. She claimed tax exemption in respect of 60% of her dividend income received from the company. Income-tax Officer, however, refused to accept X's claim and taxed the whole of her income without any exemption. Is he right?
6. Seven friends joined hands to form a company and named it as "The Saltash Watermen's Steam Packet Co. Ltd." On a bill of exchange, its name appeared as "The Saltash Watermen's Steam Packet Co. Saltash" and the acceptance as "Accepted, John Martyr, Secretary to the company." The bill is dishonoured on the due date. State who is liable to pay the amount of the bill to the payee?

7. A, B and five others are only shareholders of the fully paid-up shares of a public limited company. A's shares are sold in a Court auction and B purchases them. Assuming that this fact is known to other shareholders, what are the consequences if the company continues to carry on its business thereafter?

8. In a private limited company, it is discovered that there are, in fact, 54 members. On an enquiry, it is ascertained that 6 of such members have been employees of the company in the recent past, and that they acquired their shares while they were still employee of the company. Is it necessary to convert the company into a public limited company?

9. 35% of the paid-up share capital of A private company is held by C, a non-banking public company, incorporated in India. Does A become a public company? Give reasons for your answer.

10. Six of the seven signatures to the Memorandum of Association of a company were forged. The Memorandum was duly presented, registered and a certificate of incorporation was issued. The existence of the company was subsequently attacked on the ground that the registration was void. Decide.

11. The Memorandum and Articles of Association of a company were delivered to the Registrar of Companies for registration on January 6. On January 8, the Registrar issued the Certificate of Incorporation but dated it January 6. On that very day (Jan. 6) the company made allotment of its shares. The allotment was challenged on the ground that it was made before the actual issue of the Certificate of Incorporation. How would you decide and why?

12. The Memorandum and Articles of Association of a company was presented to the Registrar of Companies for registration and the Registrar issued the Certificate of Incorporation. The company, after complying with all the prescribed legal formalities, started a business according to the objects clause, which was clearly an illegal business. The company contends that the nature of the business cannot be gone into as the Certificate of Incorporation is conclusive. Discuss.

13. A, on the instruction of promoters of a company, prepared Memorandum and Articles of Association, paid the registration fees and got the company incorporated. A claims his costs and charges from the company. The company refuses to pay. Will A succeed?

14. A, a furniture dealer, entered into a contract with the company for the furnishing of the offices of the company. The company went into liquidation before it could obtain certificate of commencement of business. Can A prove in the winding up for the price of the furniture supplied to the company?

15. X Ltd., a cotton textile company, enters into a contract with A Ltd., an adjacent cotton textile mill, to supply electricity from their power generation plant. After supplies have been made for three months, it is discovered that this activity is beyond the scope of the objects clause of Memorandum of Association of X Ltd. Shareholders of X Ltd. ratify the contract by an *ex-post facto* General Body Resolution. A Ltd. refuses to make payment on the ground that the contract is wholly null and void. Comment.

16. X Mining Company Ltd., applied to Company Law Board for permission to add following objects in its Memorandum of Association, which earlier stated mining as its main purpose.
    (a) To sell goods on hire-purchase basis;
    (b) To do all kinds of fabrication works of steel, aluminum, copper, zinc and alloys;
    (c) To buy and sell land, buildings, hotels, restaurants and business premises; and
    (d) To enter into contracts for construction of buildings with private people or governments.

    Could the Company Law Board approve this alteration?

17. A company had been formed to permit, assist and protect the use of bicycle, tricycle and other similar vehicles on the public roads and for further objects connected with same road uses. The company proposes to alter its objects clause to include motorists as well for benefits under the schemes of this company. Should the Court confirm such an alteration?

18. Default has been made in holding the annual general meeting of a company, more than 18 months having elapsed since the date of the last such meeting. What can be done in the circumstances by any member who wishes that the meeting should be held?

19. Please explain what steps you would suggest in the following circumstances:

    (a) The last meeting of the Board of Directors was held on 17th February 2010. Majority of the directors will remain out of India till 21st of May, 2010 whereas it is necessary to convene the next Board meeting within three months within the meaning of Section 265 of the Companies Act, 1956.

    (b) In the agenda of the Board of Directors' meeting, there is an item in which four out of five directors are interested. The directors wish that the item should be considered and not dropped.

    (c) A director residing outside India has complained that as the notice of the last Board Meeting was not served on him outside India, but was simply sent to his Indian address, the last Board meeting was invalid.

20. For a special resolution in a company's general body meeting, 9 voted in favour, 2 against it and 4 abstained. The Chairman declared the resolution as passed. Is it a valid resolution?

21. A member of a company, gives a proxy to B, in pursuance of which B attends the meeting of the company, after satisfying all requirements of law, A himself attended the meeting and voted on a particular resolution. A's vote was rejected. Discuss the validity of A's vote.

22. The shareholders, in a duly convened annual meeting of a company, passed a resolution for payment of dividend at a rate higher than what was recommended by the Board of Directors. Examine the legality.

23. A company's trade has been suspended temporarily owing to the trade depression but it has bonafide intention to continue its operations when conditions improve. A prayer was made to court for winding up the company. Decide.

24. An application was made by a father as guardian of his minor daughter for shares and the company registered the shares in the name of the daughter describing her as a minor. The company went into liquidation and the father of the minor was placed on the list of contributories. The father resists this. Decide.

25. The claim of a company for the realization of the amount due on a call becomes barred by limitation. Thereafter the company goes into liquidation. Can be liquidator realize the said amount barred by limitation? Will it make any difference if the amount is due on account of goods purchased from the company on credit by the contributory?

26. On March 15, 2010, a company in consideration of past debt of ₹ 75,000 and a future advance of ₹ 25,000, issued debentures to a creditor accompanied by a floating charge over its assets. On August 20, 2010, the company is wound up. State the rights of creditor in the winding up.

❑ ❑ ❑